2ND EDI

Texas Real Estate Contracts

Ralph Tamper, DREI, GRI, CREI, CBR

This publication is designed to provide accurate and authoritative information in regard to the subject matter covered. It is sold with the understanding that the publisher is not engaged in rendering legal, accounting or other professional service. If legal advice or other assistance is required, the services of a competent professional person should be sought.

Publisher: Diana Faulhaber
Senior Development Editor: Louise Benzer
Managing Editor: Ronald J. Liszkowski
Art and Design Manager: Lucy Jenkins

Published by Real Estate Education Company®/Chicago,
a division of Dearborn Financial Publishing, Inc.®
155 North Wacker Drive
Chicago, IL 60606-1719
(312) 836-4400
http://www.REcampus.com

Printed in the United States of America.

01 02 10 9 8 7 6 5 4 3

Library of Congress Cataloging-in-Publication Data

Tamper, Ralph.
Texas real estate contracts / Ralph Tamper.—2nd. ed.
p. cm.
ISBN 0-7931-3689-X
1. Vendors and purchasers—Texas. 2. Real property—Texas—Forms.
I. Title.
KFT1326.T36 2000
346.76404'3—dc21 00–027970

Dedication

This book is dedicated to the success of all Texas real estate brokers and salespersons who are in the business of serving Texas sellers and buyers with honesty, competency and fairness.

It is also dedicated to John P. Wiedemer, DREI, and David Sirota, DREI. Both men are distinguished real estate educators and authors who have encouraged, inspired and assisted the author in countless ways throughout his career as a real estate educator.

Table of Contents

Preface

This book was created to provide a clear, practical approach to one of the most important things a Texas real estate broker or salesperson will do for a buyer or seller: filling in the blanks on the purchase agreement. The book is not designed as a definitive legal text, nor does it provide legal advice to licensees or their customers and clients. Readers are advised that it is always desirable to read every word of a legal document carefully and understand it before signing. When unusual matters arise or a party does not understand what he or she is being asked to sign, legal counsel should be sought before proceeding. Real estate licensees may not give legal advice or write documents defining legal rights and remedies of the parties. Licensees may only add business details desired by the parties.

At the conclusion of your study of the material in this volume, you will

- understand that the role of the licensee is to set down the wishes and intent of the parties and not to make decisions for them or impose the broker's or salesperson's will upon them;
- be able to state clearly the elements of a contract;
- be able to explain and comply with the provisions of the Statute of Frauds, the Texas Real Estate License Act and the Rules of the Texas Real Estate Commission as they relate to the creation of executory contracts between sellers and buyers;
- be able to write down a business detail and know the difference between a word or phrase that establishes a business detail and one that defines legal rights and remedies of the parties;

- know which form or forms are appropriate to define the agreement of the parties;
- be able to recognize potential legal problems and know when to encourage the parties to seek competent legal advice from a real estate attorney;
- be able to explain to a seller what is required by statute with regard to property disclosure requirements;
- be able to assist buyers and sellers in gaining understanding of the options available to them when a breach of contract occurs; and
- be able to estimate the bottom line accurately for the seller and the buyer.

The book is intended for use by both new licensees and seasoned practitioners. As you begin your study, remember that what others do and what is popular are not always correct, and what is correct is not always popular. Real professionals accept the responsibility of verifying and making certain that the approach being utilized is accurate and appropriate.

Learn what is correct and do not let others intimidate you or put you at risk just because they have been in the business longer than you have. Many practicing licensees have never carefully read the forms. A truly competent real estate broker or salesperson should be able to discuss in detail every one of the promulgated contracts and addenda. A competent licensee should know exactly when to use and when not to use each of the forms.

Great care has been taken to ensure that every detail about contracts that is covered on the state licensing exams has been thoroughly explored in these pages.

The Texas Real Estate Broker-Lawyer Committee and the Texas Real Estate Commission meet on a regular basis to review and modify the forms. The commission makes licensees aware of any changes and any newly adopted forms through **THE ADVISOR,** the official publication of the Texas Real Estate Commission for the distribution of important information to licensees. Carefully read every word of a new form before you use it.

If necessary, a supplement will be added to this book that will give you current information about revisions and new forms that have been promulgated since the publication of this second edition. A visit to the TREC web site at www.trec.state.tx.us offers the opportunity for you to download the latest version of the forms.

This book explores only Texas Real Estate Commission published forms. Forms made available for use by members of trade organizations such as local REALTOR® associations and the Texas Association of REALTORS® are not included because they are available only to organization members.

Acknowledgments

The author would like to thank Lloyd Hampton, Chuck Hutchinson, Carolyn Rogers and Susan Bouet, instructors at THE REAL ESTATE SCHOOL, Houston, Texas, for their invaluable input. In addition to offering valuable suggestions for the content, they field-tested the case studies. Appreciation is also expressed to Don Shrum for his assistance in preparing the manuscript.

The author also thanks the following reviewers for their valuable contributions to this edition: Harold Grimes, Tyler Real Estate College; Frankie Jefferson, Houston Community College; Rick Knowles, Capital Real Estate Training; Kevin S. Morris, San Jacinto College; Philip G. Schoewe, DREI, HomeIndex Real Estate Company; and Ken Trussell, Continuing Education for Licensing, Inc. (C.E.L.I.) and Texas A&M University—Commerce.

In addition, the author wishes to thank those who have helped with the previous edition, including Nanci Hawes, DREI, Nanci Hawes Real Estate School; Randy McKechnie, University of Texas at Arlington; and Marga Shefman, formerly with the Austin Association of REALTORS®.

About the Author

Ralph Tamper, owner and director of **THE REAL ESTATE SCHOOL** of Houston, Texas, received his real estate training at the University of Houston. He is author of *Mastering Real Estate Mathematics,* Sixth Edition, 1995, published by Real Estate Education Company® of Chicago and *MCE for Texas Real Estate Professionals 1999*, also published by Real Estate Education Company of Chicago. He is in demand as a reviewer of real estate related texts and computer software of real estate study.

Mr. Tamper is active as a presenter of continuing education classes for real estate brokers and salespersons, attorneys, appraisers and accountants. He is also a popular instructor for the Graduate Realtor Institute program in which he teaches legal issues, pricing property, contracts, technology, taxation and investments. He is a Senior Instructor for the course leading to the Certified Buyer Representative (CBR®) designation.

He has been awarded the prestigious Distinguished Real Estate Instructor (DREI) designation by the Real Estate Educator's Association. He serves on the Board of Directors, was program chairman for the 1998 Annual Conference and is president of the Real Estate Educators Association for 2000–2001. Additionally, he is a senior instructor for the Real Estate Educators Association's Instructor Development Workshops.

He is a life member of the Texas Real Estate Teachers Association and has been awarded its CREI (Certified Real Estate Instructor) designation. He also holds memberships in the national, Texas, Fort Bend and Houston Associations of REALTORS®.

PART 1

An Agreement or a Contract?

Key Terms

assignment
bilateral contract
breach of contract
competent party
contract
default
executory contract
forbearance
fraud
incompetent party
liquidated damages
minor
money damages
novation
performance
statute of frauds
unenforceable
unilateral contract
valid
void
voidable

Every day individuals enter into agreements to do or to refrain from doing specific acts. Some of these agreements can be classified as contracts; others are simply agreements. A **contract** is a legally enforceable agreement to do (**performance**) or not to do (**forbearance**) a specific thing. Our Texas statutes protect contractual rights. Those who enter a contract and fail to perform (**default**) may be sued by the other party or parties to the agreement. To be considered an enforceable contract, the agreement must meet certain requirements. The six elements of a valid real estate contract include the following:

1. ***Competent Parties***—A party who does not have legal capacity (**incompetent party**) cannot be held to the terms of an agreement. To be legally competent a party must have attained the age of majority, which

in Texas is 18 years old. A contract signed by a **minor** (younger than 18) is classified as *voidable;* that is, it can be set aside by the minor party. If the minor chooses to uphold and fulfill the terms of the agreement, the contract is binding. The parties must be in control of their mental faculties. Individuals are considered sane or mentally competent until declared otherwise by a court. The parties must also be sober and demonstrate contractual intent. Any person who meets the **competent party** test may, through a duly executed specific *power of attorney,* name and appoint another to act as an **attorney-in-fact.** The signature of the attorney-in-fact binds a party just as effectively as the party's own signature. Licensees dealing with corporate-owned real estate should remember that only an officer named in a *corporate resolution* passed at a meeting of the board of directors can sign a contract for and on behalf of the corporation.

2. ***Consideration***—To be valid a contract must specifically identify that something, usually money, is being given in exchange for something else. Texas courts have clearly defined that a promise given in exchange for a promise is adequate consideration to bind a purchase agreement. With regard to a purchase contract, the listing broker best fulfills the fiduciary duty to the seller by encouraging a substantial amount of earnest money. The earnest money may serve as **liquidated damages** in the event of a breach of contract. This is discussed more fully in Part 3.
3. ***Mutual Agreement*** *(mutual assent)*—The parties must enter the contract freely and voluntarily. Their decisions must be based on truthful, accurate information. The presence of false information or fraud, by either acts of commission or acts of omission, precludes having an enforceable agreement. Licensees should take decisive action to ensure that full disclosure is made and that the parties to a purchase agreement are making their decisions based upon truthful, accurate information.
4. ***Lawful Objective***—The provisions of an agreement must call for lawful activity. A provision that does not comply with federal, state or local law cannot be upheld by a court. Suppose a tenant signs a lease stating that if the tenant fails to pay the rent, the landlord may enter the premises, seize all of the tenant's personal possessions and immediately sell them to satisfy the rent obligation. This provision is in violation of the homestead law and therefore unenforceable.
5. ***In Writing and Signed by the Parties***—The **Statute of Frauds** requires that to be enforceable all agreements affecting title to or interest in real estate in Texas be reduced to writing and signed by the parties. An oral agreement of sale is unenforceable in Texas and it is inadvisable for licensees to conduct real estate negotiations orally. Offers and counteroffers should be in writing. One does not have a binding executory contract until an offer has been made and accepted in writing and the offeror has been notified of the acceptance. The only exception to the "in writing" rule is a lease for one year or less. All other agreements must be in writing.

6. ***Contain a Legal Description***—A street address does not constitute an adequate description of the property for contract and conveyance purposes. The Statute of Frauds calls for the agreement to have a description that is of such certainty and accuracy that one can go to and identify it. The two commonly used are (1) reference to a recorded plat (lot, block, section number, subdivision name) and (2) metes and bounds.

Valid/Void/Unenforceable/Voidable

If an agreement meets the above requirements, it is considered **valid** and will be upheld by Texas courts. If it does not meet the requirements, it is identified as a **void** (the absence of) contract. Due to a change in the law or the passage of time, a contract or certain provisions of a contract may become **unenforceable.**

As mentioned earlier, contracts can also be **voidable** (set aside at the option of one of the contracting parties). Voidable contracts exist in four instances.

1. When entered into with a minor, the agreement is voidable at the option of the minor party.
2. When **fraud** by acts of commission or acts of omission can be proven, the agreement is voidable at the option of the nonfraudulent party.
3. When the seller fails to provide and the buyer of a previously occupied single-family residence fails to receive the Texas legislature-mandated "Seller's Disclosure of Property Condition," the contract is voidable at the option of the buyer. If it is presented after the agreement is signed, the buyer may terminate the contract within seven days after receipt of the disclosure.
4. When homeowner's association information and "Resale Certificate" has not been provided to the buyer prior to creating an executory contract to purchase.

Presenting Offers

All offers should be reduced to writing and presented to the property owner as quickly as possible. No real estate broker or salesperson has the right to withhold an offer from a property owner. To do so may result in suspension or revocation of one's license under the provisions of the Texas Real Estate License Act or, worse, result in an unpleasant lawsuit for tortious interference. A tort is an act that damages another individual and gives rise to legal action. A property owner may consider the licensee's failure to present an offer in a timely manner a tortious interference with his or her ability to sell the property. The reader would do well to explore the possible consequences of this further before failing to present an offer in a timely manner.

Every licensee in Texas must successfully complete a 30-hour course in the law of agency to obtain a license. Never lose sight of your fiduciary duties to your clients when helping them negotiate contracts. In addition to obedience (finding a buyer for the property), loyalty (putting the client's best interest above all others, including your own), confidentiality (not revealing the client's personal information, although you have the duty to disclose all material facts about the property not specifically excluded by statute), reasonable care and due diligence, you owe your client disclosure and accounting. *Failure to present an offer* is certainly a breach of one's fiduciary duties, as well as the possible basis for a tortious interference lawsuit. All offers must be presented!

When an offer is unacceptable to the property owner, the owner's interest is best served when the owner gives written notice that the offer is unacceptable, thanks the offeror for the interest in the property and invites the offeror to submit another offer. The owner should give the offeror information that will shed some light upon what terms would be more acceptable to the offeree. A REALTOR® and his or her client might use the TAR form designed for this purpose or might simply create a letter to convey the message to the offeror. An example of such a letter follows.

> Dear Mr. and Mrs. Prospect:
>
> Thank you for your offer to purchase our home at 4321 Pine Hollow Drive. We cannot accept your offer as presented. We appreciate your interest and encourage you to submit another offer which will be more favorably considered if you will:
>
> - offer a purchase price more in line with current market value,
> - close within 20 to 30 days,
> - purchase the property in its present condition and
> - pay your own loan originiation costs including the fee for the survey required by your lender.
>
> We look forward to hearing from you soon and wish you a very pleasant day.
>
> Sincerely,

Although the majority of lawsuits against licensees are still brought by dissatisfied buyers after the sale closes, each year more and more suits are being brought by clients or customers who feel that the selling agent breached one or more fiduciary duties or treated them unfairly.

Failure to present an offer can also result in disciplinary action against the licensee by TREC.

The seller presented with a written offer may

- accept it,
- reject it,
- counter it or
- do nothing.

The offeror may withdraw an offer any time before the offeree's acceptance. Other things that may terminate an offer include

- lapse of reasonable time,
- destruction of the subject matter and
- death or insanity of the offeror.

Performance

When an offeror has presented an offer to a seller, the offeree has accepted it and the offeror has been notified of the acceptance, an **executory contract** exists. If and when everyone does what was promised in the agreement, closing should occur in a few days.

When closing and funding occur, the contract is considered fully **executed.** An executory contract is one that is fully negotiated and signed by the parties. The parties still have obligations to fulfill before all things called for in the agreement have been performed. A *fully executed contract* is one in which all parties have fulfilled all promises made in the agreement. When the seller has delivered the deed, received the proceeds and granted possession to the purchaser, there exists a fully executed contract.

If one of the parties violates the agreement (**breach of contract**) the nondefaulting party may

- sue for specific performance,
- accept the earnest money as liquidated damages or
- sue for **money damages.**

Bilateral versus Unilateral

Purchase contracts are **bilateral contracts** that involve a promise in exchange for a promise. The seller in a purchase agreement agrees to deliver clear title and the buyer agrees to deliver money. A **unilateral contract** involves a promise in exchange for an act. The seller agrees to pay the listing broker when and if the broker produces a ready, willing and able buyer.

Interpreting Contracts

When a court is called upon to settle a dispute between the parties to a contract, the court examines the entire agreement in an attempt to discover the intent of the parties. The court reads the preprinted form and presumes that anything added to the preprinted agreement more clearly shows the intent of the parties. Something handwritten overrides anything typewritten or preprinted, and an addendum takes precedence over the preprinted form. Once an *executory contract* has been created, the court favors upholding the agreement and applies the *parol evidence rule* when called upon to make a decision. The parol evidence rule prohibits the consideration of later written or oral agreements unless those agreements clear up any ambiguity in the original agreement. For example, if the original agreement called for closing in "late July" and a separate written agreement called for closing on "July 28," the court would accept the additional "evidence" as a more specific time to close. When parties wish to alter the provisions of an executory contract, they may execute a new contract in place of the existing agreement or amend the existing contract by using the TREC 39–2 Amendment. In legal terms, a replacement contract is known as a **novation.** The new agreement should clearly reference the original agreement and state that the new agreement replaces it.

Reasonable Time versus "Time Is of the Essence"

With regard to time frames established in contracts, Texas courts always favor upholding the provisions of the contract when the parties have acted in good faith and have performed within a *reasonable time*. The court must hold the parties to exact performance within the time specified only when the agreement has incorporated the words, *"time is of the essence."* Only two forms in this book include those words: Addendum for Sale of Other Property by Buyer (TREC form 10-3) and Addendum for "Back-Up" Contract (TREC form 11-3).

A real estate broker or salesperson should *never* add "time is of the essence" to a contract or advise a customer or client to do so. If a party wants to add the words, that party and the other party should be advised to seek the counsel of a real estate attorney before proceeding.

Assignment versus Novation

Once an executory contract has been created, a party may transfer his or her interest to another legal entity (**assignment**) unless prohibited by statute or written agreement of the parties. Purchase contracts are typically assignable. Leases, by statute, may not be assigned without the express written permission of the property owner. The assignor is the party who transfers a right and the assignee is the party to whom the right is assigned. The assignee takes on all of the rights and obligations of the contract being assigned.

Summary

To have a valid contract there must be competent parties who have reached mutual agreement and have tendered consideration. They must have agreed to lawful acts and must have reduced their agreement to writing if it involves rights and interest in real estate. Once the agreement is signed, it can be valid, void, unenforceable or voidable.

The licensee should present all offers immediately to avoid disciplinary action by the Texas Real Estate Commission or a possible suit for tortious interference brought by the property owner.

Texas courts favor upholding the provisions of contracts and apply the reasonable-time rule when interpreting contracts unless the parties have specifically stated that "time is of the essence."

PART 1 REVIEW QUESTIONS

1. What kind of contract exists when a promise is exchanged for a promise?

   A. Unilateral
   B. Executed
   C. Bilateral
   D. Defaulted

2. When all parties have signed a contract, which of the following describes what exists?

   A. Executed contract
   B. Expired contract
   C. Unenforceable contract
   D. Executory contract

3. When there is a default on the part of one party and the other party wants the defaulting party to do what was agreed in the contract, for what would the nondefaulting party sue?

   A. Money damages
   B. Specific performance
   C. Liquidated damages
   D. Injunctive relief

4. What word best describes a contract entered into with a minor?

   A. Void
   B. Voidable
   C. Valid
   D. Venued

5. Which of the following is an example of a unilateral contract?

   A. Contract for sale
   B. Lease
   C. Contract for deed
   D. Listing

6. When an agreement is unenforceable because it does not fulfill the statutory requirements of a contract, it is identified as

   A. valid.
   B. void.
   C. voidable.
   D. invalid.

7. An offer made in response to an offer is known as what?

   A. Contract
   B. Assignment
   C. Counteroffer
   D. Novation

8. The substitution of a new contract for an existing contract is known as what?

   A. Assignment
   B. Novation
   C. Cancellation
   D. Rescission

9. What do you call a deliberate act of deception for the purpose of inducing another to part with something of value or to enter into a contract?

   A. Innocent misrepresentation
   B. Duress
   C. Mistake
   D. Fraud

10. The transfer of a party's rights and obligations created by the contract to a third party is

    A. cancellation.
    B. assignment.
    C. novation.
    D. specific performance.

PART 2

The Texas Real Estate License Act and the Rules of the Texas Real Estate Commission

Key Terms

addenda
addendum
Broker-Lawyer Committee
business detail
earnest money
lease
legal right
option
promulgate
remedy
temporary lease

Under its police power, the state of Texas has the ability to enact and enforce laws to protect the health, safety and general welfare of the public. Since 1939 Texas has had a Real Estate License Act (Article 65732, *Vernon's Texas Civil Statutes*) to regulate those who, for a fee or other valuable consideration, sell, exchange, procure, prospect or inspect real property. The law holds brokers responsible for all professional and vocational acts performed by any real estate salesperson associated with or acting for the broker. Brokers should pay close attention to the activities of their licensed staff.

In Section 16 of the act, licensees are specifically prohibited from practicing law by giving opinions or counsel regarding the validity or legal sufficiency of an instrument that addresses real property rights or as to the status of title to real estate. Throughout the act, it is clearly established that the licensee should give a buyer written advice to have the abstract covering the property examined by an attorney of the buyer's selection or to obtain an owner's title insurance policy prior to closing. Failure to do so may result in disciplinary action by TREC.

Section 16 (a) and (b) clearly establish that it is illegal for the licensee to draw a deed, note, deed of trust, will or other written instrument that transfers or may transfer an interest in or title to real property. However, the act goes on to give permission for a licensee to complete a contract form that may bind the sale, exchange, option, lease or rental of any interest in real property as long as forms are used that have been prepared by or are required by the property owner or have been provided by the real estate commission, prepared by an attorney licensed by Texas and approved by that attorney for a particular type of transaction.

> SECTION 16 (a) A license granted under the provisions of this Act shall be suspended or revoked by the commission on proof that the licensee, not being licensed and authorized to practice law in this state, for a consideration, reward, pecuniary benefit, present or anticipated, direct or indirect, or in connection with or as part of his employment, agency, or fiduciary relationship as a licensee, drew a deed, note, deed of trust, will, or other written instrument that may transfer or anywise affect the title to or an interest in land, except as provided in the subsections below, or advised or counseled a person as to the validity or legal sufficiency of an instrument or as to the validity of title to real estate.
>
> (b) Notwithstanding the provisions of this Act or any other law, the completion of contract forms which bind the sale, exchange, option, lease, or rental of any interest in real property by a real estate broker or salesman incident to the performance of the acts of a broker as defined by this article does not constitute the unauthorized or illegal practice of law in this state, provided the forms have been promulgated for use by the commission for the particular kind of transaction involved, or the forms have been prepared by an attorney at law licensed by this state and approved by said attorney for the particular kind of transaction involved, or the forms have been prepared by the property owner or prepared by an attorney and required by the property owner.

The legislature created an advisory body to develop and recommend various contract forms to the Texas Real Estate Commission for use by licensees when performing the tasks for which they have been licensed. This body, the Texas Real Estate **Broker-Lawyer Committee,** does not **promulgate** or publish forms for mandatory use by licensees. Only the Texas Real Estate Commission has been given rule-making authority. The Broker-Lawyer Committee develops forms and recommends their adoption, but it is the Texas Real Estate Commission that *promulgates* the forms for mandatory use. The act clearly establishes the responsibilities of the committee, composed of six brokers appointed by TREC and six attorneys appointed by the president of the state bar of Texas.

> (c) A Texas Real Estate Broker-Lawyer Committee is hereby created which, in addition to other powers and duties delegated to it, shall draft and

revise contract forms capable of standardization for use by real estate licensees and which will expedite real estate transactions and reduce controversies to a minimum while containing safeguards adequate to protect the interest of the principals to the transaction.

(d) The Texas Real Estate Broker-Lawyer Committee shall have 12 members including six members appointed by the commission and six members of the State Bar of Texas appointed by the President of the State Bar of Texas. The members of the committee shall hold office for staggered terms of six years with the terms of two commission appointees and two State Bar appointees expiring every two years. Each member shall hold office until his successor is appointed. A vacancy for any cause shall be filled for the unexpired term by the agency making the original appointment.

Appointments to the committee shall be made without regard to race, creed, sex, religion, or national origin.

The licensee also needs to be aware that the legislature has given the commission rule-making authority and that the rules of the commission are just as binding upon licensees as are the provisions of the act. With regard to contracts, specific authority is given in Section 16 of the act.

(e) In the best interest of the public the commission may adopt rules and regulations requiring real estate brokers and salesmen to use contract forms which have been prepared by the Texas Real Estate Broker-Lawyer Committee and promulgated by the commission; provided, however, that the commission shall not prohibit a real estate broker or salesman from using a contract form or forms binding the sale, exchange, option, lease, or rental of any interest in real property which have been prepared by the property owner or prepared by an attorney and required by the property owner. For the purpose of this section, contract forms prepared by the Texas Real Estate Broker-Lawyer Committee appointed by the commission and the State Bar of Texas and promulgated by the commission prior to the effective date of this Act shall be deemed to have been prepared by the Texas Real Estate Broker-Lawyer Committee. The commission may suspend or revoke a license issued under the provisions of this article when it has determined that the licensee failed to use a contract form as required by the commission pursuant to this section.

Before engaging in the business of completing any contract forms that bind the sale, **lease, temporary lease** or rental of any real property, the licensee should become thoroughly familiar with what the rules do and do not permit.

The first part of Rule 537.11 lists the forms that are currently promulgated; that is, published for mandatory use by a licensee when the form fits a particular transaction. The following list gives the date on which the form was promulgated, as well as the name of the form and the TREC form reference number. Earlier versions of forms should not be used.

TEXAS REAL ESTATE COMMISSION FORMS

PROMULGATED

Number	Name	Promulgation Date	Page Number
CONTRACTS:			
9-4	Unimproved Property Contract—Residential	11/99	164–170
20-4	One to Four Family Residential Contract (Resale) All Cash, Assumption, Third Party Conventional or Seller Financing	11/99	106–114
21-4	One to Four Family Residential Contract (Resale) FHA Insured or VA Guaranteed Financing	11/99	142–148
23-4	New Home Contract (Incomplete Construction)	6/00	243–250
24-4	New Home Contract (Completed Construction)	6/00	200–207
25-3	Farm and Ranch Contract	11/99	174–181
30-2	Residential Condominium Contract (Resale) All Cash, Assumption, Third Party Conventional or Seller Financing	11/99	186–193
31-2	Residential Condominium Contract (Resale) FHA Insured or VA Guaranteed Financing	11/99	275–282
ADDENDA:			
10-3	Addendum for Sale of Other Property by Buyer	9/99	72
11-3	Addendum for Second or “Back-Up” Contract	6/98	73
12-1	Release of Liability on Assumption of FHA, VA or Conventional Loan, Restoration of Seller’s Entitlement for VA Guaranteed Loan	3/92	39
15-3	Seller’s Temporary Residential Lease	12/98	60–61
16-3	Buyer’s Temporary Residential Lease	12/98	62–63
26-2	Seller Financing Addendum	10/93	36
28-0	Environmental Assessment, Threatened or Endangered Species, and Wetlands Addendum	10/93	47
29-1	Addendum for Abstract of Title	9/99	44
33-0	Addendum for Coastal Area Property	12/94	45
34-0	Addendum for Property Located Seaward of the Gulf Intracoastal Waterway	12/94	46
35-1	Mediation Addendum	6/98	66
36-1	Addendum for Property Subject to Mandatory Membership in an Owner’s Association	1/00	28
39-1	Amendment	9/99	58

RESALE CERTIFICATES:			
32-0	Condominium Resale Certificate	8/94	94
37-1	Subdivision Information, Including Resale Certificate for Property Subject to Mandatory Membership in an Owner's Association	1/00	29–30
NOTICE:			
38-0	Notice of Termination of Contract	6/98	59
DISCLOSURE:			
*	Consumer Information Form 1-1	8/91	97
OPTIONAL / VOLUNTARY USE:			
*	Notice to Prospective Buyer	12/99	100
*	Seller's Disclosure of Property Condition	10/93	51–52
*	Texas Real Estate Consumer Notice Concerning Recognized Hazards	9/94	98
*	Information About Brokerage Services (Please note that the form is optional but the content must be reproduced verbatum in 10 point or larger type as dictated by section 15C of the TRELA.	1/96	99
*	Addendum for Seller's Disclosure of Information on Lead-Based Paint and Lead-Based Paint Hazards as Required by Federal Law	2/97	53

After itemizing the current inventory of available forms, the commission sets down the do's and don'ts for the completion of those forms. A careful reading of the rules tells you all you need to know. The underlining has been added for emphasis.

(b) When negotiating contracts binding the sale, exchange, option, lease or rental of any interest in real property, a real estate licensee shall use only those contract forms promulgated by the Texas Real Estate Commission for that kind of transaction with the following exceptions:

(1) transactions in which the licensee is functioning solely as a principal, not as an agent;

(2) transactions in which an agency of the United States government requires a different form to be used;

(3) transactions for which a contract form has been prepared by the property owner or prepared by an attorney and required by the property owner;

(4) transactions for which no standard contract form has been promulgated by the Texas Real Estate Commission, and the licensee uses a form prepared by an *attorney at law* licensed by this state and approved by the attorney for the particular kind of transactions involved or prepared by the

Texas Real Estate Broker-Lawyer Committee and made available for trial use by licensees with the consent of the Texas Real Estate Commission.

(c) A licensee may not practice law, offer, give nor attempt to give advice, directly or indirectly; the licensee may not act as a public conveyancer nor give advice or opinions as to the legal effect of any contracts or other such instruments which may affect the title to real estate; the licensee may not give opinions concerning the status or validity of title to real estate; and the licensee may not attempt to prevent nor in any manner whatsoever discourage any principal to a real estate transaction from employing a lawyer. However, nothing herein shall be deemed to limit the licensee's fiduciary obligation to disclose to his principals all pertinent facts which are within the knowledge of the licensee, including such facts which might affect the status of or title to real estate.

(d) A licensee may not undertake to draw or prepare documents fixing and defining the *legal rights* of the principals to a transaction. In negotiating real estate transactions, the licensee may fill in forms for such transactions, using exclusively forms which have been approved and promulgated by the Texas Real Estate Commission or such forms as are otherwise permitted by these rules. When filling in such a form, the licensee may only fill in the blanks provided and may not add to or strike matter from such form, except that licensees shall add *factual statements* and *business details* desired by the principals and shall strike only such matter as is desired by the principals and as is necessary to conform the instrument to the intent of the parties. A licensee may not add to a promulgated earnest money contract form factual statements or business details for which a contract **addendum,** lease or other form has been promulgated by the commission for mandatory use. Nothing herein shall be deemed to prevent the licensee from explaining to the principals the meaning of the factual statements and business details contained in the said instrument so long as the licensee does not offer or give legal advice. It is not the practice of law as defined in this Act for a real estate licensee to complete a contract form which is either promulgated by the Texas Real Estate Commission or prepared by the Texas Real Estate Broker-Lawyer Committee and made available for trial use by licensees with the consent of the Texas Real Estate Commission. Contract forms prepared by the Texas Real Estate Broker-Lawyer Committee for trial use may be used on a voluntary basis after being approved by the commission. Contract forms prepared by the Texas Real Estate Broker-Lawyer Committee and approved by the commission to replace previously promulgated forms may be used by licensees on a voluntary basis prior to the effective date of rules requiring use of the replacement form.

(e) Where it appears that, prior to the execution of any such instrument, there are unusual matters involved in the transaction which should be resolved by legal counsel before the instrument is executed or that the instrument is to be acknowledged and filed for record, the licensee shall advise the principals that each should consult a lawyer of the principal's choice before executing same.

(f) A licensee may not employ, directly or indirectly, a lawyer nor pay for the services of a lawyer to represent any principal to a real estate transaction in which the licensee is acting as an agent. The licensee may employ and pay for the services of a lawyer to represent only the licensee in a real estate transaction, including preparation of the contract, agreement, or other legal instruments to be executed by the principals to the transactions.

(g) A licensee shall advise the principals that the instrument they are about to execute is binding on them.

(h) Forms approved or promulgated by the commission may be reproduced only from the following sources:

(1) numbered copies obtained from the commission, whether in a printed format or electronically reproduced from the files available on the commission's Internet site;

(2) printed copies made from copies obtained from the commission;

(3) legible photocopies made from such copies; or

(4) computer-driven printers following these guidelines.

(A) The computer file or program containing the form text must not allow the end-user direct access to the text of the form and may only permit the user to insert language in blanks in the forms or to strike through language at the direction of the parties to the contract.

(B) Typefaces or fonts must appear to be identical to those used by the commission in printed copies of the particular form.

(C) The text and number of pages must be identical to that used by the commission in printed proofs of the particular form.

(D) The spacing, length of blanks, borders and placement of text on the page must appear to be identical to that used by the commission in printed copies of the form.

(E) The name and address of the person or firm responsible for developing the software program must be legibly printed below the border at the bottom of each page in no less than 6 point type and in no larger than 10 point type.

(F) The text of the form must be obtained from a copy of the form bearing a control number assigned by the commission.

(i) The control number of each copy must appear on all forms reproduced from the copy, including forms reproduced by computer-driven printers.

(j) Forms approved or promulgated by the commission must be reproduced on the same size of paper used by the commission with the following changes or additions only.

(1) The business name or logo of a broker, organization or printer may appear at the top of a form outside the border.

(2) The broker's name may be inserted in any blank provided for that purpose.

The commission and the Broker-Lawyer Committee are charged with serving the best interest of the public and have adopted the foregoing to accomplish that purpose. They are always willing to hear comments from the licensees whom they regulate. Address your suggestions for contract and addenda revisions to:

Mark A. Moseley, General Counsel
Texas Real Estate Commission
P.O. Box 12188
Austin, TX 78711-2188

From time to time the TREC ADVISOR will carry a message from TREC's enforcement division relating to the proper approach to structuring, presenting and negotiating purchase agreements. Volume 9, No. 4 addresses the proper handling of multiple offers, a common challenge in a "seller's market." In response to the commonly asked questions about the listing agent's duty to notify the seller of multiple offers, TREC responded:

> TREC rule 535.156(a) specifically requires a licensee to "convey to the principal all known information which would affect the principal's decision on whether or not to accept or reject offers." Subsection 535.156(c) further provides that "a licensee has an affirmative duty to keep the principal informed at all times of significant information applicable to the transaction or transactions in which the licensee is acting as agent for the principal." Thus the rules require the listing agent to submit all written purchase offers to the seller until a buyer and the seller have a fully executed contract.
>
> Although the general rule is that all offers must be communicated to the seller by the listing agent, there are a few exceptions. These include instances where the seller has specifically instructed the listing broker not

to bring the seller any offers below a certain price, or situations in which a binding contract has been executed between a seller and buyer. In the latter situation, Rule 535.156(a) provides that "the licensee shall have no duty to submit offers to the principal after the principal has accepted an offer." Furthermore, the listing agent is prohibited from sharing any information about one buyer's offer with another buyer. Note, however, that in the end, it is always the sellers' decision whether to accept or reject offers they receive. The listing should address the broker's duty regarding back-up offers so as to avoid confusion on the issue. Also, trade association rules may affect the brokers duty.

Summary

The purpose of the license act and the rules of the commission is to protect the public. The provisions prohibit the unauthorized practice of law by real estate licensees both in the area of structuring instruments and in the area of giving legal advice and opinions as to the legal sufficiency of instruments or the status of title.

To assist licensees, the commission has promulgated various forms for use by licensees. Remember that you must use promulgated contracts and addenda. Do not write a **business detail** addressing the business detail into the "Special Provisions" paragraph when there is a promulgated addendum. A business detail states what someone will or will not do. The licensee may only fill in the blanks provided and may not add material to or strike wording from the forms except to add business details to conform the instrument to the intent of the parties. When you describe what will happen if someone does or does not do a certain act (e.g., terminate the contract, refund earnest money), you step over the line and begin defining **legal rights** and **remedies.** A thorough discussion and example of what is and is not acceptable wording for paragraph 11 is provided in Chapter 3.

The licensee may help a customer or client read the document, but shall not give legal advice or opinions. Never discourage a customer or client from employing a competent real estate attorney. It is good practice to encourage buyers and sellers to carefully read any document before they sign it and seek legal counsel to clarify anything they do not understand.

1. Which of the following defines a legal right as opposed to simply stating a business detail?

   A. The buyer will inspect the property again during the four hours immediately preceding closing.
   B. The buyer will pay for the owner's title policy.
   C. The seller will pay for all of the buyer's normal closing costs.
   D. The buyer may terminate the contract if the foundation needs to be repaired.

2. Identify which of the following addenda is not a promulgated form.

   A. Lead-Based Paint Addendum
   B. Seller's Temporary Residential Lease
   C. Seller Financing Addendum
   D. Addendum for Abstract of Title

3. Who must notify the buyer to have the abstract examined by an attorney or obtain a policy of title insurance?

   A. The seller
   B. The licensee
   C. The lender
   D. The buyer's attorney

4. A licensee may use a contract form that has been prepared by the property owner when instructed by the property owner to do so.

   A. True
   B. False

5. What should a licensee do when there are unusual matters involved in a transaction?

   A. Explain it to the best of his/her ability before letting the prospect sign the contract.
   B. Ignore it and hope that the client understands it.
   C. Have the client sign the form and then advise him/her to talk to an attorney.
   D. Advise the client to seek legal advice before signing anything.

6. For which of the following is there *no* promulgated form?

   A. Sale of an unimproved residential lot
   B. Contract for deed
   C. Lease for temporary occupancy of a seller after the closing
   D. Request for information about an owner's association

7. As an added value to the service provided by a broker, may a broker retain and pay for the services of an attorney to provide legal counsel to a client?

   A. Yes
   B. No

8. Which of the following actions might leave a licensee open to a charge of practicing law without a license?

   A. Licensee advises the seller that the property probably won't sell because it's overpriced.
   B. Licensee advises the buyer that a title policy should be obtained as well as a survey.
   C. Licensee advises both the seller and the buyer that, in his opinion, title to the subject property is encumbered.
   D. Licensee adds factual statements and business details to a promulgated form as requested by the client.

9. Which of the following is true regarding TREC promulgated contract forms?

   A. They must be used by all real estate licensees and Texas attorneys handling real estate transactions.
   B. They must be used by real estate licensees in all transactions to which the forms are applicable unless a substitute form is required by the property owner.
   C. They contain suggested language that a licensee may include when writing an agreement of purchase between a seller and a buyer.
   D. They are written and published by the Broker-Lawyer Committee and must be used for those transactions identified by the committee.

10. When no promulgated form meets the needs of a particular transaction, the licensee may use which of the following?

    A. Any standard form sold at the office supply store
    B. Any of the State Bar standard forms
    C. A form structured and approved by a licensed attorney at law
    D. A form created by a Texas licensed attorney for that type of transaction

PART 3

Contract and Addenda Provisions

To become thoroughly familiar with the provisions of the promulgated contract forms and addenda, we shall begin with a paragraph-by-paragraph inspection and analysis of TREC form 20-4, which is the most commonly used form.

PROMULGATED BY THE TEXAS REAL ESTATE COMMISSION (TREC) 11-8-99

ONE TO FOUR FAMILY RESIDENTIAL CONTRACT (RESALE)
ALL CASH, ASSUMPTION, THIRD PARTY CONVENTIONAL OR SELLER FINANCING

NOTICE: Not For Use For Condominium Transactions

You will notice that the intended use of the form is identified in its title.

- Resale—not for use with new construction
- All cash, assumption, conventional, seller financing—not for use for FHA insured or VA guaranteed financing

Some forms also include a notice to refrain from using the form for certain types of transactions.

In the upper right hand corner of each form is the date of the Commission meeting at which the form was promulgated. To make certain that you are using correct forms, verify the date on any form against the date on the list in Part Two in this book. If you have forms with an earlier date than those found on the list, do not use them. Once an earlier version of a form has been retired it is illegal for a licensee to use it in structuring a transaction.

The various addenda designed to add specific business details, contingencies and temporary leasehold arrangements to the transaction are introduced throughout the discussion of the provisions of the basic contract form. The other seven contract forms are examined in Part Four.

Unfortunately, many licensees attempt to complete the forms without ever having read them. The best approach is to read the form carefully and simply add the appropriate business detail called for by a blank line. We shall discuss what needs to be added where blanks appear.

The completed form should reflect the desires and wishes of the parties. The salesperson or broker who makes decisions for the parties is exceeding the scope of authority granted by a listing or buyer representation agreement. The special agent should identify options and then let the client or customer set the limits.

The executory contract provides the escrow officer and all affected parties with definitive instructions for closing the real estate transaction. The executory contract serves as a blueprint for the closing. It should address every detail relating to what must be done to close the sale of the property and have a fully executed contract. There should be no reason for anyone to contact the licensee to interpret the phraseology of the special provisions or any filled in blanks if the licensee has performed competently.

As you proceed through the various provisions of the contract, remember that reasonable, realistic time frames need to be defined. One cannot close in 15 days if it is going to take 25 days to get loan approval and 20 days to get the results of an environmental inspection. It makes no sense to structure an executory contract that is contingent upon obtaining a 97 percent LTV loan at 8 percent annual interest for 40 years if only 90 percent LTV loans at 8.75 percent annual interest for 30 years are available from lenders.

1. **PARTIES:** ______________________________ (Seller)
agrees to sell and convey to ______________________________ (Buyer)
and Buyer agrees to buy from Seller the property described below.

The seller(s) and buyer(s) must be identified in the first paragraph. Because Texas is a community property state, it is important to include marital status. The following are acceptable ways to identify the marital status of parties.

Unmarried	NAME, **an unmarried person**
Married	(When spouse is not joining in the conveyance) NAME, **as separate property**

Married
(Community property)
NAME, **and spouse** NAME
Husband's NAME **and wife** wife's NAME
Wife's NAME **and husband** husband's NAME

Unmarried Persons Buying Together
NAME and NAME, **as tenants in common**
NOTE: When the parties wish to create rights of survivorship or fractional interests are involved, the parties should be advised to seek the advice of a competent real estate attorney before proceeding.

Executor or Administrator of an Estate
Executor's or administrator's NAME, **executor (administrator) of the estate of (decedent's name), deceased**

General Partnership
Business NAME, **a Texas partnership**
or
Business NAME, **a Texas partnership composed of name, name and name**

Limited Partnership
Business NAME, **a Texas limited partnership, name, as general partner acting for and on behalf of the partnership**

Corporation
Company NAME, Inc., **a Texas* corporation**
*or the name of the state in which the corporation is chartered
NOTE: A corporate resolution issued by the board of directors names the officers appointed to execute the instruments for and on behalf of the corporation. A licensee should request a copy of the corporate resolution prior to the execution of any written agreements. It is to be retained in the transaction file.

Texas Limited Liability Company
Company NAME, **a Texas limited liability company**
or
Company NAME, **LLC**

Nonprofit Corporation
NAME, NAME and NAME, **trustees for and on behalf of (corporate name)**

Make certain that all names are complete and spelled correctly. To verify sellers' names one may check the owner's title policy issued when title was taken or examine the name(s) appearing on the deed used to convey title and recorded at the county courthouse of the county in which the property is located. Remember that the tax records often contain significant errors and should not be relied upon as the final authority in these matters.

2. **PROPERTY:** Lot ________________, Block ______, ________________________________
Addition, City of ________________________________, ________________________ County,
Texas, known as ____
(Address/Zip Code), or as described on attached exhibit, together with the following items, if any: curtains and rods, draperies and rods, valances, blinds, window shades, screens, shutters, awnings, wall-to-wall carpeting, mirrors fixed in place, ceiling fans, attic fans, mail boxes, television antennas and satellite dish system with controls and equipment, permanently installed heating and air-conditioning units, window air-conditioning units, built-in security and fire detection equipment, plumbing and lighting fixtures including chandeliers, water softener, stove, built-in kitchen equipment, garage door openers with controls, built-in cleaning equipment, all swimming pool equipment and maintenance accessories, shrubbery, landscaping, permanently installed outdoor cooking equipment, built-in fireplace screens, artificial fireplace logs and all other property owned by Seller and attached to the above described real property except the following property which is not included: ________________________________
____
____
____.

All property sold by this contract is called the "Property." The Property ❑ is ❑ is not subject to mandatory membership in an owners' association. The TREC Addendum For Property Subject To Mandatory Membership In An Owners' Association ❑ is ❑ is not attached.
NOTICE TO BUYER: If the Property is subject to mandatory membership in an owner's association, Seller notifies Buyer under §5.012, Texas Property Code, that, as a purchaser of property in the residential community in which the Property is located, you are obligated to be a member of an owners' association. Restrictive covenants governing the use and occupancy of the Property and a dedicatory instrument governing the establishment, maintenance, and operation of this residential community have been or will be recorded in the Real Property Records of the county in which the Property is located. Copies of the restrictive covenants and dedicatory instrument may be obtained from the county clerk. You are obligated to pay assessments to the owners' association. The amount of the assessments is subject to change. Your failure to pay the assessments could result in a lien on and the foreclosure of the Property.

The Statute of Frauds requires that agreements affecting title to real property have a legal description, a description of such certainty and accuracy that one can go to the property and identify it. Most urban residential properties are described by reference to a plat recorded at the courthouse of the county where the property is located.

The form provides a blank for the lot number, the block number, the name of the subdivision, the name of the city and the informal street or post office address. When the subdivision has multiple sections, it is important to include the section number either before or after the name of the addition.

Example: Lot 3, Block 5, Section 2 of Shady Hollow Addition . . .

When the property is located in a city, include the name of the city. If the property is located in an unincorporated area, put N/A (not applicable) in the blank for city. Be sure to provide the zip code as called for in the contract form.

If the property is described by a metes-and-bounds description, put "N/A" in the blanks for lot and block. You may or may not have a subdivision name.

Often townhouses are located in a platted subdivision but are described by a metes-and-bounds description. Fill in any blanks that apply, put N/A in those that do not apply and be sure to attach the metes-and-bounds description as "Exhibit A."

The next part of this paragraph lists the fixtures plus the curtains, draperies and stove that usually remain with the property upon the transfer of ownership. When any of these items are to be removed by the seller, carefully list in the space provided the items that do not remain. It is not necessary to strike any words in this paragraph. Simply list any property not included. If there are no exclusions, be sure that you enter "N/A" or "none" in the space provided for the purpose of listing any exclusions.

Do not attempt in this paragraph to deal with personal property that might remain with the property. It is best to keep personal property completely out of the contract. The contract addresses the proposed transfer of real property. Personal property should be handled by a bill of sale as an entirely separate transaction between the parties. However, if the parties insist on putting personal property in the contract, it may be addressed in paragraph 11.

The final two sentences address a very big issue. You must check a box to identify whether the property is or is not subject to mandatory membership in a homeowners' association and its assessments. You must also address whether an addendum is attached.

To further address the issue, the Texas Real Estate Commission promulgated a revised addendum in 1999. The addendum (page 28) calls for a "Resale Certificate" (page 29) to be provided by the homeowners' association. The certificate is not to be completed by the homeowner; it is prepared by the governing body of the association to list suits pending against the association as well as to give the prospective buyer information about any delinquencies by the present owner, reserves and transfer fees. It further calls for attachments, such as the current operating budget, articles of incorporation, bylaws, rules and regulations and any other documents specified by the parties.

During the 1999 legislative session, the legislature enacted SB 434 to ensure that Texas homeowners can obtain information from the homeowner's association in a timely manner after filing a written request with the

PROMULGATED BY THE TEXAS REAL ESTATE COMMISSION (TREC) 09-01-99

ADDENDUM FOR PROPERTY SUBJECT TO MANDATORY MEMBERSHIP IN AN OWNERS' ASSOCIATION

(NOT FOR USE WITH CONDOMINIUMS)

ADDENDUM TO CONTRACT CONCERNING THE PROPERTY AT

____
(Street Address and City)

____
(Name of Owners' Association)

A. **SUBDIVISION INFORMATION:** "Subdivision Information" means: (i) the restrictions applying to the subdivision, (ii) the bylaws and rules of the Owners' Association, and (iii) a resale certificate, all of which were provided by the Owners' Association in compliance with Section 207.003 of the Texas Property Code no more than three months before the date of their delivery to Buyer.
(Check only one box):

☐ 1. Within ________ days after the effective date of the contract, Seller shall at Seller's expense deliver the Subdivision Information to Buyer. If Buyer does not receive the Subdivision Information, Buyer may terminate the contract at any time prior to closing. If Seller delivers the Subdivision Information, Buyer may terminate the contract for any reason within 7 days after Buyer receives the Subdivision Information or prior to closing, whichever first occurs.

☐ 2. Buyer has received and approved the Subdivision Information before signing the contract.

☐ 3. Buyer does not require delivery of the Subdivision Information **and waives the right of termination under this Addendum**.

If Seller becomes aware of any material changes in the Subdivision Information, Seller shall immediately give notice to Buyer. Buyer may terminate the contract prior to closing by giving written notice to Seller if: (i) any of the Subdivision Information provided was not true; or (ii) any material adverse change in the Subdivision Information occurs prior to closing.

B. **TRANSFER FEES:** Buyer shall pay any Owners' Association transfer fee not to exceed $ ____________, and Seller agrees to pay any excess.

NOTICE TO BUYER REGARDING REPAIRS BY THE OWNERS' ASSOCIATION: The Owners' Association may have the sole responsibility to make certain repairs to the Property. If you are concerned about the condition of any part of the Property which the Owners' Association is required to repair, you should not sign the contract unless you are satisfied that the Owners' Association will make the desired repairs.

______________________ Buyer	______________________ Seller
______________________ Buyer	______________________ Seller

The form of this addendum has been approved by the Texas Real Estate Commission for use only with similarly approved or promulgated forms of contracts. Such approval relates to this contract form only. TREC forms are intended for use only by trained real estate licensees. No representation is made as to the legal validity or adequacy of any provision in any specific transactions. It is not suitable for complex transactions.(09-99)Texas Real Estate Commission, P.O. Box 12188, Austin, TX 78711-2188, 1-800-250-8732 or (512) 459-6544 (http://www.trec.state.tx.us) TREC No. 36-1.This form replaces TREC No. 36-0.

01A TREC No. 36-1

PROMULGATED BY THE TEXAS REAL ESTATE COMMISSION (TREC) 09-01-99

SUBDIVISION INFORMATION, INCLUDING RESALE CERTIFICATE FOR PROPERTY SUBJECT TO MANDATORY MEMBERSHIP IN AN OWNERS' ASSOCIATION

(Section 207.003, Texas Property Code)

(NOT FOR USE WITH CONDOMINIUMS)

Resale Certificate concerning the Property (including any common areas assigned to the Property) located at ____ (Street Address), City of ____________________, ____________________, County, Texas, prepared by the property owners' association (the Owners' Association).

A. The Property ❑ is ❑ is not subject to a right of first refusal or other restraint contained in the restrictions or restrictive covenants that restricts the owner's right to transfer the owner's property.

B. The current regular assessment for the Property is $_______________ per _______________.

C. A special assessment for the Property due after the date the resale certificate was prepared is $_______________ payable as follows ______________________________.

D. The total of all amounts due and unpaid to the Owners' Association that are attributable to the Property is $ ________________________.

E. The capital expenditures approved by the Owners' Association for its current fiscal year are $ ________________________.

F. The amount of reserves for capital expenditures is $________________________.

G. Unsatisfied judgments against the Owners' Association total $____________________________.

H. There ❑ are ❑ are not any suits pending against the Owners' Association. The style and cause number of each pending suit is: ____.

I. The Owners' Association's board ❑ has actual knowledge ❑ has no actual knowledge of conditions on the Property in violation of the restrictions applying to the subdivision or the bylaws or rules of the Owners' Association. Known violations are: ____

J. The Owners' Association ❑ has ❑ has not received notice from any governmental authority regarding health or building code violations with respect to the Property or any common areas or common facilities owned or leased by the Owners' Association. A summary or copy of each notice is attached.

Subdivision Information Concerning ______________________________ Page Two 09-01-99
(Address)

K. The Owners' Association's administrative transfer fee is $ ____________, payable to ______________________________.

L. The Owners' Association's managing agent is ____________________, ____________________
(Name of Agent) (Mailing Address)

______________________________, ____________________, ____________________.
(Telephone Number) (Fax Number)

M. The restrictions ☐ do ☐ do not allow foreclosure of the Owners' Association's lien on the Property for failure to pay assessments.

REQUIRED ATTACHMENTS:

1. Restrictions
2. Rules
3. Bylaws
4. Current Balance Sheet
5. Current Operating Budget
6. Certificate of Insurance concerning Property and Liability Insurance for Common Areas and Facilities
7. Any Governmental Notices of Health or Housing Code Violations

NOTICE: This Subdivision Information may change at any time.

____
Name of Owners' Association

By: ______________________________

Title: ______________________________

Mailing Address: ______________________________

Date: ______________________________

association. The statute provides that the association must furnish the completed TREC 37-1 "Resale Certificate" within ten days of receipt of a written request for it from the homeowner or the owner's agent. Associations are permitted to charge a reasonable fee for the certificate.

The final paragraph contains the statutory notice to the buyer that warns that unpaid assessments to the owner's association may result in a foreclosure action. It also puts the buyer on notice that the amount of the assessment is subject to change.

You need to ask about the association transfer fee at the time you list the property so that the proper amount can be inserted in section B of the addendum.

Paragraph 3 is one of the easiest to complete correctly. Enter the sales price on line C. Add all loans that will be used to finance the purchase and enter the amount on line B. Most of the time you will deal with only one loan. Sometimes you may have a buyer assuming an existing loan and asking a seller to carry back a second.

3. SALES PRICE:
A. Cash portion of Sales Price payable by Buyer at closing. . . . . $__________
B. Sum of all financing described below
(excluding any private mortgage insurance [PMI] premium) . . . . $__________
C. Sales Price (Sum of A and B) . . . . $__________

Example: The buyer is assuming a first lien note with an outstanding balance of $83,400 and a home improvement loan with a balance of $21,680 and asking the seller to carry back a note for $30,000. To get the correct number to enter in 3B, add $83,400 + $21,680 + $30,000 for a total of $135,080. To get the correct number to put in 3A, simply subtract 3B from 3C.

If the sales price in the above example is $160,600, line 3A would be $25,520 ($160,600 minus $135,080). Make certain that the buyer realizes that 3A represents only the cash portion of the sales price to be paid at closing by the buyer. Prepaids, reserve impounds and closing costs are not included in this number.

The first part of paragraph 4 establishes how many days the buyer has after the effective date of the contract to apply for lender approval. It then defines when approval will be deemed to have been obtained and establishes the financing contingency. It is important to make certain that the number of days inserted in the second blank is carefully coordinated with the projected closing date inserted later in paragraph 9. Do not be one of the licensees who structures a contract with an effective date of June 1 that calls for a closing on June 20 and gives the buyer 45 days to obtain lender approval.

When dealing with number of days in the contract, remember that all days are counted beginning the day *after* the effective date of the contract and ending at midnight on the last day.

> ***Example:*** The contract has an effective date of October 1, 1999 (Friday) and five days for the buyer to make loan application. The five days are:
>
> Day 1 Saturday, October 2
> Day 2 Sunday, October 3
> Day 3 Monday, October 4
> Day 4 Tuesday, October 5
> Day 5 Wednesday, October 6 until midnight

> 4. **FINANCING:** Within ______ days after the effective date of this contract Buyer shall apply for all third party financing or noteholder's approval of any assumption and make every reasonable effort to obtain financing or assumption approval. Financing or assumption approval will be deemed to have been obtained when the lender determines that Buyer has satisfied all of lender's financial requirements (those items relating to Buyer's net worth, income and creditworthiness). If financing (including any financed PMI premium) or assumption approval is not obtained within ______ days after the effective date hereof, this contract will terminate and the earnest money will be refunded to Buyer. Each note to be executed hereunder must be secured by vendor's and deed of trust liens.
> The portion of Sales Price not payable in cash will be paid as follows: (Check applicable boxes below)

Subsections A through E define the contingency and are self-explanatory upon a careful reading. The only problem one might encounter is knowing what to put in the first blank of 4A(1) ". . . loan-to-value ratio not to exceed _____% as established . . .". The best approach, after you have completed paragraph 3, is to divide 3B by 3C. The result gives the correct number when you move the decimal point two places to the right. Remember that 3B ÷ 3C = LTV.

> ***Example:*** 3. A $100,000
> B $100,000
> C $200,000
>
> Divide $100,000 by $200,000 and you get .5
> .5 = 50%

If the appraisal comes in at $190,000 and you divide $100,000 by $190,000, you get .526 or 52.6 percent. The buyer now has the ability to cancel and walk away, renegotiate the sales price or proceed with the sale in spite of the low appraisal.

When dealing with an 80 percent or greater loan-to-value ratio, a low appraisal will block the approval of the loan without an adjustment to the sales price.

It may also change the loan without PMI to one requiring the buyer(s) to purchase PMI. For a thorough explanation of when private mortgage insurance may be required and why lenders require it, you may want to refer to a good finance or principles of real estate textbook.

❑ A. **THIRD PARTY FINANCING:**

❑ (1) This contract is subject to approval for Buyer of a third party first mortgage loan having a loan-to-value ratio not to exceed _____% as established by such third party (excluding any financed PMI premium), due in full in ____ year(s), with interest not to exceed ____% per annum for the first ____ year(s) of the loan. The loan will be ❑ with ❑ without PMI.

❑ (2) This contract is subject to approval for Buyer of a third party second mortgage loan having a loan-to-value ratio not to exceed _____% as established by such third party (excluding any financed PMI premium), due in full in ____ year(s), with interest not to exceed ____% per annum for the first ____ year(s) of the loan. The loan will be ❑ with ❑ without PMI.

❑ B. **TEXAS VETERANS' HOUSING ASSISTANCE PROGRAM LOAN:** This contract is subject to approval for Buyer of a Texas Veterans' Housing Assistance Program Loan (the Program Loan) of $___________ for a period of at least _______ years at the interest rate established by the Texas Veterans' Land Board at the time of closing.

❑ C. **SELLER FINANCING:** A promissory note from Buyer to Seller of $__________, bearing _____% interest per annum, secured by vendor's and deed of trust liens, in accordance with the terms and conditions set forth in the attached TREC Seller Financing Addendum. If an owner policy of title insurance is furnished, Buyer shall furnish Seller with a mortgagee policy of title insurance.

❑ D. **ASSUMPTION:**

❑ (1) Buyer shall assume the unpaid principal balance of a first lien promissory note payable to ____ which unpaid balance at closing will be $___________. The total current monthly payment including principal, interest and any reserve deposits is $___________. Buyer's initial payment will be the first payment due after closing.

❑ (2) Buyer shall assume the unpaid principal balance of a second lien promissory note payable to ____ which unpaid balance at closing will be $________________. The total current monthly payment including principal, interest and any reserve deposits is $________________. Buyer's initial payment will be the first payment due after closing.

Buyer's assumption of an existing note includes all obligations imposed by the deed of trust securing the note.

If the unpaid principal balance(s) of any assumed loan(s) as of the Closing Date varies from the loan balance(s) stated above, the ❑ cash payable at closing ❑ Sales Price will be adjusted by the amount of any variance; provided, if the total principal balance of all assumed loans varies in an amount greater than $350.00 at closing, either party may terminate this contract and the earnest money will be refunded to Buyer unless the other party elects to eliminate the excess in the variance by an appropriate adjustment at closing. If the noteholder requires (a) payment of

[Continued]

an assumption fee in excess of $____________ in D(1) above or $____________ in D(2) above and Seller declines to pay such excess, or (b) an increase in the interest rate to more than _____% in D(1) above, or _____% in D(2) above, or (c) any other modification of the loan documents, Buyer may terminate this contract and the earnest money will be refunded to Buyer. A vendor's lien and deed of trust to secure assumption will be required which shall automatically be released on execution and delivery of a release by noteholder. If Seller is released from liability on any assumed note, the vendor's lien and deed of trust to secure assumption will not be required.

NOTICE TO BUYER: The monthly payments, interest rates or other terms of some loans may be adjusted by the lender at or after closing. If you are concerned about the possibility of future adjustments, do not sign the contract without examining the notes and deeds of trust.

NOTICE TO SELLER: Your liability to pay the note assumed by Buyer will continue unless you obtain a release of liability from the lender. If you are concerned about future liability, you should use the TREC Release of Liability Addendum.

❑ E. **CREDIT APPROVAL ON ASSUMPTION OR SELLER FINANCING:** Within _____ days after the effective date of this contract, Buyer shall deliver to Seller ❑ credit report ❑ verification of employment, including salary ❑ verification of funds on deposit in financial institutions ❑ current financial statement to establish Buyer's creditworthiness for assumption approval or seller financing and ❑ ____.

If Buyer's documentation is not delivered within the specified time, Seller may terminate this contract by notice to Buyer within 7 days after expiration of the time for delivery, and the earnest money will be paid to Seller. If this contract is not so terminated, Seller will be deemed to have accepted Buyer's credit. If the documentation is timely delivered, and Seller determines in Seller's sole discretion that Buyer's credit is unacceptable, Seller may terminate this contract by notice to Buyer within 7 days after expiration of the time for delivery and the earnest money will be refunded to Buyer. If Seller does not so terminate this contract, Seller will be deemed to have accepted Buyer's credit. Buyer hereby authorizes any credit reporting agency to furnish to Seller at Buyer's sole expense copies of Buyer's credit reports.

Before using subparagraph 4B, obtain information about the Texas Veterans' Housing Assistance Program by calling (800) 252-VETS. The program has a maximum loan amount of $150,000, which may be used alone or in combination with an FHA insured, VA guaranteed or conventional loan. The interest rate can be as much as 2 percent below the going rate on other loans and can save the buyer as much as $17,000 over the term of the loan. Every buyer's agent should become informed about the program and pass the information on to any Texas buyer who might be eligible. To complete the contract form, simply enter the desired loan amount and the desired term, which cannot exceed 30 years. The interest rate is established by the Texas Veterans' Land Board. For complete information on this program, go to **www.glo.state.tx.us/vlb**

Often a seller offers financing and accepts a secured note as part of the consideration for the purchase of the property. A seller-carried note may be the sole loan or it might be a second lien note when the buyer assumes an existing first lien note or when the lender providing the first lien note permits the creation of a subordinated second lien note in place of the part of the cash needed to create the desired loan-to-value ratio. To complete paragraph 4C, insert the amount of the note in the first blank and the interest rate in the second.

The "Seller Financing Addendum" (page 36) will be added to the contract to address how the loan will be repaid, whether the note is assumable and how payment of ad valorem taxes and insurance will be handled. A prudent seller should have an attorney any time seller financing is a part of the transaction. The attorney should be experienced in real estate law and understand the potential risks to the seller's financial well-being when the buyer defaults on the payments and decisive legal action against the borrower becomes necessary. An agent who tells a seller that legal counsel is optional in this type of transaction sets himself or herself up for significant potential legal ramification if the buyer later defaults and the seller loses money or, worse yet, the property.

Although rare, occasionally a buyer will be able to complete a purchase by assuming a seller's existing financing. Many, if not most, notes and mortgages contain a due-on-sale clause and cannot be assumed. FHA insured and VA guaranteed are the exception and can be rather easily assumed.

When the buyer assumes an existing loan or loans as part of the consideration for the sale, check the box at 4D. Check box 1 for assumption of a first lien position loan and, if applicable, box 2 for assumption of a second lien position loan. To correctly complete this paragraph you must gather some very specific information about the loan or loans being assumed. You need to know

- the name of the note holder(s),
- the current unpaid principal balance(s),
- the current monthly PITI payment(s),
- the assumption fee(s) to be charged by the note holder(s),
- to what level the interest rate(s) will be adjusted at closing,
- whether the parties want the sales price or the cash payable at closing adjusted to compensate for any variance entered in the contract form, and
- the seller's wishes with regard to being released from liability for the obligations of the note being assumed. It should be noted that the liability to pay the note continues in Texas when a loan is assumed unless the seller is specifically released from liability by the lender. Be sure to carefully read the notices to both the buyer and the seller included as part of paragraph 4D. When a seller desires to be released from liability upon assumption or wants a restoration of the ability to use the VA guaranteed loan program, the "Addendum for Release of Liability on Assumption of FHA, VA or Conventional Loan/Restoration of Seller's Entitlement for VA Guaranteed Loan," TREC addendum number 12-1 (page 39), must be used.

10-25-93

SELLER FINANCING ADDENDUM

PROMULGATED BY THE TEXAS REAL ESTATE COMMISSION (TREC)

NOTICE: NOT FOR USE FOR COMPLEX TRANSACTIONS

ADDENDUM TO EARNEST MONEY CONTRACT BETWEEN THE UNDERSIGNED PARTIES CONCERNING THE PROPERTY IDENTIFIED AS ______________________________

A. **PROMISSORY NOTE.** The promissory note (the Note) described in Paragraph 4 of the Earnest Money Contract payable by Buyer (Maker) to the order of Seller (Payee) shall be payable at the place designated by Payee. The Note may be prepaid in whole or in part at any time without penalty. Any prepayments are to be applied to the payment of the installments of principal last maturing and interest shall immediately cease on the prepaid principal. The lien securing payment of the Note will be inferior to any lien securing any superior note described in the contract. The Note shall be payable as follows:

☐ (1) In one payment due ______________ after the date of the Note with interest payable ________________.

☐ (2) In ____________________ installments of $ ____________________ ☐ including interest ☐ plus interest beginning ____________________ after the date of the Note and continuing at ____________________ intervals thereafter for ____________________ when the entire balance of the Note shall be due and payable.

☐ (3) Interest only in ____________________ installments for the first ________________ year(s) and thereafter in installments of $________________ ☐ including interest ☐ plus interest beginning ________________ after the date of the Note and continuing at ________________ intervals thereafter for ________________ ________ when the entire balance of the Note shall be due and payable.

B. **DEED OF TRUST.** The deed of trust securing the Note shall provide for the following:

(1) ASSUMPTION OF NOTE OR PROHIBITIONS AGAINST ASSUMPTION: (check only one)

☐ (a) Assumption Without Consent: The Property may be sold without the consent of the Payee, provided any subsequent buyer assumes the Note.

☐ (b) Assumption With Consent: The Property may be sold to a subsequent Buyer who assumes the Note, with no change in interest rate or terms; provided the subsequent buyer obtains prior written consent from the Payee. Consent will be based on the subsequent Buyer's credit history, and shall not be unreasonably withheld. If all or any part of the Property is sold, conveyed, leased for a period longer than 3 years, leased with an option to purchase, or otherwise sold (including by contract for deed), without the prior written consent of the Payee, then the Payee may at his option declare the outstanding principal balance of the Note, plus accrued interest, to be immediately due and payable. The creation of a subordinate lien, any sale thereunder, any deed under threat or order of condemnation, any conveyance solely between makers, or the passage of title by reason of the death of a maker or by operation of law shall not be construed as a sale or conveyance of the Property.

☐ (c) Prohibition Against Assumption: If all or any part of the Property is sold, conveyed, leased for a period longer than 3 years, leased with an option to purchase, or otherwise sold (including any contract for deed), without the prior written consent of the Payee, then the Payee may at his option declare the outstanding principal balance of the Note, plus accrued interest, to be immediately due and payable. The creation of a subordinate lien, any sale thereunder, any deed under threat or order of condemnation, any conveyance solely between makers, the passage of title by reason of the death of a maker or by operation of law shall not be construed as a sale or conveyance of the Property.

(2) TAX AND INSURANCE PAYMENTS: (check only one)

☐ (a) Without Escrow: Maker shall furnish to Payee annually, before the taxes become delinquent, copies of tax receipts showing that all taxes on the Property have been paid. Maker shall furnish to Payee annually evidence of current paid-up insurance naming Payee as an insured.

☐ (b) With Escrow: Maker shall, in addition to the principal and interest installments, deposit with the Payee a pro rata part of the estimated annual ad valorem taxes on the Property and a pro rata part of the estimated annual insurance premiums for the improvements on the Property. These tax and insurance deposits are only estimates and may be insufficient to pay total taxes and insurance premiums. Maker shall pay any deficiency within 30 days after notice from Payee. Maker's failure to pay the deficiency shall constitute a default under the Deed of Trust. In the event any superior lienholder on the Property is collecting escrow payments for taxes and insurance, this Paragraph shall be inoperative so long as payments are being made to the superior lienholder.

(3) CROSS-DEFAULT: Any act or occurrence which would constitute default under the terms of any lien superior to the lien securing the Note shall constitute a default under the Deed of Trust securing the Note.

______________________	______________________
Buyer/Maker	Seller/Payee
______________________	______________________
Buyer/Maker	Seller/Payee

The form of this Addendum has been approved by the Texas Real Estate Commission for use with similarly approved or promulgated contract forms. Such approval relates to this form only. No representation is made as to the legal validity or adequacy of any provision in any specific transactions. It is not suitable for complex transactions. (10-93) TREC No. 26-2. This form replaces TREC No. 26-1.

01A TREC No. 26-2

When you have gathered the above information, read the beginning of paragraph 4D and fill in the appropriate blanks. In a blank that does not apply to the particular transaction, simply enter "N/A."

When a release of liability or restoration of entitlement is desired, use the following addendum (page 39) and check the boxes that express the wishes of the parties. Note that under both paragraphs A and B the parties may check a box to terminate the contract if the desired action is not obtained by the closing date or to close and have the buyer continue to assist the seller in obtaining the release or the restoration. In most transactions, the parties check the first box.

In the last paragraph note that the form obligates the seller to pay the cost of securing the release and/or restoration. A quick call to a loan officer will give you an answer as to what dollar amount needs to go in the blank for the seller's anticipated cost. Many licensees enter .5 percent or 1 point (remember that a point is equal to 1 percent of the loan balance) instead of using a dollar amount. This approach works well.

Before a seller agrees to seller financing or to permitting an existing loan to be assumed, the seller may want to call for the buyer to provide certain evidence of the buyer's creditworthiness. Specific items can be requested by checking the appropriate boxes. If the seller wants to be more specific and require a credit report from a particular credit reporting agency, you may need to set such business details in the "Special Provisions" paragraph.

Note that the parties must determine and specify in the blank provided how many days the buyer has to provide the required documentation to the seller. If the documentation is not furnished, the seller may terminate the contract within seven days after the time for delivery has expired. If the seller fails to terminate the contract within the time specified, the contract states that the seller is deemed to have accepted the buyer's credit and is bound to move on to closing. If the seller determines that the buyer's credit is unacceptable, the seller notifies the buyer and terminates the contract within *seven days* after expiration of the time for delivery of the documentation.

> **5. EARNEST MONEY:** Buyer shall deposit $__________ as earnest money with ______________________________ at ______________________________ (Address), as escrow agent, upon execution of this contract by both parties. Additional earnest money of $__________ must be deposited by Buyer with escrow agent on or before ______________, 19____. If Buyer fails to deposit the earnest money as required by this contract, Buyer will be in default.

The earnest money serves two purposes. The first is to show good faith and serious intent on the part of the purchaser. Note that earnest money is not necessary to bind the contract. The promise of the purchaser to buy and the promise of the seller to deliver title is adequate consideration to create a legally binding executory contract. Thus, a listing agent might want to suggest that the seller ask the buyer to show serious intent by requesting a significant deposit. Around 3 to 5 percent of the purchase price is common; however, the parties may determine that a smaller or larger amount is appropriate for their particular transaction. Please remember that the final decision is in the hands of the buyer and the seller. The second purpose of the deposited money is to serve as liquidated damages in the event of default.

The blanks calling for additional earnest money can be used when the buyer is unable to make the full desired deposit at the time of signing the agreement. This might occur when the buyer is waiting for a certificate of deposit to mature and does not want to delay signing the agreement or to cash in early and lose the interest on the instrument. It should be noted that failure to deposit the additional money constitutes a default and gives the seller the right to exercise the default remedies established by agreement of the parties in paragraph 15.

The Texas real estate licensee should note that TREC rule 535.15 requires that earnest money be deposited with the escrow agent selected by the parties by the close of the second business day following the signing of the agreement. When the buyer has tendered the offer in writing, the seller has accepted the offer by signing the contract and the buyer has been notified of the seller's acceptance, an executory contract exists, and the agent or the buyer needs to deliver the earnest money to the escrow officer named in paragraph 5 of the contract.

The contract is an agreement between the buyer and the seller and should reflect their wishes. Usually the company selected in paragraph 6 to issue the owner's title policy is the same chosen in paragraph 5 to serve as escrow officer. Who should choose the company?

Many would argue that because the seller usually pays for the title policy the seller should choose. Who pays does not and should not automatically dictate who chooses something in a real estate transaction. For example, the buyer is usually required to pay for an appraisal when the buyer is seeking a new loan, but it is the lender who selects the appraiser and is the client of the appraiser. When utilizing a loan guaranteed by the Department of Veterans Affairs, the government regulations require that the seller pay the legal fees for the preparation of the note and mortgage instrument for the borrower's loan. Before a seller or listing agent attempts to dictate the title company, it should be noted that the owner's title policy is a contract between the buyer and the title company. Also, a review of the Real Estate Settlement Procedures Act (RESPA), covering one-family to four-family residential transactions that have financing related to the federal government, reveals that federal regulation prohibits the seller from requiring the buyer to use the services of a particular

03-17-92

ADDENDUM FOR
RELEASE OF LIABILITY ON ASSUMPTION OF FHA, VA OR CONVENTIONAL LOAN
RESTORATION OF SELLER'S ENTITLEMENT FOR VA GUARANTEED LOAN

PROMULGATED BY THE TEXAS REAL ESTATE COMMISSION (TREC)

ADDENDUM TO EARNEST MONEY CONTRACT BETWEEN THE UNDERSIGNED PARTIES CONCERNING THE PROPERTY AT____
(Street Address and City)

☐ **A. RELEASE OF SELLER'S LIABILITY ON LOAN TO BE ASSUMED:**

Within __________ days from the effective date of this contract Seller and Buyer shall apply for release of Seller's liability from (a) any conventional lender, (b) VA and any lender whose loan has been guaranteed by VA, or (c) FHA and any lender whose loan has been insured by FHA. Seller and Buyer shall furnish all required information and documents. If any release of liability has not been approved by the Closing Date: (check 1 or 2 below)

☐ 1. This contract shall terminate and the Earnest Money shall be refunded to Buyer.

☐ 2. Failure to obtain release approval shall not delay closing and Seller and Buyer shall continue to seek release of Seller's liability.

☐ **B. RESTORATION OF SELLERS ENTITLEMENT FOR VA LOAN:**

Within _________ days from the effective date of this contract Seller and Buyer shall apply for restoration of Seller's VA entitlement and shall furnish all information and documents required by VA. If restoration has not been approved by the Closing Date: (check 1 or 2 below)

☐ 1. This contract shall terminate and the Earnest Money shall be refunded to Buyer.

☐ 2. Failure to obtain restoration approval shall not delay closing and Seller and Buyer shall continue to seek restoration of Seller's VA entitlement.

NOTICE: VA will not restore Seller's VA entitlement unless Buyer: (a) is a veteran, (b) has sufficient unused VA entitlement and (c) is otherwise qualified. If Seller desires release of liability from VA and the lender together with restoration of VA entitlement, paragraphs A and B should be used.

Seller shall pay the cost of securing the release and restoration. If Seller's cost will exceed $ __________________, and Buyer declines to pay the excess, Seller may (a) waive release or restoration, (b) pay the excess, or (c) terminate this contract and the Earnest Money shall be refunded to Buyer.

Seller's deed shall contain any loan assumption clause required by FHA, VA or any lender. The provisions of this addendum are enforceable after closing.

____________________ ____________________
Buyer Seller

____________________ ____________________
Buyer Seller

The form of this Addendum has been approved by the Texas Real Estate Commission for use with similarly approved or promulgated contract forms. Such approval relates to this form only. No representation is made as to the legal validity or adequacy of any provision in any specific transactions. It is not suitable for complex transactions. (03-92) TREC No. 12-1. This form replaces TREC No. 12-0.

title provider. Refer to page 17 of the HUD guide, "Settlement Costs," which is given to buyers at the time of loan application. Why should the seller really care? Providing the title policy is an economical way to show evidence of clear title, and the premium cost is the same at all title companies in the state to insure the title of the property with the same sales price.

The majority of transactions closed in Texas involve the issuance of a title policy to the buyer of the property. Local custom often calls for the owner's policy of title insurance to be furnished at the seller's expense. This is a point to be negotiated by the parties. When the parties have come to an agreement on this matter, check the appropriate box.

Licensees should let the parties choose the title company that will issue the title policy. On RESPA-covered transactions involving purchases of a one-family to four-family residential property with a federally related loan, the buyer always has the right to choose the provider of title services.

RESPA 2608

(a) No seller of property that will be purchased with the assistance of a federally related mortgage loan shall require, directly or indirectly, as a condition to selling the property, that title insurance covering the property be purchased by the buyer from any particular title company.

(b) Any seller who violates the provisions of subsection (a) shall be liable to the buyer in an amount equal to three times all charges made for such title insurance.

The reader should further consider that it is the buyer who must live with the coverage and deal with the insurance company when a title problem rears its ugly head. A buyer who is asking the seller to pay for the policy may be willing to permit the seller to choose. Licensees should not dictate in this area; they should always ask.

In addition to identifying who issues and who pays for the title policy, paragraph 6A establishes that the policy is subject to the exclusions promulgated by the state insurance board in Austin. The eight exclusions are listed in the contract.

The standard printed exception relating to discrepancies, conflicts and shortages in area or boundary lines, etc., may be deleted by the payment of an additional 15 percent to the title insurance premium and by providing a survey acceptable to the title company. When this business detail is to be added to the agreement, it is addressed in paragraph 11 by simply stating who will pay the additional premium.

6. TITLE POLICY AND SURVEY:

❑ A. **TITLE POLICY:** Seller shall furnish to Buyer at ❑ Seller's ❑ Buyer's expense an owner policy of title insurance (the Title Policy) issued by ______________________ (the Title Company) in the amount of the Sales Price, dated at or after closing, insuring Buyer against loss under the provisions of the Title Policy, subject to the promulgated exclusions (including existing building and zoning ordinances) and the following exceptions:

(1) Restrictive covenants common to the platted subdivision in which the Property is located.
(2) The standard printed exception for standby fees, taxes and assessments.
(3) Liens created as part of the financing described in Paragraph 4.
(4) Utility easements created by the dedication deed or plat of the subdivision in which the Property is located.
(5) Reservations or exceptions otherwise permitted by this contract or as may be approved by Buyer in writing.
(6) The standard printed exception as to discrepancies, conflicts, shortages in area or boundary lines, encroachments or protrusions, or overlapping improvements.
(7) The standard printed exception as to marital rights.
(8) The standard printed exception as to waters, tidelands, beaches, streams, and related matters.

Within 20 days after the Title Company receives a copy of this contract, Seller shall furnish to Buyer a commitment for title insurance (the Commitment) and, at Buyer's expense, legible copies of restrictive covenants and documents evidencing exceptions in the Commitment other than the standard printed exceptions. Seller authorizes the Title Company to mail or hand deliver the Commitment and related documents to Buyer at Buyer's address shown below. If the Commitment is not delivered to Buyer within the specified time, the time for delivery will be automatically extended up to 15 days. Buyer will have 7 days after the receipt of the Commitment to object in writing to matters disclosed in the Commitment.

❑ B. **SURVEY:** (Check one box only)

❑ (1) Within ______ days after Buyer's receipt of a survey furnished to a third-party lender at ❑ Seller's ❑ Buyer's expense, Buyer may object in writing to any matter shown on the survey which constitutes a defect or encumbrance to title.

❑ (2) Within ______ days after the effective date of this contract, Buyer may object in writing to any matter which constitutes a defect or encumbrance to title shown on a survey obtained by Buyer at Buyer's expense.

The survey must be made by a Registered Professional Land Surveyor acceptable to the Title Company and any lender. Utility easements created by the dedication deed and plat of the subdivision in which the Property is located will not be a basis for objection.

Buyer may object to existing building and zoning ordinances, items 6A(1) through (8) above and matters shown on the survey if Buyer determines that any such ordinance, items or matters prohibits the following use or activity: ______________________

______________________.

Buyer's failure to object under Paragraph 6A or 6B within the time allowed will constitute a waiver of Buyer's right to object; except that the requirements in Schedule C of the Commitment will not be deemed to have been waived. Seller shall cure the timely objections of Buyer or any third party lender within 15 days from the date Seller receives the objections and the Closing Date will be extended as necessary. If objections are not cured by the extended Closing Date, this contract will terminate and the earnest money will be refunded to Buyer unless Buyer elects to waive the objections.

NOTICE TO SELLER AND BUYER:

(1) Broker advises Buyer to have an abstract of title covering the Property examined by an attorney of Buyer's selection, or Buyer should be furnished with or obtain a Title Policy. If a Title Policy is furnished, the Commitment should be promptly reviewed by an attorney of Buyer's choice due to the time limitations on Buyer's right to object.

[*Continued*]

(2) If the Property is situated in a utility or other statutorily created district providing water, sewer, drainage, or flood control facilities and services, Chapter 49 of the Texas Water Code requires Seller to deliver and Buyer to sign the statutory notice relating to the tax rate, bonded indebtedness, or standby fee of the district prior to final execution of this contract.

(3) If the Property abuts the tidally influenced waters of the state, Section 33.135, Texas Natural Resources Code, requires a notice regarding coastal area property to be included in the contract. An addendum either promulgated by TREC or required by the parties should be used.

(4) Buyer is advised that the presence of wetlands, toxic substances, including asbestos and wastes or other environmental hazards or the presence of a threatened or endangered species or its habitat may affect Buyer's intended use of the Property. If Buyer is concerned about these matters, an addendum either promulgated by TREC or required by the parties should be used.

(5) If the Property is located outside the limits of a municipality, Seller notifies Buyer under §5.011, Texas Property Code, that the Property may now or later be included in the extraterritorial jurisdiction of a municipality and may now or later be subject to annexation by the municipality. Each municipality maintains a map that depicts its boundaries and extraterritorial jurisdiction. To determine if the Property is located within a municipality's extraterritorial jurisdiction or is likely to be located within a municipality's extraterritorial jurisdiction, contact all municipalities located in the general proximity of the Property for further information.

(6) Unless expressly prohibited in writing by the parties, Seller may continue to show the Property for sale and to receive, negotiate and accept back up offers.

(7) Any residential service contract that is purchased in connection with this transaction should be reviewed for the scope of coverage, exclusions and limitations. **The purchase of a residential service contract is optional. Similar coverage may be purchased from various companies authorized to do business in Texas.**

The agreement calls for the seller to furnish the buyer a commitment for title insurance and, at the buyer's expense, legible copies of deed restrictions and documentation of any exceptions in the commitment within 20 days. The seller requests that the title company mail or hand-deliver the commitment to the buyer's address shown in paragraph 23 of the contract form. The parties agree that if the title company is unable to deliver within 20 days, the time for delivery is automatically extended up to 15 days. After the buyer receives the commitment, the buyer has five days to object in writing to any matters disclosed in the commitment.

At the bottom of section 6 is a space in which the buyer can list anything the buyer may want to do on the property that may be prohibited by deed restrictions, zoning ordinances, etc. Examples of what may be listed here include conducting a home-based business from the premises, parking a motor home or boat in the driveway, erecting a basketball net, installing a satellite dish or erecting a ten-foot privacy fence.

When the buyer wants to request an abstract of title instead of a title policy, add addendum 29-1 (page 44), which replaces and supersedes paragraph 6A of the contract.

When the lender requires a survey, the buyer may check box 6B and box 1 under B to claim the opportunity to object in writing to any matter shown on the survey that constitutes a defect or encumbrance to title. The parties must specify the number of days after the buyer's receipt of the survey that the buyer has to make the written objection. Two or three days should be ample for any buyer to be able to review the survey and make the written objections. The parties also need to identify who will pay for the survey.

When the transaction is all cash, assumption or owner financed, there is no third party requiring a survey. The buyer may call for a survey by checking box 6B and box 2. When box 2 is used, a longer period must be entered in the blank to allow for time to secure the services of a surveyor, have the survey performed, get the survey to the buyer and give the buyer the opportunity to review and to make objections in writing. A reasonable time is 15 to 20 days.

At the end of the paragraph, note that the parties agree that if the buyer does not object within the times specified in 6A or B, the buyer is deemed to have waived rights to cancel. If objections are made, the seller has 15 days to cure them, and the parties agree that the closing date established in paragraph 9 may be extended and objections will be cured within 15 days from the date the seller receives written notice of the objections. If the seller is unable to cure, the contract comes to an end and the earnest money is refunded to the buyer.

Following the discussion of title and survey matters, seven notices are given to the seller and the buyer.

1. The buyer needs to check the title carefully before closing the transaction.
2. The seller is required by statute to furnish the buyer with relevant information about the utility district if the property lies within one.
3. Notices regarding coastal area property are to be included in the agreement between parties. See addenda (pages 45 and 46) that follow.
4. The concerned buyer should check the property for the presence of toxic materials, wetlands or endangered species. See addendum (page 47) that follows.
5. The statutory notice that property located in a city's extraterritorial jurisdiction may now or later be subject to annexation.
6. The property is still owned by the seller and may continue to be shown for backup offers.
7. Residential service contracts are optional and not all contracts are created equal.

Licensees would do well to advise buyers to inspect and evaluate the property carefully prior to final acceptance of a previously occupied property. The Broker-Lawyer Committee and TREC have designed the property condition section of the contract to remove the licensee from this part of the transaction.

09-20-99

PROMULGATED BY THE TEXAS REAL ESTATE COMMISSION (TREC)

ADDENDUM FOR ABSTRACT OF TITLE

ADDENDUM TO CONTRACT CONCERNING THE PROPERTY AT

____
(Street Address and City)

Paragraph 6A of the contract is replaced and superseded by this Addendum.

Within 30 days after ________________________________ (the Abstract Company) receives a copy of this contract, Seller shall furnish to Buyer at Seller's expense an Abstract of Title certified by the Abstract Company from the sovereignty to the effective date of this contract (Complete Abstract). If the Complete Abstract is not delivered to Buyer within the specified time, the time for delivery will be automatically extended up to 15 days. Within 30 days after Buyer's receipt of the Complete Abstract, Buyer may object in writing to matters disclosed in the Complete Abstract.

Seller shall furnish to Buyer at Seller's expense a Supplemental Abstract that supplements the Complete Abstract as of the Closing Date. Prior to closing, Buyer may object in writing to matters disclosed in the Supplemental Abstract.

The Complete Abstract and Supplemental Abstract may be examined at Buyer's expense by an attorney selected by Buyer. Buyer's failure to object within the time allowed will constitute a waiver of Buyer's right to object. If objections are made by Buyer or any third party lender, Seller shall cure the objections within 20 days after Seller receives the objections and the Closing Date will be extended as necessary. If objections are not cured by the extended Closing Date, this contract will terminate and the earnest money will be refunded to Buyer unless Buyer elects to waive the objections.

____________________	____________________
Buyer	Seller
____________________	____________________
Buyer	Seller

The form of this addendum has been approved by the Texas Real Estate Commission for use only with similarly approved or promulgated forms of contracts. TREC forms are intended for use only by trained real estate licensees. No representation is made as to the legal validity or adequacy of any provision in any specific transactions. (9-99) Texas Real Estate Commission, P.O. Box 12188, Austin, TX 78711-2188, 1-800-250-8732 or (512) 459-6544 (http://www.trec.state.tx.us) TREC No. 29-1. This form replaces TREC No. 29-0.

01A

PROMULGATED BY THE TEXAS REAL ESTATE COMMISSION (TREC)
P.O. BOX 12188, AUSTIN, TX 78711-2188

12-05-94

ADDENDUM FOR
COASTAL AREA PROPERTY

ADDENDUM TO EARNEST MONEY CONTRACT BETWEEN THE UNDERSIGNED PARTIES CONCERNING THE PROPERTY AT

____

____
(Location of Property)

IN ACCORDANCE WITH SECTION 33.1 35, TEXAS NATURAL RESOURCES CODE, THE FOLLOWING NOTICE IS INCLUDED AS PART OF THE CONTRACT:

NOTICE REGARDING COASTAL AREA PROPERTY

1. The real property described in and subject to this contract adjoins and shares a common boundary with the tidally influenced submerged lands of the state. The boundary is subject to change and can be determined accurately only by a survey on the ground made by a licensed state land surveyor in accordance with the original grant from the sovereign. The owner of the property described in this contract may gain or lose portions of the tract because of changes in the boundary.

2. The seller, transferor, or grantor has no knowledge of any prior fill as it relates to the property described in and subject to this contract except: ____
____
____.

3. State law prohibits the use, encumbrance, construction, or placing of any structure in, on, or over state-owned submerged lands below the applicable tide line, without proper permission.

4. The purchaser or grantee is hereby advised to seek the advice of an attorney or other qualified person as to the legal nature and effect of the facts set forth in this notice on the property described in and subject to this contract. Information regarding the location of the applicable tide line as to the property described in and subject to this contract may be obtained from the surveying division of the General Land Office in Austin.

______________________	______________________
Buyer	Seller
______________________	______________________
Buyer	Seller

This form has been approved by the Texas Real Estate Commission for use with similarly approved or promulgated contract forms. Such approval relates to this form only. No representation is made as to the legal validity or adequacy of any provision in any specific transactions. It is not suitable for complex transactions. (12-94) TREC No. 33-0.

12-05-94

PROMULGATED BY THE TEXAS REAL ESTATE COMMISSION (TREC)
P.O. BOX 12188, AUSTIN, TX 78711-2188

ADDENDUM FOR
PROPERTY LOCATED SEAWARD OF THE GULF INTRACOASTAL WATERWAY

ADDENDUM TO EARNEST MONEY CONTRACT BETWEEN THE UNDERSIGNED PARTIES CONCERNING THE PROPERTY AT

____

____
(Location of Property)

IN ACCORDANCE WITH SECTION 61.025, TEXAS NATURAL RESOURCES CODE, THE FOLLOWING STATEMENT IS INCLUDED AS PART OF THE CONTRACT:

The real property described in this contract is located seaward of the Gulf Intracoastal Waterway to its southernmost point and then seaward of the longitudinal line also known as 97 degrees, 12', 19" which runs southerly to the international boundary from the intersection of the centerline of the Gulf Intracoastal Waterway and the Brownsville Ship Channel. If the property is in close proximity to a beach fronting the Gulf of Mexico, the purchaser is hereby advised that the public has acquired a right of use or easement to or over the area of any public beach by prescription, dedication, or presumption, or has retained a right by virtue of continuous right in the public since time immemorial, as recognized in law and custom.

The extreme seaward boundary of natural vegetation that spreads continuously inland customarily marks the landward boundary of the public easement. If there is no clearly marked natural vegetation line, the landward boundary of the easement is as provided by Sections 61.016 and 61.017, Natural Resources Code.

State law prohibits any obstruction, barrier, restraint, or interference with the use of the public easement, including the placement of structures seaward of the landward boundary of the easement. STRUCTURES ERECTED SEAWARD OF THE VEGETATION LINE (OR OTHER APPLICABLE EASEMENT BOUNDARY) OR THAT BECOME SEAWARD OF THE VEGETATION LINE AS A RESULT OF NATURAL PROCESSES ARE SUBJECT TO A LAWSUIT BY THE STATE OF TEXAS TO REMOVE THE STRUCTURES.

The purchaser is hereby notified that the purchaser should seek the advice of an attorney or other qualified person before executing this contract or instrument of conveyance as to the relevance of these statutes and facts to the value of the property the purchaser is hereby purchasing or contracting to purchase.

Buyer	Seller
Buyer	Seller

This form has been approved by the Texas Real Estate Commission for use with similarly approved or promulgated contract forms. Such approval relates to this form only. No representation is made as to the legal validity or adequacy of any provision in any specific transactions. It is not suitable for complex transactions. (12-94) TREC No. 34-0.

10-25-93

ENVIRONMENTAL ASSESSMENT, THREATENED OR ENDANGERED SPECIES, AND WETLANDS ADDENDUM

PROMULGATED BY THE TEXAS REAL ESTATE COMMISSION (TREC)

ADDENDUM TO EARNEST MONEY CONTRACT BETWEEN THE UNDERSIGNED PARTIES CONCERNING THE PROPERTY AT ______________________________
(Address)

☐ A. ENVIRONMENTAL ASSESSMENT: Buyer, at Buyer's expense, may obtain an Environmental Assessment Report prepared by an environmental specialist.

☐ B. THREATENED OR ENDANGERED SPECIES: Buyer, at Buyer's expense, may obtain a report from a natural resources professional to determine if there are any threatened or endangered species or their habitats as defined by the Texas Parks and wildlife Department or the U.S. Fish and Wildlife Service.

☐ C. WETLANDS: Buyer, at Buyer's expense, may obtain a report from an environmental specialist to determine if there are wetlands, as defined by federal or state law or regulation.

Within _________ days after the Effective Date of the contract, Buyer may terminate the contract by furnishing Seller a copy of any report noted above that adversely affects the use of the Property and the Earnest Money shall be refunded to Buyer. If Buyer does not furnish Seller a copy of the unacceptable report within the prescribed time and give Seller notice that Buyer has terminated the contract, Buyer shall be deemed to have accepted the Property.

Buyer	Seller
Buyer	Seller

The form of this addendum has been approved by the Texas Real Estate Commission for use only with similarly approved or promulgated forms of contracts. No representation is made as to the legal validity or adequacy of any provision in any specific transactions. It is not suitable for complex transactions. (10-93) TREC No. 28-0.

7. PROPERTY CONDITION:

A. INSPECTIONS, ACCESS AND UTILITIES: Buyer may have the Property inspected by an inspector selected by Buyer, licensed by TREC or otherwise permitted by law to make such inspections. Seller shall permit access to the Property at reasonable times for inspection, repairs and treatment and for reinspection after repairs and treatment have been completed. Seller shall pay for turning on utilities for inspection and reinspection.

B. SELLER'S DISCLOSURE NOTICE PURSUANT TO SECTION 5.008, TEXAS PROPERTY CODE (Notice) (check one box only):

❑ (1) Buyer has received the Notice.

❑ (2) Buyer has not received the Notice. Within _______ days after the effective date of this contract, Seller shall deliver the Notice to Buyer. If Buyer does not receive the Notice, Buyer may terminate this contract at any time prior to the closing. If Seller delivers the Notice, Buyer may terminate this contract for any reason within 7 days after Buyer receives the Notice or prior to the closing, whichever first occurs.

❑ (3) The Texas Property Code does not require this Seller to furnish the Notice.

C. SELLER'S DISCLOSURE OF LEAD-BASED PAINT AND LEAD-BASED PAINT HAZARDS is required by Federal law for a residential dwelling constructed prior to 1978. An addendum providing such disclosure ❑ is ❑ is not attached.

D. ACCEPTANCE OF PROPERTY CONDITION: (check one box only):

❑ (1) In addition to any earnest money deposited with escrow agent, Buyer has paid Seller $____________ (the "Option Fee") for the unrestricted right to terminate this contract by giving notice of termination to Seller within _______ days after the effective date of this contract. If Buyer gives notice of termination within the time specified, the Option Fee will not be refunded, however, any earnest money will be refunded to Buyer. If Buyer does not give notice of termination within the time specified, Buyer will be deemed to have accepted the Property in its current condition and the Option Fee ❑ will ❑ will not be credited to the Sales Price at closing.

❑ (2) Buyer accepts the Property in its present condition; provided Seller, at Seller's expense, shall complete the following repairs and treatment: ______________________________

____

____

____.

E. LENDER REQUIRED REPAIRS AND TREATMENTS (REPAIRS): Unless otherwise agreed in writing, neither party is obligated to pay for lender required repairs or treatments for wood destroying insects. If the cost of lender required repairs exceeds 5% of the Sales Price, Buyer may terminate this contract.

F. COMPLETION OF REPAIRS AND TREATMENT. Unless otherwise agreed by the parties in writing, Seller shall complete all agreed repairs and treatment prior to the Closing Date. Repairs and treatments must be performed by persons who regularly provide such repairs or treatments. At Buyer's election, any transferable warranties received by Seller with respect to the repairs will be transferred to Buyer at Buyer's expense. If Seller fails to complete any agreed repairs and treatment prior to the Closing Date, Buyer may do so and the Closing Date will be extended up to 15 days, if necessary, to complete repairs and treatment or treatments for wood destroying insects.

Remember that the agreement is between the seller and the buyer and that the licensee is not a party to the contract. Also, when dealing with a resale transaction the licensee must guard against creating false expectations on the part of the buyer(s). Inform every buyer that mechanical and structural problems may be present and that it is in a buyer's best interest to select and hire professional inspectors to assist in evaluating the merits and shortcomings of the property.

Paragraph 7A grants access at reasonable times for the appropriate inspections to be done. It further agrees that the seller, at seller's expense, shall have utilities turned on for inspections.

Effective January 1, 1994, section 5.008 of the Texas Property Code requires sellers of previously occupied residential dwelling units to furnish buyers with a seller's disclosure notice with content and information required by statute. Failure to provide the notice prior to signing an executory contract to purchase creates a voidable contract that may be terminated at the sole discretion of the buyer. If it is furnished after an executory contract of purchase is signed, the buyer has a period of seven days to terminate the contract without penalty or forefeiture of earnest money.

There are 11 exceptions stated in subsection (e) of section 5.008 of the Texas Property Code.

(e) This section does not apply to a transfer:

(1) pursuant to a court order or foreclosure sale;

(2) by a trustee in bankruptcy;

(3) to a mortgagee by a mortgagor or successor in interest, or to a beneficiary of a deed of trust by a trustor or successor in interest;

(4) by a mortgagee or a beneficiary under a deed of trust who has acquired the real property at a sale conducted pursuant to a power of sale under a deed of trust or a sale pursuant to a court ordered foreclosure or has acquired the real property by a deed in lieu of foreclosure;

(5) by a fiduciary in the course of the administration of a decedent's estate, guardianship, conservatorship, or trust;

(6) from one co-owner to one or more other co-owners;

(7) made to a spouse or to a person or persons in the lineal line of consanguinity of one or more of the transferors;

(8) between spouses resulting from a decree of dissolution of marriage or a decree of legal separation or from a property settlement agreement incidental to such a decree;

(9) to or from any governmental entity;

(10) transfers of new residences of not more than one dwelling unit which have not previously been occupied for residential purposes; or

(11) transfers of real property where the value of any dwelling does not exceed five percent (5%) of the value of the property. (Note: This provision typically excludes a ranch or farm sale.)

By checking the appropriate box in 7B, the parties define whether

- the buyer has received the notice,
- the seller has a defined number of days to furnish it, or
- the property is exempt from the requirement pursuant to the Texas Property Code.

Remember also that according to this section of the code and section 15E of the TRELA, there is no duty to disclose specific information. Subsection (c) of 5.008 states:

(C) A seller or seller's agent shall have no duty to make a disclosure or release information related to whether a death by natural causes, suicide, or accident unrelated to the condition of the property occurred on the property or whether a previous occupant had, may have had, has, or may have AIDS, HIV related illnesses, or HIV infection.

The form that follows (pages 51 and 52) is the TREC version of the Seller's Disclosure Notice, which is made available for voluntary use by the customers and clients of licensees. Some licensees prefer to use a format developed by the Texas Association of REALTORS® and some use a form developed by an in-house attorney. As long as the disclosure includes the minimum content established by 5.008, it is acceptable.

Some licensees have the mistaken idea that the form must be signed by the seller, acknowledged by the buyer and attached as an addendum to the purchase contract. The statute only requires that the seller complete the written disclosure and give it to the buyer. Do not list it as an addendum in paragraph 21. It is a disclosure of what the seller knows; it is not a representation or warranty and therefore not a promise or covenant exchanged between the parties. Some lawyers we have questioned on this matter feel that to reference it as an addendum in some way converts it from being simply a disclosure to a representation and warranty of the property condition. Courts in both San Antonio and Houston have ruled that the attached seller's disclosure was a representation by the sellers and ruled in favor of the buyers. We suggest that you follow the lead of TREC and simply check the appropriate box in paragraph 7B that provides adequate documentation as to what the parties have done with regard to this matter.

Paragraph 7C establishes whether a "Lead-Based Paint" addendum (page 53) has been added to the agreement. Licensees and sellers must be certain that they follow the HUD guidelines with regard to the seller's disclosure of the

EQUAL HOUSING OPPORTUNITY

APPROVED BY THE TEXAS REAL ESTATE COMMISSION (TREC) 10-25-93

SELLER'S DISCLOSURE OF PROPERTY CONDITION

(SECTION 5.008, TEXAS PROPERTY CODE)

CONCERNING THE PROPERTY AT______________________________
(Street Address and City)

THIS NOTICE IS A DISCLOSURE OF SELLER'S KNOWLEDGE OF THE CONDITION OF THE PROPERTY AS OF THE DATE SIGNED BY SELLER AND IS NOT A SUBSTITUTE FOR ANY INSPECTIONS OR WARRANTI ES THE PURCHASER MAY WISH TO OBTAIN. IT IS NOT A WARRANTY OF ANY KIND BY SELLER OR SELLER'S AGENTS.

Seller ☐ is ☐ is not occupying the Property. If unoccupied, how long since Seller has occupied the Property? ____________

1. The Property has the items checked below [Write Yes (Y), No (N), or Unknown (U)]:

__Range	__Oven	__Microwave
__Dishwasher	__Trash Compactor	__Disposal
__Washer/Dryer Hookups	__Window Screens	__Rain Gutters
__Security System	__Fire Detection Equipment	__Intercom System
__TV Antenna	__Cable TV Wiring	__Satellite Dish
__Ceiling Fan(s)	__Attic Fan(s)	__Exhaust Fan(s)
__Central A/C	__Central Heating	__Wall/Window Air Conditioning
__Plumbing System	__Septic System	__Public Sewer System
__Patio/Decking	__Outdoor Grill	__Fences
__Pool	__Sauna	__Spa__Hot Tub
__Pool Equipment	__Pool Heater	__Automatic Lawn Sprinkler System
__Fireplace(s) & Chimney(Woodburning)	__Fireplace(s) & Chimney (Mock)	__Gas Lines (Nat./LP)
__Gas Fixtures	Garage:__Attached __Not Attached	__Carport
Garage Door Opener(s):	__Electronic	__Control(s)
Water Heater:	__Gas	__Electric

Water Supply: __City __Well __MUD __Co-op

Roof Type:______________________ Age:______________________(approx)

Are you (Seller) aware of any of the above items that are not in working condition, that have known defects, or that are in need of repair? ☐ Yes ☐ No ☐ Unknown. If yes, then describe. (Attach additional sheets if necessary): ____________
____
____

2. Are you (Seller) aware of any known defects/malfunctions in any of the following? Write Yes (Y) if you are aware, write No (N) if you are not aware.

__Interior Walls	__Ceilings	__Floors
__Exterior Walls	__Doors	__Windows
__Roof	__Foundation/Slab(s)	__Basement
__Walls/Fences	__Driveways	__Sidewalks
__Plumbing/Sewers/Septics	__Electrical Systems	__Lighting Fixtures

__Other Structural Components (Describe) ______________________________
____
____

Seller's Disclosure Notice Concerning the Property at_______________ Page 2 10-25-93
(Street Address and City)

If the answer to any of the above is yes, explain. (Attach additional sheets if necessary): ____________

3. Are you (Seller) aware of any of the following conditions? Write Yes (Y) if you are aware, write No (N) if you are not aware.

__Active Termites (includes wood-destroying insects)
__Termite or Wood Rot Damage Needing Repair
__Previous Termite Damage
__Previous Termite Treatment
__Previous Flooding
__Improper Drainage
__Water Penetration
__Located in 100-Year Floodplain
__Present Flood Insurance Coverage
__Previous Structural or Roof Repair
__Hazardous or Toxic Waste
__Asbestos Components
__Urea-formaldehyde Insulation
__Aluminum Wiring
__Landfill, Settling, Soil Movement, Fault Lines
__Radon Gas
__Previous Fires
__Subsurface Structure or Pits
__Lead Based Paint
__Unplatted Easements

If the answer to any of the above is yes, explain. (Attach additional sheets if necessary): ____________

4. Are you (Seller) aware of any item, equipment, or system in or on the Property that is in need of repair? ☐ Yes (if you are aware) ☐ No (if you are not aware). If yes, explain (attach additional sheets as necessary). ____________

5. Are you (Seller) aware of any of the following? Write Yes (Y) if you are aware, write No (N) if you are not aware.

__ Room additions, structural modifications, or other alterations or repairs made without necessary permits or not in compliance with building codes in effect at that time.

__ Homeowners' Association or maintenance fees or assessments.

__ Any "common area" (facilities such as pools, tennis courts, walkways, or other areas) co-owned in undivided interest with others.

__ Any notices of violations of deed restrictions or governmental ordinances affecting the condition or use of the Property.

__ Any lawsuits directly or indirectly affecting the Property.

__ Any condition on the Property which materially affects the physical health or safety of an individual.

If the answer to any of the above is yes, explain. (Attach additional sheets if necessary): ____________

Date ____________ Signature of Seller   Date ____________ Signature of Seller

The undersigned purchaser hereby acknowledges receipt of the foregoing notice.

Date ____________ Signature of Purchaser   Date ____________ Signature of Purchaser

1978

APPROVED BY THE
TEXAS REAL ESTATE COMMISSION

02-10-97

ADDENDUM FOR SELLER'S DISCLOSURE OF INFORMATION ON LEAD-BASED PAINT AND LEAD-BASED PAINT HAZARDS AS REQUIRED BY FEDERAL LAW

CONCERNING THE PROPERTY AT ______________________________
(Street Address and City)

A. LEAD WARNING STATEMENT: "Every purchaser of any interest in residential real property on which a residential dwelling was built prior to 1978 is notified that such property may present exposure to lead from lead-based paint that may place young children at risk of developing lead poisoning. Lead poisoning in young children may produce permanent neurological damage, including learning disabilities, reduced intelligence quotient, behavioral problems, and impaired memory. Lead poisoning also poses a particular risk to pregnant women. The seller of any interest in residential real property is required to provide the buyer with any information on lead-based paint hazards from risk assessments or inspections in the seller's possession and notify the buyer of any known lead-based paint hazards. A risk assessment or inspection for possible lead-paint hazards is recommended prior to purchase."

B. SELLER'S DISCLOSURE:

1. PRESENCE OF LEAD-BASED PAINT AND/OR LEAD-BASED PAINT HAZARDS (check one box only):
   - ❑(a) Known lead-based paint and/or lead-based paint hazards are present in the Property (explain): ______________________________.
   - ❑(b) Seller has no actual knowledge of lead-based paint and/or lead-based paint hazards in the Property.
2. RECORDS AND REPORTS AVAILABLE TO SELLER (check one box only):
   - ❑(a) Seller has provided the purchaser with all available records and reports pertaining to lead-based paint and/or lead-based paint hazards in the Property (list documents): ______________________________.
   - ❑(b) Seller has no reports or records pertaining to lead-based paint and/or lead-based paint hazards in the Property.

C. BUYER'S RIGHTS (check one box only):

❑ 1. Buyer waives the opportunity to conduct a risk assessment or inspection of the Property for the presence of lead-based paint or lead-based paint hazards.

❑ 2. Within ten days after the effective date of this contract, Buyer may have the Property inspected for the presence of lead-based paint and/or lead-based paint hazards. If lead-based paint or lead-based paint hazards are present, Buyer may terminate this contract by giving Seller written notice within 14 days after the effective date of this contract.

D. BUYER'S ACKNOWLEDGMENT (check applicable boxes) **:**

❑ 1. Buyer has received copies of all information listed above.

❑ 2. Buyer has received the pamphlet *Protect Your Family from Lead in Your Home.*

E. BROKERS' ACKNOWLEDGMENT: Brokers have informed Seller of Seller's obligations under 42 U.S.C. 4852d to: (a) provide Buyer with the federally approved pamphlet on lead poisoning prevention; (b) complete this addendum; (c) disclose any known lead-based paint and/or lead-based paint hazards in the Property; (d) deliver all records and reports to Buyer pertaining to lead-based paint and/or lead-based paint hazards in the Property; (e) provide Buyer a period of up to 10 days to have the Property inspected; and (f) retain a completed copy of this addendum for at least 3 years following the sale Brokers are aware of their responsibility to ensure compliance.

F. CERTIFICATION OF ACCURACY: The following persons have reviewed the information above and certify, to the best of their knowledge, that the information they have provided is true and accurate.

Seller	Date	Buyer	Date
Seller	Date	Buyer	Date
Listing Broker	Date	Other Broker	Date

The form of this addendum has been approved for voluntary use by the Texas Real Estate Commission for use only with similarly approved or promulgated forms of contracts. No representation is made as to the legal validity or adequacy of any provision in any specific transactions. Texas Real Estate Commission, P.O. Box 12188, Austin, TX 78711-2188, 1-800-250-8732 or (512) 459-6544.

01A TREC No. OP-L

presence of lead-based paint and/or lead hazards. If the building permits for the construction of the home were issued prior to January 1, 1978, the addendum must be used to comply with the federal regulation to furnish a lead warning statement. You may use the TREC version that follows or the HUD version.

Please notice that at several points the parties are instructed to make a choice and "check one box only." So it is with paragraph 7D, which addresses the buyer's acceptance of property condition.

Paragraph 7D offers the buyer two choices, only one of which can be selected:

1. The buyer may purchase an unrestricted right to terminate the contract within a defined time frame.
2. The buyer may accept the property in its present condition with limited repairs itemized.

When the first choice is selected, sellers must realize that for the defined option amount, the seller is granting the buyer the unrestricted right to terminate the contract within the option period. The buyer should understand that only the right to terminate is being purchased and that the seller is under absolutely no obligation to acknowledge, consider or accept any overture from the buyer to amend the contract during the option period. The length of the option period and the amount of the option fee are matters to be decided by the parties. Sellers might do well to require a reasonable and equitable amount for this powerful right being granted to the buyer rather than granting it for insignificant amounts of cash.

The buyer must further realize that an overture to amend the contract, utilizing TREC Form 39-1 that follows (page 58), during the option period does not constitute a notice of termination. If negotiations to amend are not completed prior to expiration of the option period, the contract continues. If the buyer is not prepared to accept the property in its present condition and desires to terminate the contract, TREC Form 38-0 (page 59) must be delivered to the seller per the agreement in paragraph 23 of TREC Form 20-3 prior to expiration of the option period.

To determine when the option period ends, begin counting with the day after the effective date of the contract. The option period ends at midnight on the last day.

The option becomes effective only when the contract has been accepted and the option fee has been paid by the buyer to the seller. An option fee is money spent to purchase a powerful right. It is not refundable; however, it may, at the parties' election, be credited to the sales price at closing. If, during the option period, the buyer decides that more time is needed, the buyer can approach the seller and request that the seller sell the buyer an additional option period for additional valuable consideration. Always remember that the Texas Supreme Court has ruled that if no valuable consideration is tendered, there is no legally recognized option period.

In many, if not most, transactions the buyer purchases the option to obtain a few days to exercise the rights established by paragraph 7A and to buy some time to cancel the agreement if the seller is unwilling to renegotiate the agreement.

Please carefully examine the two forms that follow. Many issues can be renegotiated using Form 39-1 if both parties agree. Make certain that buyers understand that sellers are under no obligation to reopen negotiations during the option period.

Buyers may choose to accept the property in its present condition with the proviso that the seller make some specific repairs listed in section 7D(2). Be specific and precise when itemizing the required repairs in this section. Sellers should consider the financial considerations of any itemized repairs listed *before* accepting the offer.

Finally, paragraph 7 discusses lender-required repairs and completion of repairs and treatment. Both are self-explanatory upon a careful reading of the contract provisions.

8. BROKER'S FEES: All obligations of the parties for payment of brokers' fees are contained in separate written agreements.

Licensees are always concerned about the payment of their fees. Fees are not a part of the agreement between the seller and the buyer but rather are an issue between the seller and the listing broker and the buyer and the buyer's broker. With regard to a subagent, it is a matter between the listing broker and the selling broker. Commission splits between salespersons and the brokers who sponsor them are to be defined by their employment or independent contractor agreement.

Having a clear understanding of who is being represented by whom is required by the TRELA. A box addressing this important issue is found on page 8 of the contract form and is identified as "Broker Information and Ratification of Fee." Brokers who represent sellers and buyers in the same transaction are reminded that section 15C of the TRELA requires that the broker have written permission from each of the parties to function as an intermediary. Acting as an intermediary without a listing signed by the seller(s) and a buyer representation agreement signed by the buyer(s) may result in disciplinary action by TREC.

BROKER INFORMATION AND RATIFICATION OF FEE

Listing Broker has agreed to pay Other Broker __________________ of the total sales price when Listing Broker's fee is received. Escrow Agent is authorized and directed to pay Other Broker from Listing Broker's fee at closing.

Other Broker License No.	Listing Broker License No.
represents ❑ Seller as Listing Broker's subagent ❑ Buyer only as Buyer's agent	represents ❑ Seller and Buyer as an intermediary ❑ Seller only as Seller's agent
	Listing Associate Telephone
Associate Telephone	Selling Associate Telephone
Broker Address	Broker Address
Telephone Facsimile	Telephone Facsimile

Closing and the buyer's possession of the property are important issues addressed in paragraphs 9 and 10. Closing needs to occur on or before a specific date, while possession should be granted at the happening of a defined event, such as closing or funding. If you use a specific date for possession, significant problems can arise if that date turns out to be a date prior to closing and/or funding. Most sellers will not want to give possession prior to being absolutely certain that the transaction has been brought to a successful conclusion and they have received their proceeds.

9. **CLOSING:** The closing of the sale will be on or before ______________________________, 19____, or within 7 days after objections to matters disclosed in the Commitment or by the survey have been cured, whichever date is later (the Closing Date). *If financing or assumption approval has been obtained pursuant to Paragraph 4,* the Closing Date will be extended up to 15 days if necessary to comply with lender's closing requirements (for example, appraisal, survey, insurance policies, lender-required repairs, closing documents). If either party fails to close this sale by the Closing Date, the non-defaulting party will be entitled to exercise the remedies contained in Paragraph 15. At closing Seller shall furnish tax statements or certificates showing no delinquent taxes and a general warranty deed conveying good and indefeasible title showing no additional exceptions to those permitted in Paragraph 6.

10. **POSSESSION:** Seller shall deliver possession of the Property to Buyer on ____________________ in its present or required repaired condition, ordinary wear and tear excepted. Any possession by Buyer prior to closing or by Seller after closing which is not authorized by a temporary lease form promulgated by TREC or required by the parties will establish a tenancy at sufferance relationship between the parties. *Consult your insurance agent prior to change of ownership or possession as insurance coverage may be limited or terminated. The absence of a written lease or appropriate insurance coverage may expose the parties to economic loss.*

If a buyer moves in before closing and funding or a seller remains after closing and funding, a landlord/tenant relationship exists. The relationship must be clearly defined by a seller's or buyer's temporary lease. Please examine the promulgated TREC forms that follow (pages 60–63). Pay particular attention to the provisions relating to insurance coverage on the property during the tenancy period.

When the parties need to add factual statements or business details to their agreement, they may utilize paragraph 11. When the parties want to define legal rights and remedies, they should seek competent legal advice.

> **11. SPECIAL PROVISIONS:** (Insert only factual statements and business details applicable to this sale. TREC rules prohibit licensees from adding factual statements or business details for which a contract addendum, lease or other form has been promulgated by TREC for mandatory use.)

Things that can be added in the paragraph include

- inventory list,
- preclosing walk-through inspection,
- documents available for review prior to closing and
- residential service contract information.

When the provisions are extensive and more than will fit in the space provided, the parties may need to seek the assistance of a competent attorney.

The following are examples of things that *MAY NOT* be addressed in "special provisions" paragraph 11:

- The transaction is contingent upon the sale of another property (see TREC addendum 10-2).
- The contract is in a second or backup position (see TREC addendum 11-2).
- The assumption transaction is contingent upon the seller's release of liability or, in the case of a VA-guaranteed loan, restoration of VA entitlement (see TREC addendum 12-1).
- Arrangements for the buyer to possess before closing or the seller to stay after closing (see TREC addenda 16-3 and 15-3).
- The contract is contingent upon satisfactory inspections to the buyer.
- The parties agree that in the event of a dispute they will try mediation before bringing a lawsuit (see TREC addendum 35-1).
- Any wording that defines legal rights and remedies such as "contingent upon, terminate, refund earnest money on demand, cancel, etc."
- "*Time is of the essence*" (parties should contact an attorney).

PROMULGATED BY THE TEXAS REAL ESTATE COMMISSION (TREC) 09-20-99

AMENDMENT

(for Residential Resales Only)

AMENDMENT TO CONTRACT BETWEEN THE UNDERSIGNED PARTIES
CONCERNING PROPERTY AT

____

(Street Address and City)

Seller and Buyer amend the contract as follows: (check applicable boxes below)

❑ (1) The Sales Price in Paragraph 3 of the contract is:
- A. Cash portion of Sales Price payable by Buyer at closing . . . . $ ____________
- B. Sum of financing described in the contract . . . . $ ____________
- C. Sales Price (Sum of A and B) . . . . $ ____________

❑ (2) Buyer accepts the Property in its present condition; provided Seller, at Seller's expense, shall complete the following repairs and treatment:

❑ (3) The Option Fee ❑ will ❑ will not be credited to the Sales Price at closing.

❑ (4) The date in Paragraph 9 of the contract is changed to ________________, ______.

❑ (5) Seller shall pay $ ________________ of the expenses stipulated to be paid by Buyer under the provisions of the contract.

❑ (6) The cost of the lender required repairs and treatment, as itemized on the attached list, will be paid as follows: $ ________________ by Seller; $ ________________ by Buyer.

❑ (7) Buyer has paid Seller an additional non-refundable Option Fee of $ ____________ for an extension of the unrestricted right to terminate the contract before 5:00 p.m., ____________, ______. This additional Option Fee ❑ will ❑ will not be credited to the Sales Price at closing.

❑ (8) Upon final acceptance of this Amendment, Buyer waives the right to terminate under Paragraph 7D(1) of the contract.

❑ (9) **Other Modifications**: (Note to Broker: Insert, modify or eliminate only factual statements and business details applicable to this contract that have been inserted in blanks or by check boxes in the contract, or by adding or eliminating a promulgated or approved addendum to the contract.).

EXECUTED the __________ day of ____________________, ________ (BROKER: FILL IN THE DATE OF FINAL ACCEPTANCE).

______________________ Buyer	______________________ Seller
______________________ Buyer	______________________ Seller

The form of this addendum has been approved by the Texas Real Estate Commission for use only with similarly approved or promulgated forms of contracts. Such approval relates to this contract form only. TREC forms are intended for use only by trained real estate licensees. No representation is made as to the legal validity or adequacy of any provision in any specific transactions. It is not suitable for complex transactions.(09-99)Texas Real Estate Commission, P.O. Box 12188, Austin, TX 78711-2188, 1-800-250-8732 or (512) 459-6544 (http://www.trec.state.tx.us) TREC No. 39-1. This form replaces TREC No. 39-0.

01A

06-15-98

PROMULGATED BY THE TEXAS REAL ESTATE COMMISSION (TREC)

NOTICE OF TERMINATION OF CONTRACT

(To Be Sent As Specified in Paragraph 23 of the Contract)

To: Seller(s)

In accordance with Paragraph 7D(1) of the Contract between ______________________ ______________ as Seller and ______________________________ as Buyer dated ______________ for the Property located at ______________________ ______________________________________, Buyer notifies Seller that the Contract is terminated.

Buyer	Date	Buyer	Date

This form has been approved by the Texas Real Estate Commission. Such approval relates to this form only. No representation is made as to the legal validity or adequacy of any provision in any specific transaction. It is not suitable for complex transactions. Extensive riders or additions are not to be used. (06-98)Texas Real Estate Commission, P.O. Box 12188, Austin, TX 78711-2188, 1-800-250-8732 or (512)459-6544 (http:\\www.trec.state.tx.us) TREC No. 38-0.

12-07-98

EQUAL HOUSING OPPORTUNITY

(NOTICE: For use only when SELLER occupies the property for no more than 90 days AFTER the closing)

SELLER'S TEMPORARY RESIDENTIAL LEASE

PROMULGATED BY THE TEXAS REAL ESTATE COMMISSION (TREC)

1. **PARTIES:** The parties to this Lease are ______________________________ (Landlord) and ______________________________(Tenant).
2. **LEASE:** Landlord leases to Tenant the Property described in the Contract between Landlord as Buyer and Tenant as Seller dated ________________, ______,and known as ______________________________ ______________________________(address).
3. **TERM:** The term of this Lease commences on the date the sale covered by the Contract is closed and terminates ______________________________, unless terminated earlier by reason of other provisions.
4. **RENTAL:** Tenant shall pay to Landlord as rental $______________per day with the full amount of rental for the term of the Lease to be paid at the time of funding of the sale. Tenant will not be entitled to a refund of rental if this Lease terminates early due to Tenant's default or voluntary surrender of the Property.
5. **SECURITY DEPOSIT:** Tenant shall pay to Landlord at the time of funding of the sale $ ____________ as a deposit to secure performance of this Lease by Tenant. Landlord may use the deposit to satisfy Tenant's obligations under this Lease. Landlord shall refund any unused portion of the deposit to Tenant with an itemized list of all deductions from the deposit within 30 days after Tenant (a) surrenders possession of the Property and (b) provides Landlord written notice of Tenant's forwarding address.
6. **UTILITIES:** Tenant shall pay all utility charges except______________________________, which Landlord shall pay.
7. **USE OF PROPERTY:** Tenant may use the Property only for single family dwelling purposes. Tenant may not assign this Lease or sublet any part of the Property.
8. **PETS:** Tenant may not keep pets on the Property except______________________________.
9. **CONDITION OF PROPERTY**: Tenant accepts the Property in its present condition and state of repair at the commencement of the Lease. Upon termination, Tenant shall surrender the Property to Landlord in the condition required under the Contract at the time of closing, except normal wear and tear and any casualty loss.
10. **ALTERATIONS:** Tenant may not alter the Property or install improvements or fixtures without the prior written consent of Landlord. Any improvements or fixtures placed on the Property during the Lease become the property of Landlord.
11. **SPECIAL PROVISIONS:**

12. **INSPECTIONS:** Landlord may enter at reasonable times to inspect the Property.
13. **LAWS:** Tenant shall comply with all applicable laws, restrictions, ordinances, rules and regulations with respect to the Property.
14. **REPAIRS AND MAINTENANCE:** Tenant shall bear all expense of repairing and maintaining the Property, including but not limited to yard, trees and shrubs, unless otherwise required by the Texas Property Code. Tenant shall promptly repair at Tenant's expense any damage to the Property caused directly or indirectly by any act or omission of the Tenant or any person other than Landlord, Landlord's agents or invitees.

Initialed for identification by Landlord __________ and Tenant __________ **01A** TREC NO. 15-3

Seller's Temporary Residential Lease____Page Two 12-07-98
(Address of Property)

15. **INDEMNITY:** Tenant indemnifies Landlord from the claims of all third parties for injury or damage to the person or property of such third party arising from the use or occupancy of the Property by Tenant. This indemnification includes attorney's fees, costs and expenses incurred by Landlord.
16. **INSURANCE:** Landlord and Tenant shall each maintain such insurance on the contents and Property as each party may deem appropriate during the term of this Lease. NOTE: CONSULT YOUR INSURANCE AGENT PRIOR TO CLOSING. Possession of the Property by Seller as Tenant may change insurance policy coverage.
17. **DEFAULT:** If Tenant fails to perform or observe any provision of this Lease and fails, within 24 hours after notice by Landlord, to commence and diligently pursue to remedy such failure, Tenant will be in default.
18. **TERMINATION:** This Lease terminates upon expiration of the term specified in Paragraph 3 or upon Tenant's default under this Lease.
19. **HOLDING OVER:** Tenant shall surrender possession of the Property upon termination of this Lease. Any possession by Tenant after termination creates a tenancy at sufferance and will not operate to renew or extend this Lease. Tenant shall pay $ _______________ per day during the period of any possession after termination as damages, in addition to any other remedies to which Landlord is entitled.
20. **ATTORNEY'S FEES:** The prevailing party in any legal proceeding brought under or with respect to the transaction described in this Lease is entitled to recover from the non-prevailing party all costs of such proceeding and reasonable attorney's fees.
21. **SMOKE DETECTORS:** The Texas Property Code requires Landlord to install smoke detectors in certain locations within the Property at Landlord's expense. Tenant expressly waives Landlord's duty to inspect and repair smoke detectors.
22. **SECURITY DEVICES:** The requirements of the Texas Property Code relating to security devices do not apply to a residential lease for a term of 90 days or less.
23. **CONSULT YOUR ATTORNEY:** Real estate licensees cannot give legal advice. This Lease is intended to be legally binding. READ IT CAREFULLY. If you do not understand the effect of this Lease, consult your attorney BEFORE signing.
24. **NOTICES:** All notices under this Lease from one party to the other must be in writing and are effective when delivered or transmitted by facsimile machine as follows:

To Landlord:

____

____

____

Facsimile:(_____)__________________

To Tenant:

____

____

____

Facsimile:(_____)__________________

EXECUTED the ______ day of ______________________________ .

____
Landlord

____
Tenant

____
Landlord

____
Tenant

The form of this contract has been approved by the Texas Real Estate Commission. Such approval relates to this contract form only. TREC forms are intended for use only by trained real estate licensees. No representation is made as to the legal validity or adequacy of any provision in any specific transaction. It is not suitable for complex transactions. Extensive riders or additions are not to be used. (12-98) Texas Real Estate Commission, P.O. Box 12188, Austin, TX 78711-2188, 1-800-250-8732 or (512)459-6544 (http://www.trec.state.tx.us) TREC NO. 15-3. This form replaces TREC NO. 15-2.

12-07-98

EQUAL HOUSING OPPORTUNITY

(NOTICE: For use only when BUYER occupies the property for no more than 90 days PRIOR to closing)

BUYER'S TEMPORARY RESIDENTIAL LEASE

PROMULGATED BY THE TEXAS REAL ESTATE COMMISSION (TREC)

1. **PARTIES:** The parties to this Lease are ____ (Landlord) and ____(Tenant).
2. **LEASE:** Landlord leases to Tenant the Property described in the Contract between Landlord as Seller and Tenant as Buyer dated __________________, ______,and known as ____(address).
3. **TERM:** The term of this Lease commences on ______________________________ and terminates as specified in Paragraph 18.
4. **RENTAL:** Rental will be $ ________________ per day. Upon commencement of this Lease, Tenant shall pay to Landlord the full amount of rental of $ ________________ for the anticipated term of the Lease (commencement date to the closing date specified in Paragraph 9 of the Contract). If the actual term of this Lease differs from the anticipated term, rent will be prorated and paid at closing through the actual closing date. No portion of the rental will be applied to payment of any items covered by the Contract.
5. **SECURITY DEPOSIT:** Tenant has paid to Landlord $ __________________ as a deposit to secure performance of this Lease by Tenant. If this Lease is terminated before the closing, Landlord may use the deposit to satisfy Tenant's obligations under this Lease. Landlord shall refund to Tenant any unused portion of the deposit together with an itemized list of all deductions from the deposit within 30 days after Tenant (a) surrenders possession of the Property and (b) provides Landlord written notice of Tenant's forwarding address. If this Lease is terminated by the closing of the sale of the Property, the unused portion of the deposit will be refunded to Tenant at closing, together with an itemized list of all deductions from the deposit. <u>NOTICE</u>: The security deposit must be in addition to the earnest money under the Contract.
6. **UTILITIES:** Tenant shall pay all utility connections, deposits and charges except ____, which Landlord shall pay.
7. **USE OF PROPERTY:** Tenant may use the Property only for single family dwelling purposes. Tenant may not assign this Lease or sublet any part of the Property.
8. **PETS:** Tenant may not keep pets on the Property except ______________________________
9. **CONDITION OF PROPERTY**: Tenant accepts the Property in its present condition and state of repair, but Landlord shall make all repairs and improvements required by the Contract. If this Lease is terminated prior to closing, Tenant shall surrender possession of the Property to Landlord in its present condition, as improved by Landlord, except normal wear and tear and any casualty loss.
10. **ALTERATIONS:** Tenant may not: (a) make any holes or drive nails into the woodwork, floors, walls or ceilings (b) alter, paint or decorate the Property or (c) install improvements or fixtures without the prior written consent of Landlord. Any improvements or fixtures placed on the Property during the Lease become a part of the Property.
11. **SPECIAL PROVISIONS:**

12. **INSPECTIONS:** Landlord may enter at reasonable times to inspect, replace, repair or complete the improvements.
13. **LAWS:** Tenant shall comply with all applicable laws, restrictions, ordinances, rules and regulations with respect to the Property.
14. **REPAIRS AND MAINTENANCE:** <u>Tenant shall bear all expense of repairing and maintaining the Property, including but not limited to yard, trees and shrubs, unless otherwise required by the Texas Property Code. Tenant shall promptly repair at Tenant's expense any damage to the Property caused directly or indirectly by any act or omission of the Tenant or any person other than Landlord, Landlord's agents or invitees.</u>

Buyer's Temporary Residential Lease____ Page Two 12-07-98
(Address of Property)

15. **INDEMNITY:** Tenant indemnifies Landlord from the claims of all third parties for injury or damage to the person or property of such third party arising from the use or occupancy of the Property by Tenant. This indemnification includes attorney's fees, costs and expenses incurred by Landlord.
16. **INSURANCE:** Landlord and Tenant shall each maintain such insurance on the contents and Property as each party may deem appropriate during the term of this Lease. NOTE: CONSULT YOUR INSURANCE AGENT PRIOR TO CLOSING. Possession of the Property by Buyer as Tenant may change insurance policy coverage.
17. **DEFAULT:** If Tenant fails to perform or observe any provision of this Lease and fails, within 24 hours after notice by Landlord, to commence and diligently pursue to remedy such failure, Tenant will be in default.
18. **TERMINATION:** This Lease terminates upon (a) closing of the sale under the Contract, (b) termination of the Contract prior to closing, (c) Tenant's default under this Lease, or (d) Tenant's default under the Contract, whichever occurs first. Upon termination other than by closing of the sale, Tenant shall surrender possession of the Property.
19. **HOLDING OVER:** Any possession by Tenant after termination creates a tenancy at sufferance and will not operate to renew or extend this Lease. Tenant shall pay $ ________________ per day during the period of any possession after termination as damages, in addition to any other remedies to which Landlord is entitled.
20. **ATTORNEY'S FEES:** The prevailing party in any legal proceeding brought under or with respect to the transaction described in this Lease is entitled to recover from the non-prevailing party all costs of such proceeding and reasonable attorney's fees.
21. **SMOKE DETECTORS:** The Texas Property Code requires Landlord to install smoke detectors in certain locations within the Property at Landlord's expense. Tenant expressly waives Landlord's duty to inspect and repair smoke detectors.
22. **SECURITY DEVICES:** The requirements of the Texas Property Code relating to security devices do not apply to a residential lease for a term of 90 days or less.
23. **CONSULT YOUR ATTORNEY:** Real estate licensees cannot give legal advice. This Lease is intended to be legally binding. READ IT CAREFULLY. If you do not understand the effect of this Lease, consult your attorney BEFORE signing.
24. **NOTICES:** All notices under this Lease from one party to the other must be in writing and are effective when delivered or transmitted by facsimile machine as follows:

To Landlord:	**To Tenant:**
____________________	____________________
____________________	____________________
____________________	____________________
Facsimile:(____)____________	Facsimile:(____)____________

EXECUTED the _____ day of ________________________ .

____________________ Landlord	____________________ Tenant
____________________ Landlord	____________________ Tenant

Paragraph 12 identifies whether the buyer or the seller pays for the appraisal. The parties could even agree to split the cost. After checking with lenders, the parties may agree to a cap on acceptable discount fees and, if applicable, any Texas Veterans' Housing Assistance Program fees. They then define how much will be paid by the seller. It may be

- a specific number of points,
- a percentage of the required fee or
- a specific dollar amount.

12. SETTLEMENT AND OTHER EXPENSES:

A. The following expenses must be paid at or prior to closing:

(1) Appraisal fees will be paid by ______________________________.

(2) The total of loan discount fees (including any Texas Veterans' Housing Assistance Program Participation Fee) may not exceed _____% of the loan of which Seller shall pay ____________ and Buyer shall pay the remainder. The total of any buydown fees may not exceed ___________ which will be paid by ______________________.

(3) Seller's Expenses: Releases of existing liens, including prepayment penalties and recording fees; release of Seller's loan liability; tax statements or certificates; preparation of deed; one-half of escrow fee; and other expenses stipulated to be paid by Seller under other provisions of this contract.

(4) Buyer's Expenses: Loan application, origination and commitment fees; loan assumption costs; preparation and recording of deed of trust to secure assumption; lender required expenses incident to new loans, including PMI premium, preparation of loan documents, loan related inspection fee, recording fees, tax service and research fees, warehouse or underwriting fees, copies of restrictions and easements, amortization schedule, premiums for mortgagee title policies and endorsements required by lender, credit reports, photos; required premiums for flood and hazard insurance; required reserve deposit for insurance premiums and ad valorem taxes; interest on all monthly installment notes from date of disbursements to one month prior to dates of first monthly payments; customary Program Loan costs for Buyer; one-half of escrow fee; and other expenses stipulated to be paid by Buyer under other provisions of this contract.

B. If any expense exceeds an amount expressly stated in this contract for such expense to be paid by a party, that party may terminate this contract unless the other party agrees to pay such excess. In no event will Buyer pay charges and fees expressly prohibited by the Texas Veterans' Housing Assistance Program or other governmental loan program regulations.

The seller's typical expenses are listed in 12A(3) and the buyer's in 12A(4). The parties can agree to shift any of these expenses by going to paragraph 11 and setting down their agreement. Buydown fees are also addressed in 12A(2).

The following paragraphs are self-explanatory. Please read them carefully. If the parties want to alter any of the wording, competent legal advice should be sought.

> **13. PRORATIONS:** Taxes for the current year, interest, maintenance fees, assessments, dues and rents will be prorated through the Closing Date. If taxes for the current year vary from the amount prorated at closing, the parties shall adjust the prorations when tax statements for the current year are available. *If a loan is assumed* and the lender maintains an escrow account, the escrow account must be transferred to Buyer without any deficiency. Buyer shall reimburse Seller for the amount in the transferred account. Buyer shall pay the premium for a new insurance policy. If taxes are not paid at or prior to closing, Buyer will be obligated to pay taxes for the current year.
>
> **14. CASUALTY LOSS:** If any part of the Property is damaged or destroyed by fire or other casualty loss after the effective date of the contract, Seller shall restore the Property to its previous condition as soon as reasonably possible, but in any event by the Closing Date. If Seller fails to do so due to factors beyond Seller's control, Buyer may either (a) terminate this contract and the earnest money will be refunded to Buyer, (b) extend the time for performance up to 15 days and the Closing Date will be extended as necessary or (c) accept the Property in its damaged condition and accept an assignment of insurance proceeds. Seller's obligations under this paragraph are independent of any obligations of Seller under Paragraph 7.

> **15. DEFAULT:** If Buyer fails to comply with this contract, Buyer will be in default, and Seller may either (a) enforce specific performance, seek such other relief as may be provided by law, or both, or (b) terminate this contract and receive the earnest money as liquidated damages, thereby releasing both parties from this contract. If, due to factors beyond Seller's control, Seller fails within the time allowed to make any noncasualty repairs or deliver the Commitment, Buyer may either (a) extend the time for performance up to 15 days and the Closing Date will be extended as necessary or (b) terminate this contract as the sole remedy and receive the earnest money. If Seller fails to comply with this contract for any other reason, Seller will be in default and Buyer may either (a) enforce specific performance, seek such other relief as may be provided by law, or both, or (b) terminate this contract and receive the earnest money, thereby releasing both parties from this contract.

Please carefully read the paragraph that follows relating to dispute resolution.

> **16. DISPUTE RESOLUTION:** It is the policy of the State of Texas to encourage the peaceable resolution of disputes through alternative dispute resolution procedures. The parties are encouraged to use an addendum approved by TREC to submit to mediation disputes which cannot be resolved in good faith through informal discussion.

The parties are advised and encouraged to submit to mediation disputes that cannot be resolved through informal discussion. The parties are encouraged to use TREC 35-1, the addendum relating to mediation (page 66).

Under the provisions of the Texas statute relating to alternative dispute resolution, only a judge has been given authority to compel parties to mediation. Licensees can encourage by pointing out the benefits but they cannot compel. Contrary to what some in the field believe, TREC does not, and in fact cannot, require that the addendum be a part of every transaction. Addenda should only be added at the request of the parties. The licensee should always make certain that the parties are made aware of the existence of addenda that may be applicable to their transaction.

06-15-98

PROMULGATED BY THE TEXAS REAL ESTATE COMMISSION (TREC)

AGREEMENT FOR MEDIATION

ADDENDUM TO CONTRACT CONCERNING THE PROPERTY AT

____

(Street Address and City)

The parties to the Contract and any broker who signs this addendum agree to negotiate in good faith in an effort to resolve any dispute related to the Contract that may arise between the parties or between a party and a broker.

If the dispute cannot be resolved by negotiation, the parties to the dispute shall submit the dispute to mediation before resorting to litigation.

This Agreement for Mediation will survive closing.

❑ If the need for mediation arises, the parties to the dispute shall choose a mutually acceptable mediator and shall share the cost of mediation services equally.

❑ If the need for mediation arises, mediation services will be provided by ____________________ ____________________ and the parties to the dispute shall share the cost of mediation services equally.

NOTE: Mediation is a voluntary dispute resolution process in which the parties to the dispute meet with an impartial person, called a mediator, who would help to resolve the dispute informally and confidentially. Mediators facilitate the resolution of disputes but cannot impose binding decisions. The parties to the dispute must agree before any settlement is binding.

Date: ____________________

____________________ Buyer	____________________ Seller
____________________ Buyer	____________________ Seller
____________________ Other Broker	____________________ Listing Broker
By: ____________________	By: ____________________

The form of this addendum has been approved for voluntary use by the Texas Real Estate Commission for use only with similarly approved or promulgated forms of contracts. No representation is made as to the legal validity or adequacy of any provision in any specific transactions. (06-98) Texas Real Estate Commission, P.O. Box 12188, Austin, TX 78711-2188, 1-800-250-8732 or (512)459-6544. (http://www.trec.state.tx.us) TREC No. 35-1. This form replaces TREC No. 35-0.

> **17. ATTORNEY'S FEES:** The prevailing party in any legal proceeding brought under or with respect to the transaction described in this contract is entitled to recover from the non-prevailing party all costs of such proceeding and reasonable attorney's fees.

The attorney's fee wording is straightforward and common to most real estate related agreements. It appears that the committee and TREC intended for the wording to include licensees who might become a party in a legal proceeding brought under or with respect to the subject transaction.

> **18. ESCROW:** The earnest money is deposited with escrow agent with the understanding that escrow agent is not (a) a party to this contract and does not have any liability for the performance or nonperformance of any party to this contract, (b) liable for interest on the earnest money and (c) liable for any loss of earnest money caused by the failure of any financial institution in which the earnest money has been deposited unless the financial institution is acting as escrow agent. At closing, the earnest money must be applied first to any cash down payment, then to Buyer's closing costs and any excess refunded to Buyer. If both parties make written demand for the earnest money, escrow agent may require payment of unpaid expenses incurred on behalf of the parties and a written release of liability of escrow agent from all parties. If one party makes written demand for the earnest money, escrow agent shall give notice of the demand by providing to the other party a copy of the demand. If escrow agent does not receive written objection to the demand from the other party within 30 days after notice to the other party, escrow agent may disburse the earnest money to the party making demand reduced by the amount of unpaid expenses incurred on behalf of the party receiving the earnest money and escrow agent may pay the same to the creditors. If escrow agent complies with the provisions of this paragraph, each party hereby releases escrow agent from all adverse claims related to the disbursal of the earnest money. Escrow agent's notice to the other party will be effective when deposited in the U. S. Mail, postage prepaid, certified mail, return receipt requested, addressed to the other party at such party's address shown below. Notice of objection to the demand will be deemed effective upon receipt by escrow agent.

The latest generation of TREC promulgated contracts has an interesting provision beginning with the last three words of line 9 in paragraph 18. The parties give the escrow agent the ability to, after due notice, release the earnest money to a party making a written demand for it. The parties agree to release the escrow agent from all adverse claims related to the disbursal of the earnest money when the detailed procedure is followed.

> **19. REPRESENTATIONS:** Seller represents that as of the Closing Date (a) there will be no liens, assessments, or security interests against the Property which will not be satisfied out of the sales proceeds unless securing payment of any loans assumed by Buyer and (b) assumed loans will not be in default. If any representation in this contract is untrue on the Closing Date, this contract may be terminated by Buyer and the earnest money will be refunded to Buyer. All representations contained in this contract will survive closing.

Sellers should note that all representations made in the agreement transfer to the warranty deed and survive closing. This is a good reason to keep the seller's disclosure notice addressed by section 5.008 of the property code separate from the contract.

> **20. FEDERAL TAX REQUIREMENT:** If Seller is a "foreign person," as defined by applicable law, or if Seller fails to deliver an affidavit that Seller is not a "foreign person," then Buyer shall withhold from the sales proceeds an amount sufficient to comply with applicable tax law and deliver the same to the Internal Revenue Service together with appropriate tax forms. IRS regulations require filing written reports if cash in excess of specified amounts is received in the transaction.

When closing takes place at a title company, the escrow agent makes certain that IRS regulations are followed. The parties should read the paragraph and seek answers to their questions from qualified sources.

> **21. AGREEMENT OF PARTIES:** This contract contains the entire agreement of the parties and cannot be changed except by their written agreement. Addenda which are a part of this contract are (list): ____
> ______________________________
> ______________________________
> ______________________________
> ______________________________
> ______________________________.

List all addenda, both promulgated and nonpromulgated, that are a part of the agreement in paragraph 21. The TREC addenda may be identified by title or number. If they are not a part of the promises being exchanged by the parties, do not list them.

Example: **DO NOT LIST**

- Seller's disclosure notice
- Information about brokerage services
- TAR form—027: "Notification of Intermediary Relationship"

> **22. CONSULT YOUR ATTORNEY:** Real estate licensees cannot give legal advice. This contract is intended to be legally binding. READ IT CAREFULLY. If you do not understand the effect of this contract, consult your attorney BEFORE signing.
> Buyer's Attorney is: ______________________ Seller's Attorney is: ______________________

Identify attorney for buyer and/or seller by name. You might include the address and/or telephone number also. Some clients choose to have their notices delivered to the attorney. If a party chooses not to select an attorney to consult before signing the agreement, enter the words "not selected" or "not identified."

23. NOTICES: All notices from one party to the other must be in writing and are effective when mailed to, hand-delivered at, or transmitted by facsimile machine as follows:

To Buyer at:	**To Seller at:**
____________________	____________________
____________________	____________________
____________________	____________________
Telephone: (___)____________________	Telephone: (___)____________________
Facsimile: (___)____________________	Facsimile: (___)____________________

EXECUTED the ______ day of ________________, 19___ (THE EFFECTIVE DATE). (BROKER: FILL IN THE DATE OF FINAL ACCEPTANCE.)

Ask the buyer and seller where notices are to be mailed, delivered or transmitted by facsimile machine. Texas courts do not recognize facsimile signatures, so be sure to obtain the original signature of each of the parties at the signature lines.

Please be aware that the contract specifies that notices are effective when delivered to the buyer or the seller. A notice given to a principal's agent may constitute an effective delivery to the buyer or seller. **Be careful here!**

If the buyer is a customer rather than a client, the buyer has no agent. Delivery of the notice to a coop agent, acting as a subagent, does not constitute delivery of the notice to the buyer. Remember that the subagent works for and represents the seller. When a transaction involves both a seller's agent and a buyer's agent, notifying a client's agent will generally be construed as giving constructive or imputed notice to the client.

The list that follows identifies some of the notices that may need to be delivered.

- Notice of termination during the option period
- Homeowner's association resale certificate
- Financial documentation of buyer as identified in paragraph 4E
- Title commitment
- Survey
- Lender required repairs
- Demand for release of earnest money deposit

____________________	____________________
Buyer	Seller
____________________	____________________
Buyer	Seller

The form of this contract has been approved by the Texas Real Estate Commission. Such approval relates to this contract form only. No representation is made as to the legal validity or adequacy of any provision in any specific transaction. It is not suitable for complex transactions. Extensive riders or additions are not to be used. Texas Real Estate Commission, P.O. Box 12188, Austin, TX 78711-2188, 1-800-250-8732 or (512) 459-6544 (http://www.trec.state.tx.us) TREC NO. 20-3. This form replaces TREC NO. 20-2.

Note that the receipt is issued by the escrow agent, not the listing or selling licensee. Some escrow agents may choose to use their own receipt form for the contract and the earnest money instead of the form at the end of the contract form. Brokers and salespersons are reminded that TREC rules require that the licensee deposit the earnest money with the escrow agent by the close of business on the second business day after the execution of the contract by the principals. The only exception occurs when the principals agree that a deposit may be delayed and a different time is expressly defined in the written agreement [Rule 535.159 (I)].

RECEIPT

Receipt of ❑ Contract and ❑ $________ Earnest Money in the form of ______________ is acknowledged.
Escrow Agent: ______________________________ Date: ______________________, 19____
By: ______________________________

____
Address Telephone: ( ) ______________________________

____
City State Zip Code Facsimile: ( ) ______________________________

The following two addenda do not really fit with the discussion of any particular paragraph or provision of the basic contract. Although recently revised, both were created at the time when the Texas real estate markets were very different. In a "seller's market" when demand for available properties exceeded available supply, the first addendum, Addendum for Sale of Other Property by Buyer (page 72) was created to enter into a contract of purchase but to give the buyer an out if the buyer's current property did not sell. From the seller's perspective, it is not a particularly good idea to take the property off the market while waiting for the buyer's property to sell. While the addendum permits the seller to continue to offer the property and to consider other offers, the reality of the marketplace is that licensees working with buyers show available properties first and only show pending properties with contingencies as a last resort. If you do use the addendum, be sure to give careful attention to the time frames. The wording in the addendum states that "time is of the essence" and demands strict compliance with the times set down. Do not confuse this addendum with notice (6) at the end of pararaph 6 that addresses the seller's right to continue to show the property for possible consideration of backup offers.

The second addendum, Addendum for Second or "Back-Up" Contract (page 73), is designed to be used when a desired property is under contract with another buyer. The second buyer can create an agreement of purchase in which the buyer is entitled to purchase the property only if the existing contract does not close. It creates a contingency for the seller in which it is agreed that "I'll sell you my property, if the existing contract does not close." Again, one must give careful attention to the time frames established by the addendum. For the purpose of the addendum, "time is of the essence."

Summary

When completing contract forms make certain to correctly complete all required blanks. In a blank in the main body of the contract form that is not applicable, insert **N/A.** For blanks that follow a box you have not checked, do nothing.

Carefully verify the spelling of the names of the parties, the legal and informal property descriptions and the mathematics of financial arrangements. Be sure that the property address has been added at the top of each page of the form and that all parties have initialed the bottom of each page that does not contain their complete signatures.

If the agreement went through a countering process, have all changes been properly initialed by each of the parties? Did you date the contract when the buyer was notified of the seller's written acceptance of the buyer's written offer or, if a counteroffer occurred, when the seller was notified of the buyer's written (initialed the changes) acceptance of the seller's written counteroffer? Remember that it is not a counteroffer if the seller has not responded with a signature and initials to any changes or modifications to the buyer's original offer.

09-20-99

PROMULGATED BY THE TEXAS REAL ESTATE COMMISSION (TREC)

ADDENDUM FOR SALE OF OTHER PROPERTY BY BUYER

ADDENDUM TO CONTRACT BETWEEN THE UNDERSIGNED PARTIES CONCERNING THE PROPERTY AT

____
(Street Address and City)

A. The contract is contingent upon Buyer's receipt of the proceeds from the sale of Buyer's property at ____(Address) by 5:00 p.m. on ____________________, ______ (the Contingency). If the Contingency is not satisfied or waived by Buyer by the above time and date, the contract will terminate automatically and the earnest money will be refunded to Buyer.
NOTICE: The date inserted in this Paragraph should be no later than the date inserted in Paragraph 9 of the contract.

B. If Seller accepts a written offer to sell the Property, Seller shall notify Buyer (1) of such acceptance **AND** (2) that Seller requires Buyer to waive the Contingency. Buyer mustwaive the Contingency by 5:00 p.m. on the ____________day after delivery of Seller's notice to Buyer; otherwise the contract will terminate automatically and the earnest money will be refunded to Buyer.

C. Buyer may waive the Contingency only by notifying Seller of the waiver and depositing $_________ with escrow agent as additional earnest money. All notices must be in writing and are effective when delivered in accordance with the contract.

D. If Buyer waives the Contingency and Buyer's loan or assumption approval is conditioned upon the sale of Buyer's property described in Paragraph A above, Buyer will be in default if such condition is not satisfied by the date provided for in Paragraph 4 of the contract. If such default occurs, Seller may exercise the remedies specified in Paragraph 15 of the contract. If Buyer fails to obtain loan or assumption approval for any other reason, the provisions of Paragraph 4 remain in effect.

E. For purposes of this Addendum time is of the essence; strict compliance with the times for performance stated herein is required.

______________________	______________________
Buyer	Seller
______________________	______________________
Buyer	Seller

The form of this addendum has been approved by the Texas Real Estate Commission for use only with similarly approved or promulgated forms of contracts. Such approval relates to this contract form only. TREC forms are intended for use only by trained real estate licensees. No representation is made as to the legal validity or adequacy of any provision in any specific transactions. It is not suitable for complex transactions.(09-99)Texas Real Estate Commission, P.O. Box 12188, Austin, TX 78711-2188, 1-800-250-8732 or (512) 459-6544 (http://www.trec.state.tx.us) TREC No. 10-3. This form replaces TREC No. 10-2.

PROMULGATED BY THE TEXAS REAL ESTATE COMMISSION (TREC) 06-15-98

ADDENDUM FOR "BACK-UP" CONTRACT

ADDENDUM TO CONTRACT BETWEEN THE UNDERSIGNED PARTIES CONCERNING PROPERTY AT

____

(Street Address and City)

A. The Contract to which this Addendum is attached (the "Back-Up Contract") is binding upon execution by the parties, and the earnest money and any Option Fee must be paid as provided in the Back-Up Contract. The Back-Up Contract is contingent upon the termination of a previous contract (the "First Contract") between Seller and ______________________________, dated ______________, ________, for the sale of Property. Except as provided by this Addendum, neither party is required to perform under the Back-Up Contract while it is contingent upon the First Contract.

B. If the First Contract terminates on or before 5:00 p.m. on ______________, ______ (the "Contingency Date"), the Back-Up Contract will no longer be contingent upon the termination of the First Contract. Seller must notify Buyer immediately of the termination of the First Contract. For purposes of performance, the effective date of the Back-Up Contract will be deemed to be the date Buyer receives notice of termination of the First Contract or the Contingency Date, whichever is earlier.

C. If the First Contract does not terminate by the Contingency Date, the Back-Up Contract terminates and the earnest money will be refunded to Buyer.

D. An amendment or modification of the First Contract will not terminate the First Contract.

E. If Buyer has the unrestricted right to terminate under Paragraph 7D(1), the time for giving notice of termination begins on the effective date of the Back-Up Contract, continues through the deemed effective date of the Back-Up Contract and ends upon the expiration of the number of days specified in Paragraph 7D(1).

F. For purposes of this Addendum, time is of the essence. Strict compliance with the times for performance stated herein is required.

______________________ Buyer	______________________ Seller
______________________ Buyer	______________________ Seller

The form of this addendum has been approved by the Texas Real Estate Commission. Such approval relates to this form only. No representation is made as to the legal validity or adequacy of any provision in any specific transaction. It is not suitable for complex transactions. Extensive riders or additions are not to be used. (06-98)Texas Real Estate Commission, P.O. Box 12188, Austin, TX 78711-2188, 1-800-250-8732 or (512)459-6544 (http:\\www.trec.state.tx.us) TREC No. 11-3. This form replaces TREC No. 11-2.

1. In a transaction where the seller is removing the water softener and window air-conditioning units prior to closing, the licensee should strike these items from paragraph 2 and have the parties initial.

   A. True
   B. False

2. Under current statutory requirements, within how many days after receiving a written request from the homeowner or the homeowner's agent must a homeowner's association furnish the completed TREC promulgated resale certificate?

   A. 5
   B. 10
   C. 7
   D. 20

3. When a loan is being assumed, if the actual loan balance differs in an amount greater than **$350** of the amount stated in paragraph 4 D.(1) or (2), the cash payable at closing will automatically be adjusted by the escrow officer at closing.

   A. True
   B. False

4. Which of the following is **not** directly addressed in the Seller Financing Addendum, TREC 26-2?

   A. The ability to prepay the note without penalty
   B. Consent to assume the note being created
   C. Payment of ad valorem taxes
   D. Interest rate to be charged

5. Which of the following should **not** be attached to the contract and identified as an addendum?

   A. Call for an environmental assessment
   B. Seller's disclosure of property condition
   C. Seller's disclosure of information about lead
   D. Buyer's or seller's temporary lease

6. Under the provisions of TREC 20-4, how many days does the buyer have after receipt of the title commitment to object in writing to matters disclosed in the commitment?

   A. 5
   B. 7
   C. 10
   D. 15

7. If loan approval has been received by the identified closing date in paragraph 9, for up to how many days may the contract be extended to comply with lender's closing requirements?

   A. 5
   B. 7
   C. 10
   D. 15

8. Any possession by the buyer prior to closing or by the seller after closing that is not authorized by a temporary lease form promulgated by TREC will establish a tenancy at sufferance relationship between the parties.

   A. True
   B. False

9. Which of the following is appropriate for insertion into paragraph 11 of TREC 20-3?

   A. Contract is subject to satisfactory inspections to the buyer.
   B. Contract is contingent upon appraisal greater than the amount in paragraph 3C.
   C. Buyer will pay the additional insurance premium to delete item 6A(6).
   D. Seller will deliver possession 72 hours after funding.

10. If any expense exceeds an amount expressly stated in the contract for such expense to be paid by a party, that party may terminate the contract unless the other party agrees to pay such excess.

    A. True
    B. False

Additional TREC Promulgated Contract Forms

Now that we are thoroughly familiar with the provision of TREC contract form 20-4 and all of the promulgated addenda, we focus our attention on the seven other promulgated contract forms, particularly those provisions and paragraphs that are different than form 20-4. The complete text of the forms discussed in this section is found in Appendix B.

PROMULGATED BY THE TEXAS REAL ESTATE COMMISSION (TREC) 11-08-99

ONE TO FOUR FAMILY RESIDENTIAL CONTRACT (RESALE)

FHA INSURED OR VA GUARANTEED FINANCING

NOTICE: Not For Use For Condominium Transactions

The form most similar to TREC contract form 20-4 is form 21-4. It is used for one-family to four-family residential resale transactions that are contingent upon obtaining financing insured by the FHA or guaranteed by the VA.

Frequently, buyers with limited up-front cash use the FHA insurance program. Remember that FHA does not loan money; it insures high LTV ratio loans and reduces the risk to the lenders loaning the money.

Early in 1999 the FHA greatly simplified the rules relating to FHA-insured loan amounts and down payment requirements. The maximum loan amounts are currently 48 percent of Fannie Mae's maximum conforming loan amount for low cost areas to 68 percent of Fannie Mae's maximum conforming loan amount in the highest cost areas. All but 31 counties in Texas have a maximum insured loan amount of $115,200 for a single family home.

For current limits on high cost counties, go to the HUD web site (**www.hud.gov**), which always has the most recent numbers available when changes are made.

Under current regulations, a buyer obtaining an FHA-insured loan must invest at least 3 percent in down payment and/or closing costs. If the sales price is $50,000 or less, the maximum LTV is 98.75 percent. The borrower must pay 1.25 percent down and costs equal to a minimum of 1.75 percent. When the sales price is more than $50,000, the maximum LTV is 97.75 percent. The borrower must pay 2.25 percent down and costs equal to a minimum of .75 percent. Any closing costs in excess of these amounts may be paid by the seller who is willing to pay them.

Paragraph 3 of TREC promulgated contract 21-4 is identical to paragraph 3 in form 20-4 except that subsection B excludes VA funding fee or FHA mortgage insurance premium rather than private mortgage insurance premiums.

3. SALES PRICE:
A. Cash portion of the Sales Price payable by buyer at closing . . . . $___________
B. Sum of all financing described below (excluding VA Funding Fee or FHA Mortgage Insurance Premium [MIP]) . . . . $___________
C. Sales Price (Sum of A and B). . . . . $___________

Paragraph 4 offers three financing options.

A. FHA INSURED FINANCING has six blanks that need to be completed:
1. FHA section number for the desired loan,
2. amount of the desired loan excluding any financed FHA insurance premium,
3. desired term of the loan,
4. maximum interest rate acceptable to the buyer,
5. initial term of an adjustable-rate loan, and
6. sale price for which the property must appraise. If the appraisal comes in low, the buyer may cancel without forfeiture of the earnest money or pay the difference in cash, or the seller may reduce the sales price to match the appraised value.

B. VA GUARANTEED FINANCING has four blanks to be completed:
1. desired loan amount (maximum is dictated by veteran's available entitlement and appraised value of the property),
2. term of the loan,

3. maximum acceptable interest rate, and
4. initial term of an adjustable rate loan.

C. TEXAS VETERANS' HOUSING ASSISTANCE PROGRAM LOAN has only two blanks:
1. desired loan amount (maximum available is $150,000) and
2. term.

4. FINANCING: Within ______ days after the effective date of this contract Buyer shall apply for and make every reasonable effort to obtain financing. Financing will be deemed to have been obtained when the lender has determined that Buyer has satisfied all of lender's financial requirements (those items relating to Buyer's net worth, income and creditworthiness). If financing (including any financed MIP or Funding Fee) is not obtained within ______ days after the effective date hereof, this contract will terminate and the earnest money will be refunded to Buyer. The portion of the Sales Price not payable in cash will be paid as follows:
(Check applicable boxes below)

❑ A. **FHA INSURED FINANCING:** This contract is subject to approval for Buyer of a Section _______ FHA insured loan of not less than $_______________ (excluding any financed MIP), amortizable monthly for not less than _______ years, with interest not to exceed __________% per annum for the first ____________ year(s) of the loan.
As required by HUD-FHA, if FHA valuation is unknown, *"It is expressly agreed that, notwithstanding any other provisions of this contract, the purchaser* (Buyer) *shall not be obligated to complete the purchase of the Property described herein or to incur any penalty by forfeiture of earnest money deposits or otherwise unless the purchaser* (Buyer) *has been given in accordance with HUD/FHA or VA requirements a written statement issued by the Federal Housing Commissioner, Department of Veterans Affairs, or a Direct Endorsement Lender setting forth the appraised value of the Property of not less than $_________________. The purchaser* (Buyer) *shall have the privilege and option of proceeding with consummation of the contract without regard to the amount of the appraised valuation. The appraised valuation is arrived at to determine the maximum mortgage the Department of Housing and Urban Development will insure. HUD does not warrant the value or the condition of the Property. The purchaser* (Buyer) *should satisfy himself/herself that the price and the condition of the Property are acceptable."* If the FHA appraised value of the Property (excluding closing costs and MIP) is less than the Sales Price (3C above), Seller may reduce the Sales Price to an amount equal to the FHA appraised value (excluding closing costs and MIP) and the parties to the sale shall close the sale at such lower Sales Price with appropriate adjustments to 3A and 3B above.

❑ B. **VA GUARANTEED FINANCING:** This contract is subject to approval for Buyer of a VA guaranteed loan of not less than $___________________ (excluding any financed Funding Fee), amortizable monthly for not less than _____ years, with interest not to exceed _____% per annum for the first ______ year(s) of the loan.
VA NOTICE TO BUYER: *"It is expressly agreed that, notwithstanding any other provisions of this contract, the Buyer shall not incur any penalty by forfeiture of earnest money or otherwise or be obligated to complete the purchase of the Property described herein, if the contract purchase price or cost exceeds the reasonable value of the Property established by the Department of Veterans Affairs. The Buyer shall, however, have the privilege and option of proceeding with the consummation of this contract without regard to the amount of the reasonable value established by the Department of Veterans Affairs."*

[*Continued*]

If Buyer elects to complete the purchase at an amount in excess of the reasonable value established by VA, Buyer shall pay such excess amount in cash from a source which Buyer agrees to disclose to the VA and which Buyer represents will not be from borrowed funds except as approved by VA. If VA reasonable value of the Property is less than the Sales Price (3C above), Seller may reduce the Sales Price to an amount equal to the VA reasonable value and the parties to the sale shall close at such lower Sales Price with appropriate adjustments to 3A and 3B above.

❑ C. **TEXAS VETERANS' HOUSING ASSISTANCE PROGRAM LOAN:** This contract is subject to approval for Buyer of a Texas Veterans' Housing Assistance Program Loan of $____________ for a period of at least ________ years at the interest rate established by the Texas Veterans' Land Board at the time of closing.

Paragraph 6B is shorter than in form 20-4 and only contains option (1) from form 20-4.

❑ B. **SURVEY:** Within ____________ days after Buyer's receipt of a survey furnished to a third-party lender at ❑ Seller's ❑ Buyer's expense, Buyer may object in writing to any matter shown on the survey which constitutes a defect or encumbrance to title.
The survey must be made by a Registered Professional Land Surveyor acceptable to the Title Company and any lender. Utility easements created by the dedication deed and plat of the subdivision in which the Property is located will not be a basis for objection.

Paragraph 7 of TREC 21-4 is identical to paragraph 7 of TREC 20-4; however, licensees should furnish HUD-92564-CN to buyers prior to addressing the buyer's choice at paragraph 7D. To have adequate opportunity to inspect, the buyer needs to elect 7D1 and purchase an option period.

Paragraph 12 defines a different set of closing costs and fees unique to FHA-insured and VA-guaranteed loan transactions. A careful reading of it will enable you to quickly identify the differences.

12. SETTLEMENT AND OTHER EXPENSES:

A. The following expenses must be paid at or prior to closing:

(1) Appraisal fees will be paid by ____________________________.

(2) The total of the loan discount fees (including any Texas Veterans' Housing Assistance Program Participation Fee) may not exceed _______% of the loan of which Seller shall pay ___________ and Buyer shall pay the remainder. The total of any buydown fees may not exceed ___________ which will be paid by ________________________.

(3) Seller's Expenses: Releases of existing liens, including prepayment penalties and recording fees; tax statements or certificates; preparation of deed; one-half of escrow fee; expenses FHA or VA prohibits Buyer to pay; and other expenses stipulated to be paid by Seller under other provisions of this contract.

[Continued]

US Department of Housing
and Urban Development
Office of Housing
Federal Housing Commissioner

OMB Approval No: 2502-0538
(exp. 11/30/99)

For Your Protection: Get a Home Inspection

Name of Seller ______________________________

Property Address ______________________________

____

What the FHA Does for Buyers... and What We Don't Do

What we do: FHA helps people become homeowners by insuring mortgages for lenders. This allows lenders to offer mortgages to first-time buyers and others who may not qualify for conventional loans. Because the FHA insures the loan for the lender, the buyer pays only a very low down-payment.

What we don't do: FHA does not guarantee the value or condition of your potential new home. If you find problems with your new home after closing, we can not give or lend you money for repairs, and we can not buy the home back from you.

That's why it's so important for you, the buyer, to get an independent home inspection. Before you sign a contract, ask a qualified home inspector to inspect your potential new home and give you the information you need to make a wise decision.

Appraisals and Home Inspections are Different

As part of our job insuring the loan, we require that the lender conduct an FHA appraisal. An appraisal is different from a home inspection. Appraisals are for lenders; home inspections are for buyers. The lender does an appraisal for three reasons:

- to estimate the value of a house
- to make sure that the house meets FHA minimum property standards
- to make sure that the house is marketable

Appraisals are not home inspections.

Why a Buyer Needs a Home Inspection

A home inspection gives the buyer more detailed information than an appraisal--information you need to make a wise decision. In a home inspection, a qualified inspector takes an in-depth, unbiased look at your potential new home to:

- evaluate the physical condition: structure, construction, and mechanical systems
- identify items that need to be repaired or replaced
- estimate the remaining useful life of the major systems, equipment, structure, and finishes

What Goes into a Home Inspection

A home inspection gives the buyer an impartial, physical evaluation of the overall condition of the home and items that need to be repaired or replaced. The inspection gives a detailed report on the condition of the structural components, exterior, roofing, plumbing, electrical, heating, insulation and ventilation, air conditioning, and interiors.

Be an Informed Buyer

It is your responsibility to be an informed buyer. Be sure that what you buy is satisfactory in every respect. You have the right to carefully examine your potential new home with a qualified home inspector. You should arrange to have a home inspection before you purchase your home. Make sure your contract states that the sale of the home depends on the inspection.

I understand the importance of getting an independent home inspection. I have thought about this before I signed a contract with the seller for a home.

X______________________________ X______________________________

Signature & Date Signature & Date

Form **HUD-92564-CN**
(6/99)

(4) Buyer's Expenses: Interest on the note(s) from date of disbursement to one month prior to dates of first monthly payments, expenses stipulated to be paid by Buyer under other provisions of this contract; any customary Texas Veterans' Housing Assistance Program Loan costs for Buyer; and premiums for mortgagee title policy and endorsements required by lender.

(a) FHA Buyer: All prepaid items required by applicable HUD-FHA or other regulations, including required premiums for flood and hazard insurance, reserve deposits for other insurance, ad valorem taxes and special governmental assessments; expenses incident to any loan, including preparation of loan documents, recording fees, copies of restrictions and easements, amortization schedule, loan origination fee, loan commitment fee, credit reports, photos, loan related inspection fee; and one-half of escrow fee.

(b) VA Buyer: All prepaid items, including required premiums for flood and hazard insurance, reserve deposits for other insurance, ad valorem taxes and special governmental assessments; expenses incident to any loan, including credit reports, recording fees, loan origination fee, loan related inspection fees.

B. The VA Loan Funding Fee or FHA Mortgage Insurance Premium (MIP) not to exceed ____________ will be paid by Buyer, and ❏ paid in cash at closing ❏ added to the amount of the loan or ❏ paid as follows: ____

____.

C. If any expense exceeds an amount expressly stated in this contract for such expense to be paid by a party, that party may terminate this contract unless the other party agrees to pay such excess. In no event will Buyer pay charges and fees expressly prohibited by FHA, VA or other governmental loan program regulations.

PROMULGATED BY THE TEXAS REAL ESTATE COMMISSION (TREC) 06-22-00

NEW HOME CONTRACT

(Incomplete Construction)

NOTICE: Not For Use For Condominium Transactions or Closings Prior to Completion of Construction

Prudent buyers of incomplete homes secure the services of a real estate attorney to make certain that the contract and all construction documents are complete and adequately protect the interest of the buyer. Most builders use their own contract forms; however, for those who do not, TREC has provided a workable form.

Paragraphs 2 and 7 must be examined together because both address the property and paragraph 7 is referenced in paragraph 2. Carefully read the two paragraphs and you will be able to quickly identify what is different from the form previously examined.

When new homes are sold, the buyer must be furnished with information about the insulation used (see 7-G).

2. **PROPERTY:** Lot ____________, Block ______, ____ Addition, City of ________________________________, __________________ County, Texas, known as ____ (Address/Zip Code), or as described on attached exhibit, together with the improvements, fixtures and all other property located thereon. All property sold by this contract is called the "Property."
Mandatory Membership in an Owners' Association: (Check one box only):
❑ The Property is not subject to mandatory membership in an owners' association.
❑ The TREC Addendum For Property Subject To Mandatory Membership In An Owners' Association is attached.
NOTICE TO BUYER: If the Property is subject to mandatory membership in an owner's association, Seller notifies Buyer under §5.012, Texas Property Code, that, as a purchaser of property in the residential community in which the Property is located, you are obligated to be a member of an owner's association. Restrictive covenants governing the use and occupancy of the Property and a dedicatory instrument governing the establishment, maintenance, and operation of this residential community have been or will be recorded in the Real Property Records of the county in which the Property is located. Copies of the restrictive covenants and dedicatory instrument may be obtained from the county clerk. You ar obligated to pay assessments to the owner's association. The amount of the assessments is subject to change. Your failure to pay the assessments could result in a lien on and the foreclosure of the Property.

7. **PROPERTY CONDITION:**
A. INSPECTIONS AND ACCESS: Buyer, at Buyer's expense, may have the Property inspected by inspectors selected by Buyer, licensed by TREC or otherwise permitted by law to make such inspections. Seller shall permit access to the Property at reasonable times for inspections and for reinspections.
B. CONSTRUCTION DOCUMENTS: Seller shall complete all improvements with due diligence in accordance with the plans and either specifications, finish-out schedules or allowances initialed by the parties, incorporated by reference and identified as ________________________________, together with the following changes or alternates: ____ and any other change orders agreed to in writing (all called Construction Documents).

C. COST ADJUSTMENTS: Increase in costs resulting from change orders or items selected by Buyer which exceed the allowances specified in the Construction Documents will be paid by Buyer as follows: ____
____.
A decrease in costs resulting from change orders and unused allowances will reduce Sales Price and loan amount accordingly.

D. BUYER'S SELECTIONS: If the Construction Documents permit selections by Buyer, Buyer's selections will conform to Seller's normal standards as set out in the Construction Documents or will not, in Seller's judgment, adversely affect the marketability of the Property. Buyer will make required selections within ________ days after receipt of written notice from Seller.

E. COMPLETION: Seller must commence construction no later than ________ days after loan approval. The improvements will be substantially completed in accordance with the Construction Documents and ready for occupancy not later than ________________, _____. The improvements will be deemed to be substantially completed in accordance with the Construction Documents upon the final inspection and approval by all applicable governmental authorities and any lender. Construction delays caused by Buyer's acts or omissions, acts of God, fire or other casualty, strikes, boycotts or nonavailability of materials for which no substitute of comparable quality and price is available will be added to the time allowed for substantial completion of the construction. However, in no event may the time for substantial completion extend beyond the Closing Date. Seller may substitute materials, equipment and appliances of comparable quality for those specified in the Construction Documents.

F. WARRANTIES: Except as expressly set forth in Paragraph 11, or as attached to this contract, Seller makes no other express warranties. Seller agrees to assign to Buyer at closing all assignable manufacturer warranties.

G. INSULATION: As required by Federal Trade Commission Regulations, the information relating to the insulation installed or to be installed in the home being purchased under this contract is as follows:

(1) Exterior walls of improved living areas: insulated with ______________________ insulation to a thickness of ________ inches which yields an R-Value of ______.

(2) Walls in other areas of the home: insulated with ______________________ insulation to a thickness of ________ inches which yields an R-Value of ______.

(3) Ceilings in improved living areas: insulated with ______________________ insulation to a thickness of ________ inches which yields an R-Value of ______.

(4) Floors of improved living areas not applied to a slab foundation: insulated with ______________ insulation to a thickness of ________ inches which yields an R-Value of ______.

(5) Other insulated areas: insulated with ______________________ insulation to a thickness of ________ inches which yields an R-Value of ______.

All stated R-Values are based on information provided by the manufacturer of the insulation.

Paragraph 4 contains nothing you have not previously studied. The paragraph has been reconfigured to include only those financing options that would be used for a newly constructed home.

3. SALES PRICE:

A. Cash portion of Sales Price payable by Buyer at closing . . . . $____________

B. Sum of all financing described below (excluding any FHA Mortgage Insurance Premium [MIP], VA funding fee, or Private Mortgage Insurance Premium [PMI]) . . . $____________

C. Sales Price (Sum of A and B) . . . . $____________

4. FINANCING: Within _____ days after the effective date of this contract Buyer shall apply for all third party financing and make every reasonable effort to obtain financing. Financing will be deemed to have been obtained when the lender determines that Buyer has satisfied all of lender's financial requirements (those items relating to Buyer's net worth, income and creditworthiness). If financing (including any financed PMI premium) is not obtained within ______ days after the effective date hereof, this contract will terminate and the earnest money will be refunded to Buyer. Each note to be executed hereunder must be secured by vendor's and deed of trust liens.

The portion of Sales Price not payable in cash will be paid as follows: (Check applicable boxes below)

❑ A. THIRD PARTY FINANCING:

❑ (1) This contract is subject to approval for Buyer of a third party first mortgage loan having a loan-to-value ratio not to exceed______ % as established by such third party (excluding anyfinanced PMI premium), due in full in____ year(s), with interest not to exceed _____ % per annum for the first _____ year(s) of the loan. The loan will be ❑ with ❑ without PMI.

❑ (2) This contract is subject to approval for Buyer of a third party second mortgage loan having a loan-to-value ratio not to exceed _____ % as established by such third party (excluding any financed PMI premium), due in full in _____ year(s), with interest not to exceed______ % per annum for the first _____ year(s) of the loan. The loan will be ❑ with ❑ without PMI.

❑ B. FHA INSURED FINANCING: This contract is subject to approval for Buyer of a Section______ FHA insured loan of not less than $_______________ (excluding any financed MIP), amortizable monthly for not less than ______ years, with interest not to exceed _____ % per annum for the first ______ year(s) of the Loan.

As required by HUD-FHA, if FHA valuation is unknown, "It is expressly agreed that, notwithstanding any other provisions of this contract, the purchaser (Buyer) *shall not be obligated to complete the purchase of the property described herein or to incur any penalty by forfeiture of earnest money deposits or otherwise unless the purchaser* (Buyer) *has been given in accordance with HUD/FHA or VA requirements a written statement issued by the Federal Housing Commissioner, Department of Veterans Affairs, or a Direct Endorsement Lender setting forth the appraised value of the Property of not less than $ _____________. The purchaser (Buyer) shall have the privilege and option of proceeding with consummation of the contract without regard to the amount of the appraised valuation. The appraised valuation is arrived at to determine the maximum mortgage the Department of Housing and Urban Development will insure. HUD does not warrant the value or the condition of the property. The purchaser* (Buyer) *should satisfy himself/herself that the price and the condition of the Property are acceptable."* If the FHA appraised value of the Property (excluding closing

[Continued]

costs and MIP) is less than the Sales Price (3C above), Seller may reduce the Sales Price to an amount equal to the FHA appraised value (excluding closing costs and MIP) and the parties to the sale shall close the sale at such lower Sales Price with appropriate adjustments to 3A and 3B above.

❑ C. VA GUARANTEED FINANCING: This contract is subject to approval for Buyer of a VA guaranteed loan of not less than $____________ (excluding any financed Funding Fee), amortizable monthly for not less than _____ years, with interest not to exceed _____ % per annum for the first _____ year(s) of the Loan.

VA NOTICE TO BUYER: *"It is expressly agreed that, notwithstanding any other provisions of this contract, the Buyer shall not incur any penalty by forfeiture of earnest money or otherwise or be obligated to complete the purchase of the Property described herein, if the contract purchase price or cost exceeds the reasonable value of the Property established by the Department of Veterans Affairs. The Buyer shall, however, have the privilege and option of proceeding with the consummation of this contract without regard to the amount of the reasonable value established by the Department of Veterans Affairs."*

If Buyer elects to complete the purchase at an amount in excess of the reasonable value established by VA, Buyer shall pay such excess amount in cash from a source which Buyer agrees to disclose to the VA and which Buyer represents will not be from borrowed funds except as approved by VA. If VA reasonable value of the Property is less than the Sales Price (3C above), Seller may reduce the Sales Price to an amount equal to the VA reasonable value and the parties to the sale shall close at such lower Sales Price with appropriate adjustments to 3A and 3B above.

❑ D. TEXAS VETERANS' HOUSING ASSISTANCE PROGRAM LOAN: This contract is subject to approval for Buyer of a Texas Veterans' Housing Assistance Program Loan (the Program Loan) of $____________ for a period of at least ______ years at the interest rate established by the Texas Veterans' Land Board at the time of closing.

❑ E. SELLER FINANCING: A promissory note from Buyer to Seller of $______________, bearing _______% interest per annum, secured by vendor's and deed of trust liens, in accordance with the terms and conditions set forth in the attached TREC Seller Financing Addendum. If an owner policy of title insurance is furnished, Buyer shall furnish Seller with a mortgagee policy of title insurance.

❑ F. CREDIT APPROVAL ON SELLER FINANCING: Within ________ days after the effective date of this contract, Buyer shall deliver to Seller ❑ credit report ❑ verification of employment, including salary ❑ verification of funds on deposit in financial institutions ❑ current financial statement to establish Buyer's creditworthiness for seller financing and ❑ ____________________________________
____.

If Buyer's documentation is not delivered within the specified time, Seller may terminate this contract by notice to Buyer within 7 days after expiration of the time for delivery, and the earnest money will be paid to Seller. If this contract is not so terminated, Seller will be deemed to have accepted Buyer's credit. If the documentation is timely delivered, and Seller determines in Seller's sole discretion that Buyer's credit is unacceptable, Seller may terminate this contract by notice to Buyer within 7 days after expiration of the time for delivery and the earnest money will be refunded to Buyer. If Seller does not so terminate this contract, Seller will be deemed to have accepted Buyer's credit. Buyer hereby authorizes any credit reporting agency to furnish to Seller at Buyer's sole expense copies of Buyer's credit reports.

In paragraph 13B we discover new wording, which we will encounter again when we examine TREC form 25-3 for Farm and Ranch transactions. Land that has been granted an agriculture exemption receives favorable ad valorem tax treatment. When that land's use changes, a significant penalty is charged. This could come as a big surprise to an uninformed purchaser. Paragraph 11 can be used to incorporate the negotiated agreement of the parties into the contract.

13. PRORATIONS AND ROLLBACK TAXES:

A. PRORATIONS: Taxes for the current year, maintenance fees, assessments, dues and rents will be prorated through the Closing Date. If taxes for the current year vary from the amount prorated at closing, the parties shall adjust the prorations when tax statements for the current year are available. If taxes are not paid at or prior to closing, Buyer will be obligated to pay taxes for the current year.

B. ROLLBACK TAXES: If this sale or Buyer's use of the Property after closing results in the assessment of additional taxes, penalties or interest (Assessments) for periods prior to closing, the Assessments will be the obligation of Buyer. If Seller's change in use of the Property prior to closing or denial of a special use valuation on the Property claimed by Seller results in Assessments for periods prior to closing, the Assessments will be the obligation of Seller. Obligations imposed by this paragraph will survive closing.

The other provisions have been encountered in the forms already examined.

PROMULGATED BY THE TEXAS REAL ESTATE COMMISSION (TREC) 06-22-00

NEW HOME CONTRACT

(Completed Construction)

NOTICE: Not For Use For Condominium Transactions

The contract for a new home that is already built is a hybrid of the TREC forms 20-4 and 23-4 that we just examined. Carefully examine paragraph 2 and paragraph 7.

2. **PROPERTY:** Lot ____________, Block ______, ____ Addition, City of ____, ____________________ County, Texas, known as ____ (Address/Zip Code), or as described on attached exhibit, together with the improvements, fixtures and all other property located thereon. All property sold by this contract is called the "Property."

Mandatory Membership in an Owners' Association: (Check one box only):

❑ The Property is not subject to mandatory membership in an owners' association.

❑ The TREC Addendum For Property Subject To Mandatory Membership In An Owners' Association is attached.

NOTICE TO BUYER: If the Property is subject to mandatory membership in an owner's association, Seller notifies Buyer under §5.012, Texas Property Code, that, as a purchaser of property in the residential community in which the Property is located, you are obligated to be a member of an owner's association. Restrictive covenants governing the use and occupancy of the Property and a dedicatory instrument governing the establishment, maintenance, and operation of this residential community have been or will be recorded in the Real Property Records of the county in which the Property is located. Copies of the restrictive covenants and dedicatory instrument may be obtained from the county clerk. You ar obligated to pay assessments to the owner's association. The amount of the assessments is subject to change. Your failure to pay the assessments could result in a lien on and the foreclosure of the Property.

7. **PROPERTY CONDITION:**

A. INSPECTIONS, ACCESS AND UTILITIES: Buyer, at Buyer's expense, may have the Property inspected by inspectors selected by Buyer, licensed by TREC or otherwise permitted by law to make such inspections. Seller shall permit access to the Property at reasonable times for inspections, repairs and treatment and for reinspections after repairs and treatment have been completed. Seller shall pay for turning on utilities for inspections and reinspections.

B. ACCEPTANCE OF PROPERTY CONDITION (check one box only):

❑ (1) In addition to any earnest money deposited with escrow agent, Buyer has paid Seller $________________ (the "Option Fee") for the unrestricted right to terminate this contract by giving notice of termination to Seller within ____________ days after the effective date of this contract. If Buyer gives notice of termination within the time specified, the Option Fee will not be refunded, however, any earnest money will be refunded to Buyer. If Buyer does not give notice of termination within the time specified, Buyer will be deemed to have accepted the Property in its current condition and the Option Fee ❑ will ❑ will not be credited to the Sales Price at closing.

❑ (2) Buyer accepts the Property in its present condition; provided Seller, at Seller's expense, shall complete the following repairs and treatment: ____

____

____

____.

C. LENDER REQUIRED REPAIRS AND TREATMENTS (REPAIRS): Unless otherwise agreed in writing, neither party is obligated to pay for lender required repairs or treatments for wood destroying insects. If the cost of lender required repairs exceeds 5% of the Sales Price, Buyer may terminate this contract.

D. COMPLETION OF REPAIRS AND TREATMENT: Unless otherwise agreed in writing, Seller shall complete all agreed repairs and treatment prior to the Closing Date. Repairs and treatments must be performed by persons who regularly provide such repairs or treatments. At Buyer's election, any transferable warranties received by Seller with respect to the repairs will be transferred to Buyer at Buyer's expense. If Seller fails to complete any agreed repairs and treatment prior to the Closing Date, Buyer may do so and the Closing Date will be extended up to 15 days, if necessary, to complete repairs and treatment.

E. WARRANTIES: Except as expressly set forth in Paragraph 11, or as attached to this contract, Seller makes no other express warranties. Seller agrees to assign to Buyer at closing all assignable manufacturer warranties.

F. INSULATION: As required by Federal Trade Commission Regulations, the information relating to the insulation installed or to be installed in the home being purchased under this contract is as follows:

(1) Exterior walls of improved living areas: insulated with ________________________ insulation to a thickness of ________ inches which yields an R-Value of ______.

(2) Walls in other areas of the home: insulated with ________________________ insulation to a thickness of ________ inches which yields an R-Value of ______.

(3) Ceilings in improved living areas: insulated with ________________________ insulation to a thickness of ________ inches which yields an R-Value of ______.

(4) Floors of improved living areas not applied to a slab foundation: insulated with ______________ insulation to a thickness of ________ inches which yields an R-Value of ______.

(5) Other insulated area: insulated with ________________________ insulation to a thickness of ________ inches which yields an R-Value of ______.

All stated R-Values are based on information provided by the manufacturer of the insulation.

TREC contract form 25-3 is used extensively in many counties of Texas. Farm and ranch property account for a significant amount of real estate activity. The first difference in this form comes in paragraph 2, which describes the property to be conveyed.

2. **PROPERTY:** The land situated in ________________________ County, Texas, described as follows:

or as described on attached exhibit, together with all improvements thereon and all rights, privileges and appurtenances pertaining thereto, including but not limited to: water rights, claims and permits, easements, all rights and obligations of applicable government programs and cooperative or association memberships. Included with the sale are the following items, if any: windmills and tanks, domestic water systems, curtains and rods, draperies and rods, valances, blinds, window shades, screens, shutters, awnings, wall-to-wall carpeting, mirrors fixed in place, ceiling fans, attic fans, mail boxes, television antennas and satellite dish with controls and equipment, permanently installed heating and air conditioning units, window air conditioning units, built-in security and fire detection equipment, plumbing and lighting fixtures, including chandeliers, water softener, stove, built-in kitchen equipment, garage door openers with controls, built-in cleaning equipment, all swimming pool equipment and maintenance accessories, shrubbery, landscaping, permanently installed outdoor cooking equipment, built-in fireplace screens, artificial fireplace logs and all other property owned by Seller and attached to the above described real property.

The following crops and equipment are included: ____

____.

The following property is not included: ____

____.

All property sold by this contract is called the "Property." The Property will be conveyed subject to the following exceptions, reservations, conditions and restrictions (if none, insert "none"):

A. Minerals, Royalties, and Timber Interests:
   (1) Presently outstanding in third parties:

   (2) To be additionally retained by Seller:

B. Mineral Leases:

C. Surface Leases:

D. Easements:

E. Restrictions, Zoning Ordinances or other Exceptions:

Notice that it calls for a metes-and-bounds description rather than a reference to a recorded plat. In addition to the fixtures itemized in form 20-4, it calls for all improvements and all rights, privileges and appurtenances to be conveyed. The rights and appurtenances are further defined as, but not limited to, water rights, claims and permits, easements, all rights and obligations of applicable government programs and cooperative or association memberships. Crops and equipment to be included in the sale must be itemized in the space provided.

After defining what is to be conveyed, the contract defines exceptions, reservations, conditions and restrictions to which the conveyance is subject. These include both those presently outstanding and those to be retained by the seller. The following areas are addressed:

- Minerals, royalties and timber interests
- Mineral leases
- Surface leases
- Easements
- Restrictions and/or zoning ordinances
- Other exceptions

A title commitment or an abstract of title reviewed by a competent attorney can be very helpful in identifying those interests presently outstanding. Often purchasers of farm and ranch properties will require that the seller furnish an abstract as a way of verifying the presence or absence of the items listed above. To call for an abstract, the parties will check box "C" in paragraph 6 of the contract and add TREC 29-1.

Paragraph 3 identifies two possible adjustments. Subparagraph B identifies the face amount of any lender-required stock. The lender-required stock is the preferred stock that a borrower must purchase and pledge as additional collateral when obtaining financing through a federal land bank. The second adjustment is linked to the results of the survey discussed in paragraph 6B. If the survey indicates more or less acreage than that claimed by the seller at the time of signing the contract, the parties need to have an agreement that defines whether an adjustment will be made to the sale price and how much per acre the adjustment will be.

3. SALES PRICE:

A. Cash portion of Sales Price payable by Buyer at closing. . . . . $___________

B. (1) Sum of all financing described in Paragraph 4 . . . .$___________

(2) Less: face amount of any lender required stock . . . . <___________>

(3) Difference between B(1) and B(2) . . . . $___________

C. Sales Price [sum of A and B(3)]. . . . . $___________

D. The Sales Price ❑ will ❑ will not be adjusted based on the survey required by Paragraph 6B, and the number of acres over or under _______ acres will be multiplied by $__________ per acre. The result thereof will be added to or subtracted from the Sales Price, and the cash amount set out in 3A will be adjusted accordingly; however, if the amount set out in 3A is to be adjusted by more than 10%, either party may terminate this contract and the earnest money will be refunded to Buyer.

Paragraph 4 is a combination of financing options previously encountered in the other forms studied.

The survey paragraph, 6B, offers an additional option not found in the previous forms. You will find the same additional option in TREC contract

❑ B. SURVEY: (Check one box only)
❑ (1) Within _________ days after the effective date of this contract, Buyer shall obtain a survey at Buyer's expense.
❑ (2) Within _________ days after the effective date of this contract, Seller shall cause a survey to be delivered to Buyer at Seller's expense.
❑ (3) Within _________ days after the effective date of this contract, Seller will deliver to Buyer the existing survey plat of the Property dated ______________________, ______, which ❑ will ❑ will not be recertified to a date subsequent to the effective date of this contract at the expense of ❑ Buyer ❑ Seller.

The survey must be made by a Registered Professional Land Surveyor acceptable to the Title Company and any lender.

Buyer will have 7 days after the receipt of the latter of the Commitment or survey to object in writing to matters disclosed in the Commitment or survey except for those matters specifically described in Paragraph 2. Buyer's failure to object under Paragraph 6 within the time allowed will constitute a waiver of Buyer's right to object; except that the requirements in Schedule C of the Commitment will not be deemed to have been waived. Seller shall cure the timely objections of Buyer or any third party lender within 20 days after Seller receives the objections and the Closing Date will be extended as necessary. If objections are not cured by the extended Closing Date, this contract will terminate and the earnest money will be refunded to Buyer unless Buyer elects to waive the objections.

❑ C. ABSTRACT OF TITLE: TREC Addendum for Abstract of Title, or an addendum required by the parties, is attached.

NOTICE TO SELLER AND BUYER:

(1) Broker advises Buyer to have an abstract of title covering the Property examined by an attorney of Buyer's selection, or Buyer should be furnished with or obtain a Title Policy. If a Title Policy is furnished, the Commitment should be promptly reviewed by an attorney of Buyer's choice due to the time limitations on Buyer's right to object.

(2) If the Property is situated in a utility or other statutorily created district providing water, sewer, drainage, or flood control facilities and services, Chapter 49 of the Texas Water Code requires Seller to deliver and the Buyer to sign the statutory notice relating to the tax rate, bonded indebtedness, or standby fee of the district prior to final execution of this contract.

(3) Eligibility for government farm program benefits may depend upon compliance with a soil conservation plan for the Property. Buyer is advised to determine whether the property is subject to and in compliance with a plan before signing this contract.

(4) Buyer is advised that the presence of wetlands, toxic substances, including asbestos and wastes or other environmental hazards or the presence of a threatened or endangered species or its habitat may affect Buyer's intended use of the Property. If Buyer is concerned about these matters, an addendum either promulgated by TREC or required by the parties should be used.

(5) If the Property is located outside the limits of a municipality, Seller notifies Buyer under §5.011, Texas Property Code, that the Property may now or later be included in the extraterritorial jurisdiction of a municipality maintains a map that depicts its boundaries and extraterritorial jurisdiction. To determine if the Property is located within a municipality's extraterritorial jurisdiction or is likely to be located within a municipality's extraterritorial jurisdiction, contact all municipalities located in the general proximity of the Property for further information.

(6) If the Property abuts the tidally influenced submerged lands of the state, Section 33.135, Texas Natural Resources Code, requires a notice regarding coastal area property to be included in the contract. An addendum either promulgated by TREC or required by the parties should be used.

(7) Unless expressly prohibited in writing by the parties, Seller may continue to show the Property for sale and to receive, negotiate and accept back-up offers.

(8) Any residential service contract that is purchased in connection with this transaction should be reviewed for the scope of coverage, exclusions and limitations. **The purchase of a residential service contract is optional. Similar coverage may be purchased from various companies authorized to do business in Texas.**

form 9-4, which is used when selling an unimproved residential building lot. Paragraph 6 also offers a check-box to identify that an addendum calling for an abstract of title is attached.

In the notices at the end of the paragraph, the third one is found only in TREC contract 25-3. The four notices following it are identical to notices 3, 4, 5 and 6 in the contracts already studied, but have been renumbered in this contract.

EQUAL HOUSING OPPORTUNITY

Notice: Not For Use Where Seller Owns Fee Simple Title To Land Beneath Unit 11-08-99

PROMULGATED BY THE TEXAS REAL ESTATE COMMISSION (TREC)

RESIDENTIAL CONDOMINIUM CONTRACT (RESALE)
ALL CASH, ASSUMPTION, THIRD PARTY CONVENTIONAL OR SELLER FINANCING

1. **PARTIES:** ______________________________ (Seller) agrees to sell and convey to ______________________________ (Buyer) and Buyer agrees to buy from Seller the property described below.

and

Notice: Not For Use Where Seller Owns Fee Simple Title To Land Beneath Unit 11-08-99

PROMULGATED BY THE TEXAS REAL ESTATE COMMISSION (TREC)

RESIDENTIAL CONDOMINIUM CONTRACT (RESALE)
FHA INSURED OR VA GUARANTEED FINANCING

The contracts for the resale of a condominium are very similar contracts for the resale of a one-family to four-family residential property. The differences are found in paragraph 2 (on page 93), which addresses the passing of condominium documents from the seller to the buyer.

Texas statute requires that the owners' association complete and furnish a resale certificate (page 94) prepared no more than three months prior to the date it is delivered to a prospective owner. The information must be furnished on a form promulgated by the Texas Real Estate Commission.

The absence of real property improvements in the proposed conveyance addressed when this form is used dictates different wording in paragraphs 2 (page 93) and 7 (page 93) than TREC 20-3 and 21-3 that contain the words ". . . . together with the following items. . . " Paragraph 6 does not contain the notice about residential service contracts.

2. **PROPERTY AND CONDOMINIUM DOCUMENTS:**

A. Condominium Unit ___________, in Building _________, of _________________________________, a condominium project, located at ____ (Address/Zip Code), City of ________________________________, ________________ County, Texas, described in the Condominium Declaration and Plat and any amendments thereto of record in said County; together with such Unit's undivided interest in the Common Elements designated by the Declaration, including those areas reserved as Limited Common Elements appurtenant to the Unit and such other rights to use the Common Elements which have been specifically assigned to the Unit in any other manner. Parking areas assigned to the Unit are: _____ ______________________________. The property includes the following items owned by Seller, if any: curtains and rods, draperies and rods, valances, blinds, window shades, screens, shutters, awnings, wall-to-wall carpeting, mirrors fixed in place, ceiling fans, attic fans, mail boxes, television antennas and satellite dish system with controls and equipment, permanently installed heating and air conditioning units, window air conditioning units, built-in security and fire detection equipment, plumbing and lighting fixtures including chandeliers, water softener, stove, built-in kitchen equipment, garage door openers with controls, built-in cleaning equipment, all swimming pool equipment and maintenance accessories, shrubbery, landscaping, permanently installed outdoor cooking equipment, built-in fireplace screens, artificial fireplace logs and all other personal property owned by Seller and attached to the Unit or located in the Unit and given as collateral for any indebtedness which will remain in effect after closing except the following property which is not included:____
____.
All property sold by this contract is called the "Property".

B. The Declaration, Bylaws and any Rules of the Association are called "Documents". (Check one box only):

❑ (1) Buyer has received a copy of the Documents. Buyer is advised to read the Documents before signing the contract.

❑ (2) Buyer has not received a copy of the Documents. Seller shall deliver the Documents to Buyer within __________ days after the effective date of the contract. Buyer may cancel the contract before the sixth day after Buyer receives the Documents by hand-delivering or mailing written notice of cancellation to Seller by certified United States mail, return receipt requested.

C. The Resale Certificate from the condominium owners association (the Association) is called the "Certificate". The Certificate must be in a form promulgated by TREC or required by the parties. The Certificate must have been prepared no more than three months before the date it is delivered to Buyer and must contain at a minimum the information required by Section 82.157 of the Texas Property Code. (Check one box only):

❑ (1) Buyer has received the Certificate.

❑ (2) Buyer has not received the Certificate. Seller shall deliver the Certificate to Buyer within _________ days after the effective date of the contract. Buyer may cancel the contract before the sixth day after the date Buyer receives the Certificate by hand-delivering or mailing written notice of cancellation to Seller by certified United States mail, return receipt requested.

❑ (3) Buyer has received Seller's affidavit that Seller requested information from the Association concerning its financial condition as required by the Texas Property Code, and that the Association did not provide a Certificate or information required in the Certificate. Buyer and Seller agree to waive the requirement to furnish the Certificate.

EQUAL HOUSING OPPORTUNITY

CONDOMINIUM RESALE CERTIFICATE

04-18-94

PROMULGATED BY THE TEXAS REAL ESTATE COMMISSION (TREC)

Condominium Certificate concerning Condominium Unit ________, in Building __________, of __________ ________________________________, a condominium project, located at ______________________ ______________________ (Address), City of ______________________, ______________________, County, Texas, on behalf of the condominium owners association (the Association) by the Association's governing body (the Board).

A. The Declaration ☐ does ☐ does not contain a right of first refusal or other restraint that restricts the right to transfer the Unit. If a right of first refusal or other restraint exists, see Section _____ of the Declaration.

B. The periodic common expense assessment for the Unit is $____________ per __________.

C. There ☐ is ☐ is not a common expense or special assessment due and unpaid by the Seller to the Association. The total unpaid amount is $____________ and is for ______________________________.

D. Other amounts ☐ are ☐ are not payable by Seller to the Association. The total unpaid amount is $__________ and is for ______________________________.

E. Capital expenditures approved by the Association for the next 12 months are $____________.

F. Reserves for capital expenditures are $______________; of this amount $______________ has been designated for ______________________________.

G. The current operating budget of the Association is attached.

H. The amount of unsatisfied judgments against the Association is $________________.

I. There ☐ are ☐ are not any suits pending against the Association. The nature of the suits is __________ ______________________________.

J. The Association ☐ does ☐ does not provide insurance coverage for the benefit of unit owners as per the attached summary from the Association's insurance agent.

K. The Board ☐ has ☐ has no knowledge of alterations or improvements to the Unit or to the limited common elements assigned to the Unit or any portion of the project that violate any provision of the Declaration, by-laws or rules of the Association. Known violations are: ______________________________ ______________________________.

L. The Board ☐ has ☐ has not received notice from a governmental authority concerning violations of health or building codes with respect to the Unit, the limited common elements assigned to the Unit, or any other portion of the condominium project. Notices received are: ______________________________ ______________________________.

M. The remaining term of any leasehold estate that affects the condominium is ________________ and the provisions governing an extension or renewal of the lease are: ______________________________ ______________________________ ______________________________.

N. The name, mailing address and telephone number of the Association's managing agent are:

____
(Name) (Telephone Number)

____
(Mailing Address)

REQUIRED ATTACHMENTS:
1. Operating Budget
2. Insurance Summary

____
(Name of Condominium Owners Association)

NOTICE: The Certificate must be prepared no more than three months before the date it is delivered to Buyer.

Received:______________________________19___

____
Buyer

____
Buyer

By: ______________________________

____
Title

____
Mailing Address

____
Date Phone No.

The form of this certificate has been approved by the Texas Real Estate Commission for use only with similarly approved or promulgated forms of contracts. No representation is made as to the legal validity or adequacy of any provision in any specific transactions. (04-94) TREC No. 32-0.

PROMULGATED BY THE TEXAS REAL ESTATE COMMISSION (TREC) 11-08-99

UNIMPROVED PROPERTY CONTRACT

Notice: Not For Use For Condominium Transactions

1. **PARTIES:** ________________ (Seller) agrees to sell and convey to ________________ (Buyer) and Buyer agrees to buy from Seller the property described below.

2. **PROPERTY:** Lot __________, Block ______, ________________ Addition, City of ________________, ____________ County, Texas, known as ________________ (Address/Zip Code), or as described on attached exhibit, (the Property). The Property ❑ is ❑ is not subject to mandatory membership in an owners' association. The TREC Addendum For Property Subject To Mandatory Membership In An Owners' Association ❑ is ❑ is not attached.

7. **PROPERTY CONDITION:**
   A. INSPECTIONS, ACCESS AND UTILITIES: Buyer may have the Property inspected by an inspector selected by Buyer, licensed by TREC or otherwise permitted by law to make such inspections. Seller shall permit access to the Property at reasonable times for inspection, repairs and treatment and for reinspection after repairs and treatment have been completed. Seller shall pay for turning on utilities for inspection and reinspection.
   B. ACCEPTANCE OF PROPERTY CONDITION: NOTICE: Buyer should determine the availability of utilities to the Property suitable to satisfy the Buyer's needs. (check one box only):
   ❑ (1) In addition to any earnest money deposited with escrow agent, Buyer has paid Seller $______________ (the "Option Fee") for the unrestricted right to terminate this contract by giving notice of termination to Seller within ______ days after the effective date of this contract. If Buyer gives notice of termination within the time specified, the Option Fee will not be refunded, however, any earnest money will be refunded to Buyer. If Buyer does not give notice of termination within the time specified, Buyer will be deemed to have accepted the Property in its current condition and the Option Fee ❑ will ❑ will not be credited to the Sales Price at closing.
   ❑ (2) Buyer accepts the Property in its present condition.

The following forms (pages 97 through 100) are published by TREC but are not a part of any contract. The first is the promulgated "Consumer Information Form," TREC 1-1 (page 97), which is to be posted in the office of every licensed inspector and broker of Texas. Brokers who sell residential property should also prominently display the HUD poster informing consumers of their rights under the federal fair housing laws. Of course the licenses of the broker and all salesperson must be displayed. All of these might best be displayed in one locking window case in the lobby of the office.

The following approved "Notice Concerning Recognized Hazards" form (page 98) warns the consumer that injury or property loss can result from a variety of improperly installed or malfunctioning mechanical equipment. It is not a promulgated for mandatory use form, but rather a convenient tool for the licensee to use to assist the parties in making informed decisions.

Section 15C of the license law addresses agency relationships between licensees and the public. One provision requires that a licensee, at the first face-to-face meeting, provide the prospect with information about brokerage services (see TREC OP-K form on page 99). A face-to-face meeting is defined as the first meeting at which substantive discussion about a particular property or a prospect's ability to buy or lease occurs.

The words, the minimum size of type (10 point) and the requirement to give it at the proper time are mandated by statute.

The form that follows (TREC OP-C on page 100) is published by TREC for voluntary use by licensees. It is not a TREC or a statutory requirement that the person receiving it sign it. It is not an addendum to the contract.

The Texas licensing law requires that a licensee notify every buyer, prior to the closing of a sale, that the abstract should be examined by an attorney of the buyer's selection or that the buyer should be furnished with or obtain a policy of title insurance. When the agreement of purchase between the seller and the buyer has been reduced to writing by using one of the TREC promulgated contract forms, this notice requirement has been fulfilled by the wording of the first in the group of notices at the end of paragraph 6.

When the contract is drawn by a party's attorney, the form on page 86 may be used to give the notice. The form is not promulgated. It is published for voluntary use by licensees to make it easier to comply with the law. Failure to deliver this notice when required can lead to loss of the broker's ability to collect a brokerage fee under the provisions of section 20 of the TRELA and possible disciplinary action by TREC under section 15 of the TRELA.

Remember that before you attempt to use any TREC promulgated contract and addendum or any voluntary-use form, carefully read it and understand its content. Help the parties identify the business details that need to be addressed and then carefully fill in the appropriate blanks, check the appropriate boxes and enter N/A where necessary.

Encourage each party to carefully read the agreement, and advise that competent legal counsel should be consulted if unusual matters are present. It is a good practice to always read paragraph 22 to a party before the contract is signed. Encouraging people to seek legal advice is an effective way to reduce your risk of being sued. Stick to defining the business details. Let attorneys address the legal rights and remedies.

THIS FIRM IS

LICENSED AND REGULATED

BY THE

TEXAS REAL ESTATE

COMMISSION (TREC)

TREC ADMINISTERS TWO RECOVERY FUNDS

WHICH MAY BE USED TO SATISFY JUDGMENTS

AGAINST INSPECTORS AND REAL ESTATE

LICENSEES INVOLVING A VIOLATION OF THE LAW.

COMPLAINTS OR INQUIRIES SHOULD

BE DIRECTED TO

TEXAS REAL ESTATE COMMISSION
P.O. BOX 12188
AUSTIN, TEXAS 78711-2188

(512) 465-3960

Consumer Information Form 1-1 (8-91)

09-23-94

TEXAS REAL ESTATE CONSUMER NOTICE CONCERNING RECOGNIZED HAZARDS

APPROVED BY THE TEXAS REAL ESTATE COMMISSION (TREC)

Each year in Texas, people are injured and property losses occur from: improperly installed water heaters in garages, faulty temperature and pressure relief valves on water heaters, and improperly installed (or the lack of) ground fault circuit protection for electrical receptacles in garages, outdoors, bathrooms and kitchen sink areas. In recognition of the studies and recommendations from the U.S. Consumer Products Safety Commission (U.S. CPSC), the Texas Real Estate Commission (TREC) has adopted a rule requiring licensed inspectors to report the above listed hazardous conditions as "in need of repair" when performing an inspection for a buyer or seller.

These conditions may not be a building code violation in a particular city or locale, or may be "grandfathered" because they were present prior to the adoption of city ordinances prohibiting such conditions. TREC has considered the potential for injury or property loss to be significant enough to warrant this notice. The effect of this rule is not to mandate these conditions be remedied, but rather to insure that the consumer be made aware of these significant hazards when revealed by inspection. Once notified, a buyer can decide whether or not to add them to the prioritized list of repairs that is typically provided to a seller under a Texas Earnest Money Contract and the Property Condition Addendum. The decision to correct the hazard is left to the parties involved in the transaction.

This form is approved by the Texas Real Estate Commission for voluntary use by its licensees. Copies of TREC rules governing real estate brokers and salesmen and real estate inspectors are available at nominal cost from TREC, P.O. Box 12188, Austin, Texas 78711-2188. TREC Consumer Notice Concerning Recognized Hazards (09-94).

Approved by the Texas Real Estate Commission for Voluntary Use

Texas law requires all real estate licensees to give the following information about brokerage services to prospective buyers, tenants, sellers and landlords.

Information About Brokerage Services

Before working with a real estate broker, you should know that the duties of a broker depend on whom the broker represents. If you are a prospective seller or landlord (owner) or a prospective buyer or tenant (buyer), you should know that the broker who lists the property for sale or lease is the owner's agent. A broker who acts as a subagent represents the owner in cooperation with the listing broker. A broker who acts as a buyer's agent represents the buyer. A broker may act as an intermediary between the parties if the parties consent in writing. A broker can assist you in locating a property, preparing a contract or lease, or obtaining financing without representing you. A broker is obligated by law to treat you honestly.

IF THE BROKER REPRESENTS THE OWNER:
The broker becomes the owner's agent by entering into an agreement with the owner, usually through a written - listing agreement, or by agreeing to act as a subagent by accepting an offer of subagency from the listing broker. A subagent may work in a different real estate office. A listing broker or subagent can assist the buyer but does not represent the buyer and must place the interests of the owner first. The buyer should not tell the owner's agent anything the buyer would not want the owner to know because an owner's agent must disclose to the owner any material information known to the agent.

IF THE BROKER REPRESENTS THE BUYER:
The broker becomes the buyer's agent by entering into an agreement to represent the buyer, usually through a written buyer representation agreement. A buyer's agent can assist the owner but does not represent the owner and must place the interests of the buyer first. The owner should not tell a buyer's agent anything the owner would not want the buyer to know because a buyer's agent must disclose to the buyer any material information known to the agent.

IF THE BROKER ACTS AS AN INTERMEDIARY:
A broker may act as an intermediary between the parties if the broker complies with The Texas Real Estate License Act. The broker must obtain the written consent of each party to the transaction to act as an intermediary. The written consent must state who will pay the broker and, in conspicuous bold or underlined print, set forth the broker's obligations as an intermediary. The broker is required to treat each party honestly and fairly and to comply with The Texas Real Estate License Act. A broker who acts as an intermediary in a transaction:

(1) shall treat all parties honestly;
(2) may not disclose that the owner will accept a price less than the asking price unless authorized in writing to do so by the owner;
(3) may not disclose that the buyer will pay a price greater than the price submitted in a written offer unless authorized in writing to do so by the buyer; and
(4) may not disclose any confidential information or any information that a party specifically instructs the broker in writing not to disclose unless authorized in writing to disclose the information or required to do so by The Texas Real Estate License Act or a court order or if the information materially relates to the condition of the property.

With the parties' consent, a broker acting as an intermediary between the parties may appoint a person who is licensed under The Texas Real Estate License Act and associated with the broker to communicate with and carry out instructions of one party and another person who is licensed under that Act and associated with the broker to communicate with and carry out instructions of the other party.

If you choose to have a broker represent you,
you should enter into a written agreement with the broker that clearly establishes the broker's obligations and your obligations. The agreement should state how and by whom the broker will be paid. You have the right to choose the type of representation, if any, you wish to receive. Your payment of a fee to a broker does not necessarily establish that the broker represents you. If you have any questions regarding the duties and responsibilities of the broker, you should resolve those questions before proceeding.

Real estate licensee asks that you acknowledge receipt of this information about brokerage services for the licensee's records.

____
Buyer, Seller, Landlord or Tenant — Date

Texas Real Estate Brokers and Salesmen are licensed and regulated by the Texas Real Estate Commission (TREC). If you have a question or complaint regarding a real estate licensee, you should contact TREC at P.O. Box 12188, Austin, Texas 78711-2188 or 512-465-3960.

01A TREC No. OP-K

APPROVED BY THE TEXAS REAL ESTATE COMMISSION

NOTICE TO PROSPECTIVE BUYER

As required by law, I advise you to have the abstract covering the property known as ____ (Address) examined by an attorney of your own selection OR you should be furnished with or obtain a policy of title insurance.

If the property is situated in a Utility District, Chapter 49 of the Texas Water Code requires you to sign and acknowledge the statutory notice from the seller of the property relating to the tax rate, bonded indebtedness or standby fee of the District.

DATED: ______________________, __________.

____
Brokerage Company Name

____
Broker or Sales Associate

I have received a copy of this **NOTICE TO PROSPECTIVE BUYER.**

____
Prospective Buyer

____
Prospective Buyer

This form has been approved by the Texas Real Estate Commission (TREC) for use when a contract of sale has not been promulgated by TREC. The form should be presented before an offer to purchase is signed by the prospective buyer. Texas Real Estate Commission, P.O. Box 12188, Austin, Texas 78711-2188, 1-800-250-8732 or (512) 459-6544 (http://www.trec.state.tx.us). TREC Notice to Prospective Buyer.(12/99) OP-C replaces MA-C.

01A TREC NO. OP-C

1. The dollar amount entered in paragraph 3B of the TREC 21-4 form includes any financed MIP or VA funding fee.

   A. True
   B. False

2. In form 21-4 the seller agrees to pay expenses that FHA or VA prohibits the buyer to pay.

   A. True
   B. False

3. Which of the following is **not** listed as an expense to be paid by the seller in paragraph 12 of TREC 21-4?

   A. Preparation of the deed
   B. Premium for mortgagee title policy
   C. Tax statements or certificates
   D. One-half of escrow fee

4. A Texas Veterans' Housing Assistance Program Loan can be used in conjunction with another loan insured by FHA or guaranteed by VA to purchase a home for an eligible veteran.

   A. True
   B. False

5. If the buyer's use of the property after closing results in the assessment of rollback taxes, penalties or interest for periods prior to closing, the assessments will be the obligation of the seller.

   A. True
   B. False

6. How much time does the buyer obtaining an FHA-insured loan legally have to have the property inspected by an inspector selected by the buyer?

   A. Five days after the effective date of the contract
   B. Seven days prior to the closing of the contract
   C. Only during the option period stated in 7D(1)
   D. During the entire time between contract and closing

7. In which TREC promulgated contract form is there a provision to adjust the sales price based on the survey required by paragraph 6B?

   A. TREC 20-4
   B. TREC 25-3
   C. TREC 24-3
   D. TREC 30-2

8. The "Information About Brokerage Services" is a promulgated addendum that must be signed by the parties and attached to every contract.

   A. True
   B. False

9. For what purpose would a licensee use the TREC approved "Notice to Prospective Buyer" form?

   A. To notify a buyer to have the property inspected
   B. To disclose to the purchaser of a new home what type of insulation is being installed
   C. To advise the buyer to have the abstract examined by an attorney
   D. To advise buyers purchasing coastal area property of the Texas open beaches act

10. All townhomes are condominiums and require the use of TREC form 30-2.

    A. True
    B. False

PART 5

Practice Makes Perfect

Now that we have reviewed some of the basic legal concepts, the contract and addenda forms, the provisions of the license act and the rules of TREC, let us continue our learning by completing some case studies.

Every transaction is unique. It may have special considerations that may be addressed by promulgated addenda or that may require the services of a real estate attorney to structure language to address certain issues. In the case studies that follow you have the opportunity to complete each promulgated contract and addendum. Your instructor may provide additional information for some of the cases or have you experience the countering process. Few addresses are furnished other than the property address. You will need to provide missing addresses. Be creative.

1. Read the case information carefully.
2. Complete the forms using a pencil. When your instructor walks through the transaction with you, you can make corrections easily.
3. Be sure to put **N/A** in blanks that are not needed for the particular transaction.
4. Be sure to list all addenda in paragraph 21.
5. **Have fun!**

Transaction 1: 80% Conventional Fixed Rate Loan

Utilizing: TREC 20-4, 28-0, 36-1, 39-1

John Paul Gordon and his wife, Mary Anne Gordon, want to purchase a home owned by Isabelle Gertrude Gerhard, an unmarried resident of Houston, Texas.

The property is identified as Lot 6, Block 10 in Section 1 of the Windswept Addition of Harris County, Texas. It is more commonly known as 2615 Pleasure Point Drive, Houston, Texas 77084. The property is subject to the rules and assessments of a mandatory owners' association.

The buyers have received and approved a copy of the owners' association resale certificate prior to signing the purchase agreement. The buyers are willing to pay $50 of the $100 transfer fee charged by the owners' association. The seller has ten days to obtain and deliver a notice to the buyer that the owners' association will repair the damage to the association-owned fence at the back property line. The annual assessment is $300 and is paid in January of each year to Smith Management Company, Inc., at 3610 West Loop South, Houston 77056. Its phone number is 713-666-7777.

Ms. Gerhard will remove the draperies from the master bedroom prior to closing. She will leave all other items listed in paragraph 2 of the standard purchase agreement.

Although Ms. Gerhard is asking $106,000 for the property, the buyers have decided to offer $96,000. Within four days after the effective date of the contract they will make a loan application and expect that they can have financing approval within 25 days after the effective date of the contract. They agree to apply for an 80 percent conventional loan at 8 percent with a 15-year amortization and with no private mortgage insurance required.

To show their serious intent, the buyers deposit $10,000 earnest money with No Cloud Title Company at 1700 South Main, Houston, Texas 77001. They feel that it would be unreasonable for the seller to require that any additional earnest money be deposited.

The buyers are willing to pay for the survey required by their lender and ask that the seller pay for the owner's title policy to demonstrate that the title is free of encumbrances as of the date of closing. The buyers want to review the title commitment and the deed restrictions to make certain that they can park their recreational vehicle in the driveway of their new home. They want three days to review the survey.

Prior to signing the offer to purchase, the buyers receive and review the seller's property disclosure form required by section 5.008 of the Texas Property Code.

The Gordons are willing to pay Ms. Gerhard $100 for a 7-day option period. The $100 will be credited to the sale price if they complete the transaction. By attaching the appropriate addendum, the parties agree that the buyers will have 20 days to have environmental assessments performed. Because the home was built in 1985, they have not attached the lead paint/hazard addendum. They do not feel that lead is an issue.

They want to close on or before the 30th day after the date of the contract and want possession to be granted at closing or the funding of their loan, whichever is later.

The buyers will pay for all typical loan costs, including any appraisal required by the lender. They do not anticipate that the lender will charge any discount points to originate their loan.

The property has been listed by Smooth Sales Realty Company (TREC# 7657321) and is being sold by a company that represents only buyers, Buyer's Broker Realty (TREC# 1234567). The agents obtain the correct addresses and numbers to be entered in paragraph 23 of the purchase contract. The listing broker, through the local MLS, has agreed to pay the selling broker a fee equal to 3 percent of the sale price. Both agents offered the parties the opportunity to add the agreement for mediation, but the parties declined.

* * *

Five days into the option period the buyer decides to approach the seller and ask the seller to replace the defective flooring in the kitchen. The seller agrees to do so providing the buyers will choose the new vinyl covering and pay any amount in excess of $1,400. The seller will only sign the amendment if the buyers will end the option period upon the execution of the amendment.

PROMULGATED BY THE TEXAS REAL ESTATE COMMISSION (TREC) 11-8-99

ONE TO FOUR FAMILY RESIDENTIAL CONTRACT (RESALE) ALL CASH, ASSUMPTION, THIRD PARTY CONVENTIONAL OR SELLER FINANCING

NOTICE: Not For Use For Condominium Transactions

1. **PARTIES:** ____ (Seller) agrees to sell and convey to ______________________________________(Buyer) and Buyer agrees to buy from Seller the property described below.

2. **PROPERTY:** Lot ____________, Block _____, ______________________________ Addition, City of ______________________________, ________________________ County, Texas, known as ____ (Address/Zip Code), or as described on attached exhibit, together with the following items, if any: curtains and rods, draperies and rods, valances, blinds, window shades, screens, shutters, awnings, wall-to-wall carpeting, mirrors fixed in place, ceiling fans, attic fans, mail boxes, television antennas and satellite dish system with controls and equipment, permanently installed heating and air-conditioning units, window air-conditioning units, built-in security and fire detection equipment, plumbing and lighting fixtures including chandeliers, water softener, stove, built-in kitchen equipment, garage door openers with controls, built-in cleaning equipment, all swimming pool equipment and maintenance accessories, shrubbery, landscaping, permanently installed outdoor cooking equipment, built-in fireplace screens, artificial fireplace logs and all other property owned by Seller and attached to the above described real property except the following property which is not included: ______________________________
____
____
____.

   All property sold by this contract is called the "Property." The Property ❑ is ❑ is not subject to mandatory membership in an owners' association. The TREC Addendum For Property Subject To Mandatory Membership In An Owners' Association ❑ is ❑ is not attached.

   NOTICE TO BUYER: If the Property is subject to mandatory membership in an owners' association, Seller notifies Buyer under §5.012, Texas Property Code, that, as a purchaser of property in the residential community in which the Property is located, you are obligated to be a member of an owners' association. Restrictive covenants governing the use and occupancy of the Property and a dedicatory instrument governing the establishment, maintenance, and operation of this residential community have been or will be recorded in the Real Property Records of the county in which the Property is located. Copies of the restrictive covenants and dedicatory instrument may be obtained from the county clerk. You are obligated to pay assessments to the owners' association. The amount of the assessments is subject to change. Your failure to pay the assessments could result in a lien on and the foreclosure of the Property.

3. **SALES PRICE:**
   A. Cash portion of Sales Price payable by Buyer at closing . . . . $____________
   B. Sum of all financing described below
   (excluding any private mortgage insurance [PMI] premium) . . . . $____________
   C. Sales Price (Sum of A and B) . . . . $____________

4. **FINANCING:** Within _____ days after the effective date of this contract Buyer shall apply for all third party financing or noteholder's approval of any assumption and make every reasonable effort to obtain financing or assumption approval. Financing or assumption approval will be deemed to have been obtained when the lender determines that Buyer has satisfied all of lender's financial requirements (those items relating to Buyer's net worth, income and creditworthiness). If financing (including any financed PMI premium) or assumption approval is not obtained within ______ days after the effective

date hereof, this contract will terminate and the earnest money will be refunded to Buyer. Each note to be executed hereunder must be secured by vendor's and deed of trust liens.

The portion of Sales Price not payable in cash will be paid as follows: (Check applicable boxes below)

❑ A. THIRD PARTY FINANCING:

❑ (1) This contract is subject to approval for Buyer of a third party first mortgage loan having a loan-to-value ratio not to exceed _____ % as established by such third party (excluding any financed PMI premium), due in full in _____ year(s), with interest not to exceed _____ % per annum for the first _____ year(s) of the loan. The loan will be ❑ with ❑ without PMI.

❑ (2) This contract is subject to approval for Buyer of a third party second mortgage loan having a loan-to-value ratio not to exceed ______ % as established by such third party (excluding any financed PMI premium), due in full in ______ year(s), with interest not to exceed _______ % per annum for the first _____ year(s) of the loan. The loan will be ❑ with ❑ without PMI.

❑ B. TEXAS VETERANS' HOUSING ASSISTANCE PROGRAM LOAN: This contract is subject to approval for Buyer of a Texas Veterans' Housing Assistance Program Loan (the Program Loan) of $________________ for a period of at least ____________ years at the interest rate established by the Texas Veterans' Land Board at the time of closing.

❑ C. SELLER FINANCING: A promissory note from Buyer to Seller of $_____________, bearing _____ % interest per annum, secured by vendor's and deed of trust liens, in accordance with the terms and conditions set forth in the attached TREC Seller Financing Addendum. If an owner policy of title insurance is furnished, Buyer shall furnish Seller with a mortgagee policy of title insurance.

❑ D. ASSUMPTION:

❑ (1) Buyer shall assume the unpaid principal balance of a first lien promissory note payable to ____
which unpaid balance at closing will be $ ______________ . The total current monthly payment including principal, interest and any reserve deposits is $ ________________ .
Buyer's initial payment will be the first payment due after closing.

❑ (2) Buyer shall assume the unpaid principal balance of a second lien promissory note payable to ____
which unpaid balance at closing will be $ ________________ . The total current monthly payment including principal, interest and any reserve deposits is $ ________________ .
Buyer's initial payment will be the first payment due after closing.

Buyer's assumption of an existing note includes all obligations imposed by the deed of trust securing the note.

If the unpaid principal balance(s) of any assumed loan(s) as of the Closing Date varies from the loan balance(s) stated above, the ❑ cash payable at closing ❑ Sales Price will be adjusted by the amount of any variance; provided, if the total principal balance of all assumed loans varies in an amount greater than $350.00 at closing, either party may terminate this contract and the earnest money will be refunded to Buyer unless the other party elects to eliminate the excess in the variance by an appropriate adjustment at closing. If the noteholder requires (a) payment of an assumption fee in excess of $ _____________in D(1) above or $ _________________ in D(2) above and Seller declines to pay such excess, or (b) an increase in the interest rate to more than _____ % in D(1) above, or _____ % in D(2) above, or (c) any other modification of the loan documents, Buyer may terminate this contract and the earnest money will be refunded to Buyer. A vendor's lien and deed of trust to secure assumption will be required which shall automatically be released on execution and delivery of a release by noteholder. If Seller is released from liability on any assumed note, the vendor's lien and deed of trust to secure assumption will not be required.

NOTICE TO BUYER: The monthly payments, interest rates or other terms of some loans may be adjusted by the lender at or after closing. If you are concerned about the possibility of future adjustments, do not sign the contract without examining the notes and deeds of trust.
NOTICE TO SELLER: Your liability to pay the note assumed by Buyer will continue unless you obtain a release of liability from the lender. If you are concerned about future liability, you should use the TREC Release of Liability Addendum.

❑ E. CREDIT APPROVAL ON ASSUMPTION OR SELLER FINANCING: Within _____ days after the effective date of this contract, Buyer shall deliver to Seller ❑ credit report ❑ verification of employment, including salary ❑ verification of funds on deposit in financial institutions ❑ current financial statement to establish Buyer's creditworthiness for assumption approval or seller financing and ❑ ____
____
____.
If Buyer's documentation is not delivered within the specified time, Seller may terminate this contract by notice to Buyer within 7 days after expiration of the time for delivery, and the earnest money will be paid to Seller. If this contract is not so terminated, Seller will be deemed to have accepted Buyer's credit. If the documentation is timely delivered, and Seller determines in Seller's sole discretion that Buyer's credit is unacceptable, Seller may terminate this contract by notice to Buyer within 7 days after expiration of the time for delivery and the earnest money will be refunded to Buyer. If Seller does not so terminate this contract, Seller will be deemed to have accepted Buyer's credit. Buyer hereby authorizes any credit reporting agency to furnish to Seller at Buyer's sole expense copies of Buyer's credit reports.

5. **EARNEST MONEY:** Buyer shall deposit $_______________ as earnest money with ___________ ___________________________________ at _____________________________________ (Address), as escrow agent, upon execution of this contract by both parties. Additional earnest money of $______________ must be deposited by Buyer with escrow agent on or before _________________, ________. If Buyer fails to deposit the earnest money as required by this contract, Buyer will be in default.

6. **TITLE POLICY AND SURVEY:**

❑ A. TITLE POLICY: Seller shall furnish to Buyer at ❑ Seller's ❑ Buyer's expense an owner policy of title insurance (the Title Policy) issued by ______________________________ (the Title Company) in the amount of the Sales Price, dated at or after closing, insuring Buyer against loss under the provisions of the Title Policy, subject to the promulgated exclusions (including existing building and zoning ordinances) and the following exceptions:

(1) Restrictive covenants common to the platted subdivision in which the Property is located.
(2) The standard printed exception for standby fees, taxes and assessments.
(3) Liens created as part of the financing described in Paragraph 4.
(4) Utility easements created by the dedication deed or plat of the subdivision in which the Property is located.
(5) Reservations or exceptions otherwise permitted by this contract or as may be approved by Buyer in writing.
(6) The standard printed exception as to discrepancies, conflicts, shortages in area or boundary lines, encroachments or protrusions, or overlapping improvements.
(7) The standard printed exception as to marital rights.
(8) The standard printed exception as to waters, tidelands, beaches, streams, and related matters.

Within 20 days after the Title Company receives a copy of this contract, Seller shall furnish to Buyer a commitment for title insurance (the Commitment) and, at Buyer's expense, legible copies of restrictive covenants and documents evidencing exceptions in the Commitment other than the

One to Four Family Residential Contract Concerning______________________________ Page Four 11-8-99
(Address of Property)

standard printed exceptions. Seller authorizes the Title Company to mail or hand deliver the Commitment and related documents to Buyer at Buyer's address shown below. If the Commitment is not delivered to Buyer within the specified time, the time for delivery will be automatically extended up to 15 days. Buyer will have 7 days after the receipt of the Commitment to object in writing to matters disclosed in the Commitment.

❑ B. SURVEY: (Check one box only)

❑ (1) Within _____ days after Buyer's receipt of a survey furnished to a third-party lender at ❑ Seller's ❑ Buyer's expense, Buyer may object in writing to any matter shown on the survey which constitutes a defect or encumbrance to title.

❑ (2) Within _____ days after the effective date of this contract, Buyer may object in writing to any matter which constitutes a defect or encumbrance to title shown on a survey obtained by Buyer at Buyer's expense.

The survey must be made by a Registered Professional Land Surveyor acceptable to the Title Company and any lender. Utility easements created by the dedication deed and plat of the subdivision in which the Property is located will not be a basis for objection.

Buyer may object to existing building and zoning ordinances, items 6A(1) through (8) above and matters shown on the survey if Buyer determines that any such ordinance, items or matters prohibits the following use or activity: ____
____
____.

Buyer's failure to object under Paragraph 6A or 6B within the time allowed will constitute a waiver of Buyer's right to object; except that the requirements in Schedule C of the Commitment will not be deemed to have been waived. Seller shall cure the timely objections of Buyer or any third party lender within 15 days from the date Seller receives the objections and the Closing Date will be extended as necessary. If objections are not cured by the extended Closing Date, this contract will terminate and the earnest money will be refunded to Buyer unless Buyer elects to waive the objections.

NOTICE TO SELLER AND BUYER:

(1) Broker advises Buyer to have an abstract of title covering the Property examined by an attorney of Buyer's selection, or Buyer should be furnished with or obtain a Title Policy. If a Title Policy is furnished, the Commitment should be promptly reviewed by an attorney of Buyer's choice due to the time limitations on Buyer's right to object.

(2) If the Property is situated in a utility or other statutorily created district providing water, sewer, drainage, or flood control facilities and services, Chapter 49 of the Texas Water Code requires Seller to deliver and Buyer to sign the statutory notice relating to the tax rate, bonded indebtedness, or standby fee of the district prior to final execution of this contract.

(3) If the Property abuts the tidally influenced waters of the state, Section 33.135, Texas Natural Resources Code, requires a notice regarding coastal area property to be included in the contract. An addendum either promulgated by TREC or required by the parties should be used.

(4) Buyer is advised that the presence of wetlands, toxic substances, including asbestos and wastes or other environmental hazards or the presence of a threatened or endangered species or its habitat may affect Buyer's intended use of the Property. If Buyer is concerned about these matters, an addendum either promulgated by TREC or required by the parties should be used.

(5) If the Property is located outside the limits of a municipality, Seller notifies Buyer under §5.011, Texas Property Code, that the Property may now or later be included in the extraterritorial jurisdiction of a municipality and may now or later be subject to annexation by the municipality. Each municipality maintains a map that depicts its boundaries and extraterritorial jurisdiction. To determine if the Property is located within a municipality's extraterritorial jurisdiction or is likely to be located within a municipality's extraterritorial jurisdiction, contact all municipalities located in the general proximity of the Property for further information.

(6) Unless expressly prohibited in writing by the parties, Seller may continue to show the Property for sale and to receive, negotiate and accept back up offers.

Initialed for identification by Buyer__________ and Seller__________ 01A TREC NO. 20-4

(7) Any residential service contract that is purchased in connection with this transaction should be reviewed for the scope of coverage, exclusions and limitations. **The purchase of a residential service contract is optional. Similar coverage may be purchased from various companies authorized to do business in Texas.**

7. **PROPERTY CONDITION:**

A. INSPECTIONS, ACCESS AND UTILITIES: Buyer may have the Property inspected by an inspector selected by Buyer, licensed by TREC or otherwise permitted by law to make such inspections. Seller shall permit access to the Property at reasonable times for inspection, repairs and treatment and for reinspection after repairs and treatment have been completed. Seller shall pay for turning on utilities for inspection and reinspection.

B. SELLER'S DISCLOSURE NOTICE PURSUANT TO SECTION 5.008, TEXAS PROPERTY CODE (Notice) (check one box only):

❑ (1) Buyer has received the Notice.

❑ (2) Buyer has not received the Notice. Within _______ days after the effective date of this contract, Seller shall deliver the Notice to Buyer. If Buyer does not receive the Notice, Buyer may terminate this contract at any time prior to the closing. If Seller delivers the Notice, Buyer may terminate this contract for any reason within 7 days after Buyer receives the Notice or prior to the closing, whichever first occurs.

❑ (3) The Texas Property Code does not require this Seller to furnish the Notice.

C. SELLER'S DISCLOSURE OF LEAD-BASED PAINT AND LEAD-BASED PAINT HAZARDS is required by Federal law for a residential dwelling constructed prior to 1978. An addendum providing such disclosure ❑ is ❑ is not attached.

D. ACCEPTANCE OF PROPERTY CONDITION: (check one box only):

❑ (1) In addition to any earnest money deposited with escrow agent, Buyer has paid Seller $____________ (the "Option Fee") for the unrestricted right to terminate this contract by giving notice of termination to Seller within _______ days after the effective date of this contract. If Buyer gives notice of termination within the time specified, the Option Fee will not be refunded, however, any earnest money will be refunded to Buyer. If Buyer does not give notice of termination within the time specified, Buyer will be deemed to have accepted the Property in its current condition and the Option Fee ❑ will ❑ will not be credited to the Sales Price at closing.

❑ (2) Buyer accepts the Property in its present condition; provided Seller, at Seller's expense, shall complete the following repairs and treatment: ______________________________

____

____

____.

E. LENDER REQUIRED REPAIRS AND TREATMENTS (REPAIRS): Unless otherwise agreed in writing, neither party is obligated to pay for lender required repairs or treatments for wood destroying insects. If the cost of lender required repairs exceeds 5% of the Sales Price, Buyer may terminate this contract.

F. COMPLETION OF REPAIRS AND TREATMENT. Unless otherwise agreed by the parties in writing, Seller shall complete all agreed repairs and treatment prior to the Closing Date. Repairs and treatments must be performed by persons who regularly provide such repairs or treatments. At Buyer's election, any transferable warranties received by Seller with respect to the repairs will be transferred to Buyer at Buyer's expense. If Seller fails to complete any agreed repairs and treatment prior to the Closing Date, Buyer may do so and the Closing Date will be extended up to 15 days, if necessary, to complete repairs and treatment or treatments for wood destroying insects.

8. **BROKERS' FEES:** All obligations of the parties for payment of brokers' fees are contained in separate written agreements.

One to Four Family Residential Contract Concerning_______________________________ Page Six 11-8-99
(Address of Property)

9. **CLOSING:** The closing of the sale will be on or before ____________________, _____, or within 7 days after objections to matters disclosed in the Commitment or by the survey have been cured, whichever date is later (the Closing Date). *If financing or assumption approval has been obtained pursuant to Paragraph 4,* the Closing Date will be extended up to 15 days if necessary to comply with lender's closing requirements (for example, appraisal, survey, insurance policies, lender-required repairs, closing documents). If either party fails to close this sale by the Closing Date, the non-defaulting party will be entitled to exercise the remedies contained in Paragraph 15. At closing Seller shall furnish tax statements or certificates showing no delinquent taxes and a general warranty deed conveying good and indefeasible title showing no additional exceptions to those permitted in Paragraph 6.

10. **POSSESSION:** Seller shall deliver possession of the Property to Buyer on ______________ in its present or required repaired condition, ordinary wear and tear excepted. Any possession by Buyer prior to closing or by Seller after closing which is not authorized by a temporary lease form promulgated by TREC or required by the parties will establish a tenancy at sufferance relationship between the parties. *Consult your insurance agent prior to change of ownership or possession as insurance coverage may be limited or terminated. The absence of a written lease or appropriate insurance coverage may expose the parties to economic loss.*

11. **SPECIAL PROVISIONS:** (Insert only factual statements and business details applicable to this sale. TREC rules prohibit licensees from adding factual statements or business details for which a contract addendum, lease or other form has been promulgated by TREC for mandatory use.)

12. **SETTLEMENT AND OTHER EXPENSES:**
    A. The following expenses must be paid at or prior to closing:
    (1) Appraisal fees will be paid by ______________________________.
    (2) The total of loan discount fees (including any Texas Veterans' Housing Assistance Program Participation Fee) may not exceed ________% of the loan of which Seller shall pay ____________ and Buyer shall pay the remainder. The total of any buydown fees may not exceed ____________which will be paid by ______________________.
    (3) Seller's Expenses: Releases of existing liens, including prepayment penalties and recording fees; release of Seller's loan liability; tax statements or certificates; preparation of deed; one-half of escrow fee; and other expenses stipulated to be paid by Seller under other provisions of this contract.
    (4) Buyer's Expenses: Loan application, origination and commitment fees; loan assumption costs; preparation and recording of deed of trust to secure assumption; lender required expenses

incident to new loans, including PMI premium, preparation of loan documents, loan related inspection fee, recording fees, tax service and research fees, warehouse or underwriting fees, copies of restrictions and easements, amortization schedule, premiums for mortgagee title policies and endorsements required by lender, credit reports, photos; required premiums for flood and hazard insurance; required reserve deposit for insurance premiums and ad valorem taxes; interest on all monthly installment notes from date of disbursements to one month prior to dates of first monthly payments; customary Program Loan costs for Buyer; one-half of escrow fee; and other expenses stipulated to be paid by Buyer under other provisions of this contract.

B. If any expense exceeds an amount expressly stated in this contract for such expense to be paid by a party, that party may terminate this contract unless the other party agrees to pay such excess. In no event will Buyer pay charges and fees expressly prohibited by the Texas Veterans' Housing Assistance Program or other governmental loan program regulations.

13. **PRORATIONS**: Taxes for the current year, interest, maintenance fees, assessments, dues and rents will be prorated through the Closing Date. If taxes for the current year vary from the amount prorated at closing, the parties shall adjust the prorations when tax statements for the current year are available. *If a loan is assumed* and the lender maintains an escrow account, the escrow account must be transferred to Buyer without any deficiency. Buyer shall reimburse Seller for the amount in the transferred account. Buyer shall pay the premium for a new insurance policy. If taxes are not paid at or prior to closing, Buyer will be obligated to pay taxes for the current year.

14. **CASUALTY LOSS**: If any part of the Property is damaged or destroyed by fire or other casualty loss after the effective date of the contract, Seller shall restore the Property to its previous condition as soon as reasonably possible, but in any event by the Closing Date. If Seller fails to do so due to factors beyond Seller's control, Buyer may either (a) terminate this contract and the earnest money will be refunded to Buyer (b) extend the time for performance up to 15 days and the Closing Date will be extended as necessary or (c) accept the Property in its damaged condition and accept an assignment of insurance proceeds. Seller's obligations under this paragraph are independent of any obligations of Seller under Paragraph 7.

15. **DEFAULT**: If Buyer fails to comply with this contract, Buyer will be in default, and Seller may either (a) enforce specific performance, seek such other relief as may be provided by law, or both, or (b) terminate this contract and receive the earnest money as liquidated damages, thereby releasing both parties from this contract. If, due to factors beyond Seller's control, Seller fails within the time allowed to make any non-casualty repairs or deliver the Commitment, Buyer may either (a) extend the time for performance up to 15 days and the Closing Date will be extended as necessary or (b) terminate this contract as the sole remedy and receive the earnest money. If Seller fails to comply with this contract for any other reason, Seller will be in default and Buyer may either (a) enforce specific performance, seek such other relief as may be provided by law, or both, or (b) terminate this contract and receive the earnest money, thereby releasing both parties from this contract.

16. **DISPUTE RESOLUTION**: It is the policy of the State of Texas to encourage the peaceable resolution of disputes through alternative dispute resolution procedures. The parties are encouraged to use an addendum approved by TREC to submit to mediation disputes which cannot be resolved in good faith through informal discussion.

17. **ATTORNEY'S FEES**: The prevailing party in any legal proceeding brought under or with respect to the transaction described in this contract is entitled to recover from the non-prevailing party all costs of such proceeding and reasonable attorney's fees.

One to Four Family Residential Contract Concerning____ Page Eight 11-8-99
(Address of Property)

18. **ESCROW:** The earnest money is deposited with escrow agent with the understanding that escrow agent is not (a) a party to this contract and does not have any liability for the performance or nonperformance of any party to this contract, (b) liable for interest on the earnest money and (c) liable for any loss of earnest money caused by the failure of any financial institution in which the earnest money has been deposited unless the financial institution is acting as escrow agent. At closing, the earnest money must be applied first to any cash down payment, then to Buyer's closing costs and any excess refunded to Buyer. If both parties make written demand for the earnest money, escrow agent may require payment of unpaid expenses incurred on behalf of the parties and a written release of liability of escrow agent from all parties. If one party makes written demand for the earnest money, escrow agent shall give notice of the demand by providing to the other party a copy of the demand. If escrow agent does not receive written objection to the demand from the other party within 30 days after notice to the other party, escrow agent may disburse the earnest money to the party making demand reduced by the amount of unpaid expenses incurred on behalf of the party receiving the earnest money and escrow agent may pay the same to the creditors. If escrow agent complies with the provisions of this paragraph, each party hereby releases escrow agent from all adverse claims related to the disbursal of the earnest money. Escrow agent's notice to the other party will be effective when deposited in the U. S. Mail, postage prepaid, certified mail, return receipt requested, addressed to the other party at such party's address shown below. Notice of objection to the demand will be deemed effective upon receipt by escrow agent.

19. **REPRESENTATIONS:** Seller represents that as of the Closing Date (a) there will be no liens, assessments, or security interests against the Property which will not be satisfied out of the sales proceeds unless securing payment of any loans assumed by Buyer and (b) assumed loans will not be in default. If any representation in this contract is untrue on the Closing Date, this contract may be terminated by Buyer and the earnest money will be refunded to Buyer. All representations contained in this contract will survive closing.

20. **FEDERAL TAX REQUIREMENT:** If Seller is a "foreign person," as defined by applicable law, or if Seller fails to deliver an affidavit that Seller is not a "foreign person," then Buyer shall withhold from the sales proceeds an amount sufficient to comply with applicable tax law and deliver the same to the Internal Revenue Service together with appropriate tax forms. IRS regulations require filing written reports if cash in excess of specified amounts is received in the transaction.

21. **AGREEMENT OF PARTIES:** This contract contains the entire agreement of the parties and cannot be changed except by their written agreement. Addenda which are a part of this contract are (list):
____
____
____
____
____
____.

22. **CONSULT YOUR ATTORNEY:** Real estate licensees cannot give legal advice. This contract is intended to be legally binding. READ IT CAREFULLY. If you do not understand the effect of this contract, consult your attorney BEFORE signing.

Buyer's
Attorney is:______________________________

Seller's
Attorney is:______________________________

One to Four Family Residential Contract Concerning________________________ Page Nine 11-8-99
(Address of Property)

23. **NOTICES:** All notices from one party to the other must be in writing and are effective when mailed to, hand-delivered at, or transmitted by facsimile machine as follows:

To Buyer at: ______________________ ______________________ ______________________

Telephone:(___)______________________

Facsimile:(___) ______________________

To Seller at: ______________________ ______________________ ______________________

Telephone:(___)______________________

Facsimile:(___) ______________________

EXECUTED the _____day of ____________________, ______ (THE EFFECTIVE DATE). (BROKER: FILL IN THE DATE OF FINAL ACCEPTANCE.)

______________________ Buyer ______________________ Seller

______________________ Buyer ______________________ Seller

The form of this contract has been approved by the Texas Real Estate Commission. TREC forms are intended for use only by trained real estate licensees. No representation is made as to the legal validity or adequacy of any provision in any specific transactions. It is not suitable for complex transactions. Texas Real Estate Commission, P.O. Box 12188, Austin, TX 78711-2188, 1-800-250-8732 or (512) 459-6544 (http://www.trec.state.tx.us)TREC NO. 20-4. This form replaces TREC NO. 20-3.

BROKER INFORMATION AND RATIFICATION OF FEE

Listing Broker has agreed to pay Other Broker ____________________ of the total sales price when Listing Broker's fee is received. Escrow Agent is authorized and directed to pay Other Broker from Listing Broker's fee at closing.

______________________ Other Broker License No.

represents ❑ Seller as Listing Broker's subagent ❑ Buyer only as Buyer's agent

______________________ Associate Telephone

______________________ Broker Address

______________________ Telephone Facsimile

______________________ Listing Broker License No.

represents ❑ Seller and Buyer as an intermediary ❑ Seller only as Seller's agent

______________________ Listing Associate Telephone

______________________ Selling Associate Telephone

______________________ Broker Address

______________________ Telephone Facsimile

RECEIPT

Receipt of ❑ Contract and ❑ $__________ Earnest Money in the form of ______________________ is acknowledged.

Escrow Agent: ______________________ Date: ______________________, ________

By: ______________________

______________________ Address

______________________ City State Zip

Telephone: (____) ______________________

Facsimile: (____) ______________________

10-25-93

ENVIRONMENTAL ASSESSMENT, THREATENED OR ENDANGERED SPECIES, AND WETLANDS ADDENDUM

PROMULGATED BY THE TEXAS REAL ESTATE COMMISSION (TREC)

ADDENDUM TO EARNEST MONEY CONTRACT BETWEEN THE UNDERSIGNED PARTIES CONCERNING THE PROPERTY AT ______________________________
(Address)

☐ A. ENVIRONMENTAL ASSESSMENT: Buyer, at Buyer's expense, may obtain an Environmental Assessment Report prepared by an environmental specialist.

☐ B. THREATENED OR ENDANGERED SPECIES: Buyer, at Buyer's expense, may obtain a report from a natural resources professional to determine if there are any threatened or endangered species or their habitats as defined by the Texas Parks and wildlife Department or the U.S. Fish and Wildlife Service.

☐ C. WETLANDS: Buyer, at Buyer's expense, may obtain a report from an environmental specialist to determine if there are wetlands, as defined by federal or state law or regulation.

Within _________ days after the Effective Date of the contract, Buyer may terminate the contract by furnishing Seller a copy of any report noted above that adversely affects the use of the Property and the Earnest Money shall be refunded to Buyer. If Buyer does not furnish Seller a copy of the unacceptable report within the prescribed time and give Seller notice that Buyer has terminated the contract, Buyer shall be deemed to have accepted the Property.

______________________________ ______________________________
Buyer Seller

______________________________ ______________________________
Buyer Seller

The form of this addendum has been approved by the Texas Real Estate Commission for use only with similarly approved or promulgated forms of contracts. No representation is made as to the legal validity or adequacy of any provision in any specific transactions. It is not suitable for complex transactions. (10-93) TREC No. 28-0.

01A TREC No. 28-0

PROMULGATED BY THE TEXAS REAL ESTATE COMMISSION (TREC) 09-01-99

ADDENDUM FOR PROPERTY SUBJECT TO MANDATORY MEMBERSHIP IN AN OWNERS' ASSOCIATION

(NOT FOR USE WITH CONDOMINIUMS)

ADDENDUM TO CONTRACT CONCERNING THE PROPERTY AT

____

(Street Address and City)

____

(Name of Owners' Association)

A. **SUBDIVISION INFORMATION:** "Subdivision Information" means: (i) the restrictions applying to the subdivision, (ii) the bylaws and rules of the Owners' Association, and (iii) a resale certificate, all of which were provided by the Owners' Association in compliance with Section 207.003 of the Texas Property Code no more than three months before the date of their delivery to Buyer.

(Check only one box):

❑ 1. Within ________ days after the effective date of the contract, Seller shall at Seller's expense deliver the Subdivision Information to Buyer. If Buyer does not receive the Subdivision Information, Buyer may terminate the contract at any time prior to closing. If Seller delivers the Subdivision Information, Buyer may terminate the contract for any reason within 7 days after Buyer receives the Subdivision Information or prior to closing, whichever first occurs.

❑ 2. Buyer has received and approved the Subdivision Information before signing the contract.

❑ 3. Buyer does not require delivery of the Subdivision Information **and waives the right of termination under this Addendum**.

If Seller becomes aware of any material changes in the Subdivision Information, Seller shall immediately give notice to Buyer. Buyer may terminate the contract prior to closing by giving written notice to Seller if: (i) any of the Subdivision Information provided was not true; or (ii) any material adverse change in the Subdivision Information occurs prior to closing.

B. **TRANSFER FEES:** Buyer shall pay any Owners' Association transfer fee not to exceed $ ____________, and Seller agrees to pay any excess.

NOTICE TO BUYER REGARDING REPAIRS BY THE OWNERS' ASSOCIATION: The Owners' Association may have the sole responsibility to make certain repairs to the Property. If you are concerned about the condition of any part of the Property which the Owners' Association is required to repair, you should not sign the contract unless you are satisfied that the Owners' Association will make the desired repairs.

______________________	______________________
Buyer	Seller
______________________	______________________
Buyer	Seller

The form of this addendum has been approved by the Texas Real Estate Commission for use only with similarly approved or promulgated forms of contracts. Such approval relates to this contract form only. TREC forms are intended for use only by trained real estate licensees. No representation is made as to the legal validity or adequacy of any provision in any specific transactions. It is not suitable for complex transactions.(09-99)Texas Real Estate Commission, P.O. Box 12188, Austin, TX 78711-2188, 1-800-250-8732 or (512) 459-6544 (http://www.trec.state.tx.us) TREC No. 36-1.This form replaces TREC No. 36-0.

PROMULGATED BY THE TEXAS REAL ESTATE COMMISSION (TREC) 09-20-99

AMENDMENT

(for Residential Resales Only)

AMENDMENT TO CONTRACT BETWEEN THE UNDERSIGNED PARTIES CONCERNING PROPERTY AT

____

(Street Address and City)

Seller and Buyer amend the contract as follows: (check applicable boxes below)

❑ (1) The Sales Price in Paragraph 3 of the contract is:

A. Cash portion of Sales Price payable by Buyer at closing . . . . $ ____________

B. Sum of financing described in the contract . . . . $ ____________

C. Sales Price (Sum of A and B) . . . . $ ____________

❑ (2) Buyer accepts the Property in its present condition; provided Seller, at Seller's expense, shall complete the following repairs and treatment:

❑ (3) The Option Fee ❑ will ❑ will not be credited to the Sales Price at closing.

❑ (4) The date in Paragraph 9 of the contract is changed to __________________, _______.

❑ (5) Seller shall pay $ __________________ of the expenses stipulated to be paid by Buyer under the provisions of the contract.

❑ (6) The cost of the lender required repairs and treatment, as itemized on the attached list, will be paid as follows: $ __________________ by Seller; $ ____________________ by Buyer.

❑ (7) Buyer has paid Seller an additional non-refundable Option Fee of $ _____________ for an extension of the unrestricted right to terminate the contract before 5:00 p.m., _______________, _______. This additional Option Fee ❑ will ❑ will not be credited to the Sales Price at closing.

❑ (8) Upon final acceptance of this Amendment, Buyer waives the right to terminate under Paragraph 7D(1) of the contract.

❑ (9) **Other Modifications**: (Note to Broker: Insert, modify or eliminate only factual statements and business details applicable to this contract that have been inserted in blanks or by check boxes in the contract, or by adding or eliminating a promulgated or approved addendum to the contract.).

EXECUTED the __________ day of ____________________, ________ (BROKER: FILL IN THE DATE OF FINAL ACCEPTANCE).

______________________	______________________
Buyer	Seller
______________________	______________________
Buyer	Seller

01A

Transaction 2: 90% Conventional Fixed Rate Loan with PMI

Utilizing: TREC 20-4, Lead-Based Paint Addendum

John Charles Wayne and his spouse, Sharon Sidekick Wayne, want to buy the home owned by Thomas Arnold Smith and his wife, Molly Bea Smith. Although the property is subject to mandatory membership in an owners' association, the Waynes do not attach the addendum regarding association membership. There are no excluded fixtures at 3510 Memosa Lane in Bellaire, Harris County, 77404. On the plat of Shadyacres Addition, the property is identified as Lot 7, Block 7.

The Waynes are willing to pay $80,000 for the property and will apply for a 90 percent, 30-year fixed-rate loan at 7.5 percent annual interest within four days after the effective date of the contract. They anticipate that all lender requirements can be met and approval can be received within 40 days and they can close within 45 days. They anticipate that they may have to pay up to one discount point to obtain the desired interest rate, and request that the seller be liable for one-half of any discount required by the lender.

To show good faith, they deposit $4,000 earnest money with Protective Title Company and will deposit another $4,000 thirty days after the effective date of this contract. As previously agreed at the time of listing, the sellers will pay for the owner's title policy. The buyers want two days to review the survey that their lender requires. They are willing to pay for the survey and appraisal.

Prior to making their offer, the buyers receive the sellers' disclosure form. Their purchase agreement contains the lead-based paint addendum because the house was built in 1965. They ask for a ten-day option period and have given the agent a check in the amount of $100 to compensate the sellers for granting the option. The option fee will be credited to the sale price at closing. They plan to have a variety of structural and mechanical evaluations done.

The buyers reserve the opportunity to do a walk-through during the four hours prior to closing and want to be granted possession at funding, which they anticipate will be at the closing table.

The buyers are customers who are purchasing the property at an open house being held by the sellers' agent, Sarah Listalot (TREC# 0234567).

With regard to the lead-based paint addendum, the seller has no knowledge of lead-based paint or hazards and buyers have no plans to conduct a risk assessment. The buyers have been furnished the HUD lead pamphlet.

PROMULGATED BY THE TEXAS REAL ESTATE COMMISSION (TREC) 11-8-99

ONE TO FOUR FAMILY RESIDENTIAL CONTRACT (RESALE)
ALL CASH, ASSUMPTION, THIRD PARTY CONVENTIONAL OR SELLER FINANCING

NOTICE: Not For Use For Condominium Transactions

1. **PARTIES:** ______________________________ (Seller) agrees to sell and convey to ______________________________ (Buyer) and Buyer agrees to buy from Seller the property described below.

2. **PROPERTY:** Lot __________, Block _____, ______________________________ Addition, City of ______________________________, ____________________ County, Texas, known as ______________________________ (Address/Zip Code), or as described on attached exhibit, together with the following items, if any: curtains and rods, draperies and rods, valances, blinds, window shades, screens, shutters, awnings, wall-to-wall carpeting, mirrors fixed in place, ceiling fans, attic fans, mail boxes, television antennas and satellite dish system with controls and equipment, permanently installed heating and air-conditioning units, window air-conditioning units, built-in security and fire detection equipment, plumbing and lighting fixtures including chandeliers, water softener, stove, built-in kitchen equipment, garage door openers with controls, built-in cleaning equipment, all swimming pool equipment and maintenance accessories, shrubbery, landscaping, permanently installed outdoor cooking equipment, built-in fireplace screens, artificial fireplace logs and all other property owned by Seller and attached to the above described real property except the following property which is not included: ______________________________
____
____
______________________________.
All property sold by this contract is called the "Property." The Property ❑ is ❑ is not subject to mandatory membership in an owners' association. The TREC Addendum For Property Subject To Mandatory Membership In An Owners' Association ❑ is ❑ is not attached.
NOTICE TO BUYER: If the Property is subject to mandatory membership in an owners' association, Seller notifies Buyer under §5.012, Texas Property Code, that, as a purchaser of property in the residential community in which the Property is located, you are obligated to be a member of an owners' association. Restrictive covenants governing the use and occupancy of the Property and a dedicatory instrument governing the establishment, maintenance, and operation of this residential community have been or will be recorded in the Real Property Records of the county in which the Property is located. Copies of the restrictive covenants and dedicatory instrument may be obtained from the county clerk. You are obligated to pay assessments to the owners' association. The amount of the assessments is subject to change. Your failure to pay the assessments could result in a lien on and the foreclosure of the Property.

3. **SALES PRICE:**
   A. Cash portion of Sales Price payable by Buyer at closing . . . . $__________
   B. Sum of all financing described below (excluding any private mortgage insurance [PMI] premium) . . . . $__________
   C. Sales Price (Sum of A and B) . . . . $__________

4. **FINANCING:** Within _____ days after the effective date of this contract Buyer shall apply for all third party financing or noteholder's approval of any assumption and make every reasonable effort to obtain financing or assumption approval. Financing or assumption approval will be deemed to have been obtained when the lender determines that Buyer has satisfied all of lender's financial requirements (those items relating to Buyer's net worth, income and creditworthiness). If financing (including any financed PMI premium) or assumption approval is not obtained within ______ days after the effective

date hereof, this contract will terminate and the earnest money will be refunded to Buyer. Each note to be executed hereunder must be secured by vendor's and deed of trust liens.

The portion of Sales Price not payable in cash will be paid as follows: (Check applicable boxes below)

❑ A. THIRD PARTY FINANCING:

❑ (1) This contract is subject to approval for Buyer of a third party first mortgage loan having a loan-to-value ratio not to exceed ____ % as established by such third party (excluding any financed PMI premium), due in full in _____ year(s), with interest not to exceed _____ % per annum for the first _____ year(s) of the loan. The loan will be ❑ with ❑ without PMI.

❑ (2) This contract is subject to approval for Buyer of a third party second mortgage loan having a loan-to-value ratio not to exceed ______ % as established by such third party (excluding any financed PMI premium), due in full in ______ year(s), with interest not to exceed _______ % per annum for the first _____ year(s) of the loan. The loan will be ❑ with ❑ without PMI.

❑ B. TEXAS VETERANS' HOUSING ASSISTANCE PROGRAM LOAN: This contract is subject to approval for Buyer of a Texas Veterans' Housing Assistance Program Loan (the Program Loan) of $_______________ for a period of at least ____________ years at the interest rate established by the Texas Veterans' Land Board at the time of closing.

❑ C. SELLER FINANCING: A promissory note from Buyer to Seller of $____________, bearing ____ % interest per annum, secured by vendor's and deed of trust liens, in accordance with the terms and conditions set forth in the attached TREC Seller Financing Addendum. If an owner policy of title insurance is furnished, Buyer shall furnish Seller with a mortgagee policy of title insurance.

❑ D. ASSUMPTION:

❑ (1) Buyer shall assume the unpaid principal balance of a first lien promissory note payable to ____ which unpaid balance at closing will be $ ______________ . The total current monthly payment including principal, interest and any reserve deposits is $ _______________ . Buyer's initial payment will be the first payment due after closing.

❑ (2) Buyer shall assume the unpaid principal balance of a second lien promissory note payable to ____ which unpaid balance at closing will be $ _______________ . The total current monthly payment including principal, interest and any reserve deposits is $ _______________ . Buyer's initial payment will be the first payment due after closing.

Buyer's assumption of an existing note includes all obligations imposed by the deed of trust securing the note.

If the unpaid principal balance(s) of any assumed loan(s) as of the Closing Date varies from the loan balance(s) stated above, the ❑ cash payable at closing ❑ Sales Price will be adjusted by the amount of any variance; provided, if the total principal balance of all assumed loans varies in an amount greater than $350.00 at closing, either party may terminate this contract and the earnest money will be refunded to Buyer unless the other party elects to eliminate the excess in the variance by an appropriate adjustment at closing. If the noteholder requires (a) payment of an assumption fee in excess of $ ____________ in D(1) above or $ ________________ in D(2) above and Seller declines to pay such excess, or (b) an increase in the interest rate to more than _____ % in D(1) above, or _____ % in D(2) above, or (c) any other modification of the loan documents, Buyer may terminate this contract and the earnest money will be refunded to Buyer. A vendor's lien and deed of trust to secure assumption will be required which shall automatically be released on execution and delivery of a release by noteholder. If Seller is released from liability on any assumed note, the vendor's lien and deed of trust to secure assumption will not be required.

One to Four Family Residential Contract Concerning____________________ Page Three 11-8-99
(Address of Property)

NOTICE TO BUYER: The monthly payments, interest rates or other terms of some loans may be adjusted by the lender at or after closing. If you are concerned about the possibility of future adjustments, do not sign the contract without examining the notes and deeds of trust.
NOTICE TO SELLER: Your liability to pay the note assumed by Buyer will continue unless you obtain a release of liability from the lender. If you are concerned about future liability, you should use the TREC Release of Liability Addendum.

❑ E. CREDIT APPROVAL ON ASSUMPTION OR SELLER FINANCING: Within _____ days after the effective date of this contract, Buyer shall deliver to Seller ❑ credit report ❑ verification of employment, including salary ❑ verification of funds on deposit in financial institutions ❑ current financial statement to establish Buyer's creditworthiness for assumption approval or seller financing and ❑ ____
____
____.

If Buyer's documentation is not delivered within the specified time, Seller may terminate this contract by notice to Buyer within 7 days after expiration of the time for delivery, and the earnest money will be paid to Seller. If this contract is not so terminated, Seller will be deemed to have accepted Buyer's credit. If the documentation is timely delivered, and Seller determines in Seller's sole discretion that Buyer's credit is unacceptable, Seller may terminate this contract by notice to Buyer within 7 days after expiration of the time for delivery and the earnest money will be refunded to Buyer. If Seller does not so terminate this contract, Seller will be deemed to have accepted Buyer's credit. Buyer hereby authorizes any credit reporting agency to furnish to Seller at Buyer's sole expense copies of Buyer's credit reports.

5. **EARNEST MONEY:** Buyer shall deposit $_______________ as earnest money with ____________ ______________________________ at ___________________________________ (Address), as escrow agent, upon execution of this contract by both parties. Additional earnest money of $______________ must be deposited by Buyer with escrow agent on or before __________________, ________. If Buyer fails to deposit the earnest money as required by this contract, Buyer will be in default.

6. **TITLE POLICY AND SURVEY:**

❑ A. TITLE POLICY: Seller shall furnish to Buyer at ❑ Seller's ❑ Buyer's expense an owner policy of title insurance (the Title Policy) issued by ___________________________________ (the Title Company) in the amount of the Sales Price, dated at or after closing, insuring Buyer against loss under the provisions of the Title Policy, subject to the promulgated exclusions (including existing building and zoning ordinances) and the following exceptions:

(1) Restrictive covenants common to the platted subdivision in which the Property is located.
(2) The standard printed exception for standby fees, taxes and assessments.
(3) Liens created as part of the financing described in Paragraph 4.
(4) Utility easements created by the dedication deed or plat of the subdivision in which the Property is located.
(5) Reservations or exceptions otherwise permitted by this contract or as may be approved by Buyer in writing.
(6) The standard printed exception as to discrepancies, conflicts, shortages in area or boundary lines, encroachments or protrusions, or overlapping improvements.
(7) The standard printed exception as to marital rights.
(8) The standard printed exception as to waters, tidelands, beaches, streams, and related matters.

Within 20 days after the Title Company receives a copy of this contract, Seller shall furnish to Buyer a commitment for title insurance (the Commitment) and, at Buyer's expense, legible copies of restrictive covenants and documents evidencing exceptions in the Commitment other than the

standard printed exceptions. Seller authorizes the Title Company to mail or hand deliver the Commitment and related documents to Buyer at Buyer's address shown below. If the Commitment is not delivered to Buyer within the specified time, the time for delivery will be automatically extended up to 15 days. Buyer will have 7 days after the receipt of the Commitment to object in writing to matters disclosed in the Commitment.

❑ B. SURVEY: (Check one box only)

❑ (1) Within _____ days after Buyer's receipt of a survey furnished to a third-party lender at ❑ Seller's ❑ Buyer's expense, Buyer may object in writing to any matter shown on the survey which constitutes a defect or encumbrance to title.

❑ (2) Within _____ days after the effective date of this contract, Buyer may object in writing to any matter which constitutes a defect or encumbrance to title shown on a survey obtained by Buyer at Buyer's expense.

The survey must be made by a Registered Professional Land Surveyor acceptable to the Title Company and any lender. Utility easements created by the dedication deed and plat of the subdivision in which the Property is located will not be a basis for objection.

Buyer may object to existing building and zoning ordinances, items 6A(1) through (8) above and matters shown on the survey if Buyer determines that any such ordinance, items or matters prohibits the following use or activity: ____

____

____.

Buyer's failure to object under Paragraph 6A or 6B within the time allowed will constitute a waiver of Buyer's right to object; except that the requirements in Schedule C of the Commitment will not be deemed to have been waived. Seller shall cure the timely objections of Buyer or any third party lender within 15 days from the date Seller receives the objections and the Closing Date will be extended as necessary. If objections are not cured by the extended Closing Date, this contract will terminate and the earnest money will be refunded to Buyer unless Buyer elects to waive the objections.

NOTICE TO SELLER AND BUYER:

(1) Broker advises Buyer to have an abstract of title covering the Property examined by an attorney of Buyer's selection, or Buyer should be furnished with or obtain a Title Policy. If a Title Policy is furnished, the Commitment should be promptly reviewed by an attorney of Buyer's choice due to the time limitations on Buyer's right to object.

(2) If the Property is situated in a utility or other statutorily created district providing water, sewer, drainage, or flood control facilities and services, Chapter 49 of the Texas Water Code requires Seller to deliver and Buyer to sign the statutory notice relating to the tax rate, bonded indebtedness, or standby fee of the district prior to final execution of this contract.

(3) If the Property abuts the tidally influenced waters of the state, Section 33.135, Texas Natural Resources Code, requires a notice regarding coastal area property to be included in the contract. An addendum either promulgated by TREC or required by the parties should be used.

(4) Buyer is advised that the presence of wetlands, toxic substances, including asbestos and wastes or other environmental hazards or the presence of a threatened or endangered species or its habitat may affect Buyer's intended use of the Property. If Buyer is concerned about these matters, an addendum either promulgated by TREC or required by the parties should be used.

(5) If the Property is located outside the limits of a municipality, Seller notifies Buyer under §5.011, Texas Property Code, that the Property may now or later be included in the extraterritorial jurisdiction of a municipality and may now or later be subject to annexation by the municipality. Each municipality maintains a map that depicts its boundaries and extraterritorial jurisdiction. To determine if the Property is located within a municipality's extraterritorial jurisdiction or is likely to be located within a municipality's extraterritorial jurisdiction, contact all municipalities located in the general proximity of the Property for further information.

(6) Unless expressly prohibited in writing by the parties, Seller may continue to show the Property for sale and to receive, negotiate and accept back up offers.

(7) Any residential service contract that is purchased in connection with this transaction should be reviewed for the scope of coverage, exclusions and limitations. **The purchase of a residential service contract is optional. Similar coverage may be purchased from various companies authorized to do business in Texas.**

7. PROPERTY CONDITION:

A. INSPECTIONS, ACCESS AND UTILITIES: Buyer may have the Property inspected by an inspector selected by Buyer, licensed by TREC or otherwise permitted by law to make such inspections. Seller shall permit access to the Property at reasonable times for inspection, repairs and treatment and for reinspection after repairs and treatment have been completed. Seller shall pay for turning on utilities for inspection and reinspection.

B. SELLER'S DISCLOSURE NOTICE PURSUANT TO SECTION 5.008, TEXAS PROPERTY CODE (Notice) (check one box only):

❑ (1) Buyer has received the Notice.

❑ (2) Buyer has not received the Notice. Within _______ days after the effective date of this contract, Seller shall deliver the Notice to Buyer. If Buyer does not receive the Notice, Buyer may terminate this contract at any time prior to the closing. If Seller delivers the Notice, Buyer may terminate this contract for any reason within 7 days after Buyer receives the Notice or prior to the closing, whichever first occurs.

❑ (3) The Texas Property Code does not require this Seller to furnish the Notice.

C. SELLER'S DISCLOSURE OF LEAD-BASED PAINT AND LEAD-BASED PAINT HAZARDS is required by Federal law for a residential dwelling constructed prior to 1978. An addendum providing such disclosure ❑ is ❑ is not attached.

D. ACCEPTANCE OF PROPERTY CONDITION: (check one box only):

❑ (1) In addition to any earnest money deposited with escrow agent, Buyer has paid Seller $____________ (the "Option Fee") for the unrestricted right to terminate this contract by giving notice of termination to Seller within _______ days after the effective date of this contract. If Buyer gives notice of termination within the time specified, the Option Fee will not be refunded, however, any earnest money will be refunded to Buyer. If Buyer does not give notice of termination within the time specified, Buyer will be deemed to have accepted the Property in its current condition and the Option Fee ❑ will ❑ will not be credited to the Sales Price at closing.

❑ (2) Buyer accepts the Property in its present condition; provided Seller, at Seller's expense, shall complete the following repairs and treatment: ______________________________
____
____
____.

E. LENDER REQUIRED REPAIRS AND TREATMENTS (REPAIRS): Unless otherwise agreed in writing, neither party is obligated to pay for lender required repairs or treatments for wood destroying insects. If the cost of lender required repairs exceeds 5% of the Sales Price, Buyer may terminate this contract.

F. COMPLETION OF REPAIRS AND TREATMENT. Unless otherwise agreed by the parties in writing, Seller shall complete all agreed repairs and treatment prior to the Closing Date. Repairs and treatments must be performed by persons who regularly provide such repairs or treatments. At Buyer's election, any transferable warranties received by Seller with respect to the repairs will be transferred to Buyer at Buyer's expense. If Seller fails to complete any agreed repairs and treatment prior to the Closing Date, Buyer may do so and the Closing Date will be extended up to 15 days, if necessary, to complete repairs and treatment or treatments for wood destroying insects.

8. BROKERS' FEES: All obligations of the parties for payment of brokers' fees are contained in separate written agreements.

9. **CLOSING:** The closing of the sale will be on or before ______________________, ______, or within 7 days after objections to matters disclosed in the Commitment or by the survey have been cured, whichever date is later (the Closing Date). *If financing or assumption approval has been obtained pursuant to Paragraph 4,* the Closing Date will be extended up to 15 days if necessary to comply with lender's closing requirements (for example, appraisal, survey, insurance policies, lender-required repairs, closing documents). If either party fails to close this sale by the Closing Date, the non-defaulting party will be entitled to exercise the remedies contained in Paragraph 15. At closing Seller shall furnish tax statements or certificates showing no delinquent taxes and a general warranty deed conveying good and indefeasible title showing no additional exceptions to those permitted in Paragraph 6.

10. **POSSESSION:** Seller shall deliver possession of the Property to Buyer on ______________ in its present or required repaired condition, ordinary wear and tear excepted. Any possession by Buyer prior to closing or by Seller after closing which is not authorized by a temporary lease form promulgated by TREC or required by the parties will establish a tenancy at sufferance relationship between the parties. *Consult your insurance agent prior to change of ownership or possession as insurance coverage may be limited or terminated. The absence of a written lease or appropriate insurance coverage may expose the parties to economic loss.*

11. **SPECIAL PROVISIONS:** (Insert only factual statements and business details applicable to this sale. TREC rules prohibit licensees from adding factual statements or business details for which a contract addendum, lease or other form has been promulgated by TREC for mandatory use.)

12. **SETTLEMENT AND OTHER EXPENSES:**
    A. The following expenses must be paid at or prior to closing:
    (1) Appraisal fees will be paid by ______________________________________.
    (2) The total of loan discount fees (including any Texas Veterans' Housing Assistance Program Participation Fee) may not exceed ________% of the loan of which Seller shall pay ____________ and Buyer shall pay the remainder. The total of any buydown fees may not exceed ____________which will be paid by ______________________.
    (3) Seller's Expenses: Releases of existing liens, including prepayment penalties and recording fees; release of Seller's loan liability; tax statements or certificates; preparation of deed; one-half of escrow fee; and other expenses stipulated to be paid by Seller under other provisions of this contract.
    (4) Buyer's Expenses: Loan application, origination and commitment fees; loan assumption costs; preparation and recording of deed of trust to secure assumption; lender required expenses

One to Four Family Residential Contract Concerning_______________ Page Seven 11-8-99
(Address of Property)

incident to new loans, including PMI premium, preparation of loan documents, loan related inspection fee, recording fees, tax service and research fees, warehouse or underwriting fees, copies of restrictions and easements, amortization schedule, premiums for mortgagee title policies and endorsements required by lender, credit reports, photos; required premiums for flood and hazard insurance; required reserve deposit for insurance premiums and ad valorem taxes; interest on all monthly installment notes from date of disbursements to one month prior to dates of first monthly payments; customary Program Loan costs for Buyer; one-half of escrow fee; and other expenses stipulated to be paid by Buyer under other provisions of this contract.

B. If any expense exceeds an amount expressly stated in this contract for such expense to be paid by a party, that party may terminate this contract unless the other party agrees to pay such excess. In no event will Buyer pay charges and fees expressly prohibited by the Texas Veterans' Housing Assistance Program or other governmental loan program regulations.

13. **PRORATIONS**: Taxes for the current year, interest, maintenance fees, assessments, dues and rents will be prorated through the Closing Date. If taxes for the current year vary from the amount prorated at closing, the parties shall adjust the prorations when tax statements for the current year are available. *If a loan is assumed* and the lender maintains an escrow account, the escrow account must be transferred to Buyer without any deficiency. Buyer shall reimburse Seller for the amount in the transferred account. Buyer shall pay the premium for a new insurance policy. If taxes are not paid at or prior to closing, Buyer will be obligated to pay taxes for the current year.

14. **CASUALTY LOSS**: If any part of the Property is damaged or destroyed by fire or other casualty loss after the effective date of the contract, Seller shall restore the Property to its previous condition as soon as reasonably possible, but in any event by the Closing Date. If Seller fails to do so due to factors beyond Seller's control, Buyer may either (a) terminate this contract and the earnest money will be refunded to Buyer (b) extend the time for performance up to 15 days and the Closing Date will be extended as necessary or (c) accept the Property in its damaged condition and accept an assignment of insurance proceeds. Seller's obligations under this paragraph are independent of any obligations of Seller under Paragraph 7.

15. **DEFAULT**: If Buyer fails to comply with this contract, Buyer will be in default, and Seller may either (a) enforce specific performance, seek such other relief as may be provided by law, or both, or (b) terminate this contract and receive the earnest money as liquidated damages, thereby releasing both parties from this contract. If, due to factors beyond Seller's control, Seller fails within the time allowed to make any non-casualty repairs or deliver the Commitment, Buyer may either (a) extend the time for performance up to 15 days and the Closing Date will be extended as necessary or (b) terminate this contract as the sole remedy and receive the earnest money. If Seller fails to comply with this contract for any other reason, Seller will be in default and Buyer may either (a) enforce specific performance, seek such other relief as may be provided by law, or both, or (b) terminate this contract and receive the earnest money, thereby releasing both parties from this contract.

16. **DISPUTE RESOLUTION**: It is the policy of the State of Texas to encourage the peaceable resolution of disputes through alternative dispute resolution procedures. The parties are encouraged to use an addendum approved by TREC to submit to mediation disputes which cannot be resolved in good faith through informal discussion.

17. **ATTORNEY'S FEES**: The prevailing party in any legal proceeding brought under or with respect to the transaction described in this contract is entitled to recover from the non-prevailing party all costs of such proceeding and reasonable attorney's fees.

One to Four Family Residential Contract Concerning________________________________Page Eight 11-8-99
(Address of Property)

18. **ESCROW:** The earnest money is deposited with escrow agent with the understanding that escrow agent is not (a) a party to this contract and does not have any liability for the performance or nonperformance of any party to this contract, (b) liable for interest on the earnest money and (c) liable for any loss of earnest money caused by the failure of any financial institution in which the earnest money has been deposited unless the financial institution is acting as escrow agent. At closing, the earnest money must be applied first to any cash down payment, then to Buyer's closing costs and any excess refunded to Buyer. If both parties make written demand for the earnest money, escrow agent may require payment of unpaid expenses incurred on behalf of the parties and a written release of liability of escrow agent from all parties. If one party makes written demand for the earnest money, escrow agent shall give notice of the demand by providing to the other party a copy of the demand. If escrow agent does not receive written objection to the demand from the other party within 30 days after notice to the other party, escrow agent may disburse the earnest money to the party making demand reduced by the amount of unpaid expenses incurred on behalf of the party receiving the earnest money and escrow agent may pay the same to the creditors. If escrow agent complies with the provisions of this paragraph, each party hereby releases escrow agent from all adverse claims related to the disbursal of the earnest money. Escrow agent's notice to the other party will be effective when deposited in the U. S. Mail, postage prepaid, certified mail, return receipt requested, addressed to the other party at such party's address shown below. Notice of objection to the demand will be deemed effective upon receipt by escrow agent.

19. **REPRESENTATIONS:** Seller represents that as of the Closing Date (a) there will be no liens, assessments, or security interests against the Property which will not be satisfied out of the sales proceeds unless securing payment of any loans assumed by Buyer and (b) assumed loans will not be in default. If any representation in this contract is untrue on the Closing Date, this contract may be terminated by Buyer and the earnest money will be refunded to Buyer. All representations contained in this contract will survive closing.

20. **FEDERAL TAX REQUIREMENT:** If Seller is a "foreign person," as defined by applicable law, or if Seller fails to deliver an affidavit that Seller is not a "foreign person," then Buyer shall withhold from the sales proceeds an amount sufficient to comply with applicable tax law and deliver the same to the Internal Revenue Service together with appropriate tax forms. IRS regulations require filing written reports if cash in excess of specified amounts is received in the transaction.

21. **AGREEMENT OF PARTIES:** This contract contains the entire agreement of the parties and cannot be changed except by their written agreement. Addenda which are a part of this contract are (list):

____
____
____
____
____
____.

22. **CONSULT YOUR ATTORNEY:** Real estate licensees cannot give legal advice. This contract is intended to be legally binding. READ IT CAREFULLY. If you do not understand the effect of this contract, consult your attorney BEFORE signing.

Buyer's
Attorney is:______________________________

Seller's
Attorney is:______________________________

One to Four Family Residential Contract Concerning____ Page Nine 11-8-99
(Address of Property)

23. **NOTICES:** All notices from one party to the other must be in writing and are effective when mailed to, hand-delivered at, or transmitted by facsimile machine as follows:

To Buyer at:

____
____
____

Telephone:(___)______________________

Facsimile:(___) ______________________

To Seller at:

____
____
____

Telephone:(___)______________________

Facsimile:(___) ______________________

EXECUTED the ______day of ___________________, ______ (THE EFFECTIVE DATE). (BROKER: FILL IN THE DATE OF FINAL ACCEPTANCE.)

______________________________ Buyer

______________________________ Seller

______________________________ Buyer

______________________________ Seller

The form of this contract has been approved by the Texas Real Estate Commission. TREC forms are intended for use only by trained real estate licensees. No representation is made as to the legal validity or adequacy of any provision in any specific transactions. It is not suitable for complex transactions. Texas Real Estate Commission, P.O. Box 12188, Austin, TX 78711-2188, 1-800-250-8732 or (512) 459-6544 (http://www.trec.state.tx.us)TREC NO. 20-4. This form replaces TREC NO. 20-3.

BROKER INFORMATION AND RATIFICATION OF FEE

Listing Broker has agreed to pay Other Broker ______________________ of the total sales price when Listing Broker's fee is received. Escrow Agent is authorized and directed to pay Other Broker from Listing Broker's fee at closing.

____
Other Broker License No.

represents ❑ Seller as Listing Broker's subagent
❑ Buyer only as Buyer's agent

____
Associate Telephone

____
Broker Address

____
Telephone Facsimile

____
Listing Broker License No.

represents ❑ Seller and Buyer as an intermediary
❑ Seller only as Seller's agent

____
Listing Associate Telephone

____
Selling Associate Telephone

____
Broker Address

____
Telephone Facsimile

RECEIPT

Receipt of ❑ Contract and ❑ $ __________ Earnest Money in the form of ________________________ is acknowledged.

Escrow Agent: ______________________________

By: ______________________________

____
Address

____
City State Zip

Date: ______________________, ______

Telephone: (____) ______________________

Facsimile: (____) ______________________

APPROVED BY THE
TEXAS REAL ESTATE COMMISSION

02-10-97

ADDENDUM FOR SELLER'S DISCLOSURE OF INFORMATION ON LEAD-BASED PAINT AND LEAD-BASED PAINT HAZARDS AS REQUIRED BY FEDERAL LAW

CONCERNING THE PROPERTY AT ______________________________
(Street Address and City)

A. **LEAD WARNING STATEMENT:** "Every purchaser of any interest in residential real property on which a residential dwelling was built prior to 1978 is notified that such property may present exposure to lead from lead-based paint that may place young children at risk of developing lead poisoning. Lead poisoning in young children may produce permanent neurological damage, including learning disabilities, reduced intelligence quotient, behavioral problems, and impaired memory. Lead poisoning also poses a particular risk to pregnant women. The seller of any interest in residential real property is required to provide the buyer with any information on lead-based paint hazards from risk assessments or inspections in the seller's possession and notify the buyer of any known lead-based paint hazards. A risk assessment or inspection for possible lead-paint hazards is recommended prior to purchase."

B. **SELLER'S DISCLOSURE:**

1. PRESENCE OF LEAD-BASED PAINT AND/OR LEAD-BASED PAINT HAZARDS (check one box only):

   ❑(a) Known lead-based paint and/or lead-based paint hazards are present in the Property (explain): ______________________________.

   ❑(b) Seller has no actual knowledge of lead-based paint and/or lead-based paint hazards in the Property.

2. RECORDS AND REPORTS AVAILABLE TO SELLER (check one box only):

   ❑(a) Seller has provided the purchaser with all available records and reports pertaining to lead-based paint and/or lead-based paint hazards in the Property (list documents): ______________________________.

   ❑(b) Seller has no reports or records pertaining to lead-based paint and/or lead-based paint hazards in the Property.

C. **BUYER'S RIGHTS** (check one box only):

❑ 1. Buyer waives the opportunity to conduct a risk assessment or inspection of the Property for the presence of lead-based paint or lead-based paint hazards.

❑ 2. Within ten days after the effective date of this contract, Buyer may have the Property inspected for the presence of lead-based paint and/or lead-based paint hazards. If lead-based paint or lead-based paint hazards are present, Buyer may terminate this contract by giving Seller written notice within 14 days after the effective date of this contract.

D. **BUYER'S ACKNOWLEDGMENT** (check applicable boxes):

❑ 1. Buyer has received copies of all information listed above.

❑ 2. Buyer has received the pamphlet *Protect Your Family from Lead in Your Home.*

E. **BROKERS' ACKNOWLEDGMENT:** Brokers have informed Seller of Seller's obligations under 42 U.S.C. 4852d to: (a) provide Buyer with the federally approved pamphlet on lead poisoning prevention; (b) complete this addendum; (c) disclose any known lead-based paint and/or lead-based paint hazards in the Property; (d) deliver all records and reports to Buyer pertaining to lead-based paint and/or lead-based paint hazards in the Property; (e) provide Buyer a period of up to 10 days to have the Property inspected; and (f) retain a completed copy of this addendum for at least 3 years following the sale. Brokers are aware of their responsibility to ensure compliance.

F. **CERTIFICATION OF ACCURACY:** The following persons have reviewed the information above and certify, to the best of their knowledge, that the information they have provided is true and accurate.

Seller	Date	Buyer	Date
Seller	Date	Buyer	Date
Listing Broker	Date	Other Broker	Date

The form of this addendum has been approved for voluntary use by the Texas Real Estate Commission for use only with similarly approved or promulgated forms of contracts. No representation is made as to the legal validity or adequacy of any provision in any specific transactions. Texas Real Estate Commission, P.O. Box 12188, Austin, TX 78711-2188, 1-800-250-8732 or (512) 459-6544.

01A TREC No. OP-L

Transaction 3: 80% Conventional ARM without PMI

Utilizing: TREC 20-4, 35-1

Susan Helen Seller, an unmarried woman, will sell her lake home to Henry Arnold Homebuyer and his spouse, Hanna Sue Homebuyer. Not being located in a city, town or village, the property is described by metes and bounds as evidenced in the purchase agreement by attached Exhibit A. The property is not in a platted subdivision. It is located in Harrison County and has a mailing address of 42 Pleasure Lake Drive, Podunk, Texas 77072. Ms. Seller will have the leased security system and the water softener removed prior to closing.

The buyers will pay $126,000 for the property and apply for an 80 percent ARM loan within 5 days after the effective date of the contract. They feel they can get approval within 20 days and close within 25 days after the effective date of the contract. They have researched the market and know they can get a 15-year ARM loan with an interest rate of 5 percent or less for the first three years of the loan.

The Homebuyers have written a check for $1,500 made payable to Buyer's Choice Title Company. They will pay for the owner's title policy as well as the survey. They want three days to review the survey that will be furnished to their lender.

The house was built in 1979, so the lead addendum is not attached. The buyers received the seller's disclosure notice. The buyers accept the property in its present condition, provided the seller will repair the septic system and bring it up to current county code.

The buyers want possession at funding and will pay for the appraisal required by the lender. The buyers want all of their notices delivered to their attorney's office at 2225 High Street, Podunk, Texas 77071. Attorney Michael Phelps will review the offer prior to signing by the buyers.

The seller will receive her notices at the property address.

The buyers are customers who were shown the property by salesperson Sam Smith, from Happy Buyer Realty. The property was promoted through the MLS by Seller's Choice Realty Services. Lester Listor is the listing associate. The selling commission is 3.5 percent of the sales price.

The parties feel that it is a good idea to agree to try mediation before resorting to litigation. They sign the appropriate addendum and agree to select a mutually acceptable mediator if it becomes necessary.

PROMULGATED BY THE TEXAS REAL ESTATE COMMISSION (TREC) 11-8-99

ONE TO FOUR FAMILY RESIDENTIAL CONTRACT (RESALE)
ALL CASH, ASSUMPTION, THIRD PARTY CONVENTIONAL OR SELLER FINANCING

NOTICE: Not For Use For Condominium Transactions

1. **PARTIES:** ______________________________ (Seller) agrees to sell and convey to ______________________________ (Buyer) and Buyer agrees to buy from Seller the property described below.

2. **PROPERTY:** Lot ____________, Block _____, ______________________________ Addition, City of ______________________, ____________________ County, Texas, known as ______________________________ (Address/Zip Code), or as described on attached exhibit, together with the following items, if any: curtains and rods, draperies and rods, valances, blinds, window shades, screens, shutters, awnings, wall-to-wall carpeting, mirrors fixed in place, ceiling fans, attic fans, mail boxes, television antennas and satellite dish system with controls and equipment, permanently installed heating and air-conditioning units, window air-conditioning units, built-in security and fire detection equipment, plumbing and lighting fixtures including chandeliers, water softener, stove, built-in kitchen equipment, garage door openers with controls, built-in cleaning equipment, all swimming pool equipment and maintenance accessories, shrubbery, landscaping, permanently installed outdoor cooking equipment, built-in fireplace screens, artificial fireplace logs and all other property owned by Seller and attached to the above described real property except the following property which is not included: ______________________________
____
____
______________________________.

   All property sold by this contract is called the "Property." The Property ☐ is ☐ is not subject to mandatory membership in an owners' association. The TREC Addendum For Property Subject To Mandatory Membership In An Owners' Association ☐ is ☐ is not attached.

   NOTICE TO BUYER: If the Property is subject to mandatory membership in an owners' association, Seller notifies Buyer under §5.012, Texas Property Code, that, as a purchaser of property in the residential community in which the Property is located, you are obligated to be a member of an owners' association. Restrictive covenants governing the use and occupancy of the Property and a dedicatory instrument governing the establishment, maintenance, and operation of this residential community have been or will be recorded in the Real Property Records of the county in which the Property is located. Copies of the restrictive covenants and dedicatory instrument may be obtained from the county clerk. You are obligated to pay assessments to the owners' association. The amount of the assessments is subject to change. Your failure to pay the assessments could result in a lien on and the foreclosure of the Property.

3. **SALES PRICE:**
   A. Cash portion of Sales Price payable by Buyer at closing . . . . $____________
   B. Sum of all financing described below
      (excluding any private mortgage insurance [PMI] premium) . . . . $____________
   C. Sales Price (Sum of A and B) . . . . $____________

4. **FINANCING:** Within _____ days after the effective date of this contract Buyer shall apply for all third party financing or noteholder's approval of any assumption and make every reasonable effort to obtain financing or assumption approval. Financing or assumption approval will be deemed to have been obtained when the lender determines that Buyer has satisfied all of lender's financial requirements (those items relating to Buyer's net worth, income and creditworthiness). If financing (including any financed PMI premium) or assumption approval is not obtained within ______ days after the effective

One to Four Family Residential Contract Concerning______________________________ Page Two 11-8-99
(Address of Property)

date hereof, this contract will terminate and the earnest money will be refunded to Buyer. Each note to be executed hereunder must be secured by vendor's and deed of trust liens.

The portion of Sales Price not payable in cash will be paid as follows: (Check applicable boxes below)

❑ A. THIRD PARTY FINANCING:

❑ (1) This contract is subject to approval for Buyer of a third party first mortgage loan having a loan-to-value ratio not to exceed ____ % as established by such third party (excluding any financed PMI premium), due in full in _____ year(s), with interest not to exceed _____ % per annum for the first _____ year(s) of the loan. The loan will be ❑ with ❑ without PMI.

❑ (2) This contract is subject to approval for Buyer of a third party second mortgage loan having a loan-to-value ratio not to exceed ______ % as established by such third party (excluding any financed PMI premium), due in full in ______ year(s), with interest not to exceed _______ % per annum for the first _____ year(s) of the loan. The loan will be ❑ with ❑ without PMI.

❑ B. TEXAS VETERANS' HOUSING ASSISTANCE PROGRAM LOAN: This contract is subject to approval for Buyer of a Texas Veterans' Housing Assistance Program Loan (the Program Loan) of $_______________ for a period of at least ____________ years at the interest rate established by the Texas Veterans' Land Board at the time of closing.

❑ C. SELLER FINANCING: A promissory note from Buyer to Seller of $____________, bearing ____ % interest per annum, secured by vendor's and deed of trust liens, in accordance with the terms and conditions set forth in the attached TREC Seller Financing Addendum. If an owner policy of title insurance is furnished, Buyer shall furnish Seller with a mortgagee policy of title insurance.

❑ D. ASSUMPTION:

❑ (1) Buyer shall assume the unpaid principal balance of a first lien promissory note payable to ____
which unpaid balance at closing will be $ ______________. The total current monthly payment including principal, interest and any reserve deposits is $ ________________.
Buyer's initial payment will be the first payment due after closing.

❑ (2) Buyer shall assume the unpaid principal balance of a second lien promissory note payable to ____
which unpaid balance at closing will be $ _______________. The total current monthly payment including principal, interest and any reserve deposits is $ _______________.
Buyer's initial payment will be the first payment due after closing.

Buyer's assumption of an existing note includes all obligations imposed by the deed of trust securing the note.

If the unpaid principal balance(s) of any assumed loan(s) as of the Closing Date varies from the loan balance(s) stated above, the ❑ cash payable at closing ❑ Sales Price will be adjusted by the amount of any variance; provided, if the total principal balance of all assumed loans varies in an amount greater than $350.00 at closing, either party may terminate this contract and the earnest money will be refunded to Buyer unless the other party elects to eliminate the excess in the variance by an appropriate adjustment at closing. If the noteholder requires (a) payment of an assumption fee in excess of $ ____________in D(1) above or $ ________________ in D(2) above and Seller declines to pay such excess, or (b) an increase in the interest rate to more than _____ % in D(1) above, or ____ % in D(2) above, or (c) any other modification of the loan documents, Buyer may terminate this contract and the earnest money will be refunded to Buyer. A vendor's lien and deed of trust to secure assumption will be required which shall automatically be released on execution and delivery of a release by noteholder. If Seller is released from liability on any assumed note, the vendor's lien and deed of trust to secure assumption will not be required.

Initialed for identification by Buyer___________and Seller__________ 01A TREC NO. 20-4

One to Four Family Residential Contract Concerning________________________________ Page Three 11-8-99
(Address of Property)

NOTICE TO BUYER: The monthly payments, interest rates or other terms of some loans may be adjusted by the lender at or after closing. If you are concerned about the possibility of future adjustments, do not sign the contract without examining the notes and deeds of trust.
NOTICE TO SELLER: Your liability to pay the note assumed by Buyer will continue unless you obtain a release of liability from the lender. If you are concerned about future liability, you should use the TREC Release of Liability Addendum.

❑ E. CREDIT APPROVAL ON ASSUMPTION OR SELLER FINANCING: Within _____ days after the effective date of this contract, Buyer shall deliver to Seller ❑ credit report ❑ verification of employment, including salary ❑ verification of funds on deposit in financial institutions ❑ current financial statement to establish Buyer's creditworthiness for assumption approval or seller financing and ❑ ____
____
____.
If Buyer's documentation is not delivered within the specified time, Seller may terminate this contract by notice to Buyer within 7 days after expiration of the time for delivery, and the earnest money will be paid to Seller. If this contract is not so terminated, Seller will be deemed to have accepted Buyer's credit. If the documentation is timely delivered, and Seller determines in Seller's sole discretion that Buyer's credit is unacceptable, Seller may terminate this contract by notice to Buyer within 7 days after expiration of the time for delivery and the earnest money will be refunded to Buyer. If Seller does not so terminate this contract, Seller will be deemed to have accepted Buyer's credit. Buyer hereby authorizes any credit reporting agency to furnish to Seller at Buyer's sole expense copies of Buyer's credit reports.

5. **EARNEST MONEY:** Buyer shall deposit $______________ as earnest money with ____________ ______________________________ at ______________________________ (Address), as escrow agent, upon execution of this contract by both parties. Additional earnest money of $______________ must be deposited by Buyer with escrow agent on or before ________________, ________. If Buyer fails to deposit the earnest money as required by this contract, Buyer will be in default.

6. **TITLE POLICY AND SURVEY:**

❑ A. TITLE POLICY: Seller shall furnish to Buyer at ❑ Seller's ❑ Buyer's expense an owner policy of title insurance (the Title Policy) issued by ______________________________ (the Title Company) in the amount of the Sales Price, dated at or after closing, insuring Buyer against loss under the provisions of the Title Policy, subject to the promulgated exclusions (including existing building and zoning ordinances) and the following exceptions:

(1) Restrictive covenants common to the platted subdivision in which the Property is located.
(2) The standard printed exception for standby fees, taxes and assessments.
(3) Liens created as part of the financing described in Paragraph 4.
(4) Utility easements created by the dedication deed or plat of the subdivision in which the Property is located.
(5) Reservations or exceptions otherwise permitted by this contract or as may be approved by Buyer in writing.
(6) The standard printed exception as to discrepancies, conflicts, shortages in area or boundary lines, encroachments or protrusions, or overlapping improvements.
(7) The standard printed exception as to marital rights.
(8) The standard printed exception as to waters, tidelands, beaches, streams, and related matters.

Within 20 days after the Title Company receives a copy of this contract, Seller shall furnish to Buyer a commitment for title insurance (the Commitment) and, at Buyer's expense, legible copies of restrictive covenants and documents evidencing exceptions in the Commitment other than the

One to Four Family Residential Contract Concerning_______________________________________ Page Four 11-8-99
(Address of Property)

standard printed exceptions. Seller authorizes the Title Company to mail or hand deliver the Commitment and related documents to Buyer at Buyer's address shown below. If the Commitment is not delivered to Buyer within the specified time, the time for delivery will be automatically extended up to 15 days. Buyer will have 7 days after the receipt of the Commitment to object in writing to matters disclosed in the Commitment.

❑ B. SURVEY: (Check one box only)

❑ (1) Within ______ days after Buyer's receipt of a survey furnished to a third-party lender at ❑ Seller's ❑ Buyer's expense, Buyer may object in writing to any matter shown on the survey which constitutes a defect or encumbrance to title.

❑ (2) Within _____ days after the effective date of this contract, Buyer may object in writing to any matter which constitutes a defect or encumbrance to title shown on a survey obtained by Buyer at Buyer's expense.

The survey must be made by a Registered Professional Land Surveyor acceptable to the Title Company and any lender. Utility easements created by the dedication deed and plat of the subdivision in which the Property is located will not be a basis for objection.

Buyer may object to existing building and zoning ordinances, items 6A(1) through (8) above and matters shown on the survey if Buyer determines that any such ordinance, items or matters prohibits the following use or activity: ____

____

____.

Buyer's failure to object under Paragraph 6A or 6B within the time allowed will constitute a waiver of Buyer's right to object; except that the requirements in Schedule C of the Commitment will not be deemed to have been waived. Seller shall cure the timely objections of Buyer or any third party lender within 15 days from the date Seller receives the objections and the Closing Date will be extended as necessary. If objections are not cured by the extended Closing Date, this contract will terminate and the earnest money will be refunded to Buyer unless Buyer elects to waive the objections.

NOTICE TO SELLER AND BUYER:

(1) Broker advises Buyer to have an abstract of title covering the Property examined by an attorney of Buyer's selection, or Buyer should be furnished with or obtain a Title Policy. If a Title Policy is furnished, the Commitment should be promptly reviewed by an attorney of Buyer's choice due to the time limitations on Buyer's right to object.

(2) If the Property is situated in a utility or other statutorily created district providing water, sewer, drainage, or flood control facilities and services, Chapter 49 of the Texas Water Code requires Seller to deliver and Buyer to sign the statutory notice relating to the tax rate, bonded indebtedness, or standby fee of the district prior to final execution of this contract.

(3) If the Property abuts the tidally influenced waters of the state, Section 33.135, Texas Natural Resources Code, requires a notice regarding coastal area property to be included in the contract. An addendum either promulgated by TREC or required by the parties should be used.

(4) Buyer is advised that the presence of wetlands, toxic substances, including asbestos and wastes or other environmental hazards or the presence of a threatened or endangered species or its habitat may affect Buyer's intended use of the Property. If Buyer is concerned about these matters, an addendum either promulgated by TREC or required by the parties should be used.

(5) If the Property is located outside the limits of a municipality, Seller notifies Buyer under §5.011, Texas Property Code, that the Property may now or later be included in the extraterritorial jurisdiction of a municipality and may now or later be subject to annexation by the municipality. Each municipality maintains a map that depicts its boundaries and extraterritorial jurisdiction. To determine if the Property is located within a municipality's extraterritorial jurisdiction or is likely to be located within a municipality's extraterritorial jurisdiction, contact all municipalities located in the general proximity of the Property for further information.

(6) Unless expressly prohibited in writing by the parties, Seller may continue to show the Property for sale and to receive, negotiate and accept back up offers.

Initialed for identification by Buyer__________ and Seller__________ 01A TREC NO. 20-4

(7) Any residential service contract that is purchased in connection with this transaction should be reviewed for the scope of coverage, exclusions and limitations. **The purchase of a residential service contract is optional. Similar coverage may be purchased from various companies authorized to do business in Texas.**

7. **PROPERTY CONDITION:**

A. INSPECTIONS, ACCESS AND UTILITIES: Buyer may have the Property inspected by an inspector selected by Buyer, licensed by TREC or otherwise permitted by law to make such inspections. Seller shall permit access to the Property at reasonable times for inspection, repairs and treatment and for reinspection after repairs and treatment have been completed. Seller shall pay for turning on utilities for inspection and reinspection.

B. SELLER'S DISCLOSURE NOTICE PURSUANT TO SECTION 5.008, TEXAS PROPERTY CODE (Notice) (check one box only):

❑ (1) Buyer has received the Notice.

❑ (2) Buyer has not received the Notice. Within _______ days after the effective date of this contract, Seller shall deliver the Notice to Buyer. If Buyer does not receive the Notice, Buyer may terminate this contract at any time prior to the closing. If Seller delivers the Notice, Buyer may terminate this contract for any reason within 7 days after Buyer receives the Notice or prior to the closing, whichever first occurs.

❑ (3) The Texas Property Code does not require this Seller to furnish the Notice.

C. SELLER'S DISCLOSURE OF LEAD-BASED PAINT AND LEAD-BASED PAINT HAZARDS is required by Federal law for a residential dwelling constructed prior to 1978. An addendum providing such disclosure ❑ is ❑ is not attached.

D. ACCEPTANCE OF PROPERTY CONDITION: (check one box only):

❑ (1) In addition to any earnest money deposited with escrow agent, Buyer has paid Seller $____________ (the "Option Fee") for the unrestricted right to terminate this contract by giving notice of termination to Seller within _______ days after the effective date of this contract. If Buyer gives notice of termination within the time specified, the Option Fee will not be refunded, however, any earnest money will be refunded to Buyer. If Buyer does not give notice of termination within the time specified, Buyer will be deemed to have accepted the Property in its current condition and the Option Fee ❑ will ❑ will not be credited to the Sales Price at closing.

❑ (2) Buyer accepts the Property in its present condition; provided Seller, at Seller's expense, shall complete the following repairs and treatment: ________________________________
____
____
____.

E. LENDER REQUIRED REPAIRS AND TREATMENTS (REPAIRS): Unless otherwise agreed in writing, neither party is obligated to pay for lender required repairs or treatments for wood destroying insects. If the cost of lender required repairs exceeds 5% of the Sales Price, Buyer may terminate this contract.

F. COMPLETION OF REPAIRS AND TREATMENT. Unless otherwise agreed by the parties in writing, Seller shall complete all agreed repairs and treatment prior to the Closing Date. Repairs and treatments must be performed by persons who regularly provide such repairs or treatments. At Buyer's election, any transferable warranties received by Seller with respect to the repairs will be transferred to Buyer at Buyer's expense. If Seller fails to complete any agreed repairs and treatment prior to the Closing Date, Buyer may do so and the Closing Date will be extended up to 15 days, if necessary, to complete repairs and treatment or treatments for wood destroying insects.

8. **BROKERS' FEES:** All obligations of the parties for payment of brokers' fees are contained in separate written agreements.

One to Four Family Residential Contract Concerning______________________________Page Six 11-8-99
(Address of Property)

9. **CLOSING:** The closing of the sale will be on or before ______________________, ______, or within 7 days after objections to matters disclosed in the Commitment or by the survey have been cured, whichever date is later (the Closing Date). *If financing or assumption approval has been obtained pursuant to Paragraph 4,* the Closing Date will be extended up to 15 days if necessary to comply with lender's closing requirements (for example, appraisal, survey, insurance policies, lender-required repairs, closing documents). If either party fails to close this sale by the Closing Date, the non-defaulting party will be entitled to exercise the remedies contained in Paragraph 15. At closing Seller shall furnish tax statements or certificates showing no delinquent taxes and a general warranty deed conveying good and indefeasible title showing no additional exceptions to those permitted in Paragraph 6.

10. **POSSESSION:** Seller shall deliver possession of the Property to Buyer on ______________ in its present or required repaired condition, ordinary wear and tear excepted. Any possession by Buyer prior to closing or by Seller after closing which is not authorized by a temporary lease form promulgated by TREC or required by the parties will establish a tenancy at sufferance relationship between the parties. *Consult your insurance agent prior to change of ownership or possession as insurance coverage may be limited or terminated. The absence of a written lease or appropriate insurance coverage may expose the parties to economic loss.*

11. **SPECIAL PROVISIONS:** (Insert only factual statements and business details applicable to this sale. TREC rules prohibit licensees from adding factual statements or business details for which a contract addendum, lease or other form has been promulgated by TREC for mandatory use.)

12. **SETTLEMENT AND OTHER EXPENSES:**
   A. The following expenses must be paid at or prior to closing:
      (1) Appraisal fees will be paid by ______________________________.
      (2) The total of loan discount fees (including any Texas Veterans' Housing Assistance Program Participation Fee) may not exceed ________% of the loan of which Seller shall pay _____________ and Buyer shall pay the remainder. The total of any buydown fees may not exceed _____________which will be paid by ______________________.
      (3) Seller's Expenses: Releases of existing liens, including prepayment penalties and recording fees; release of Seller's loan liability; tax statements or certificates; preparation of deed; one-half of escrow fee; and other expenses stipulated to be paid by Seller under other provisions of this contract.
      (4) Buyer's Expenses: Loan application, origination and commitment fees; loan assumption costs; preparation and recording of deed of trust to secure assumption; lender required expenses

incident to new loans, including PMI premium, preparation of loan documents, loan related inspection fee, recording fees, tax service and research fees, warehouse or underwriting fees, copies of restrictions and easements, amortization schedule, premiums for mortgagee title policies and endorsements required by lender, credit reports, photos; required premiums for flood and hazard insurance; required reserve deposit for insurance premiums and ad valorem taxes; interest on all monthly installment notes from date of disbursements to one month prior to dates of first monthly payments; customary Program Loan costs for Buyer; one-half of escrow fee; and other expenses stipulated to be paid by Buyer under other provisions of this contract.

B. If any expense exceeds an amount expressly stated in this contract for such expense to be paid by a party, that party may terminate this contract unless the other party agrees to pay such excess. In no event will Buyer pay charges and fees expressly prohibited by the Texas Veterans' Housing Assistance Program or other governmental loan program regulations.

13. **PRORATIONS**: Taxes for the current year, interest, maintenance fees, assessments, dues and rents will be prorated through the Closing Date. If taxes for the current year vary from the amount prorated at closing, the parties shall adjust the prorations when tax statements for the current year are available. *If a loan is assumed* and the lender maintains an escrow account, the escrow account must be transferred to Buyer without any deficiency. Buyer shall reimburse Seller for the amount in the transferred account. Buyer shall pay the premium for a new insurance policy. If taxes are not paid at or prior to closing, Buyer will be obligated to pay taxes for the current year.

14. **CASUALTY LOSS:** If any part of the Property is damaged or destroyed by fire or other casualty loss after the effective date of the contract, Seller shall restore the Property to its previous condition as soon as reasonably possible, but in any event by the Closing Date. If Seller fails to do so due to factors beyond Seller's control, Buyer may either (a) terminate this contract and the earnest money will be refunded to Buyer (b) extend the time for performance up to 15 days and the Closing Date will be extended as necessary or (c) accept the Property in its damaged condition and accept an assignment of insurance proceeds. Seller's obligations under this paragraph are independent of any obligations of Seller under Paragraph 7.

15. **DEFAULT:** If Buyer fails to comply with this contract, Buyer will be in default, and Seller may either (a) enforce specific performance, seek such other relief as may be provided by law, or both, or (b) terminate this contract and receive the earnest money as liquidated damages, thereby releasing both parties from this contract. If, due to factors beyond Seller's control, Seller fails within the time allowed to make any non-casualty repairs or deliver the Commitment, Buyer may either (a) extend the time for performance up to 15 days and the Closing Date will be extended as necessary or (b) terminate this contract as the sole remedy and receive the earnest money. If Seller fails to comply with this contract for any other reason, Seller will be in default and Buyer may either (a) enforce specific performance, seek such other relief as may be provided by law, or both, or (b) terminate this contract and receive the earnest money, thereby releasing both parties from this contract.

16. **DISPUTE RESOLUTION:** It is the policy of the State of Texas to encourage the peaceable resolution of disputes through alternative dispute resolution procedures. The parties are encouraged to use an addendum approved by TREC to submit to mediation disputes which cannot be resolved in good faith through informal discussion.

17. **ATTORNEY'S FEES:** The prevailing party in any legal proceeding brought under or with respect to the transaction described in this contract is entitled to recover from the non-prevailing party all costs of such proceeding and reasonable attorney's fees.

One to Four Family Residential Contract Concerning____ Page Eight 11-8-99
(Address of Property)

18. **ESCROW:** The earnest money is deposited with escrow agent with the understanding that escrow agent is not (a) a party to this contract and does not have any liability for the performance or nonperformance of any party to this contract, (b) liable for interest on the earnest money and (c) liable for any loss of earnest money caused by the failure of any financial institution in which the earnest money has been deposited unless the financial institution is acting as escrow agent. At closing, the earnest money must be applied first to any cash down payment, then to Buyer's closing costs and any excess refunded to Buyer. If both parties make written demand for the earnest money, escrow agent may require payment of unpaid expenses incurred on behalf of the parties and a written release of liability of escrow agent from all parties. If one party makes written demand for the earnest money, escrow agent shall give notice of the demand by providing to the other party a copy of the demand. If escrow agent does not receive written objection to the demand from the other party within 30 days after notice to the other party, escrow agent may disburse the earnest money to the party making demand reduced by the amount of unpaid expenses incurred on behalf of the party receiving the earnest money and escrow agent may pay the same to the creditors. If escrow agent complies with the provisions of this paragraph, each party hereby releases escrow agent from all adverse claims related to the disbursal of the earnest money. Escrow agent's notice to the other party will be effective when deposited in the U. S. Mail, postage prepaid, certified mail, return receipt requested, addressed to the other party at such party's address shown below. Notice of objection to the demand will be deemed effective upon receipt by escrow agent.

19. **REPRESENTATIONS:** Seller represents that as of the Closing Date (a) there will be no liens, assessments, or security interests against the Property which will not be satisfied out of the sales proceeds unless securing payment of any loans assumed by Buyer and (b) assumed loans will not be in default. If any representation in this contract is untrue on the Closing Date, this contract may be terminated by Buyer and the earnest money will be refunded to Buyer. All representations contained in this contract will survive closing.

20. **FEDERAL TAX REQUIREMENT:** If Seller is a "foreign person," as defined by applicable law, or if Seller fails to deliver an affidavit that Seller is not a "foreign person," then Buyer shall withhold from the sales proceeds an amount sufficient to comply with applicable tax law and deliver the same to the Internal Revenue Service together with appropriate tax forms. IRS regulations require filing written reports if cash in excess of specified amounts is received in the transaction.

21. **AGREEMENT OF PARTIES:** This contract contains the entire agreement of the parties and cannot be changed except by their written agreement. Addenda which are a part of this contract are (list):
____
____
____
____
____
____.

22. **CONSULT YOUR ATTORNEY:** Real estate licensees cannot give legal advice. This contract is intended to be legally binding. READ IT CAREFULLY. If you do not understand the effect of this contract, consult your attorney BEFORE signing.

Buyer's
Attorney is:____________________________

Seller's
Attorney is:____________________________

Initialed for identification by Buyer__________ and Seller__________ 01A TREC NO. 20-4

One to Four Family Residential Contract Concerning________________________________ Page Nine 11-8-99
(Address of Property)

23. **NOTICES:** All notices from one party to the other must be in writing and are effective when mailed to, hand-delivered at, or transmitted by facsimile machine as follows:

To Buyer at: **To Seller at:**

________________________ ________________________

________________________ ________________________

________________________ ________________________

Telephone:(___)________________ Telephone:(___)________________

Facsimile:(___) ________________ Facsimile:(___) ________________

EXECUTED the ______day of ____________________, ______ (THE EFFECTIVE DATE). (BROKER: FILL IN THE DATE OF FINAL ACCEPTANCE.)

________________________ ________________________
Buyer Seller

________________________ ________________________
Buyer Seller

The form of this contract has been approved by the Texas Real Estate Commission. TREC forms are intended for use only by trained real estate licensees. No representation is made as to the legal validity or adequacy of any provision in any specific transactions. It is not suitable for complex transactions. Texas Real Estate Commission, P.O. Box 12188, Austin, TX 78711-2188, 1-800-250-8732 or (512) 459-6544 (http://www.trec.state.tx.us)TREC NO. 20-4. This form replaces TREC NO. 20-3.

BROKER INFORMATION AND RATIFICATION OF FEE

Listing Broker has agreed to pay Other Broker ________________ of the total sales price when Listing Broker's fee is received. Escrow Agent is authorized and directed to pay Other Broker from Listing Broker's fee at closing.

________________________ ________________________
Other Broker License No. Listing Broker License No.

represents ❑ Seller as Listing Broker's subagent
❑ Buyer only as Buyer's agent

represents ❑ Seller and Buyer as an intermediary
❑ Seller only as Seller's agent

____
Listing Associate Telephone

________________________ ________________________
Associate Telephone Selling Associate Telephone

________________________ ________________________
Broker Address Broker Address

________________________ ________________________
Telephone Facsimile Telephone Facsimile

RECEIPT

Receipt of ❑ Contract and ❑ $ __________ Earnest Money in the form of ____________________ is acknowledged.

Escrow Agent: ________________________ Date: ________________, ______

By: ________________________

________________________ Telephone: (____) ________________
Address

________________________ Facsimile: (____) ________________
City State Zip

06-15-98

PROMULGATED BY THE TEXAS REAL ESTATE COMMISSION (TREC)

AGREEMENT FOR MEDIATION

ADDENDUM TO CONTRACT CONCERNING THE PROPERTY AT

____

(Street Address and City)

The parties to the Contract and any broker who signs this addendum agree to negotiate in good faith in an effort to resolve any dispute related to the Contract that may arise between the parties or between a party and a broker.

If the dispute cannot be resolved by negotiation, the parties to the dispute shall submit the dispute to mediation before resorting to litigation.

This Agreement for Mediation will survive closing.

❑ If the need for mediation arises, the parties to the dispute shall choose a mutually acceptable mediator and shall share the cost of mediation services equally.

❑ If the need for mediation arises, mediation services will be provided by ______________________ ____________________and the parties to the dispute shall share the cost of mediation services equally.

NOTE: Mediation is a voluntary dispute resolution process in which the parties to the dispute meet with an impartial person, called a mediator, who would help to resolve the dispute informally and confidentially. Mediators facilitate the resolution of disputes but cannot impose binding decisions. The parties to the dispute must agree before any settlement is binding.

Date: ______________________________

______________________ Buyer	______________________ Seller
______________________ Buyer	______________________ Seller
______________________ Other Broker	______________________ Listing Broker
By: ______________________	By: ______________________

The form of this addendum has been approved for voluntary use by the Texas Real Estate Commission for use only with similarly approved or promulgated forms of contracts. No representation is made as to the legal validity or adequacy of any provision in any specific transactions. (06-98) Texas Real Estate Commission, P.O. Box 12188, Austin, TX 78711-2188, 1-800-250-8732 or (512)459-6544. (http://www.trec.state.tx.us) TREC No. 35-1. This form replaces TREC No. 35-0.

Transaction 4: FHA 203b Acquisition Cost

Utilizing: TREC 21-4, Lead-Based Paint Addendum

Manuel Moritz and his wife, Estella Moritz, are first-time buyers with limited funds who want to utilize a FHA 203b loan. They want to buy the property owned by Barbara Johnson, who owns it as her separate property.

Ms. Johnson is asking $52,000 but the Moritzes offer $48,000. They will apply for the FHA insured loan within five days after the date of the contract and anticipate that they can get loan approval within 40 days and close within 45 days after the effective date of the contract. Knowing that it will table fund, the Moritzes request possession at funding.

The property is located in Section 2 of the Rivermont Addition of Houston, Harris County, Texas. It is identified as Lot 17, Block 5 on the plat and is commonly known as 2129 Bingle Road. The property receives mail in zip code 77027 and is not subject to mandatory membership in an owners' association.

The Moritzes will utilize an FHA 203b insured loan, which will enable them to move in with minimal cash up front. They can obtain a 30-year fixed rate loan at 7.75 percent annual interest.

$800 is deposited with Buyer's Choice Title Company at the time the contract is negotiated. The buyers will deposit an additional $1,000 twenty days after the effective date of the contract.

Ms. Johnson will pay for the owner's title policy, as well as the survey required by the lender. The buyers want two days to review the survey.

The buyers have received the disclosure notice required by section 5.008 of the Texas Property Code prior to making their offer. The house was built in 1955. Ms. Johnson had a lead assessment done and furnished the buyers with a copy. The lead addendum is made a part of the contract to furnish the HUD required lead notice language.

Mr. Moritz has been involved in repairing homes for several years. Although the agent advised that they have a professional inspection done, the buyers choose to accept the property in its present condition and ask that no repairs be done by the seller.

The buyers will pay for the appraisal. They ask the seller to pay one-half of any required discount points. The research by their agent shows that the maximum number of discount points anyone is charging is 2. They will pay the 2.25 points of mortgage insurance premium by adding it to their loan.

The sale is being handled by John Denton of John Denton, REALTORS®, license #0343567. Mr. Denton has been authorized in writing by both parties to function as an intermediary. Mr. Denton does not choose to appoint associates to communicate with and advise the parties.

11-08-99

PROMULGATED BY THE TEXAS REAL ESTATE COMMISSION (TREC)

ONE TO FOUR FAMILY RESIDENTIAL CONTRACT (RESALE)
FHA INSURED OR VA GUARANTEED FINANCING

Notice: Not For Use For Condominium Transactions

1. **PARTIES:** ______________________________ (Seller) agrees to sell and convey to ______________________________ (Buyer) and Buyer agrees to buy from Seller the Property described below.

2. **PROPERTY:** Lot _______, Block _______, ______________________________Addition, City of ______________________, ______________________ County, Texas, known as ______________________________ (Address/Zip Code), or as described on attached exhibit, together with the following items, if any: curtains and rods, draperies and rods, valances, blinds, window shades, screens, shutters, awnings, wall-to-wall carpeting, mirrors fixed in place, ceiling fans, attic fans, mail boxes, television antennas and satellite dish system with controls and equipment, permanently installed heating and air conditioning units, window air conditioning units, built-in security and fire detection equipment, plumbing and lighting fixtures, including chandeliers, water softener, stove, built-in kitchen equipment, garage door openers with controls, built-in cleaning equipment, all swimming pool equipment and maintenance accessories, shrubbery, landscaping, permanently installed outdoor cooking equipment, built-in fireplace screens, artificial fireplace logs and all other property owned by Seller and attached to the above described real property except the following property which is not included:______________________________
______________________________.
All property sold by this contract is called the "Property." The Property ❑ is ❑ is not subject to mandatory membership in an owners' association. The TREC Addendum For Property Subject To Mandatory Membership In An Owners' Association ❑ is ❑ is not attached.
NOTICE TO BUYER: If the Property is subject to mandatory membership in an owners' association, Seller notifies Buyer under §5.012, Texas Property Code, that, as a purchaser of property in the residential community in which the Property is located, you are obligated to be a member of an owners' association. Restrictive covenants governing the use and occupancy of the Property and a dedicatory instrument governing the establishment, maintenance, and operation of this residential community have been or will be recorded in the Real Property Records of the county in which the Property is located. Copies of the restrictive covenants and dedicatory instrument may be obtained from the county clerk. You are obligated to pay assessments to the owners' association. The amount of the assessments is subject to change. Your failure to pay the assessments could result in a lien on and the foreclosure of the Property.

3. **SALES PRICE:**
   A. Cash portion of the Sales Price payable by Buyer at closing . . . . $______________
   B. Sum of all financing described below (excluding VA Funding Fee or FHA Mortgage Insurance Premium [MIP]) . . . . $______________
   C. Sales Price (Sum of A and B) . . . . $______________

4. **FINANCING:** Within _______ days after the effective date of this contract Buyer shall apply for and make every reasonable effort to obtain financing. Financing will be deemed to have been obtained when the lender has determined that Buyer has satisfied all of lender's financial requirements (those items relating to Buyer's net worth, income and creditworthiness). If financing (including any financed MIP or Funding Fee) is not obtained within _______ days after the effective date hereof, this contract will terminate and the earnest money will refunded to Buyer. The portion of the Sales Price not payable in cash will be paid as follows: (Check applicable boxes below)
   ❑ A. FHA INSURED FINANCING: This contract is subject to approval for Buyer of a Section ________ FHA insured loan of not less than $_____________ (excluding any financed MIP), amortizable monthly for not less than _____ years, with interest not to exceed _______% per annum for the first ________year(s) of the loan.
   As required by HUD-FHA, if FHA valuation is unknown, *"It is expressly agreed that, notwithstanding any other provisions of this contract, the purchaser* (Buyer) *shall not be obligated to complete the purchase of the Property described herein or to incur any penalty by forfeiture of earnest money*

FHA or VA Residential Contract Concerning____Page Two 11-08-99
(Address of Property)

deposits or otherwise unless the purchaser (Buyer) *has been given in accordance with HUD/FHA or VA requirements a written statement issued by the Federal Housing Commissioner, Department of Veterans Affairs, or a Direct Endorsement Lender setting forth the appraised value of the Property of not less than $_______________. The purchaser* (Buyer) *shall have the privilege and option of proceeding with consummation of the contract without regard to the amount of the appraised valuation. The appraised valuation is arrived at to determine the maximum mortgage the Department of Housing and Urban Development will insure. HUD does not warrant the value or the condition of the Property. The purchaser* (Buyer) *should satisfy himself/herself that the price and the condition of the Property are acceptable."* If the FHA appraised value of the Property (excluding closing costs and MIP) is less than the Sales Price (3C above), Seller may reduce the Sales Price to an amount equal to the FHA appraised value (excluding closing costs and MIP) and the parties to the sale shall close the sale at such lower Sales Price with appropriate adjustments to 3A and 3B above.

❑ B. VA GUARANTEED FINANCING: This contract is subject to approval for Buyer of a VA guaranteed loan of not less than $___________(excluding any financed Funding Fee), amortizable monthly for not less than_____ years, with interest not to exceed _____ % per annum for the first _____ year(s) of the loan.

VA NOTICE TO BUYER: *"It is expressly agreed that, notwithstanding any other provisions of this contract, the Buyer shall not incur any penalty by forfeiture of earnest money or otherwise or be obligated to complete the purchase of the Property described herein, if the contract purchase price or cost exceeds the reasonable value of the Property established by the Department of Veterans Affairs. The Buyer shall, however, have the privilege and option of proceeding with the consummation of this contract without regard to the amount of the reasonable value established by the Department of Veterans Affairs."*

If Buyer elects to complete the purchase at an amount in excess of the reasonable value established by VA, Buyer shall pay such excess amount in cash from a source which Buyer agrees to disclose to the VA and which Buyer represents will not be from borrowed funds except as approved by VA. If VA reasonable value of the Property is less than the Sales Price (3C above), Seller may reduce the Sales Price to an amount equal to the VA reasonable value and the parties to the sale shall close at such lower Sales Price with appropriate adjustments to 3A and 3B above.

❑ C. TEXAS VETERANS' HOUSING ASSISTANCE PROGRAM LOAN: This contract is subject to approval for Buyer of a Texas Veterans' Housing Assistance Program Loan of $______________ for a period of at least ______ years at the interest rate established by the Texas Veterans' Land Board at the time of closing.

5. **EARNEST MONEY:** Buyer shall deposit $______________ as earnest money with ________________ ________________________________ at ____ (Address), as escrow agent, upon execution of this contract by both parties. Additional earnest money of $ __________________ must be deposited by Buyer with escrow agent on or before ___________________ , _____. If Buyer fails to deposit the earnest money as required by this contract, Buyer will be in default.

6. **TITLE POLICY AND SURVEY:**

❑ A. TITLE POLICY: Seller shall furnish to Buyer at ❑ Seller's ❑ Buyer's expense an owner policy of title insurance (the Title Policy) issued by ____ (the Title Company) in the amount of the Sales Price, dated at or after closing, insuring Buyer against loss under the provisions of the Title Policy, subject to the promulgated exclusions (including existing building and zoning ordinances) and the following exceptions:

(1) Restrictive covenants common to the platted subdivision in which the Property is located.
(2) The standard printed exception for standby fees, taxes and assessments.
(3) Liens created as part of the financing described in Paragraph 4.
(4 Utility easements created by the dedication deed or plat of the subdivision in which the Property is located.
(5) Reservations or exceptions otherwise permitted by this contract or as may be approved by Buyer in writing.
(6) The standard printed exception as to discrepancies, conflicts, shortages in area or boundary lines, encroachments or protrusions, or overlapping improvements.
(7) The standard printed exception as to marital rights.
(8) The standard printed exception as to waters, tidelands, beaches, streams, and related matters.

FHA or VA Residential Contract Concerning____ Page Three 11-08-99
(Address of Property)

Within 20 days after the Title Company receives a copy of this contract, Seller shall furnish to Buyer a commitment for title insurance (the Commitment) and, at Buyer's expense, legible copies of restrictive covenants and documents evidencing exceptions in the Commitment other than the standard printed exceptions. Seller authorizes the Title Company to mail or hand deliver the Commitment and related documents to Buyer at Buyer's address shown below. If the Commitment is not delivered to Buyer within the specified time, the time for delivery will be automatically extended up to 15 days. Buyer will have 7 days after the receipt of the Commitment to object in writing to matters disclosed in the Commitment.

❑ B. SURVEY: Within ________ days after Buyer's receipt of a survey furnished to a third-party lender at ❑ Seller's ❑ Buyer's expense, Buyer may object in writing to any matter shown on the survey which constitutes a defect or encumbrance to title.
The survey must be made by a Registered Professional Land Surveyor acceptable to the Title Company and any lender. Utility easements created by the dedication deed and plat of the subdivision in which the Property is located will not be a basis for objection.

Buyer may object to existing building and zoning ordinances, items 6A(1) through (8) above and matters shown on the survey if Buyer determines that any such ordinance, items or matters prohibits the following use or activity:____
____.

Buyer's failure to object under Paragraph 6A or 6B within the time allowed will constitute a waiver of Buyer's right to object; except that the requirements in Schedule C of the Commitment will not be deemed to have been waived. Seller shall cure the timely objections of Buyer or any third party lender within 15 days from the date Seller receives the objections and the Closing Date will be extended as necessary. If objections are not cured by the extended Closing Date, this contract will terminate and the earnest money will be refunded to Buyer unless Buyer elects to waive the objections.

NOTICE TO SELLER AND BUYER:

(1) Broker advises Buyer to have an abstract of title covering the Property examined by an attorney of Buyer's selection, or Buyer should be furnished with or obtain a Title Policy. If a Title Policy is furnished, the Commitment should be promptly reviewed by an attorney of Buyer's choice due to the time limitations on Buyer's right to object.

(2) If the Property is situated in a utility or other statutorily created district providing water, sewer, drainage, or flood control facilities and services, Chapter 49 of the Texas Water Code requires Seller to deliver and Buyer to sign the statutory notice relating to the tax rate, bonded indebtedness, or standby fee of the district prior to final execution of this contract.

(3) If the Property abuts the tidally influenced waters of the state, Section 33.135, Texas Natural Resources Code, requires a notice regarding coastal area property to be included in the contract. An addendum either promulgated by TREC or required by the parties should be used.

(4) Buyer is advised that the presence of wetlands, toxic substances including asbestos and wastes or other environmental hazards or the presence of a threatened or endangered species or its habitat may affect Buyer's intended use of the Property. If Buyer is concerned about these matters, an addendum either promulgated by TREC or required by the parties should be used.

(5) If the Property is located outside the limits of a municipality, Seller notifies Buyer under §5.011, Texas Property Code, that the Property may now or later be included in the extraterritorial jurisdiction of a municipality and may now or later be subject to annexation by the municipality. Each municipality maintains a map that depicts its boundaries and extraterritorial jurisdiction. To determine if the Property is located within a municipality's extraterritorial jurisdiction or is likely to be located within a municipality's extraterritorial jurisdiction, contact all municipalities located in the general proximity of the Property for further information.

(6) Unless expressly prohibited in writing by the parties, Seller may continue to show the Property for sale and to receive, negotiate and accept back-up offers.

(7) Any residential service contract that is purchased in connection with this transaction should be reviewed for the scope of coverage, exclusions and limitations. **The purchase of a residential service contract is optional. Similar coverage may be purchased from various companies authorized to do business in Texas.**

7. **PROPERTY CONDITION:**

A. INSPECTIONS, ACCESS AND UTILITIES: Buyer may have the Property inspected by an inspector

selected by Buyer, licensed by TREC or otherwise permitted by law to make such inspections. Seller shall permit access to the Property at reasonable times for inspection, repairs and treatment and for reinspection after repairs and treatment have been completed. Seller shall pay for turning on utilities for inspection and reinspection.

B. SELLER'S DISCLOSURE NOTICE PURSUANT TO SECTION 5.008, TEXAS PROPERTY CODE (Notice) (check one box only):

❑ (1) Buyer has received the Notice.

❑ (2) Buyer has not received the Notice. Within _______ days after the effective date of this contract, Seller shall deliver the Notice to Buyer. If Buyer does not receive the Notice, Buyer may terminate this contract at any time prior to the closing. If Seller delivers the Notice, Buyer may terminate this contract for any reason within 7 days after Buyer receives the Notice or prior to the closing, whichever first occurs.

❑ (3) The Texas Property Code does not require this Seller to furnish the Notice.

C. SELLER'S DISCLOSURE OF LEAD-BASED PAINT AND LEAD-BASED PAINT HAZARDS is required by Federal law for a residential dwelling constructed prior to 1978. An addendum providing such disclosure ❑ is ❑ is not attached.

D. ACCEPTANCE OF PROPERTY CONDITION: (check one box only):

❑ (1) In addition to any earnest money deposited with escrow agent, Buyer has paid Seller $_____________ (the "Option Fee") for the unrestricted right to terminate this contract by giving notice of termination to Seller within _______ days after the effective date of this contract. If Buyer gives notice of termination within the time specified, the Option Fee will not be refunded, however, any earnest money will be refunded to Buyer. If Buyer does not give notice of termination within the time specified, Buyer will be deemed to have accepted the Property in its current condition and the Option Fee ❑ will ❑ will not be credited to the Sales Price at closing.

❑ (2) Buyer accepts the Property in its present condition; provided Seller, at Seller's expense, shall complete the following repairs and treatment: ______________________________
____
____.

E. LENDER REQUIRED REPAIRS AND TREATMENTS (REPAIRS): Unless otherwise agreed in writing, neither party is obligated to pay for lender required repairs or treatments for wood destroying insects. If the cost of lender required repairs exceeds 5% of the Sales Price, Buyer may terminate this contract.

F. COMPLETION OF REPAIRS AND TREATMENT. Unless otherwise agreed by the parties in writing, Seller shall complete all agreed repairs and treatment prior to the Closing Date. Repairs and treatments must be performed by persons who regularly provide such repairs or treatments. At Buyer's election, any transferable warranties received by Seller with respect to the repairs will be transferred to Buyer at Buyer's expense. If Seller fails to complete any agreed repairs and treatment prior to the Closing Date, Buyer may do so and the Closing Date will be extended up to 15 days, if necessary, to complete repairs and treatment.

8. **BROKERS' FEES:** All obligations of the parties for payment of brokers' fees are contained in separate written agreements.

9. **CLOSING:** The closing of the sale will be on or before ____________________________, ______, or within 7 days after objections to matters disclosed in the Commitment or by the survey have been cured, whichever date is later (the Closing Date). *If financing has been obtained pursuant to Paragraph 4,* the Closing Date will be extended up to 15 days if necessary to comply with lender's closing requirements, for example: appraisal, survey, insurance policies, lender-required repairs, closing documents). If either party fails to close this sale by the Closing Date, the non-defaulting party will be entitled to exercise the remedies contained in Paragraph 15. At closing Seller shall furnish tax statements or certificates showing no delinquent taxes and a general warranty deed conveying good and indefeasible title showing no additional exceptions to those permitted in Paragraph 6.

10. **POSSESSION:** Seller shall deliver possession of the Property to Buyer on ____________________ in its present or required repaired condition, ordinary wear and tear excepted. Any possession by Buyer prior to closing or by Seller after closing which is not authorized by a temporary lease form promulgated by TREC or required by the parties will establish a tenancy at sufferance relationship between the parties. *Consult your insurance agent prior to change of ownership or possession as insurance*

coverage may be limited or terminated. The absence of a written lease or appropriate insurance coverage may expose the parties to economic loss.

11. **SPECIAL PROVISIONS:** (Insert only factual statements and business details applicable to this sale. TREC rules prohibit licensees from adding factual statements or business details for which a contract addendum, lease or other form has been promulgated by TREC for mandatory use.)

12. **SETTLEMENT AND OTHER EXPENSES:**
   A. The following expenses must be paid at or prior to closing:
      (1) Appraisal fees will be paid by ______________________________.
      (2) The total of the loan discount fees (including any Texas Veterans' Housing Assistance Program Participation Fee) may not exceed _________% of the loan of which Seller shall pay ___________and Buyer shall pay the remainder. The total of any buydown fees may not exceed _______________ which will be paid by ______________________________.
      (3) Seller's Expenses: Releases of existing liens, including prepayment penalties and recording fees; tax statements or certificates; preparation of deed; one-half of escrow fee; expenses FHA or VA prohibits Buyer to pay; and other expenses stipulated to be paid by Seller under other provisions of this contract.
      (4) Buyer's Expenses: Interest on the note(s) from date of disbursement to one month prior to dates of first monthly payments, expenses stipulated to be paid by Buyer under other provisions of this contract; any customary Texas Veterans' Housing Assistance Program Loan costs for Buyer; and premiums for mortgagee title policy and endorsements required by lender.
         (a) FHA Buyer: All prepaid items required by applicable HUD-FHA or other regulations, including required premiums for flood and hazard insurance, reserve deposits for other insurance, ad valorem taxes and special governmental assessments; expenses incident to any loan, including preparation of loan documents, recording fees, copies of restrictions and easements, amortization schedule, loan origination fee, loan commitment fee, credit reports, photos, loan related inspection fee; and one-half of escrow fee.
         (b) VA Buyer: All prepaid items, including required premiums for flood and hazard insurance, reserve deposits for other insurance, ad valorem taxes and special governmental assessments; expenses incident to any loan, including credit reports, recording fees, loan origination fee, loan related inspection fees.
   B. The VA Loan Funding Fee or FHA Mortgage Insurance Premium (MIP) not to exceed ___________ will be paid by Buyer, and ❑ paid in cash at closing ❑ added to the amount of the loan or ❑ paid as follows: ______________________________
   ______________________________.
   C. If any expense exceeds an amount expressly stated in this contract for such expense to be paid by a party, that party may terminate this contract unless the other party agrees to pay such excess. In no event will Buyer pay charges and fees expressly prohibited by FHA, VA or other governmental loan program regulations.

13. **PRORATIONS**: Taxes for the current year, maintenance fees, assessments, dues and rents will be prorated through the Closing Date. If taxes for the current year vary from the amount prorated at closing, the parties will adjust the prorations when tax statements for the current year are available. If taxes are not paid at or prior to closing, Buyer will be obligated to pay taxes for the current year.

14. **CASUALTY LOSS:** If any part of the Property is damaged or destroyed by fire or other casualty loss after the effective date of the contract, Seller shall restore the Property to its previous condition as soon as

FHA or VA Residential Contract Concerning____Page Six 11-08-99
(Address of Property)

reasonably possible, but in any event by the Closing Date. If Seller fails to do so due to factors beyond Seller's control, Buyer may either (a) terminate this contract and the earnest money will be refunded to Buyer (b) extend the time for performance up to 15 days and the Closing Date will be extended as necessary or (c) accept the Property in its damaged condition and accept an assignment of insurance proceeds. Seller's obligations under this paragraph are independent of any obligations of Seller under Paragraph 7.

15. **DEFAULT:** If Buyer fails to comply with this contract, Buyer will be in default, and Seller may either (a) enforce specific performance, seek such other relief as may be provided by law, or both, or (b) terminate this contract and receive the earnest money as liquidated damages, thereby releasing both parties from this contract. If, due to factors beyond Seller's control, Seller fails within the time allowed to make any non-casualty repairs or deliver the Commitment, Buyer may either (a) extend the time for performance up to 15 days and the Closing Date will be extended as necessary or (b) terminate this contract as the sole remedy and receive the earnest money. If Seller fails to comply with this contract for any other reason, Seller will be in default and Buyer may either (a) enforce specific performance, seek such other relief as may be provided by law, or both, or (b) terminate this contract and receive the earnest money, thereby releasing both parties from this contract.

16. **DISPUTE RESOLUTION:** It is the policy of the State of Texas to encourage the peaceable resolution of disputes through alternative dispute resolution procedures. The parties are encouraged to use an addendum approved by TREC to submit to mediation disputes which cannot be resolved in good faith through informal discussion.

17. **ATTORNEY'S FEES:** The prevailing party in any legal proceeding brought under or with respect to the transaction described in this contract is entitled to recover from the non-prevailing party all costs of such proceeding and reasonable attorney's fees.

18. **ESCROW:** The earnest money is deposited with escrow agent with the understanding that escrow agent is not (a) a party to this contract and does not have any liability for the performance or nonperformance of any party to this contract, (b) liable for interest on the earnest money and (c) liable for any loss of earnest money caused by the failure of any financial institution in which the earnest money has been deposited unless the financial institution is acting as escrow agent. At closing, the earnest money must be applied first to any cash down payment, then to Buyer's closing costs and any excess refunded to Buyer. If both parties make written demand for the earnest money, escrow agent may require payment of unpaid expenses incurred on behalf of the parties and a written release of liability of escrow agent from all parties. If one party makes written demand for the earnest money, escrow agent shall give notice of the demand by providing to the other party a copy of the demand. If escrow agent does not receive written objection to the demand from the other party within 30 days after notice to the other party, escrow agent may disburse the earnest money to the party making demand reduced by the amount of unpaid expenses incurred on behalf of the party receiving the earnest money and escrow agent may pay the same to the creditors. If escrow agent complies with the provisions of this paragraph, each party hereby releases escrow agent from all adverse claims related to the disbursal of the earnest money. Escrow agent's notice to the other party will be effective when deposited in the U. S. Mail, postage prepaid, certified mail, return receipt requested, addressed to the other party at such party's address shown below. Notice of objection to the demand will be deemed effective upon receipt by escrow agent.

19. **REPRESENTATIONS:** Seller represents that as of the Closing Date there will be no liens, assessments, or security interests against the Property which will not be satisfied out of the sales proceeds. If any representation in this contract is untrue on the Closing Date, this contract may be terminated by Buyer and the earnest money will be refunded to Buyer. All representations contained in this contract will survive closing.

20. **FEDERAL TAX REQUIREMENT:** If Seller is a "foreign person", as defined by applicable law, or if Seller fails to deliver an affidavit that Seller is not a "foreign person", then Buyer shall withhold from the sales proceeds an amount sufficient to comply with applicable tax law and deliver the same to the Internal Revenue Service together with appropriate tax forms. IRS regulations require filing written reports if cash in excess of specified amounts is received in the transaction.

21. **AGREEMENT OF PARTIES:** This contract contains the entire agreement of the parties and cannot be changed except by their written agreement. Addenda which are a part of this contract are (list): ______
____.

Initialed for identification by Buyer________ and Seller________ 01A TREC NO. 21-4

FHA or VA Residential Contract Concerning______________________________ Page Seven 11-08-99
(Address of Property)

22. **CONSULT YOUR ATTORNEY:** Real estate licensees cannot give legal advice. This contract is intended to be legally binding. READ IT CAREFULLY. If you do not understand the effect of this contract, consult your attorney BEFORE signing.

Buyer's Attorney is: ______________________ Seller's Attorney is: ______________________

23. **NOTICES:** All notices from one party to the other must be in writing and are effective when mailed to, hand-delivered at, or transmitted by facsimile machine as follows:

To Buyer at: ______________________

Telephone:(___)______________________

Facsimile:(___)______________________

To Seller at: ______________________

Telephone:(___)______________________

Facsimile: (___)______________________

EXECUTED the ________day of ______________________, ______ (THE EFFECTIVE DATE). (BROKER: FILL IN THE DATE OF FINAL ACCEPTANCE.)

______________________ Buyer

______________________ Seller

______________________ Buyer

______________________ Seller

The form of this contract has been approved by the Texas Real Estate Commission. Such approval relates to this contract form only. TREC forms are intended for use only by trained real estate licensees. No representation is made as to the legal validity or adequacy of any provision in any specific transaction. It is not suitable for complex transactions. Extensive riders or additions are not to be used. Texas Real Estate Commission, P.O. Box 12188, Austin, TX 78711-2188, 1-800-250-8732 or (512) 459-6544 (http://www.trec.state.tx.us) TREC NO. 21-4. This form replaces TREC NO. 21-3.

BROKER INFORMATION AND RATIFICATION OF FEE

Listing Broker has agreed to pay Other Broker ______________________ of the total sales price when Listing Broker's fee is received. Escrow Agent is authorized and directed to pay Other Broker from Listing Broker's fee at closing.

____
Other Broker License No.

represents
- ❑ Seller as Listing Broker's subagent
- ❑ Buyer only as Buyer's agent

____
Associate Telephone

____
Broker Address

____
Telephone Facsimile

____
Listing Broker License No.

represents
- ❑ Seller and Buyer as an intermediary
- ❑ Seller only as Seller's agent

____
Listing Associate Telephone

____
Selling Associate Telephone

____
Broker Address

____
Telephone Facsimile

RECEIPT

Receipt of ❑ Contract and ❑ $________ Earnest Money in the form of______________________is acknowledged.

Escrow Agent: ______________________ Date: ______________________,______

By:______________________

Telephone: (___)______________________

____
Address

Facsimile: (___)______________________

____
City State Zip Code

01A TREC NO. 21-4

APPROVED BY THE
TEXAS REAL ESTATE COMMISSION

02-10-97

ADDENDUM FOR SELLER'S DISCLOSURE OF INFORMATION ON LEAD-BASED PAINT AND LEAD-BASED PAINT HAZARDS AS REQUIRED BY FEDERAL LAW

CONCERNING THE PROPERTY AT____
(Street Address and City)

A. **LEAD WARNING STATEMENT:** "Every purchaser of any interest in residential real property on which a residential dwelling was built prior to 1978 is notified that such property may present exposure to lead from lead-based paint that may place young children at risk of developing lead poisoning. Lead poisoning in young children may produce permanent neurological damage, including learning disabilities, reduced intelligence quotient, behavioral problems, and impaired memory. Lead poisoning also poses a particular risk to pregnant women. The seller of any interest in residential real property is required to provide the buyer with any information on lead-based paint hazards from risk assessments or inspections in the seller's possession and notify the buyer of any known lead-based paint hazards. A risk assessment or inspection for possible lead-paint hazards is recommended prior to purchase."

B. **SELLER'S DISCLOSURE:**

1. PRESENCE OF LEAD-BASED PAINT AND/OR LEAD-BASED PAINT HAZARDS (check one box only):
   - ☐ (a) Known lead-based paint and/or lead-based paint hazards are present in the Property (explain): ________
     ____.
   - ☐ (b) Seller has no actual knowledge of lead-based paint and/or lead-based paint hazards in the Property.
2. RECORDS AND REPORTS AVAILABLE TO SELLER (check one box only):
   - ☐ (a) Seller has provided the purchaser with all available records and reports pertaining to lead-based paint and/or lead-based paint hazards in the Property (list documents): ________________
     ____.
   - ☐ (b) Seller has no reports or records pertaining to lead-based paint and/or lead-based paint hazards in the Property.

C. **BUYER'S RIGHTS** (check one box only):

☐ 1. Buyer waives the opportunity to conduct a risk assessment or inspection of the Property for the presence of lead-based paint or lead-based paint hazards.

☐ 2. Within ten days after the effective date of this contract, Buyer may have the Property inspected for the presence of lead-based paint and/or lead-based paint hazards. If lead-based paint or lead-based paint hazards are present, Buyer may terminate this contract by giving Seller written notice within 14 days after the effective date of this contract.

D. **BUYER'S ACKNOWLEDGMENT** (check applicable boxes) **:**

☐ 1. Buyer has received copies of all information listed above.

☐ 2. Buyer has received the pamphlet *Protect Your Family from Lead in Your Home.*

E. **BROKERS' ACKNOWLEDGMENT:** Brokers have informed Seller of Seller's obligations under 42 U.S.C. 4852d to: (a) provide Buyer with the federally approved pamphlet on lead poisoning prevention; (b) complete this addendum; (c) disclose any known lead-based paint and/or lead-based paint hazards in the Property; (d) deliver all records and reports to Buyer pertaining to lead-based paint and/or lead-based paint hazards in the Property; (e) provide Buyer a period of up to 10 days to have the Property inspected; and (f) retain a completed copy of this addendum for at least 3 years following the sale. Brokers are aware of their responsibility to ensure compliance.

F. **CERTIFICATION OF ACCURACY:** The following persons have reviewed the information above and certify, to the best of their knowledge, that the information they have provided is true and accurate.

Seller	Date	Buyer	Date
Seller	Date	Buyer	Date
Listing Broker	Date	Other Broker	Date

The form of this addendum has been approved for voluntary use by the Texas Real Estate Commission for use only with similarly approved or promulgated forms of contracts. No representation is made as to the legal validity or adequacy of any provision in any specific transactions. Texas Real Estate Commission, P.O. Box 12188, Austin, TX 78711-2188, 1-800-250-8732 or (512) 459-6544.

01A TREC No. OP-L

Transaction 5: VA Guaranteed Loan

Utilizing: TREC 21-4, 10-3, 15-3, Lead Addendum

Freddie Mac, an unmarried man, has listed his home at 2365 Veterans Boulevard for sale with Friendly Agent Company. He gives the agent permission to put it in the local multiple listing service and offer other companies the opportunity to function as subagents. Sam Smith, an associate at Peter Finch Realty, shows the property to Victor and Victoria Vet who make an offer of purchase. Although Sam has offered them the opportunity for representation, they choose to be customers and understand that anything they say to Sam may be repeated to the listing agent and the seller. Sam will be paid 2.75 percent of the sales price as the selling commission.

The property is legally identified as Lot 64, Block 83 in Section 2 of the Friendly Hills Addition of Austin, Travis County, Texas. Although it is subject to mandatory membership in the owners' association, the buyers elect not to use the HOA addendum to call for the seller to provide information. They have spoken to an officer of the association and feel that they have learned everything they need to know. The property receives mail at zip code 78711.

The buyers write a check for $1,000 to Buyer's Choice Title Company as earnest money and $100 to the seller as an option fee to have eight days to have the property inspected and back out if they find any significant problems. The option fee will be credited to the sale price at closing.

The seller will pay for the owner's title policy, as well as the survey. The buyers will pay for the appraisal and the VA funding fee, which will be something less than 1 point. They will pay for it with cash at closing. They want three days to examine the lender-required survey.

The lead-based paint addendum is made a part of the contract. The buyer has not yet received the seller's disclosure notice, but asks the seller to furnish it within three days after the effective date of the contract.

The buyers are willing to pay $78,000 for the property. Although Mrs. Vet has full entitlement, the Vets have decided to borrow only $62,400 in order to keep their payments at a comfortable level. They will apply for the loan within four days of the effective date of the agreement and anticipate that they can get loan approval within 30 days and close on or before October 20. They can obtain a 30-year fixed-rate loan at 7.25 percent annual interest rate.

They would like possession at closing and table funding. They compromise and agree to permit the seller to remain four days after funding because they are making the transaction contingent upon selling their present home at 1565 Travis Lane. It is under contract and should close on or before October 1. The buyers agree to permit the seller to continue to show the property. If the seller receives and accepts a satisfactory offer from another buyer, the seller shall waive the contingency by 5:00 PM on the third day after the buyers receive the seller's notice. To waive the contingency, the buyers agree that an additional $5,000 earnest money will be deposited with the escrow agent.

For the seller's temporary leasehold, Mr. Mac will pay $50 per day and tender a security deposit of $1,000.

11-08-99

PROMULGATED BY THE TEXAS REAL ESTATE COMMISSION (TREC)

ONE TO FOUR FAMILY RESIDENTIAL CONTRACT (RESALE)
FHA INSURED OR VA GUARANTEED FINANCING

Notice: Not For Use For Condominium Transactions

1. **PARTIES:** ________________________________ (Seller) agrees to sell and convey to ________________________________ (Buyer) and Buyer agrees to buy from Seller the Property described below.

2. **PROPERTY:** Lot _______, Block _______, ________________________Addition, City of ____________________, ________________ County, Texas, known as ________________________________ (Address/Zip Code), or as described on attached exhibit, together with the following items, if any: curtains and rods, draperies and rods, valances, blinds, window shades, screens, shutters, awnings, wall-to-wall carpeting, mirrors fixed in place, ceiling fans, attic fans, mail boxes, television antennas and satellite dish system with controls and equipment, permanently installed heating and air conditioning units, window air conditioning units, built-in security and fire detection equipment, plumbing and lighting fixtures, including chandeliers, water softener, stove, built-in kitchen equipment, garage door openers with controls, built-in cleaning equipment, all swimming pool equipment and maintenance accessories, shrubbery, landscaping, permanently installed outdoor cooking equipment, built-in fireplace screens, artificial fireplace logs and all other property owned by Seller and attached to the above described real property except the following property which is not included:____
____.

All property sold by this contract is called the "Property." The Property ❑ is ❑ is not subject to mandatory membership in an owners' association. The TREC Addendum For Property Subject To Mandatory Membership In An Owners' Association ❑ is ❑ is not attached.

NOTICE TO BUYER: If the Property is subject to mandatory membership in an owners' association, Seller notifies Buyer under §5.012, Texas Property Code, that, as a purchaser of property in the residential community in which the Property is located, you are obligated to be a member of an owners' association. Restrictive covenants governing the use and occupancy of the Property and a dedicatory instrument governing the establishment, maintenance, and operation of this residential community have been or will be recorded in the Real Property Records of the county in which the Property is located. Copies of the restrictive covenants and dedicatory instrument may be obtained from the county clerk. You are obligated to pay assessments to the owners' association. The amount of the assessments is subject to change. Your failure to pay the assessments could result in a lien on and the foreclosure of the Property.

3. **SALES PRICE:**
   A. Cash portion of the Sales Price payable by Buyer at closing . . . . $______________
   B. Sum of all financing described below (excluding VA Funding Fee or FHA Mortgage Insurance Premium [MIP]) . . . . $______________
   C. Sales Price (Sum of A and B) . . . . $______________

4. **FINANCING:** Within _______ days after the effective date of this contract Buyer shall apply for and make every reasonable effort to obtain financing. Financing will be deemed to have been obtained when the lender has determined that Buyer has satisfied all of lender's financial requirements (those items relating to Buyer's net worth, income and creditworthiness). If financing (including any financed MIP or Funding Fee) is not obtained within _______ days after the effective date hereof, this contract will terminate and the earnest money will refunded to Buyer. The portion of the Sales Price not payable in cash will be paid as follows: (Check applicable boxes below)

   ❑ A. FHA INSURED FINANCING: This contract is subject to approval for Buyer of a Section ________ FHA insured loan of not less than $_____________ (excluding any financed MIP), amortizable monthly for not less than _____ years, with interest not to exceed _______% per annum for the first ________year(s) of the loan.

   As required by HUD-FHA, if FHA valuation is unknown, *"It is expressly agreed that, notwithstanding any other provisions of this contract, the purchaser* (Buyer) *shall not be obligated to complete the purchase of the Property described herein or to incur any penalty by forfeiture of earnest money*

FHA or VA Residential Contract Concerning____Page Two 11-08-99
(Address of Property)

deposits or otherwise unless the purchaser (Buyer) *has been given in accordance with HUD/FHA or VA requirements a written statement issued by the Federal Housing Commissioner, Department of Veterans Affairs, or a Direct Endorsement Lender setting forth the appraised value of the Property of not less than $_______________. The purchaser* (Buyer) *shall have the privilege and option of proceeding with consummation of the contract without regard to the amount of the appraised valuation. The appraised valuation is arrived at to determine the maximum mortgage the Department of Housing and Urban Development will insure. HUD does not warrant the value or the condition of the Property. The purchaser* (Buyer) *should satisfy himself/herself that the price and the condition of the Property are acceptable."* If the FHA appraised value of the Property (excluding closing costs and MIP) is less than the Sales Price (3C above), Seller may reduce the Sales Price to an amount equal to the FHA appraised value (excluding closing costs and MIP) and the parties to the sale shall close the sale at such lower Sales Price with appropriate adjustments to 3A and 3B above.

❑ B. VA GUARANTEED FINANCING: This contract is subject to approval for Buyer of a VA guaranteed loan of not less than $___________(excluding any financed Funding Fee), amortizable monthly for not less than_____ years, with interest not to exceed _____ % per annum for the first _____ year(s) of the loan.

VA NOTICE TO BUYER: *"It is expressly agreed that, notwithstanding any other provisions of this contract, the Buyer shall not incur any penalty by forfeiture of earnest money or otherwise or be obligated to complete the purchase of the Property described herein, if the contract purchase price or cost exceeds the reasonable value of the Property established by the Department of Veterans Affairs. The Buyer shall, however, have the privilege and option of proceeding with the consummation of this contract without regard to the amount of the reasonable value established by the Department of Veterans Affairs."*

If Buyer elects to complete the purchase at an amount in excess of the reasonable value established by VA, Buyer shall pay such excess amount in cash from a source which Buyer agrees to disclose to the VA and which Buyer represents will not be from borrowed funds except as approved by VA. If VA reasonable value of the Property is less than the Sales Price (3C above), Seller may reduce the Sales Price to an amount equal to the VA reasonable value and the parties to the sale shall close at such lower Sales Price with appropriate adjustments to 3A and 3B above.

❑ C. TEXAS VETERANS' HOUSING ASSISTANCE PROGRAM LOAN: This contract is subject to approval for Buyer of a Texas Veterans' Housing Assistance Program Loan of $______________ for a period of at least ______ years at the interest rate established by the Texas Veterans' Land Board at the time of closing.

5. **EARNEST MONEY:** Buyer shall deposit $_______________ as earnest money with ________________ ______________________________ at ____ (Address), as escrow agent, upon execution of this contract by both parties. Additional earnest money of $ __________________ must be deposited by Buyer with escrow agent on or before ________________ , _____. If Buyer fails to deposit the earnest money as required by this contract, Buyer will be in default.

6. **TITLE POLICY AND SURVEY:**

❑ A. TITLE POLICY: Seller shall furnish to Buyer at ❑ Seller's ❑ Buyer's expense an owner policy of title insurance (the Title Policy) issued by ____ (the Title Company) in the amount of the Sales Price, dated at or after closing, insuring Buyer against loss under the provisions of the Title Policy, subject to the promulgated exclusions (including existing building and zoning ordinances) and the following exceptions:

(1) Restrictive covenants common to the platted subdivision in which the Property is located.
(2) The standard printed exception for standby fees, taxes and assessments.
(3) Liens created as part of the financing described in Paragraph 4.
(4 Utility easements created by the dedication deed or plat of the subdivision in which the Property is located.
(5) Reservations or exceptions otherwise permitted by this contract or as may be approved by Buyer in writing.
(6) The standard printed exception as to discrepancies, conflicts, shortages in area or boundary lines, encroachments or protrusions, or overlapping improvements.
(7) The standard printed exception as to marital rights.
(8) The standard printed exception as to waters, tidelands, beaches, streams, and related matters.

Within 20 days after the Title Company receives a copy of this contract, Seller shall furnish to Buyer a commitment for title insurance (the Commitment) and, at Buyer's expense, legible copies of restrictive covenants and documents evidencing exceptions in the Commitment other than the standard printed exceptions. Seller authorizes the Title Company to mail or hand deliver the Commitment and related documents to Buyer at Buyer's address shown below. If the Commitment is not delivered to Buyer within the specified time, the time for delivery will be automatically extended up to 15 days. Buyer will have 7 days after the receipt of the Commitment to object in writing to matters disclosed in the Commitment.

❑ B. SURVEY: Within ________ days after Buyer's receipt of a survey furnished to a third-party lender at ❑ Seller's ❑ Buyer's expense, Buyer may object in writing to any matter shown on the survey which constitutes a defect or encumbrance to title.
The survey must be made by a Registered Professional Land Surveyor acceptable to the Title Company and any lender. Utility easements created by the dedication deed and plat of the subdivision in which the Property is located will not be a basis for objection.

Buyer may object to existing building and zoning ordinances, items 6A(1) through (8) above and matters shown on the survey if Buyer determines that any such ordinance, items or matters prohibits the following use or activity:____
____.

Buyer's failure to object under Paragraph 6A or 6B within the time allowed will constitute a waiver of Buyer's right to object; except that the requirements in Schedule C of the Commitment will not be deemed to have been waived. Seller shall cure the timely objections of Buyer or any third party lender within 15 days from the date Seller receives the objections and the Closing Date will be extended as necessary. If objections are not cured by the extended Closing Date, this contract will terminate and the earnest money will be refunded to Buyer unless Buyer elects to waive the objections.

NOTICE TO SELLER AND BUYER:

(1) Broker advises Buyer to have an abstract of title covering the Property examined by an attorney of Buyer's selection, or Buyer should be furnished with or obtain a Title Policy. If a Title Policy is furnished, the Commitment should be promptly reviewed by an attorney of Buyer's choice due to the time limitations on Buyer's right to object.

(2) If the Property is situated in a utility or other statutorily created district providing water, sewer, drainage, or flood control facilities and services, Chapter 49 of the Texas Water Code requires Seller to deliver and Buyer to sign the statutory notice relating to the tax rate, bonded indebtedness, or standby fee of the district prior to final execution of this contract.

(3) If the Property abuts the tidally influenced waters of the state, Section 33.135, Texas Natural Resources Code, requires a notice regarding coastal area property to be included in the contract. An addendum either promulgated by TREC or required by the parties should be used.

(4) Buyer is advised that the presence of wetlands, toxic substances including asbestos and wastes or other environmental hazards or the presence of a threatened or endangered species or its habitat may affect Buyer's intended use of the Property. If Buyer is concerned about these matters, an addendum either promulgated by TREC or required by the parties should be used.

(5) If the Property is located outside the limits of a municipality, Seller notifies Buyer under §5.011, Texas Property Code, that the Property may now or later be included in the extraterritorial jurisdiction of a municipality and may now or later be subject to annexation by the municipality. Each municipality maintains a map that depicts its boundaries and extraterritorial jurisdiction. To determine if the Property is located within a municipality's extraterritorial jurisdiction or is likely to be located within a municipality's extraterritorial jurisdiction, contact all municipalities located in the general proximity of the Property for further information.

(6) Unless expressly prohibited in writing by the parties, Seller may continue to show the Property for sale and to receive, negotiate and accept back-up offers.

(7) Any residential service contract that is purchased in connection with this transaction should be reviewed for the scope of coverage, exclusions and limitations. **The purchase of a residential service contract is optional. Similar coverage may be purchased from various companies authorized to do business in Texas.**

7. PROPERTY CONDITION:

A. INSPECTIONS, ACCESS AND UTILITIES: Buyer may have the Property inspected by an inspector

selected by Buyer, licensed by TREC or otherwise permitted by law to make such inspections. Seller shall permit access to the Property at reasonable times for inspection, repairs and treatment and for reinspection after repairs and treatment have been completed. Seller shall pay for turning on utilities for inspection and reinspection.

B. SELLER'S DISCLOSURE NOTICE PURSUANT TO SECTION 5.008, TEXAS PROPERTY CODE (Notice) (check one box only):

❑ (1) Buyer has received the Notice.

❑ (2) Buyer has not received the Notice. Within _______ days after the effective date of this contract, Seller shall deliver the Notice to Buyer. If Buyer does not receive the Notice, Buyer may terminate this contract at any time prior to the closing. If Seller delivers the Notice, Buyer may terminate this contract for any reason within 7 days after Buyer receives the Notice or prior to the closing, whichever first occurs.

❑ (3) The Texas Property Code does not require this Seller to furnish the Notice.

C. SELLER'S DISCLOSURE OF LEAD-BASED PAINT AND LEAD-BASED PAINT HAZARDS is required by Federal law for a residential dwelling constructed prior to 1978. An addendum providing such disclosure ❑ is ❑ is not attached.

D. ACCEPTANCE OF PROPERTY CONDITION: (check one box only):

❑ (1) In addition to any earnest money deposited with escrow agent, Buyer has paid Seller $_____________ (the "Option Fee") for the unrestricted right to terminate this contract by giving notice of termination to Seller within _______ days after the effective date of this contract. If Buyer gives notice of termination within the time specified, the Option Fee will not be refunded, however, any earnest money will be refunded to Buyer. If Buyer does not give notice of termination within the time specified, Buyer will be deemed to have accepted the Property in its current condition and the Option Fee ❑ will ❑ will not be credited to the Sales Price at closing.

❑ (2) Buyer accepts the Property in its present condition; provided Seller, at Seller's expense, shall complete the following repairs and treatment: ______________________________________
____
____.

E. LENDER REQUIRED REPAIRS AND TREATMENTS (REPAIRS): Unless otherwise agreed in writing, neither party is obligated to pay for lender required repairs or treatments for wood destroying insects. If the cost of lender required repairs exceeds 5% of the Sales Price, Buyer may terminate this contract.

F. COMPLETION OF REPAIRS AND TREATMENT. Unless otherwise agreed by the parties in writing, Seller shall complete all agreed repairs and treatment prior to the Closing Date. Repairs and treatments must be performed by persons who regularly provide such repairs or treatments. At Buyer's election, any transferable warranties received by Seller with respect to the repairs will be transferred to Buyer at Buyer's expense. If Seller fails to complete any agreed repairs and treatment prior to the Closing Date, Buyer may do so and the Closing Date will be extended up to 15 days, if necessary, to complete repairs and treatment.

8. **BROKERS' FEES:** All obligations of the parties for payment of brokers' fees are contained in separate written agreements.

9. **CLOSING:** The closing of the sale will be on or before ____________________________,______, or within 7 days after objections to matters disclosed in the Commitment or by the survey have been cured, whichever date is later (the Closing Date). *If financing has been obtained pursuant to Paragraph 4,* the Closing Date will be extended up to 15 days if necessary to comply with lender's closing requirements, for example: appraisal, survey, insurance policies, lender-required repairs, closing documents). If either party fails to close this sale by the Closing Date, the non-defaulting party will be entitled to exercise the remedies contained in Paragraph 15. At closing Seller shall furnish tax statements or certificates showing no delinquent taxes and a general warranty deed conveying good and indefeasible title showing no additional exceptions to those permitted in Paragraph 6.

10. **POSSESSION:** Seller shall deliver possession of the Property to Buyer on ____________________ in its present or required repaired condition, ordinary wear and tear excepted. Any possession by Buyer prior to closing or by Seller after closing which is not authorized by a temporary lease form promulgated by TREC or required by the parties will establish a tenancy at sufferance relationship between the parties. *Consult your insurance agent prior to change of ownership or possession as insurance*

coverage may be limited or terminated. The absence of a written lease or appropriate insurance coverage may expose the parties to economic loss.

11. **SPECIAL PROVISIONS:** (Insert only factual statements and business details applicable to this sale. TREC rules prohibit licensees from adding factual statements or business details for which a contract addendum, lease or other form has been promulgated by TREC for mandatory use.)

12. **SETTLEMENT AND OTHER EXPENSES:**

A. The following expenses must be paid at or prior to closing:

(1) Appraisal fees will be paid by ____.

(2) The total of the loan discount fees (including any Texas Veterans' Housing Assistance Program Participation Fee) may not exceed _________% of the loan of which Seller shall pay ____________and Buyer shall pay the remainder. The total of any buydown fees may not exceed ________________ which will be paid by ____.

(3) Seller's Expenses: Releases of existing liens, including prepayment penalties and recording fees; tax statements or certificates; preparation of deed; one-half of escrow fee; expenses FHA or VA prohibits Buyer to pay; and other expenses stipulated to be paid by Seller under other provisions of this contract.

(4) Buyer's Expenses: Interest on the note(s) from date of disbursement to one month prior to dates of first monthly payments, expenses stipulated to be paid by Buyer under other provisions of this contract; any customary Texas Veterans' Housing Assistance Program Loan costs for Buyer; and premiums for mortgagee title policy and endorsements required by lender.

(a) FHA Buyer: All prepaid items required by applicable HUD-FHA or other regulations, including required premiums for flood and hazard insurance, reserve deposits for other insurance, ad valorem taxes and special governmental assessments; expenses incident to any loan, including preparation of loan documents, recording fees, copies of restrictions and easements, amortization schedule, loan origination fee, loan commitment fee, credit reports, photos, loan related inspection fee; and one-half of escrow fee.

(b) VA Buyer: All prepaid items,including required premiums for flood and hazard insurance, reserve deposits for other insurance, ad valorem taxes and special governmental assessments; expenses incident to any loan, including credit reports, recording fees, loan origination fee, loan related inspection fees.

B. The VA Loan Funding Fee or FHA Mortgage Insurance Premium (MIP) not to exceed ___________ will be paid by Buyer, and ❑ paid in cash at closing ❑ added to the amount of the loan or ❑ paid as follows: ____.

C. If any expense exceeds an amount expressly stated in this contract for such expense to be paid by a party, that party may terminate this contract unless the other party agrees to pay such excess. In no event will Buyer pay charges and fees expressly prohibited by FHA, VA or other governmental loan program regulations.

13. **PRORATIONS**: Taxes for the current year, maintenance fees, assessments, dues and rents will be prorated through the Closing Date. If taxes for the current year vary from the amount prorated at closing, the parties will adjust the prorations when tax statements for the current year are available. If taxes are not paid at or prior to closing, Buyer will be obligated to pay taxes for the current year.

14. **CASUALTY LOSS:** If any part of the Property is damaged or destroyed by fire or other casualty loss after the effective date of the contract, Seller shall restore the Property to its previous condition as soon as

reasonably possible, but in any event by the Closing Date. If Seller fails to do so due to factors beyond Seller's control, Buyer may either (a) terminate this contract and the earnest money will be refunded to Buyer (b) extend the time for performance up to 15 days and the Closing Date will be extended as necessary or (c) accept the Property in its damaged condition and accept an assignment of insurance proceeds. Seller's obligations under this paragraph are independent of any obligations of Seller under Paragraph 7.

15. **DEFAULT:** If Buyer fails to comply with this contract, Buyer will be in default, and Seller may either (a) enforce specific performance, seek such other relief as may be provided by law, or both, or (b) terminate this contract and receive the earnest money as liquidated damages, thereby releasing both parties from this contract. If, due to factors beyond Seller's control, Seller fails within the time allowed to make any non-casualty repairs or deliver the Commitment, Buyer may either (a) extend the time for performance up to 15 days and the Closing Date will be extended as necessary or (b) terminate this contract as the sole remedy and receive the earnest money. If Seller fails to comply with this contract for any other reason, Seller will be in default and Buyer may either (a) enforce specific performance, seek such other relief as may be provided by law, or both, or (b) terminate this contract and receive the earnest money, thereby releasing both parties from this contract.

16. **DISPUTE RESOLUTION:** It is the policy of the State of Texas to encourage the peaceable resolution of disputes through alternative dispute resolution procedures. The parties are encouraged to use an addendum approved by TREC to submit to mediation disputes which cannot be resolved in good faith through informal discussion.

17. **ATTORNEY'S FEES:** The prevailing party in any legal proceeding brought under or with respect to the transaction described in this contract is entitled to recover from the non-prevailing party all costs of such proceeding and reasonable attorney's fees.

18. **ESCROW:** The earnest money is deposited with escrow agent with the understanding that escrow agent is not (a) a party to this contract and does not have any liability for the performance or nonperformance of any party to this contract, (b) liable for interest on the earnest money and (c) liable for any loss of earnest money caused by the failure of any financial institution in which the earnest money has been deposited unless the financial institution is acting as escrow agent. At closing, the earnest money must be applied first to any cash down payment, then to Buyer's closing costs and any excess refunded to Buyer. If both parties make written demand for the earnest money, escrow agent may require payment of unpaid expenses incurred on behalf of the parties and a written release of liability of escrow agent from all parties. If one party makes written demand for the earnest money, escrow agent shall give notice of the demand by providing to the other party a copy of the demand. If escrow agent does not receive written objection to the demand from the other party within 30 days after notice to the other party, escrow agent may disburse the earnest money to the party making demand reduced by the amount of unpaid expenses incurred on behalf of the party receiving the earnest money and escrow agent may pay the same to the creditors. If escrow agent complies with the provisions of this paragraph, each party hereby releases escrow agent from all adverse claims related to the disbursal of the earnest money. Escrow agent's notice to the other party will be effective when deposited in the U. S. Mail, postage prepaid, certified mail, return receipt requested, addressed to the other party at such party's address shown below. Notice of objection to the demand will be deemed effective upon receipt by escrow agent.

19. **REPRESENTATIONS:** Seller represents that as of the Closing Date there will be no liens, assessments, or security interests against the Property which will not be satisfied out of the sales proceeds. If any representation in this contract is untrue on the Closing Date, this contract may be terminated by Buyer and the earnest money will be refunded to Buyer. All representations contained in this contract will survive closing.

20. **FEDERAL TAX REQUIREMENT:** If Seller is a "foreign person", as defined by applicable law, or if Seller fails to deliver an affidavit that Seller is not a "foreign person", then Buyer shall withhold from the sales proceeds an amount sufficient to comply with applicable tax law and deliver the same to the Internal Revenue Service together with appropriate tax forms. IRS regulations require filing written reports if cash in excess of specified amounts is received in the transaction.

21. **AGREEMENT OF PARTIES:** This contract contains the entire agreement of the parties and cannot be changed except by their written agreement. Addenda which are a part of this contract are (list): ______
____.

FHA or VA Residential Contract Concerning____Page Seven 11-08-99
(Address of Property)

22. **CONSULT YOUR ATTORNEY:** Real estate licensees cannot give legal advice. This contract is intended to be legally binding. READ IT CAREFULLY. If you do not understand the effect of this contract, consult your attorney BEFORE signing.

Buyer's Attorney is: ______________________________ Seller's Attorney is: ______________________________

23. **NOTICES:** All notices from one party to the other must be in writing and are effective when mailed to, hand-delivered at, or transmitted by facsimile machine as follows:

To Buyer at: **To Seller at:**

______________________________ ______________________________

______________________________ ______________________________

______________________________ ______________________________

Telephone:(___)______________________ Telephone:(___)______________________

Facsimile:(___)______________________ Facsimile: (___)______________________

EXECUTED the __________day of ______________________, _____ (THE EFFECTIVE DATE).
(BROKER: FILL IN THE DATE OF FINAL ACCEPTANCE.)

______________________________ ______________________________
Buyer Seller

______________________________ ______________________________
Buyer Seller

The form of this contract has been approved by the Texas Real Estate Commission. Such approval relates to this contract form only. TREC forms are intended for use only by trained real estate licensees. No representation is made as to the legal validity or adequacy of any provision in any specific transaction. It is not suitable for complex transactions. Extensive riders or additions are not to be used. Texas Real Estate Commission, P.O. Box 12188, Austin, TX 78711-2188, 1-800-250-8732 or (512) 459-6544 (http://www.trec.state.tx.us) TREC NO. 21-4. This form replaces TREC NO. 21-3.

BROKER INFORMATION AND RATIFICATION OF FEE

Listing Broker has agreed to pay Other Broker ______________________ of the total sales price when Listing Broker's fee is received. Escrow Agent is authorized and directed to pay Other Broker from Listing Broker's fee at closing.

____
Other Broker License No.
represents ❑ Seller as Listing Broker's subagent
❑ Buyer only as Buyer's agent

____
Associate Telephone

____
Broker Address

____
Telephone Facsimile

____
Listing Broker License No.
represents ❑ Seller and Buyer as an intermediary
❑ Seller only as Seller's agent

____
Listing Associate Telephone

____
Selling Associate Telephone

____
Broker Address

____
Telephone Facsimile

RECEIPT

Receipt of ❑ Contract and ❑ $_________ Earnest Money in the form of__________________________is acknowledged.

Escrow Agent: ______________________________ Date: ______________________,_____

By:______________________________

Telephone: (___)______________________

____
Address

Facsimile: (___)______________________

____
City State Zip Code

APPROVED BY THE
TEXAS REAL ESTATE COMMISSION

02-10-97

ADDENDUM FOR SELLER'S DISCLOSURE OF INFORMATION ON LEAD-BASED PAINT AND LEAD-BASED PAINT HAZARDS AS REQUIRED BY FEDERAL LAW

CONCERNING THE PROPERTY AT____
(Street Address and City)

A. LEAD WARNING STATEMENT: "Every purchaser of any interest in residential real property on which a residential dwelling was built prior to 1978 is notified that such property may present exposure to lead from lead-based paint that may place young children at risk of developing lead poisoning. Lead poisoning in young children may produce permanent neurological damage, including learning disabilities, reduced intelligence quotient, behavioral problems, and impaired memory. Lead poisoning also poses a particular risk to pregnant women. The seller of any interest in residential real property is required to provide the buyer with any information on lead-based paint hazards from risk assessments or inspections in the seller's possession and notify the buyer of any known lead-based paint hazards. A risk assessment or inspection for possible lead-paint hazards is recommended prior to purchase."

B. SELLER'S DISCLOSURE:

1. PRESENCE OF LEAD-BASED PAINT AND/OR LEAD-BASED PAINT HAZARDS (check one box only):
   - ☐(a) Known lead-based paint and/or lead-based paint hazards are present in the Property (explain): ________
     ____.
   - ☐(b) Seller has no actual knowledge of lead-based paint and/or lead-based paint hazards in the Property.
2. RECORDS AND REPORTS AVAILABLE TO SELLER (check one box only):
   - ☐(a) Seller has provided the purchaser with all available records and reports pertaining to lead-based paint and/or lead-based paint hazards in the Property (list documents): ________________
     ____.
   - ☐(b) Seller has no reports or records pertaining to lead-based paint and/or lead-based paint hazards in the Property.

C. BUYER'S RIGHTS (check one box only)**:**

☐ 1. Buyer waives the opportunity to conduct a risk assessment or inspection of the Property for the presence of lead-based paint or lead-based paint hazards.

☐ 2. Within ten days after the effective date of this contract, Buyer may have the Property inspected for the presence of lead-based paint and/or lead-based paint hazards. If lead-based paint or lead-based paint hazards are present, Buyer may terminate this contract by giving Seller written notice within 14 days after the effective date of this contract.

D. BUYER'S ACKNOWLEDGMENT (check applicable boxes) **:**

☐ 1. Buyer has received copies of all information listed above.

☐ 2. Buyer has received the pamphlet *Protect Your Family from Lead in Your Home.*

E. BROKERS' ACKNOWLEDGMENT: Brokers have informed Seller of Seller's obligations under 42 U.S.C. 4852d to: (a) provide Buyer with the federally approved pamphlet on lead poisoning prevention; (b) complete this addendum; (c) disclose any known lead-based paint and/or lead-based paint hazards in the Property; (d) deliver all records and reports to Buyer pertaining to lead-based paint and/or lead-based paint hazards in the Property; (e) provide Buyer a period of up to 10 days to have the Property inspected; and (f) retain a completed copy of this addendum for at least 3 years following the sale Brokers are aware of their responsibility to ensure compliance.

F. CERTIFICATION OF ACCURACY: The following persons have reviewed the information above and certify, to the best of their knowledge, that the information they have provided is true and accurate.

Seller	Date	Buyer	Date
Seller	Date	Buyer	Date
Listing Broker	Date	Other Broker	Date

The form of this addendum has been approved for voluntary use by the Texas Real Estate Commission for use only with similarly approved or promulgated forms of contracts. No representation is made as to the legal validity or adequacy of any provision in any specific transactions. Texas Real Estate Commission, P.O. Box 12188, Austin, TX 78711-2188, 1-800-250-8732 or (512) 459-6544.

01A TREC No. OP-L

09-20-99

PROMULGATED BY THE TEXAS REAL ESTATE COMMISSION (TREC)

ADDENDUM FOR SALE OF OTHER PROPERTY BY BUYER

ADDENDUM TO CONTRACT BETWEEN THE UNDERSIGNED PARTIES CONCERNING THE PROPERTY AT

____

(Street Address and City)

A. The contract is contingent upon Buyer's receipt of the proceeds from the sale of Buyer's property at ____(Address) by 5:00 p.m. on ____________________, ______ (the Contingency). If the Contingency is not satisfied or waived by Buyer by the above time and date, the contract will terminate automatically and the earnest money will be refunded to Buyer.
NOTICE: The date inserted in this Paragraph should be no later than the date inserted in Paragraph 9 of the contract.

B. If Seller accepts a written offer to sell the Property, Seller shall notify Buyer (1) of such acceptance **AND** (2) that Seller requires Buyer to waive the Contingency. Buyer mustwaive the Contingency by 5:00 p.m. on the ____________day after delivery of Seller's notice to Buyer; otherwise the contract will terminate automatically and the earnest money will be refunded to Buyer.

C. Buyer may waive the Contingency only by notifying Seller of the waiver and depositing $__________ with escrow agent as additional earnest money. All notices must be in writing and are effective when delivered in accordance with the contract.

D. If Buyer waives the Contingency and Buyer's loan or assumption approval is conditioned upon the sale of Buyer's property described in Paragraph A above, Buyer will be in default if such condition is not satisfied by the date provided for in Paragraph 4 of the contract. If such default occurs, Seller may exercise the remedies specified in Paragraph 15 of the contract. If Buyer fails to obtain loan or assumption approval for any other reason, the provisions of Paragraph 4 remain in effect.

E. For purposes of this Addendum time is of the essence; strict compliance with the times for performance stated herein is required.

______________________ Buyer	______________________ Seller
______________________ Buyer	______________________ Seller

The form of this addendum has been approved by the Texas Real Estate Commission for use only with similarly approved or promulgated forms of contracts. Such approval relates to this contract form only. TREC forms are intended for use only by trained real estate licensees. No representation is made as to the legal validity or adequacy of any provision in any specific transactions. It is not suitable for complex transactions.(09-99)Texas Real Estate Commission, P.O. Box 12188, Austin, TX 78711-2188, 1-800-250-8732 or (512) 459-6544 (http://www.trec.state.tx.us) TREC No. 10-3. This form replaces TREC No. 10-2.

(NOTICE: For use only when SELLER occupies the property for no more than 90 days AFTER the closing) 12-07-98

SELLER'S TEMPORARY RESIDENTIAL LEASE

PROMULGATED BY THE TEXAS REAL ESTATE COMMISSION (TREC)

1. **PARTIES:** The parties to this Lease are ______________________________ (Landlord) and ______________________________(Tenant).
2. **LEASE:** Landlord leases to Tenant the Property described in the Contract between Landlord as Buyer and Tenant as Seller dated __________________, ______,and known as ______________________________(address).
3. **TERM:** The term of this Lease commences on the date the sale covered by the Contract is closed and terminates ______________________________, unless terminated earlier by reason of other provisions.
4. **RENTAL:** Tenant shall pay to Landlord as rental $_______________per day with the full amount of rental for the term of the Lease to be paid at the time of funding of the sale. Tenant will not be entitled to a refund of rental if this Lease terminates early due to Tenant's default or voluntary surrender of the Property.
5. **SECURITY DEPOSIT:** Tenant shall pay to Landlord at the time of funding of the sale $ ______________ as a deposit to secure performance of this Lease by Tenant. Landlord may use the deposit to satisfy Tenant's obligations under this Lease. Landlord shall refund any unused portion of the deposit to Tenant with an itemized list of all deductions from the deposit within 30 days after Tenant (a) surrenders possession of the Property and (b) provides Landlord written notice of Tenant's forwarding address.
6. **UTILITIES:** Tenant shall pay all utility charges except______________________________, which Landlord shall pay.
7. **USE OF PROPERTY:** Tenant may use the Property only for single family dwelling purposes. Tenant may not assign this Lease or sublet any part of the Property.
8. **PETS:** Tenant may not keep pets on the Property except______________________________.
9. **CONDITION OF PROPERTY**: Tenant accepts the Property in its present condition and state of repair at the commencement of the Lease. Upon termination, Tenant shall surrender the Property to Landlord in the condition required under the Contract at the time of closing, except normal wear and tear and any casualty loss.
10. **ALTERATIONS:** Tenant may not alter the Property or install improvements or fixtures without the prior written consent of Landlord. Any improvements or fixtures placed on the Property during the Lease become the property of Landlord.
11. **SPECIAL PROVISIONS:**

12. **INSPECTIONS:** Landlord may enter at reasonable times to inspect the Property.
13. **LAWS:** Tenant shall comply with all applicable laws, restrictions, ordinances, rules and regulations with respect to the Property.
14. **REPAIRS AND MAINTENANCE:** Tenant shall bear all expense of repairing and maintaining the Property, including but not limited to yard, trees and shrubs, unless otherwise required by the Texas Property Code. Tenant shall promptly repair at Tenant's expense any damage to the Property caused directly or indirectly by any act or omission of the Tenant or any person other than Landlord, Landlord's agents or invitees.

Initialed for identification by Landlord __________ and Tenant __________

Seller's Temporary Residential Lease____Page Two 12-07-98
(Address of Property)

15. **INDEMNITY:** Tenant indemnifies Landlord from the claims of all third parties for injury or damage to the person or property of such third party arising from the use or occupancy of the Property by Tenant. This indemnification includes attorney's fees, costs and expenses incurred by Landlord.
16. **INSURANCE:** Landlord and Tenant shall each maintain such insurance on the contents and Property as each party may deem appropriate during the term of this Lease. NOTE: CONSULT YOUR INSURANCE AGENT PRIOR TO CLOSING. Possession of the Property by Seller as Tenant may change insurance policy coverage.
17. **DEFAULT:** If Tenant fails to perform or observe any provision of this Lease and fails, within 24 hours after notice by Landlord, to commence and diligently pursue to remedy such failure, Tenant will be in default.
18. **TERMINATION:** This Lease terminates upon expiration of the term specified in Paragraph 3 or upon Tenant's default under this Lease.
19. **HOLDING OVER:** Tenant shall surrender possession of the Property upon termination of this Lease. Any possession by Tenant after termination creates a tenancy at sufferance and will not operate to renew or extend this Lease. Tenant shall pay $ _______________ per day during the period of any possession after termination as damages, in addition to any other remedies to which Landlord is entitled.
20. **ATTORNEY'S FEES:** The prevailing party in any legal proceeding brought under or with respect to the transaction described in this Lease is entitled to recover from the non-prevailing party all costs of such proceeding and reasonable attorney's fees.
21. **SMOKE DETECTORS:** The Texas Property Code requires Landlord to install smoke detectors in certain locations within the Property at Landlord's expense. Tenant expressly waives Landlord's duty to inspect and repair smoke detectors.
22. **SECURITY DEVICES:** The requirements of the Texas Property Code relating to security devices do not apply to a residential lease for a term of 90 days or less.
23. **CONSULT YOUR ATTORNEY:** Real estate licensees cannot give legal advice. This Lease is intended to be legally binding. READ IT CAREFULLY. If you do not understand the effect of this Lease, consult your attorney BEFORE signing.
24. **NOTICES:** All notices under this Lease from one party to the other must be in writing and are effective when delivered or transmitted by facsimile machine as follows:

To Landlord:	**To Tenant:**
______________________________	______________________________
______________________________	______________________________
______________________________	______________________________
Facsimile:(_____)________________	Facsimile:(_____)________________

EXECUTED the ______ day of ______________________________ .

______________________________	______________________________
Landlord	Tenant
______________________________	______________________________
Landlord	Tenant

Transaction 6: Seller Finance on Unimproved One-Family to Four-Family Lot

Utilizing: TREC 9-4, 26-2, 28-0

Thomas John Swanson and his wife, Sarah Jane Swanson, will purchase a vacant lot known as Lot 6, Block 8 of the Happily-Ever-After Addition of Waco, McLennan County, Texas. They are willing to pay $23,500 for the lot if the owner, Samuel Jay Johnson (a bachelor), will owner finance $15,000 for five years at 7 percent annual interest. The buyers will pay monthly interest only until maturity, when the principal balance is due. They agree to a due-on-sale clause in the deed of trust and will provide paid tax receipts by February 1 of each year the loan is outstanding.

The Swansons request a title policy issued by Secure Title Company and a survey showing no encroachments or easements other than the 10-foot utility easement at the rear of the lot. The seller will pay for the title policy and the survey. The Swansons plan to build a duplex and want to make certain that electric, public water and sewer, natural gas, telephone and cable TV services are available.

The property is not subject to a mandatory homeowners' association assessment. It is listed with Smooth Sails Realty through whom the buyers purchase it without representation. They will close on or before May 27, which is within 15 days of the effective date of the contract. The seller requests that the buyers furnish a current credit report within five days after the effective date of the contract as evidence of good credit.

The street number has not yet been assigned to this lot on Paradise Avenue in Waco, Texas 76710. The buyer wants deletion of the common title policy exclusion relating to discrepancies, conflicts and shortages in area or boundary, and is willing to pay the additional 15 percent policy premium required by the title company. $2,000 earnest money has been tendered. The buyers will inspect the survey within 10 days of the effective date of the contract. The purchasers want to have an environmental assessment performed to make certain there is no contamination or toxic materials present. This they will do within ten days after the effective date of the contract.

11-8-99

PROMULGATED BY THE TEXAS REAL ESTATE COMMISSION (TREC)

EQUAL HOUSING OPPORTUNITY

UNIMPROVED PROPERTY CONTRACT

NOTICE: Not For Use For Condominium Transactions

1. **PARTIES:** _______________ (Seller) agrees to sell and convey to _______________(Buyer) and Buyer agrees to buy from Seller the property described below.

2. **PROPERTY:** Lot __________, Block _____, _______________Addition, City of _______________, _______________ County, Texas, known as _______________(Address/Zip Code), or as described on attached exhibit, (the Property). The Property ❑ is ❑ is not subject to mandatory membership in an owners' association. The TREC Addendum For Property Subject To Mandatory Membership In An Owners' Association ❑ is ❑ is not attached.
NOTICE TO BUYER: If the Property is subject to mandatory membership in an owners' association, Seller notifies Buyer under §5.012, Texas Property Code, that, as a purchaser of property in the residential community in which the Property is located, you are obligated to be a member of an owners' association. Restrictive covenants governing the use and occupancy of the Property and a dedicatory instrument governing the establishment, maintenance, and operation of this residential community have been or will be recorded in the Real Property Records of the county in which the Property is located. Copies of the restrictive covenants and dedicatory instrument may be obtained from the county clerk. You are obligated to pay assessments to the owners' association. The amount of the assessments is subject to change. Your failure to pay the assessments could result in a lien on and the foreclosure of the Property.

3. **SALES PRICE:**
A. Cash portion of Sales Price payable by Buyer at closing . . . . $__________
B. Sum of all financing described below . . . . $__________
C. Sales Price (Sum of A and B) . . . . $__________

4. **FINANCING:** Within _____ days after the effective date of this contract Buyer shall apply for all third party financing or noteholder's approval of any assumption and make every reasonable effort to obtain financing or assumption approval. Financing or assumption approval will be deemed to have been obtained when the lender determines that Buyer has satisfied all of lender's financial requirements (those items relating to Buyer's net worth, income and creditworthiness). If financing or assumption approval is not obtained within _______ days after the effective date hereof, this contract will terminate and the earnest money will be refunded to Buyer. Each note to be executed hereunder must be secured by vendor's and deed of trust liens. The portion of Sales Price not payable in cash will be paid as follows: (Check applicable boxes below)
❑ A. THIRD PARTY FINANCING:
❑ (1) This contract is subject to approval for Buyer of a third party loan in an amount not to exceed _____ % of the Sales Price, evidenced by a third party first lien promissory note of not less than $ _______________, due in full in _____ year(s), with interest not to exceed _____ % per annum for the first _____ year(s) of the loan.
❑ (2) This contract is subject to approval for Buyer of a third party loan in an amount not to exceed _____ % of the Sales Price, evidenced by a third party second lien promissory note of not less than $ ____________, due in full in _____year(s), with interest not to exceed _____ % per annum for the first _____ year(s) of the loan.
❑ B. SELLER FINANCING: A promissory note from Buyer to Seller of $___________, bearing _____% interest per annum, secured by vendor's and deed of trust liens, in accordance with the terms and conditions set forth in the attached TREC Seller Financing Addendum. If an owner policy of title insurance is furnished, Buyer shall furnish Seller with a mortgagee policy of title insurance.
❑ C. ASSUMPTION:
❑ (1) Buyer shall assume the unpaid principal balance of a first lien promissory note payable to _______________ which unpaid balance at closing will be $ ____________. The total current monthly payment including principal, interest and any reserve deposits is $ ______________. Buyer's initial payment will be the first payment due after closing.

Unimproved Property Contract Concerning_______________________________________ Page Two 11-8-99
(Address of Property)

❑ (2) Buyer shall assume the unpaid principal balance of a second lien promissory note payable to ____________________________________ which unpaid balance at closing will be $ ______________. The total current monthly payment including principal, interest and any reserve deposits is $______________. Buyer's initial payment will be the first payment due after closing.

Buyer's assumption of an existing note includes all obligations imposed by the deed of trust securing the note.

If the unpaid principal balance(s) of any assumed loan(s) as of the Closing Date varies from the loan balance(s) stated above, the ❑ cash payable at closing ❑ Sales Price will be adjusted by the amount of any variance; provided, if the total principal balance of all assumed loans varies in an amount greater than $350.00 at closing, either party may terminate this contract and the earnest money will be refunded to Buyer unless the other party elects to eliminate the excess in the variance by an appropriate adjustment at closing. If the noteholder requires (a) payment of an assumption fee in excess of $ ______________ in C(1) above or $ ______________ in C(2) above and Seller declines to pay such excess, or (b) an increase in the interest rate to more than ______ % in C(1) above, or ______ % in C(2) above, or (c) any other modification of the loan documents, Buyer may terminate this contract and the earnest money will be refunded to Buyer. A vendor's lien and deed of trust to secure assumption will be required which shall automatically be released on execution and delivery of a release by noteholder. If Seller is released from liability on any assumed note, the vendor's lien and deed of trust to secure assumption will not be required.

NOTICE TO BUYER: The monthly payments, interest rates or other terms of some loans may be adjusted by the lender at or after closing. If you are concerned about the possibility of future adjustments, do not sign the contract without examining the notes and deeds of trust.

NOTICE TO SELLER: Your liability to pay the note assumed by Buyer will continue unless you obtain a release of liability from the lender. If you are concerned about future liability, you should use the TREC Release of Liability Addendum.

❑ D. CREDIT APPROVAL ON ASSUMPTION OR SELLER FINANCING: Within ______ days after the effective date of this contract, Buyer shall deliver to Seller ❑ credit report ❑ verification of employment, including salary ❑ verification of funds on deposit in financial institutions ❑ current financial statement to establish Buyer's creditworthiness or assumption approval or seller financing and ❑ ____.

If Buyer's documentation is not delivered within the specified time, Seller may terminate this contract by notice to Buyer within 7 days after expiration of the time for delivery, and the earnest money will be paid to Seller. If this contract is not so terminated, Seller will be deemed to have accepted Buyer's credit. If the documentation is timely delivered, and Seller determines in Seller's sole discretion that Buyer's credit is unacceptable, Seller may terminate this contract by notice to Buyer within 7 days after expiration of the time for delivery and the earnest money will be refunded to Buyer. If Seller does not so terminate this contract, Seller will be deemed to have accepted Buyer's credit. Buyer hereby authorizes any credit reporting agency to furnish to Seller at Buyer's sole expense copies of Buyer's credit reports.

5. **EARNEST MONEY:** Buyer shall deposit $__________ as earnest money with ______________________________ at ______________________________ (Address), as escrow agent, upon execution of this contract by both parties. Additional earnest money of $______________must be deposited by Buyer with escrow agent on or before ________________, ______. If Buyer fails to deposit the earnest money as required by this contract, Buyer will be in default.

6. **TITLE POLICY AND SURVEY:**

❑ A. TITLE POLICY: Seller shall furnish to Buyer at ❑ Seller's ❑ Buyer's expense an owner policy of title insurance (the Title Policy) issued by____________________________________ (the Title Company) in the amount of the Sales Price, dated at or after closing, insuring Buyer against loss under the provisions of the Title Policy, subject to the promulgated exclusions (including existing building and zoning ordinances) and the following exceptions:

(1) Restrictive covenants common to the platted subdivision in which the Property is located.

(2) The standard printed exception for standby fees, taxes and assessments.

Initialed for identification by Buyer__________and Seller__________ **01A** TREC NO. 9-4

Unimproved Property Contract Concerning____Page Three 11-8-99
(Address of Property)

(3) Liens created as part of the financing described in Paragraph 4.
(4) Utility easements created by the dedication deed or plat of the subdivision in which the Property is located.
(5) Reservations or exceptions otherwise permitted by this contract or as may be approved by Buyer in writing.
(6) The standard printed exception as to discrepancies, conflicts, shortages in area or boundary lines, encroachments or protrusions, or overlapping improvements.
(7) The standard printed exception as to marital rights.
(8) The standard printed exception as to waters, tidelands, beaches, streams, and related matters.

Within 20 days after the Title Company receives a copy of this contract, Seller shall furnish to Buyer a commitment for title insurance (the Commitment) and, at Buyer's expense, legible copies of restrictive covenants and documents evidencing exceptions in the Commitment other than the standard printed exceptions. Seller authorizes the Title Company to mail or hand deliver the Commitment and related documents to Buyer at Buyer's address shown below. If the Commitment is not delivered to Buyer within the specified time, the time for delivery will be automatically extended up to 15 days.

❑ B. SURVEY: (Check one box only)

❑ (1) Within ______ days after the effective date of this contract, Buyer shall obtain a survey at Buyer's expense.

❑ (2) Within _____ days after the effective date of this contract, Seller shall cause a survey to be delivered to Buyer at Seller's expense.

❑ (3) Within _____ days after the effective date of this contract, Seller will deliver to Buyer the existing survey plat of the Property dated ___________________________, ________, which ❑ will ❑ will not be recertified to a date subsequent to the effective date of this contract at the expense of ❑ Buyer ❑ Seller.

The survey must be made by a Registered Professional Land Surveyor acceptable to the Title Company and any lender.

Buyer may object to existing building and zoning ordinances, items 6A(1) through (8) above and matters shown on the survey if Buyer determines that any such ordinance, items or matters prohibits the following use or activity: ____.

Buyer will have 7 days after the receipt of the latter of the Commitment or survey to object in writing to matters disclosed in the Commitment or survey. Buyer's failure to object under Paragraph 6 within the time allowed will constitute a waiver of Buyer's right to object; except that the requirements in Schedule C of the Commitment will not be deemed to have been waived. Seller shall cure the timely objections of Buyer or any third party lender within 20 days after Seller receives the objections and the Closing Date will be extended as necessary. If objections are not cured by the extended Closing Date, this contract will terminate and the earnest money will be refunded to Buyer unless Buyer elects to waive the objections.

NOTICE TO SELLER AND BUYER:

(1) Broker advises Buyer to have an abstract of title covering the Property examined by an attorney of Buyer's selection, or Buyer should be furnished with or obtain a Title Policy. If a Title Policy is furnished, the Commitment should be promptly reviewed by an attorney of Buyer's choice due to the time limitations on Buyer's right to object.
(2) If the Property is situated in a utility or other statutorily created district providing water, sewer, drainage, or flood control facilities and services, Chapter 49 of the Texas Water Code requires Seller to deliver and Buyer to sign the statutory notice relating to the tax rate, bonded indebtedness, or standby fee of the district prior to final execution of this contract.
(3) If the Property abuts the tidally influenced waters of the state, Section 33.135, Texas Natural Resources Code, requires a notice regarding coastal area property to be included in the contract. An addendum either promulgated by TREC or required by the parties should be used.
(4) Buyer is advised that the presence of wetlands, toxic substances, including asbestos and wastes or other environmental hazards or the presence of a threatened or endangered species or its habitat may affect Buyer's intended use of the Property. If Buyer is concerned about these matters, an addendum either promulgated by TREC or required by the parties should be used.

Unimproved Property Contract Concerning____Page Four 11-8-99
(Address of Property)

(5) If the Property is located outside the limits of a municipality, Seller notifies Buyer under §5.011, Texas Property Code, that the Property may now or later be included in the extraterritorial jurisdiction of a municipality and may now or later be subject to annexation by the municipality. Each municipality maintains a map that depicts its boundaries and extraterritorial jurisdiction. To determine if the Property is located within a municipality's extraterritorial jurisdiction or is likely to be located within a municipality's extraterritorial jurisdiction, contact all municipalities located in the general proximity of the Property for further information.

(6) Unless expressly prohibited in writing by the parties, Seller may continue to show the Property for sale and to receive, negotiate and accept back-up offers.

7. **PROPERTY CONDITION:**

A. INSPECTIONS, ACCESS AND UTILITIES: Buyer may have the Property inspected by an inspector selected by Buyer, licensed by TREC or otherwise permitted by law to make such inspections. Seller shall permit access to the Property at reasonable times for inspection, repairs and treatment and for reinspection after repairs and treatment have been completed. Seller shall pay for turning on utilities for inspection and reinspection.

B. ACCEPTANCE OF PROPERTY CONDITION: NOTICE: Buyer should determine the availability of utilities to the Property suitable to satisfy Buyer's needs. (check one box only):

❑ (1) In addition to any earnest money deposited with escrow agent, Buyer has paid Seller $____________ (the "Option Fee") for the unrestricted right to terminate this contract by giving notice of termination to Seller within _____ days after the effective date of this contract. If Buyer gives notice of termination within the time specified, the Option Fee will not be refunded, however, any earnest money will be refunded to Buyer. If Buyer does not give notice of termination within the time specified, Buyer will be deemed to have accepted the Property in its current condition and the Option Fee ❑ will ❑ will not be credited to the Sales Price at closing.

❑ (2) Buyer accepts the Property in its present condition.

8. **BROKERS' FEES:** All obligations of the parties for payment of brokers' fees are contained in separate written agreements.

9. **CLOSING:** The closing of the sale will be on or before ______________________________,_______, or within 7 days after objections to matters disclosed in the Commitment or by the survey have been cured, whichever date is later (the Closing Date). *If financing or assumption approval has been obtained pursuant to Paragraph 4,* the Closing Date will be extended up to 15 days if necessary to comply with lender's closing requirements. If either party fails to close this sale by the Closing Date, the non-defaulting party will be entitled to exercise the remedies contained in Paragraph 15. At closing Seller shall furnish tax statements or certificates showing no delinquent taxes and a general warranty deed conveying good and indefeasible title showing no additional exceptions to those permitted in Paragraph 6.

10. **POSSESSION:** Seller shall deliver possession of the Property to Buyer at closing and funding.

11. **SPECIAL PROVISIONS:** (Insert only factual statements and business details applicable to this sale. TREC rules prohibit licensees from adding factual statements or business details for which a contract addendum, lease or other form has been promulgated by TREC for mandatory use.)

Initialed for identification by Buyer__________ and Seller__________ **01A** TREC NO. 9-4

12. **SETTLEMENT AND OTHER EXPENSES:**

A. The following expenses must be paid at or prior to closing:

(1) Appraisal fees will be paid by ________________________________.

(2) The total of loan discount fees may not exceed ______ % of the loan of which Seller shall pay _____________ and Buyer shall pay the remainder. The total of any buydown fees may not exceed ___________ which will be paid by ____________________________.

(3) Seller's Expenses: Releases of existing liens, including prepayment penalties and recording fees; release of Seller's loan liability; tax statements or certificates; preparation of deed; one-half of escrow fee; and other expenses stipulated to be paid by Seller under other provisions of this contract.

(4) Buyer's Expenses: Loan application, origination and commitment fees; loan assumption costs; preparation and recording of deed of trust to secure assumption; lender required expenses incident to new loans, including preparation of loan documents, recording fees, tax service and research fees, warehouse or underwriting fees, copies of restrictions and easements, amortization schedule, premiums for mortgagee title policies and endorsements required by lender, credit reports, photos; required premiums for flood and hazard insurance; required reserve deposit for insurance premiums and ad valorem taxes; interest on all monthly installment notes from date of disbursements to one month prior to dates of first monthly payments; one-half of escrow fee; and other expenses stipulated to be paid by Buyer under other provisions of this contract.

B. If any expense exceeds an amount expressly stated in this contract for such expense to be paid by a party, that party may terminate this contract unless the other party agrees to pay such excess. In no event will Buyer pay charges and fees expressly prohibited by governmental loan program regulations.

13. **PRORATIONS AND ROLLBACK TAXES**:

A. PRORATIONS: Taxes for the current year, interest, maintenance fees, assessments, dues and rents will be prorated through the Closing Date. If taxes for the current year vary from the amount prorated at closing, the parties shall adjust the prorations when tax statements for the current year are available. *If a loan is assumed* and the lender maintains an escrow account, the escrow account must be transferred to Buyer without any deficiency. Buyer shall reimburse Seller for the amount in the transferred account. Buyer shall pay the premium for a new insurance policy. If taxes are not paid at or prior to closing, Buyer will be obligated to pay taxes for the current year.

B. ROLLBACK TAXES: If this sale or Buyer's use of the Property after closing results in the assessment of additional taxes, penalties or interest (Assessments) for periods prior to closing, the Assessments will be the obligation of Buyer. If Seller's change in use of the Property prior to closing or denial of a special use valuation on the Property claimed by Seller results in Assessments for periods prior to closing, the Assessments will be the obligation of Seller. Obligations imposed by this paragraph will survive closing.

14. **CASUALTY LOSS:** If any part of the Property is damaged or destroyed by fire or other casualty loss after the effective date of the contract, Seller shall restore the Property to its previous condition as soon as reasonably possible, but in any event by the Closing Date. If Seller fails to do so due to factors beyond Seller's control, Buyer may either (a) terminate this contract and the earnest money will be refunded to Buyer (b) extend the time for performance up to 15 days and the Closing Date will be extended as necessary or (c) accept the Property in its damaged condition and accept an assignment of insurance proceeds. Seller's obligations under this paragraph are independent of any obligations of Seller under Paragraph 7.

15. **DEFAULT:** If Buyer fails to comply with this contract, Buyer will be in default, and Seller may either (a) enforce specific performance, seek such other relief as may be provided by law, or both, or (b) terminate this contract and receive the earnest money as liquidated damages, thereby releasing both parties from this contract. If, due to factors beyond Seller's control, Seller fails within the time allowed to make any non-casualty repairs or deliver the Commitment, Buyer may either (a) extend the time for performance up to 15 days and the Closing Date will be extended as necessary or (b) terminate this contract as the sole remedy and receive the earnest money. If Seller fails to comply with this contract for any other reason, Seller will be in default and Buyer may either (a) enforce specific performance, seek such other relief as may be provided by law, or both, or (b) terminate this contract and receive the earnest money, thereby releasing both parties from this contract.

Unimproved Property Contract Concerning____Page Six 11-8-99
(Address of Property)

16. **DISPUTE RESOLUTION:** It is the policy of the State of Texas to encourage the peaceable resolution of disputes through alternative dispute resolution procedures. The parties are encouraged to use an addendum approved by TREC to submit to mediation disputes which cannot be resolved in good faith through informal discussion.

17. **ATTORNEY'S FEES:** The prevailing party in any legal proceeding brought under or with respect to the transaction described in this contract is entitled to recover from the non-prevailing party all costs of such proceeding and reasonable attorney's fees.

18. **ESCROW:** The earnest money is deposited with escrow agent with the understanding that escrow agent is not (a) a party to this contract and does not have any liability for the performance or nonperformance of any party to this contract, (b) liable for interest on the earnest money and (c) liable for any loss of earnest money caused by the failure of any financial institution in which the earnest money has been deposited unless the financial institution is acting as escrow agent. At closing, the earnest money must be applied first to any cash down payment, then to Buyer's closing costs and any excess refunded to Buyer. If both parties make written demand for the earnest money, escrow agent may require payment of unpaid expenses incurred on behalf of the parties and a written release of liability of escrow agent from all parties. If one party makes written demand for the earnest money, escrow agent shall give notice of the demand by providing to the other party a copy of the demand. If escrow agent does not receive written objection to the demand from the other party within 30 days after notice to the other party, escrow agent may disburse the earnest money to the party making demand reduced by the amount of unpaid expenses incurred on behalf of the party receiving the earnest money and escrow agent may pay the same to the creditors. If escrow agent complies with the provisions of this paragraph, each party hereby releases escrow agent from all adverse claims related to the disbursal of the earnest money. Escrow agent's notice to the other party will be effective when deposited in the U. S. Mail, postage prepaid, certified mail, return receipt requested, addressed to the other party at such party's address shown below. Notice of objection to the demand will be deemed effective upon receipt by escrow agent.

19. **REPRESENTATIONS:** Seller represents that as of the Closing Date (a) there will be no liens, assessments, or security interests against the Property which will not be satisfied out of the sales proceeds unless securing payment of any loans assumed by Buyer and (b) assumed loans will not be in default. If any representation in this contract is untrue on the Closing Date, this contract may be terminated by Buyer and the earnest money will be refunded to Buyer. All representations contained in this contract will survive closing.

20. **FEDERAL TAX REQUIREMENT:** If Seller is a "foreign person", as defined by applicable law, or if Seller fails to deliver an affidavit that Seller is not a "foreign person", then Buyer shall withhold from the sales proceeds an amount sufficient to comply with applicable tax law and deliver the same to the Internal Revenue Service together with appropriate tax forms. IRS regulations require filing written reports if cash in excess of specified amounts is received in the transaction.

21. **AGREEMENT OF PARTIES:** This contract contains the entire agreement of the parties and cannot be changed except by their written agreement. Addenda which are a part of this contract are (list): ________
____
____
____.

22. **CONSULT YOUR ATTORNEY:** Real estate licensees cannot give legal advice. This contract is intended to be legally binding. READ IT CAREFULLY. If you do not understand the effect of this contract, consult your attorney BEFORE signing.

Buyer's Attorney is:______________________________ Seller's Attorney is:______________________________

Unimproved Property Contract Concerning ______________________________ Page Seven 11-8-99
(Address of Property)

23. **NOTICES:** All notices from one party to the other must be in writing and are effective when mailed to, hand-delivered at, or transmitted by facsimile machine as follows:

To Buyer at:	**To Seller at:**
______________________	______________________
______________________	______________________
______________________	______________________
Telephone: (___)______________	Telephone: (___)______________
Facsimile: (___)______________	Facsimile: (___)______________

EXECUTED the _____ day of ________________, ______ (THE EFFECTIVE DATE). (BROKER: FILL IN THE DATE OF FINAL ACCEPTANCE.)

______________________ Buyer	______________________ Seller
______________________ Buyer	______________________ Seller

The form of this contract has been approved by the Texas Real Estate Commission. Such approval relates to this contract form only. TREC forms are intended for use only by trained real estate licensees. No representation is made as to the legal validity or adequacy of any provision in any specific transaction. It is not suitable for complex transactions. Extensive riders or additions are not to be used. Texas Real Estate Commission, P.O. Box 12188, Austin, TX 78711-2188, 1-800-250-8732 or (512) 459-6544 (http://www.trec.state.tx.us) TREC NO. 9-4. This form replaces TREC NO. 9-3.

BROKER INFORMATION AND RATIFICATION OF FEE

Listing Broker has agreed to pay Other Broker ____________________ of the total sales price when Listing Broker's fee is received. Escrow Agent is authorized and directed to pay Other Broker from Listing Broker's fee at closing.

______________________ Other Broker License No. represents ❑ Seller as Listing Broker's subagent ❑ Buyer only as Buyer's agent	______________________ Listing Broker License No. represents ❑ Seller and Buyer as an intermediary ❑ Seller only as Seller's agent
	______________________ Listing Associate Telephone
______________________ Associate Telephone	______________________ Selling Associate Telephone
______________________ Broker Address	______________________ Broker Address
______________________ Telephone Facsimile	______________________ Telephone Facsimile

RECEIPT

Receipt of ❑ Contract and ❑ $________ Earnest Money in the form of ____________________ is acknowledged.

Escrow Agent: ______________________ Date: ________________, ________

By: ______________________

______________________ Telephone: (___) ______________
Address

______________________ Facsimile: (___) ______________
City State Zip Code

10-25-93

SELLER FINANCING ADDENDUM

PROMULGATED BY THE TEXAS REAL ESTATE COMMISSION (TREC)
NOTICE: NOT FOR USE FOR COMPLEX TRANSACTIONS

ADDENDUM TO EARNEST MONEY CONTRACT BETWEEN THE UNDERSIGNED PARTIES CONCERNING THE PROPERTY IDENTIFIED AS ______________________________

A. **PROMISSORY NOTE.** The promissory note (the Note) described in Paragraph 4 of the Earnest Money Contract payable by Buyer (Maker) to the order of Seller (Payee) shall be payable at the place designated by Payee. The Note may be prepaid in whole or in part at any time without penalty. Any prepayments are to be applied to the payment of the installments of principal last maturing and interest shall immediately cease on the prepaid principal. The lien securing payment of the Note will be inferior to any lien securing any superior note described in the contract. The Note shall be payable as follows:

☐ (1) In one payment due ______________ after the date of the Note with interest payable ______________.

☐ (2) In ______________ installments of $ ______________ ☐ including interest ☐ plus interest beginning ______________ after the date of the Note and continuing at ______________ intervals thereafter for ______________ when the entire balance of the Note shall be due and payable.

☐ (3) Interest only in ______________ installments for the first ______________ year(s) and thereafter in installments of $______________ ☐ including interest ☐ plus interest beginning ______________ after the date of the Note and continuing at ______________ intervals thereafter for ______________ when the entire balance of the Note shall be due and payable.

B. **DEED OF TRUST.** The deed of trust securing the Note shall provide for the following:

(1) ASSUMPTION OF NOTE OR PROHIBITIONS AGAINST ASSUMPTION: (check only one)

☐ (a) Assumption Without Consent: The Property may be sold without the consent of the Payee, provided any subsequent buyer assumes the Note.

☐ (b) Assumption With Consent: The Property may be sold to a subsequent Buyer who assumes the Note, with no change in interest rate or terms; provided the subsequent buyer obtains prior written consent from the Payee. Consent will be based on the subsequent Buyer's credit history, and shall not be unreasonably withheld. If all or any part of the Property is sold, conveyed, leased for a period longer than 3 years, leased with an option to purchase, or otherwise sold (including by contract for deed), without the prior written consent of the Payee, then the Payee may at his option declare the outstanding principal balance of the Note, plus accrued interest, to be immediately due and payable. The creation of a subordinate lien, any sale thereunder, any deed under threat or order of condemnation, any conveyance solely between makers, or the passage of title by reason of the death of a maker or by operation of law shall not be construed as a sale or conveyance of the Property.

☐ (c) Prohibition Against Assumption: If all or any part of the Property is sold, conveyed, leased for a period longer than 3 years, leased with an option to purchase, or otherwise sold (including any contract for deed), without the prior written consent of the Payee, then the Payee may at his option declare the outstanding principal balance of the Note, plus accrued interest, to be immediately due and payable. The creation of a subordinate lien, any sale thereunder, any deed under threat or order of condemnation, any conveyance solely between makers, the passage of title by reason of the death of a maker or by operation of law shall not be construed as a sale or conveyance of the Property.

(2) TAX AND INSURANCE PAYMENTS: (check only one)

☐ (a) Without Escrow: Maker shall furnish to Payee annually, before the taxes become delinquent, copies of tax receipts showing that all taxes on the Property have been paid. Maker shall furnish to Payee annually evidence of current paid-up insurance naming Payee as an insured.

☐ (b) With Escrow: Maker shall, in addition to the principal and interest installments, deposit with the Payee a pro rata part of the estimated annual ad valorem taxes on the Property and a pro rata part of the estimated annual insurance premiums for the improvements on the Property. These tax and insurance deposits are only estimates and may be insufficient to pay total taxes and insurance premiums. Maker shall pay any deficiency within 30 days after notice from Payee. Maker's failure to pay the deficiency shall constitute a default under the Deed of Trust. In the event any superior lienholder on the Property is collecting escrow payments for taxes and insurance, this Paragraph shall be inoperative so long as payments are being made to the superior lienholder.

(3) CROSS-DEFAULT: Any act or occurrence which would constitute default under the terms of any lien superior to the lien securing the Note shall constitute a default under the Deed of Trust securing the Note.

______________________________ Buyer/Maker	______________________________ Seller/Payee
______________________________ Buyer/Maker	______________________________ Seller/Payee

The form of this Addendum has been approved by the Texas Real Estate Commission for use with similarly approved or promulgated contract forms. Such approval relates to this form only. No representation is made as to the legal validity or adequacy of any provision in any specific transactions. It is not suitable for complex transactions. (10-93) TREC No. 26-2. This form replaces TREC No. 26-1.

10-25-93

ENVIRONMENTAL ASSESSMENT, THREATENED OR ENDANGERED SPECIES, AND WETLANDS ADDENDUM

PROMULGATED BY THE TEXAS REAL ESTATE COMMISSION (TREC)

ADDENDUM TO EARNEST MONEY CONTRACT BETWEEN THE UNDERSIGNED PARTIES CONCERNING THE PROPERTY AT ______________________________
(Address)

☐ A. ENVIRONMENTAL ASSESSMENT: Buyer, at Buyer's expense, may obtain an Environmental Assessment Report prepared by an environmental specialist.

☐ B. THREATENED OR ENDANGERED SPECIES: Buyer, at Buyer's expense, may obtain a report from a natural resources professional to determine if there are any threatened o r endangered species or their habitats as defined by the Texas Parks and wildlife Department or the U.S. Fish and Wildlife Service.

☐ C. WETLANDS: Buyer, at Buyer's expense, may obtain a report from an environmental specialist to determine if there are wetlands, as defined by federal or state law or regulation.

Within _________ days after the Effective Date of the contract, Buyer may terminate the contract by furnishing Seller a copy of any report noted above that adversely affects the use of the Property and the Earnest Money shall be refunded to Buyer. If Buyer does not furnish Seller a copy of the unacceptable report within the prescribed time and give Seller notice that Buyer has terminated the contract, Buyer shall be deemed to have accepted the Property.

______________________________ ______________________________
Buyer Seller

______________________________ ______________________________
Buyer Seller

The form of this addendum has been approved by the Texas Real Estate Commission for use only with similarly approved o r promulgated forms of contracts. No representation is made as to the legal validity or adequacy of any provision in any specific transactions. It is not suitable for complex transactions. (10-93) TREC No. 28-0.

Transaction 7: All Cash

Utilizing: TREC 25-3, 29-1, Lead-Based Paint Addendum

Fannie Phyllis Farmer, a widow, will sell her Pecos County ranch to William Robert (Billy Bob) Richman and his wife, Mae Bea Richman. The property is described by a rather lengthy metes-and-bounds description, which is attached to the purchase agreement and identified as Exhibit A.

There are no crops or equipment included in the sale. There are no outstanding mineral or timber interests; however, Fannie will retain 50 percent of the gas and oil interests at closing. The buyers request that the seller furnish, at her own expense, a survey of the property within ten days after the effective date of the contract. They call for an abstract to be furnished within 30 days after the effective date of the contract, and will have it reviewed by their real estate attorney, Ronald Hawkeye Redundant.

The buyers will pay $895,000 cash for the property. According to the seller, the farm is 350 acres. If, after reviewing the survey, it is found to be more or less than 350 acres, the sale price will be adjusted $2,500 per acre over or under. They tender $100,000 earnest money with Pecos County Abstract Company, who will close the transaction in about 30 days on December 23. Possession will be granted at closing and funding, which will occur on December 23.

The buyers choose not to have any inspections done and accept the property in its present condition. They have received the seller's disclosure of property condition form. They have also waived their right to have the farmhouse inspected for lead-based paint hazards. They will have all of the present ramshackle buildings demolished to make way for a new 12,000-square-foot house. Rollback taxes will not be an issue because the buyers plan no change in the use of the property.

The listing broker is Don Shrum Country Properties. The buyers are represented by Colby Carter, an independent broker. The buyer's broker will be paid a selling fee of $10,000, which will be paid from the listing broker's fee at closing.

11-08-99

EQUAL HOUSING OPPORTUNITY

PROMULGATED BY THE TEXAS REAL ESTATE COMMISSION (TREC)

FARM AND RANCH CONTRACT

1. **PARTIES:** ______________________________ (Seller) agrees to sell and convey to ______________________________(Buyer) and Buyer agrees to buy from Seller the property described below.

2. **PROPERTY:** The land situated in ____________________County, Texas, described as follows:

or as described on attached exhibit, together with all improvements thereon and all rights, privileges and appurtenances pertaining thereto, including but not limited to: water rights, claims and permits, easements, all rights and obligations of applicable government programs and cooperative or association memberships. Included with the sale are the following items, if any: windmills and tanks, domestic water systems, curtains and rods, draperies and rods, valances, blinds, window shades, screens, shutters, awnings, wall-to-wall carpeting, mirrors fixed in place, ceiling fans, attic fans, mail boxes, television antennas and satellite dish with controls and equipment, permanently installed heating and air conditioning units, window air conditioning units, built-in security and fire detection equipment, plumbing and lighting fixtures, including chandeliers, water softener, stove, built-in kitchen equipment, garage door openers with controls, built-in cleaning equipment, all swimming pool equipment and maintenance accessories, shrubbery, landscaping, permanently installed outdoor cooking equipment, built-in fireplace screens, artificial fireplace logs and all other property owned by Seller and attached to the above described real property.

The following crops and equipment are included:______________________________
______________________________.

The following property is not included:______________________________
______________________________.

All property sold by this contract is called the "Property." The Property will be conveyed subject to the following exceptions, reservations, conditions and restrictions (if none, insert "none"):

A. Minerals, Royalties, and Timber Interests:

(1) Presently outstanding in third parties:

(2) To be additionally retained by Seller:

B. Mineral Leases:

C. Surface Leases:

D. Easements:

Initialed for identification by Buyer__________ and Seller__________ **01A** TREC NO.25-3

Farm and Ranch Contract Page Two 11-08-99

E. Restrictions, Zoning Ordinances or other Exceptions:

3. SALES PRICE:

A. Cash portion of Sales Price payable by Buyer at closing . . . . $____________
B. (1) Sum of all financing described in Paragraph 4 . . . . $__________
(2) Less: face amount of any lender required stock . . . . <__________>
(3) Difference between B(1) and B(2) . . . . $____________
C. Sales Price [sum of A and B(3)] . . . . $____________
D. The Sales Price ❑ will ❑ will not be adjusted based on the survey required by Paragraph 6B, and the number of acres over or under ______ acres will be multiplied by $__________ per acre. The result thereof will be added to or subtracted from the Sales Price, and the cash amount set out in 3A will be adjusted accordingly; however, if the amount set out in 3A is to be adjusted by more than 10%, either party may terminate this contract and the earnest money will be refunded to Buyer.

4. FINANCING: Within _____ days after the effective date of this contract Buyer shall apply for all third party financing or noteholder's approval of any assumption and make every reasonable effort to obtain financing or assumption approval. Financing or assumption approval will be deemed to have been obtained when the lender determines that Buyer has satisfied all of lender's financial requirements (those items relating to Buyer's net worth, income and creditworthiness). If financing (including the face amount of any lender required stock) or assumption approval is not obtained within______ days after the effective date hereof, this contract will terminate and the earnest money will be refunded to Buyer. Each note to be executed hereunder must be secured by vendor's and deed of trust liens.
The portion of Sales Price not payable in cash will be paid as follows: (Check applicable boxes below)

❑ A. THIRD PARTY FINANCING:

❑ (1) This contract is subject to approval for Buyer of a third party first lien note of $__________ (including the face amount of any lender required stock) payable at ________ intervals for not less than _____ years with the initial interest rate not to exceed _____ % per annum.

❑ (2) This contract is subject to approval for Buyer of a third party second lien note of $________________ (including the face amount of any lender required stock) payable at _________ intervals for not less than ______ years with the initial interest rate not to exceed _____ % per annum.

❑ B. SELLER FINANCING: A promissory note from Buyer to Seller of $__________________, bearing _____% interest per annum, secured by vendor's and deed of trust liens, in accordance with the terms and conditions set forth in the attached TREC Seller Financing Addendum. If an owner policy of title insurance is furnished, Buyer shall furnish Seller with a mortgagee policy of title insurance.

❑ C. ASSUMPTION:

❑ (1) Buyer shall assume the unpaid principal balance of a first lien promissory note payable to ______________________________ dated _________________, which unpaid balance at closing will be $_____________ (including the face amount of any lender required stock). The total current monthly payment including principal, interest and any reserve deposits is $ ___________. Buyer's initial payment will be the first payment due after closing.

❑ (2) Buyer shall assume the unpaid principal balance of a second lien promissory note payable to ______________________________dated ___________________, which unpaid balance at closing will be $___________ (including the face amount of any lender required stock). The total current monthly payment including principal, interest and any reserve deposits is $ ______________. Buyer's initial payment will be the first payment due after closing.

If any assumed loan initially required the purchase of lender's stock, the sale of the Property will include such stock.

Buyer's assumption of an existing note includes all obligations imposed by the deed of trust securing the note. If the unpaid principal balance(s) of any assumed loan(s) as of the Closing Date varies from the loan balance(s) stated above, the ❑ cash payable at closing ❑ Sales Price will be adjusted by the amount of any variance; provided, if the total principal balance of all assumed loans varies in an amount greater than $500.00 at closing, either party may terminate this contract and the earnest money will

Initialed for identification by Buyer__________and Seller__________ **01A** TREC NO.25-3 be refunded to Buyer unless the other party elects to eliminate the excess in the variance by an appropriate adjustment at closing. If the noteholder on assumption requires (a) Buyer to pay an assumption fee in excess of $__________ in C(l) above or $__________ in C(2) above, and Seller declines to pay such excess or (b) an increase in the interest rate to more than _____% in C(l) above or ______% in C(2) above, or (c) any other modification of the loan documents, Buyer may terminate this contract and the earnest money will be refunded to Buyer. A vendor's lien and deed of trust to secure assumption will be required, which will automatically be released on execution and delivery of a release by noteholder. If Seller is released from liability on any assumed note, the vendor's lien and deed of trust to secure assumption will not be required.

NOTICE TO BUYER: The payments, interest rates or other terms of some loans may be adjusted by the lender at or after closing. If you are concerned about the possibility of future adjustments, do not sign the contract without examining the notes and deeds of trust.

NOTICE TO SELLER: Your liability to pay the note assumed by Buyer will continue unless you obtain a release of liability from the lender. If you are concerned about future liability, you should use the TREC Release of Liability Addendum.

❑ D. CREDIT APPROVAL ON ASSUMPTION OR SELLER FINANCING: Within _______ days after the effective date of this contract, Buyer shall deliver to Seller ❑ credit report ❑ verification of employment, including salary ❑ verification of funds on deposit in financial institutions ❑ current financial statement to establish Buyer's creditworthiness for assumption approval or seller financing and ❑ __________

____

____.

If Buyer's documentation is not delivered within the specified time, Seller may terminate this contract by notice to Buyer within 7 days after expiration of the time for delivery, and the earnest money will be paid to Seller. If this contract is not so terminated, Seller will be deemed to have accepted Buyer's credit. If the documentation is timely delivered, and Seller determines in Seller's sole discretion that Buyer's credit is unacceptable, Seller may terminate this contract by notice to Buyer within 7 days after expiration of the time for delivery and the earnest money will be refunded to Buyer. If Seller does not so terminate this contract, Seller will be deemed to have accepted Buyer's credit. Buyer hereby authorizes any credit reporting agency to furnish to Seller at Buyer's sole expense copies of Buyer's credit reports.

5. **EARNEST MONEY:** Buyer shall deposit $______________ as earnest money with ______________ ______________________________ at ______________________________ (Address), as escrow agent, upon execution of this contract by both parties. Additional earnest money of $___________ must be deposited by Buyer with escrow agent on or before __________________, ______. If Buyer fails to deposit the earnest money as required by this contract, Buyer will be in default.

6. **TITLE POLICY AND SURVEY:**

❑ A. TITLE POLICY: Seller shall furnish to Buyer at ❑ Seller's ❑ Buyer's expense an owner policy of title insurance (the Title Policy) issued by ____(the Title Company) in the amount of the Sales Price, dated at or after closing, insuring Buyer against loss under the provisions of the Title Policy, subject to the promulgated exclusions (including existing building and zoning ordinances) and the following exceptions:

(1) The standard printed exception for standby fees, taxes and assessments.
(2) Liens created as part of the financing described in Paragraph 4.
(3) Those matters specifically described in Paragraph 2.
(4) The standard printed exception as to discrepancies, conflicts, shortages in area or boundary lines, encroachments or protrusions, or overlapping improvements.
(5) The standard printed exception as to marital rights.
(6) The standard printed exception as to waters, tidelands, beaches, streams, and related matters.

Within 20 days after the Title Company receives a copy of this contract, Seller shall furnish to Buyer a commitment for title insurance (the Commitment) and, at Buyer's expense, legible copies of restrictive covenants and documents evidencing exceptions in the Commitment other than the standard printed exceptions. Seller authorizes the Title Company to mail or hand deliver the Commitment and related documents to Buyer at Buyer's address shown below. If the Commitment is not delivered to Buyer within the specified time, the time for delivery will be automatically extended up to 15 days.

❑ B. SURVEY: (Check one box only)

❑ (1) Within _____ days after the effective date of this contract, Buyer shall obtain a survey at Buyer's expense.

❑ (2) Within _____ days after the effective date of this contract, Seller shall cause a survey to be delivered to Buyer at Seller's expense.

❑ (3) Within _____ days after the effective date of this contract, Seller will deliver to Buyer the existing survey plat of the Property dated __________________________, _____, which ❑ will ❑ will not be recertified to a date subsequent to the effective date of this contract at the expense of ❑ Buyer ❑ Seller.

The survey must be made by a Registered Professional Land Surveyor acceptable to the Title Company and any lender.

Buyer will have 7 days after the receipt of the latter of the Commitment or survey to object in writing to matters disclosed in the Commitment or survey except for those matters specifically described in Paragraph 2. Buyer's failure to object under Paragraph 6 within the time allowed will constitute a waiver of Buyer's right to object; except that the requirements in Schedule C of the Commitment will not be deemed to have been waived. Seller shall cure the timely objections of Buyer or any third party lender within 20 days after Seller receives the objections and the Closing Date will be extended as necessary. If objections are not cured by the extended Closing Date, this contract will terminate and the earnest money will be refunded to Buyer unless Buyer elects to waive the objections.

❑ C. ABSTRACT OF TITLE: TREC Addendum for Abstract of Title, or an addendum required by the parties, is attached.

NOTICE TO SELLER AND BUYER:

(1) Broker advises Buyer to have an abstract of title covering the Property examined by an attorney of Buyer's selection, or Buyer should be furnished with or obtain a Title Policy. If a Title Policy is furnished, the Commitment should be promptly reviewed by an attorney of Buyer's choice due to the time limitations on Buyer's right to object.

(2) If the Property is situated in a utility or other statutorily created district providing water, sewer, drainage, or flood control facilities and services, Chapter 49 of the Texas Water Code requires Seller to deliver and the Buyer to sign the statutory notice relating to the tax rate, bonded indebtedness, or standby fee of the district prior to final execution of this contract.

(3) Eligibility for government farm program benefits may depend upon compliance with a soil conservation plan for the Property. Buyer is advised to determine whether the property is subject to and in compliance with a plan before signing this contract.

(4) Buyer is advised that the presence of wetlands, toxic substances, including asbestos and wastes or other environmental hazards or the presence of a threatened or endangered species or its habitat may affect Buyer's intended use of the Property. If Buyer is concerned about these matters, an addendum either promulgated by TREC or required by the parties should be used.

(5) If the Property is located outside the limits of a municipality, Seller notifies Buyer under §5.011, Texas Property Code, that the Property may now or later be included in the extraterritorial jurisdiction of a municipality and may now or later be subject to annexation by the municipality. Each municipality maintains a map that depicts its boundaries and extraterritorial jurisdiction. To determine if the Property is located within a municipality's extraterritorial jurisdiction or is likely to be located within a municipality's extraterritorial jurisdiction, contact all municipalities located in the general proximity of the Property for further information.

(6) If the Property abuts the tidally influenced submerged lands of the state, Section 33.135, Texas Natural Resources Code, requires a notice regarding coastal area property to be included in the contract. An addendum either promulgated by TREC or required by the parties should be used.

(7) Unless expressly prohibited in writing by the parties, Seller may continue to show the Property for sale and to receive, negotiate and accept back-up offers.

(8) Any residential service contract that is purchased in connection with this transaction should be reviewed for the scope of coverage, exclusions and limitations. **The purchase of a residential service contract is optional. Similar coverage may be purchased from various companies authorized to do business in Texas.**

7. **PROPERTY CONDITION:**

A. INSPECTIONS, ACCESS AND UTILITIES: Buyer may have the Property inspected by an inspector selected by Buyer, licenced by TREC or otherwise permitted by law to make suchinspections. Seller shall permit access to the Property at reasonable times for inspection, repairs and treatment and for reinspection after repairs and treatment have been completed. Seller shall pay for turning on utilities for inspection and reinspection.

B. SELLER'S DISCLOSURE NOTICE PURSUANT TO SECTION 5.008, TEXAS PROPERTY CODE (Notice) (check one box only):

❑ (1) Buyer has received the Notice.

❑ (2) Buyer has not received the Notice. Within _____ days after the effective date of this contract, Seller shall deliver the Notice to Buyer. If Buyer does not receive the Notice, Buyer may terminate this contract at any time prior to the closing. If Seller delivers the Notice, Buyer may terminate this contract for any reason within 7 days after Buyer receives the Notice or prior to the closing, whichever first occurs.

❑ (3) The Texas Property Code does not require this Seller to furnish the Notice.

C. SELLER'S DISCLOSURE OF LEAD-BASED PAINT AND LEAD-BASED PAINT HAZARDS is required by Federal law for a residential dwelling constructed prior to 1978. An addendum providing such disclosure ❑ is ❑ is not attached.

D. ACCEPTANCE OF PROPERTY CONDITION: (check one box only):

❑ (1) In addition to any earnest money deposited with escrow agent, Buyer has paid Seller $_____________ (the "Option Fee") for the (i) right to inspect the Property at Buyer's cost, (ii) right to conduct feasibility studies as Buyer deems necessary and (iii) unrestricted right to terminate this contract by giving notice of termination to Seller within ________ days after the effective date of this contract. If Buyer gives notice of termination within the time specified, the Option Fee will not be refunded, however, any earnest money will be refunded to Buyer. If Buyer does not give notice of termination within the time specified, Buyer will be deemed to have accepted the Property in its current condition and the Option Fee ❑ will ❑ will not be credited to the Sales Price at closing.

❑ (2) Buyer accepts the Property in its present condition; provided Seller, at Seller's expense, shall complete the following repairs and treatment: ____
____
____.

E. LENDER REQUIRED REPAIRS AND TREATMENTS (REPAIRS): Unless otherwise agreed in writing, neither party is obligated to pay for lender required repairs or treatments for wood destroying insects. If the cost of lender required repairs exceeds 5% of the Sales Price, Buyer may terminate this contract.

F. COMPLETION OF REPAIRS AND TREATMENT. Unless otherwise agreed by the parties in writing, Seller shall complete all agreed repairs and treatment prior to the Closing Date. Repairs and treatments must be performed by persons who regularly provide such repairs or treatments. At Buyer's election, any transferable warranties received by Seller with respect to the repairs will be transferred to Buyer at Buyer's expense. If Seller fails to complete any agreed repairs and treatment prior to the Closing Date, Buyer may do so and the Closing Date will be extended up to 15 days, if necessary, to complete repairs and treatment.

8. **BROKERS' FEES:** All obligations of the parties for payment of brokers' fees are contained in separate written agreements.

9. **CLOSING:** The closing of the sale will be on or before ____________________________,_________, or within 7 days after objections to matters disclosed in the Commitment or by the survey have been cured, whichever date is later (the Closing Date). *If financing or assumption approval has been obtained pursuant to Paragraph 4,* the Closing Date will be extended up to 15 days if necessary to comply with lender's closing requirements (for example, appraisal, survey, insurance policies, lender-required repairs, closing documents). If either party fails to close this sale by the Closing Date, the non-defaulting party will be entitled to exercise the remedies contained in Paragraph 15. At closing Seller shall furnish tax statements or certificates showing no delinquent taxes, and a general warranty deed conveying good and indefeasible title showing no additional exceptions to those permitted in Paragraph 6.

10. **POSSESSION:** Seller shall deliver possession of the Property to Buyer on ______________________ in its present or required repaired condition, ordinary wear and tear excepted. Any possession by Buyer prior to closing or by Seller after closing which is not authorized by a temporary lease form promulgated by TREC or required by the parties will establish a tenancy at sufferance relationship between the parties. *Consult your insurance agent prior to change of ownership or possession as insurance coverage may be limited or terminated. The absence of a written lease or appropriate insurance coverage may expose the parties to economic loss.*

Farm and Ranch Contract

Page Six 11-08-99

11. SPECIAL PROVISIONS: (Insert only factual statements and business details applicable to this sale. TREC rules prohibit licensees from adding factual statements or business details for which a contract addendum, lease or other form has been promulgated by TREC for mandatory use.)

12. SETTLEMENT AND OTHER EXPENSES:

A. The following expenses must be paid at or prior to closing:

(1) Appraisal fees will be paid by ______________________________.

(2) The total of loan discount fees (including any Texas Veterans' Housing Assistance Program Participation Fee) may not exceed_____% of the loan of which Seller shall pay ___________ and Buyer shall pay the remainder. The total of any buydown fees may not exceed ___________which will be paid by ______________________________.

(3) Seller's Expenses: Releases of existing liens, including prepayment penalties and recording fees; release of Seller's loan liability; tax statements or certificates; preparation of deed; one-half of escrow fee; and other expenses stipulated to be paid by Seller under other provisions of this contract.

(4) Buyer's Expenses: Loan application, origination and commitment fees; loan assumption costs; preparation and recording of deed of trust to secure assumption; lender required expenses incident to new loans, including PMI premium, preparation of loan documents, recording fees, tax service and research fees, warehouse or underwriting fees, copies of restrictions and easements, amortization schedule, premiums for mortgagee title policies and endorsements required by lender, credit reports, photos; required premiums for flood and hazard insurance; required reserve deposit for insurance premiums and ad valorem taxes; interest on all monthly installment notes from date of disbursements to one month prior to dates of first monthly payments; customary Program Loan costs for Buyer; one-half of escrow fee; and other expenses stipulated to be paid by Buyer under other provisions of this contract.

B. If any expense exceeds an amount expressly stated in this contract for such expense to be paid by a party, that party may terminate this contract unless the other party agrees to pay such excess. In no event will Buyer pay charges and fees expressly prohibited by the Texas Veterans' Housing Assistance Program or other governmental loan program regulations.

13. PRORATIONS AND ROLLBACK TAXES:

A. PRORATIONS: Taxes for the current year, interest, maintenance fees, assessments, dues and rents will be prorated through the Closing Date. If taxes for the current year vary from the amount prorated at closing, the parties shall adjust the prorations when tax statements for the current year are available. *If a loan is assumed* and the lender maintains an escrow account, the escrow account must be transferred to Buyer without any deficiency. Buyer shall reimburse Seller for the amount in the transferred account. Buyer shall pay the premium for a new insurance policy. If taxes are not paid at or prior to closing, Buyer will be obligated to pay taxes for the current year.

B. ROLLBACK TAXES: If this sale or Buyer's use of the Property after closing results in the assessment of additional taxes, penalties or interest (Assessments) for periods prior to closing, the Assessments will be the obligation of Buyer. If Seller's change in use of the Property prior to closing or denial of a special use valuation on the Property claimed by Seller results in Assessments for periods prior to closing, the Assessments will be the obligation of Seller. Obligations imposed by this paragraph will survive closing.

14. CASUALTY LOSS: If any part of the Property is damaged or destroyed by fire or other casualty loss after the effective date of the contract, Seller shall restore the Property to its previous condition as soon as reasonably possible, but in any event by the Closing Date. If Seller fails to do so due to factors beyond Seller's control, Buyer may either (a) terminate this contract and the earnest money will be refunded to Buyer (b) extend the time for performance up to 15 days and the Closing Date will be extended as necessary or (c) accept the Property in its damaged condition and accept an assignment of insurance proceeds. Seller's obligations under this paragraph are independent of any obligations of Seller under Paragraph 7.

Initialed for identification by Buyer_________ and Seller_________ **01A** TREC NO.25-3

15. **DEFAULT:** If Buyer fails to comply with this contract, Buyer will be in default, and Seller may either (a) enforce specific performance, seek such other relief as may be provided by law, or both, or (b) terminate this contract and receive the earnest money as liquidated damages, thereby releasing both parties from this contract. If, due to factors beyond Seller's control, Seller fails within the time allowed to make any non-casualty repairs or deliver the Commitment, Buyer may either (a) extend the time for performance up to 15 days and the Closing Date will be extended as necessary or (b) terminate this contract as the sole remedy and receive the earnest money. If Seller fails to comply with this contract for any other reason, Seller will be in default and Buyer may either (a) enforce specific performance, seek such other relief as may be provided by law, or both, or (b) terminate this contract and receive the earnest money, thereby releasing both parties from this contract.

16. **DISPUTE RESOLUTION:** It is the policy of the State of Texas to encourage the peaceable resolution of disputes through alternative dispute resolution procedures. The parties are encouraged to use an addendum approved by TREC to submit to mediation disputes which cannot be resolved in good faith through informal discussion.

17. **ATTORNEY'S FEES:** The prevailing party in any legal proceeding brought under or with respect to the transaction described in this contract is entitled to recover from the non-prevailing party all costs of such proceeding and reasonable attorney's fees.

18. **ESCROW:** The earnest money is deposited with escrow agent with the understanding that escrow agent is not (a) a party to this contract and does not have any liability for the performance or nonperformance of any party to this contract, (b) liable for interest on the earnest money and (c) liable for any loss of earnest money caused by the failure of any financial institution in which the earnest money has been deposited unless the financial institution is acting as escrow agent. At closing, the earnest money must be applied first to any cash down payment, then to Buyer's closing costs and any excess refunded to Buyer. If both parties make written demand for the earnest money, escrow agent may require payment of unpaid expenses incurred on behalf of the parties and a written release of liability of escrow agent from all parties. If one party makes written demand for the earnest money, escrow agent shall give notice of the demand by providing to the other party a copy of the demand. If escrow agent does not receive written objection to the demand from the other party within 30 days after notice to the other party, escrow agent may disburse the earnest money to the party making demand reduced by the amount of unpaid expenses incurred on behalf of the party receiving the earnest money and escrow agent may pay the same to the creditors. If escrow agent complies with the provisions of this paragraph, each party hereby releases escrow agent from all adverse claims related to the disbursal of the earnest money. Escrow agent's notice to the other party will be effective when deposited in the U. S. Mail, postage prepaid, certified mail, return receipt requested, addressed to the other party at such party's address shown below. Notice of objection to the demand will be deemed effective upon receipt by escrow agent.

19. **REPRESENTATIONS:** Seller represents that as of the Closing Date (a) there will be no liens, assessments, or security interests against the Property which will not be satisfied out of the Sales Price unless securing payment of any loans assumed by Buyer and (b) assumed loans will be without default. If any representation in this contract is untrue on the Closing Date, this contract may be terminated by Buyer and the Earnest Money will be refunded to Buyer. All representations contained in this contract will survive closing.

20. **FEDERAL TAX REQUIREMENT:** If Seller is a "foreign person", as defined by applicable law, or if Seller fails to deliver an affidavit that Seller is not a "foreign person", then Buyer shall withhold from the sales proceeds an amount sufficient to comply with applicable tax law and deliver the same to the Internal Revenue Service together with appropriate tax forms. IRS regulations require filing written reports if cash in excess of specified amounts is received in the transaction.

21. **AGREEMENT OF PARTIES:** This contract contains the entire agreement of the parties and cannot be changed except by their written agreement. Addenda which are a part of this contract are (list):________
____
____
____.

22. **CONSULT YOUR ATTORNEY:** Real estate licensees cannot give legal advice. This is intended to be a legally binding contract. READ IT CAREFULLY. If you do not understand the effect of this contract, consult

Farm and Ranch Contract Page Eight 11-08-99

your attorney BEFORE signing.

Buyer's Attorney is:______________________________ Seller's Attorney is:______________________________

23. NOTICES: All notices from the parties to each other must be in writing and are effective when mailed to, hand-delivered at, or transmitted by facsimile machine as follows:

To Buyer at:

____

____

____

Telephone: (___)______________________

Facsimile: (___)______________________

To Seller at:

____

____

____

Telephone: (___) ______________________

Facsimile:(___) ______________________

EXECUTED the _____day of _________________, _____ (THE EFFECTIVE DATE). (BROKER: FILL IN THE DATE OF FINAL ACCEPTANCE.)

______________________________ Buyer ______________________________ Seller

______________________________ Buyer ______________________________ Seller

The form of this contract has been approved by the Texas Real Estate Commission. Such approval relates to this contract form only. TREC forms are intended for use only by trained real estate licensees. No representation is made as to the legal validity or adequacy of any provision in any specific transaction. It is not suitable for complex transactions. Extensive riders or additions are not to be used. Texas Real Estate Commission, P.O. Box 12188, Austin, TX 78711-2188, 1-800-250-8732 or (512) 459-6544 (http://www.trec.state.tx.us) TREC NO. 25-3. This form replaces TREC NO. 25-2.

BROKER INFORMATION AND RATIFICATION OF FEE

Listing Broker has agreed to pay Other Broker ______________________ of the total sales price when Listing Broker's fee is received. Escrow Agent is authorized and directed to pay Other Broker from Listing Broker's fee at closing.

____
Other Broker License No.
represents ❑ Seller as Listing Broker's subagent
❑ Buyer only as Buyer's agent

____
Associate Telephone

____
Broker Address

____
Telephone Facsimile

____
Listing Broker License No.
represents ❑ Seller and Buyer as an intermediary
❑ Seller only as Seller's agent

____
Listing Associate Telephone

____
Selling Associate Telephone

____
Broker Address

____
Telephone Facsimile

RECEIPT

Receipt of ❑ Contract and ❑ $__________ Earnest Money in the form of______________________is acknowledged.

Escrow Agent: ______________________________ Date: ______________________, ________

By:______________________________

____
Address

Telephone: (_____)______________________

____
City State Zip Code

Facsimile: (_____) ______________________

09-20-99

PROMULGATED BY THE TEXAS REAL ESTATE COMMISSION (TREC)

ADDENDUM FOR ABSTRACT OF TITLE

ADDENDUM TO CONTRACT CONCERNING THE PROPERTY AT

____
(Street Address and City)

Paragraph 6A of the contract is replaced and superseded by this Addendum.

Within 30 days after ______________________________ (the Abstract Company) receives a copy of this contract, Seller shall furnish to Buyer at Seller's expense an Abstract of Title certified by the Abstract Company from the sovereignty to the effective date of this contract (Complete Abstract). If the Complete Abstract is not delivered to Buyer within the specified time, the time for delivery will be automatically extended up to 15 days. Within 30 days after Buyer's receipt of the Complete Abstract, Buyer may object in writing to matters disclosed in the Complete Abstract.

Seller shall furnish to Buyer at Seller's expense a Supplemental Abstract that supplements the Complete Abstract as of the Closing Date. Prior to closing, Buyer may object in writing to matters disclosed in the Supplemental Abstract.

The Complete Abstract and Supplemental Abstract may be examined at Buyer's expense by an attorney selected by Buyer. Buyer's failure to object within the time allowed will constitute a waiver of Buyer's right to object. If objections are made by Buyer or any third party lender, Seller shall cure the objections within 20 days after Seller receives the objections and the Closing Date will be extended as necessary. If objections are not cured by the extended Closing Date, this contract will terminate and the earnest money will be refunded to Buyer unless Buyer elects to waive the objections.

Buyer	Seller
Buyer	Seller

APPROVED BY THE
TEXAS REAL ESTATE COMMISSION

02-10-97

ADDENDUM FOR SELLER'S DISCLOSURE OF INFORMATION ON LEAD-BASED PAINT AND LEAD-BASED PAINT HAZARDS AS REQUIRED BY FEDERAL LAW

CONCERNING THE PROPERTY AT ______________________________
(Street Address and City)

A. LEAD WARNING STATEMENT: "Every purchaser of any interest in residential real property on which a residential dwelling was built prior to 1978 is notified that such property may present exposure to lead from lead-based paint that may place young children at risk of developing lead poisoning. Lead poisoning in young children may produce permanent neurological damage, including learning disabilities, reduced intelligence quotient, behavioral problems, and impaired memory. Lead poisoning also poses a particular risk to pregnant women. The seller of any interest in residential real property is required to provide the buyer with any information on lead-based paint hazards from risk assessments or inspections in the seller's possession and notify the buyer of any known lead-based paint hazards. A risk assessment or inspection for possible lead-paint hazards is recommended prior to purchase."

B. SELLER'S DISCLOSURE:

1. PRESENCE OF LEAD-BASED PAINT AND/OR LEAD-BASED PAINT HAZARDS (check one box only):
   - ☐ (a) Known lead-based paint and/or lead-based paint hazards are present in the Property (explain): ______________________________.
   - ☐ (b) Seller has no actual knowledge of lead-based paint and/or lead-based paint hazards in the Property.
2. RECORDS AND REPORTS AVAILABLE TO SELLER (check one box only):
   - ☐ (a) Seller has provided the purchaser with all available records and reports pertaining to lead-based paint and/or lead-based paint hazards in the Property (list documents): ______________________________.
   - ☐ (b) Seller has no reports or records pertaining to lead-based paint and/or lead-based paint hazards in the Property.

C. BUYER'S RIGHTS (check one box only)**:**

☐ 1. Buyer waives the opportunity to conduct a risk assessment or inspection of the Property for the presence of lead-based paint or lead-based paint hazards.

☐ 2. Within ten days after the effective date of this contract, Buyer may have the Property inspected for the presence of lead-based paint and/or lead-based paint hazards. If lead-based paint or lead-based paint hazards are present, Buyer may terminate this contract by giving Seller written notice within 14 days after the effective date of this contract.

D. BUYER'S ACKNOWLEDGMENT (check applicable boxes)**:**

☐ 1. Buyer has received copies of all information listed above.

☐ 2. Buyer has received the pamphlet *Protect Your Family from Lead in Your Home.*

E. BROKERS' ACKNOWLEDGMENT: Brokers have informed Seller of Seller's obligations under 42 U.S.C. 4852d to: (a) provide Buyer with the federally approved pamphlet on lead poisoning prevention; (b) complete this addendum; (c) disclose any known lead-based paint and/or lead-based paint hazards in the Property; (d) deliver all records and reports to Buyer pertaining to lead-based paint and/or lead-based paint hazards in the Property; (e) provide Buyer a period of up to 10 days to have the Property inspected; and (f) retain a completed copy of this addendum for at least 3 years following the sale. Brokers are aware of their responsibility to ensure compliance.

F. CERTIFICATION OF ACCURACY: The following persons have reviewed the information above and certify, to the best of their knowledge, that the information they have provided is true and accurate.

Seller ______ Date	Buyer ______ Date
Seller ______ Date	Buyer ______ Date
Listing Broker ______ Date	Other Broker ______ Date

The form of this addendum has been approved for voluntary use by the Texas Real Estate Commission for use only with similarly approved or promulgated forms of contracts. No representation is made as to the legal validity or adequacy of any provision in any specific transactions. Texas Real Estate Commission, P.O. Box 12188, Austin, TX 78711-2188, 1-800-250-8732 or (512) 459-6544.

01A TREC No. OP-L

Transaction 8: Assumption with Release of Liability

Utilizing: TREC 30-2, 11-3, 12-1, 33-0, 34-0

Unit 623 of Building B of the condominium project known as Freedom Flats, Phase II in Corpus Christi, Nueces County, Texas, is being sold to Bernie Bryan Buyer and spouse, Beverly Barbara Buyer, by Peter Paul Pastor and his wife, Sarah Sue Pastor. The property is more commonly known as 1215 Market Street, Apartment 623. Ownership of the unit includes two parking spaces identified as numbers 1654 and 1658 in the adjoining parking garage. The zip code is 78411.

Prior to signing the agreement of purchase, the buyers received, reviewed and accepted all of the condominium documents, as well as the Condominium Resale Certificate (TREC No. 32-0), which was prepared and signed by the secretary of the homeowners' association 20 days ago.

The buyers will pay $68,200 for the unit and assume the seller's existing conventional loan with an outstanding balance of $51,800. The loan is held by Deep Pocket Mortgage Company, Inc. The buyers will apply for assumption approval within three days after the effective date of the contract. They will close within 30 days of the effective date of this contract, which will allow for closing on June 16. The current loan is at 6.75 percent and may be escalated to 7.25 percent upon assumption. If the loan balance is a few dollars more or less at closing, the cash payable at closing will be adjusted to compensate for any variance. The lender will charge a 1 point transfer fee, which will be paid by thc buycr.

The buyers will pay for the owner's title policy. The buyer received the seller's disclosure notice and accepts the property in its present condition, provided the seller, at seller's expense, shall replace the nonfunctioning garbage disposal and the broken faucet in the bathroom. Because the project was built in 1979, it is not subject to the HUD lead-based paint disclosure requirement. No repairs to any of the common elements are required.

The seller has informed the buyers that the monthly PITI payment is $785 and that the monthly maintenance fee is $236. The amount of the maintenance fee was confirmed by the resale certificate furnished by the secretary of the homeowner's association. Any transfer or processing fee charged by the homeowner's association will be paid solely by the buyer.

The seller will have the purchase agreement reviewed by attorney Michael Holmes prior to signing the agreement.

The unit has been listed with Skyline Realty. The listing company will pay the subagent, Downhome Realty, a selling fee equal to 3.25 percent of the selling price of the property.

$2,000 earnest money is delivered to Buyer's Choice Title Company, who will issue an owner's policy at closing.

The sellers will deliver a copy of the note and deed of trust to the buyer for review within three days after the effective date of the purchase agreement. The buyers also request that copies of every document they will be asked to sign at closing be delivered to them for review a minimum of 48 hours prior to closing.

The sellers will permit the loan to be assumed only if they are released from liability and will not close if the lender refuses to release them. The buyers and the sellers will apply for the release within three days after the effective date of the contract.

There is already an existing contract in place, dated May 5, between the sellers and a bachelor by the name of Gordon Robinson. If the seller notifies the buyers on or before 5 P.M. on May 20 that the contract with Mr. Robinson is terminated, this agreement is no longer subject to the contingency, and the effective date of this contract will be amended to be the date of termination of the previous contract.

The seller has no knowledge of any prior fill as it relates to the property.

NOTICE: Not For Use Where Seller Owns Fee Simple Title To Land Beneath Unit 11-8-99
PROMULGATED BY THE TEXAS REAL ESTATE COMMISSION (TREC)

EQUAL HOUSING OPPORTUNITY

RESIDENTIAL CONDOMINIUM CONTRACT (RESALE)
ALL CASH, ASSUMPTION, THIRD PARTY CONVENTIONAL OR SELLER FINANCING

1. **PARTIES:** ____________________ (Seller) agrees to sell and convey to ____________________ (Buyer) and Buyer agrees to buy from Seller the property described below.

2. **PROPERTY AND CONDOMINIUM DOCUMENTS:**
   A. Condominium Unit ________, in Building ________, of ____________________, a condominium project, located at ____________________ (Address/Zip Code), City of ____________________, ____________________ County, Texas, described in the Condominium Declaration and Plat and any amendments thereto of record in said County; together with such Unit's undivided interest in the Common Elements designated by the Declaration, including those areas reserved as Limited Common Elements appurtenant to the Unit and such other rights to use the Common Elements which have been specifically assigned to the Unit in any other manner. Parking areas assigned to the Unit are: ____________________.
   The property includes the following items owned by Seller, if any: curtains and rods, draperies and rods, valances, blinds, window shades, screens, shutters, awnings, wall-to-wall carpeting, mirrors fixed in place, ceiling fans, attic fans, mail boxes, television antennas and satellite dish system with controls and equipment, permanently installed heating and air conditioning units, window air conditioning units, built-in security and fire detection equipment, plumbing and lighting fixtures including chandeliers, water softener, stove, built-in kitchen equipment, garage door openers with controls, built-in cleaning equipment, all swimming pool equipment and maintenance accessories, shrubbery, landscaping, permanently installed outdoor cooking equipment, built-in fireplace screens, artificial fireplace logs and all other personal property owned by Seller and attached to the Unit or located in the Unit and given as collateral for any indebtedness which will remain in effect after closing except the following property which is not included:
   ____
   ____________________.
   All property sold by this contract is called the "Property".
   B. The Declaration, Bylaws and any Rules of the Association are called "Documents". (Check one box only):
      ☐ (1) Buyer has received a copy of the Documents. Buyer is advised to read the Documents before signing the contract.
      ☐ (2) Buyer has not received a copy of the Documents. Seller shall deliver the Documents to Buyer within ______ days after the effective date of the contract. Buyer may cancel the contract before the sixth day after Buyer receives the Documents by hand-delivering or mailing written notice of cancellation to Seller by certified United States mail, return receipt requested.
   C. The Resale Certificate from the condominium owners association (the Association) is called the "Certificate". The Certificate must be in a form promulgated by TREC or required by the parties. The Certificate must have been prepared no more than three months before the date it is delivered to Buyer and must contain at a minimum the information required by Section 82.157 of the Texas Property Code. (Check one box only):
      ☐ (1) Buyer has received the Certificate.
      ☐ (2) Buyer has not received the Certificate. Seller shall deliver the Certificate to Buyer within _____ days after the effective date of the contract. Buyer may cancel the contract before the sixth day after the date Buyer receives the Certificate by hand-delivering or mailing written notice of cancellation to Seller by certified United States mail, return receipt requested.
      ☐ (3) Buyer has received Seller's affidavit that Seller requested information from the Association concerning its financial condition as required by the Texas Property Code, and that the Association did not provide a Certificate or information required in the Certificate. Buyer and Seller agree to waive the requirement to furnish the Certificate.

3. **SALES PRICE:**
   A. Cash portion of Sales Price payable by Buyer at closing . . . . $____________
   B. Sum of all financing described below
   (excluding any private mortgage insurance [PMI] premium) . . . . $____________
   C. Sales Price (Sum of A and B) . . . . $____________

Residential Condominium Contract Concerning____Page Two 11-8-99
(Address of Property)

4. **FINANCING:** Within _____ days after the effective date of this contract Buyer shall apply for all third party financing or noteholder's approval of any assumption and make every reasonable effort to obtain financing or assumption approval. Financing or assumption approval will be deemed to have been obtained when the lender determines that Buyer has satisfied all of lender's financial requirements (those items relating to Buyer's net worth, income and creditworthiness). If financing (including any financed PMI premium) or assumption approval is not obtained within _____ days after the effective date hereof, this contract will terminate and the earnest money will be refunded to Buyer. Each note to be executed hereunder must be secured by vendor's and deed of trust liens.
The portion of Sales Price not payable in cash will be paid as follows: (Check applicable boxes below)

❑ A. THIRD PARTY FINANCING:

❑ (1) This contract is subject to approval for Buyer of a third party first mortgage loan having a loan-to-value ratio not to exceed _______ % as established by such third party (excluding any financed PMI premium), due in full in _____ year(s), with interest not to exceed _____ % per annum for the first _____ year(s) of the loan. The loan will be ❑ with ❑ without PMI.

❑ (2) This contract is subject to approval for Buyer of a third party second mortgage loan having a loan-to-value ratio not to exceed _____ % as established by such third party (excluding any financed PMI premium), due in full in _______ year(s), with interest not to exceed _______ % per annum for the first _____ year(s) of the loan. The loan will be ❑ with ❑ without PMI.

❑ B. TEXAS VETERANS' HOUSING ASSISTANCE PROGRAM LOAN: This contract is subject to approval for Buyer of a Texas Veterans' Housing Assistance Program Loan (the Program Loan) of $_________________for a period of at least ________ years at the interest rate established by the Texas Veterans' Land Board at the time of closing.

❑ C. SELLER FINANCING: A promissory note from Buyer to Seller of $__________________, bearing _______ % interest per annum, secured by vendor's and deed of trust liens, in accordance with the terms and conditions set forth in the attached TREC Seller Financing Addendum. If an owner policy of title insurance is furnished, Buyer shall furnish Seller with a mortgagee policy of title insurance.

❑ D. ASSUMPTION:

❑ (1) Buyer shall assume the unpaid principal balance of a first lien promissory note payable to ____ which unpaid balance at closing will be $ ______________ . The total current monthly payment including principal, interest and any reserve deposits is $ _______________ . Buyer's initial payment will be the first payment due after closing.

❑ (2) Buyer shall assume the unpaid principal balance of a second lien promissory note payable to ____ which unpaid balance at closing will be $ _______________ . The total current monthly payment including principal, interest and any reserve deposits is $ ______________ . Buyer's initial payment will be the first payment due after closing.

Buyer's assumption of an existing note includes all obligations imposed by the deed of trust securing the note.

If the unpaid principal balance(s) of any assumed loan(s) as of the Closing Date varies from the loan balance(s) stated above, the ❑ cash payable at closing ❑ Sales Price will be adjusted by the amount of any variance; provided, if the total principal balance of all assumed loans varies in an amount greater than $350.00 at closing, either party may terminate this contract and the earnest money will be refunded to Buyer unless the other party elects to eliminate the excess in the variance by an appropriate adjustment at closing. If the noteholder requires (a) payment of an assumption fee in excess of $ _______________in D(1) above or $ _______________ in D(2) above and Seller declines to pay such excess, or (b) an increase in the interest rate to more than _____ % in D(1) above, or _____ % in D(2) above, or (c) any other modification of the loan documents, Buyer may terminate this contract and the earnest money will be refunded to Buyer. A vendor's lien and deed of trust to secure assumption will be required which shall automatically be released on execution and delivery of a release by noteholder. If Seller is released from liability on any assumed note, the vendor's lien and deed of trust to secure assumption will not be required.

NOTICE TO BUYER: The monthly payments, interest rates or other terms of some loans may be adjusted by the lender at or after closing. If you are concerned about the possibility of

future adjustments, do not sign the contract without examining the notes and deeds of trust.
NOTICE TO SELLER: Your liability to pay the note assumed by Buyer will continue unless you obtain a release of liability from the lender. If you are concerned about future liability, you should use the TREC Release of Liability Addendum.

❑ E. CREDIT APPROVAL ON ASSUMPTION OR SELLER FINANCING: Within ______ days after the effective date of this contract, Buyer shall deliver to Seller ❑ credit report ❑ verification of employment, including salary ❑ verification of funds on deposit in financial institutions ❑ current financial statement to establish Buyer's creditworthiness for assumption approval or seller financing and ❑ ____
____
____.
If Buyer's documentation is not delivered within the specified time, Seller may terminate this contract by notice to Buyer within 7 days after expiration of the time for delivery, and the earnest money will be paid to Seller. If this contract is not so terminated, Seller will be deemed to have accepted Buyer's credit. If the documentation is timely delivered, and Seller determines in Seller's sole discretion that Buyer's credit is unacceptable, Seller may terminate this contract by notice to Buyer within 7 days after expiration of the time for delivery and the earnest money will be refunded to Buyer. If Seller does not so terminate this contract, Seller will be deemed to have accepted Buyer's credit. Buyer hereby authorizes any credit reporting agency to furnish to Seller at Buyer's sole expense copies of Buyer's credit reports.

5. **EARNEST MONEY:** Buyer shall deposit $___________ as earnest money with ____________________ ___________________________________ at ____ (Address), as escrow agent, upon execution of this contract by both parties. Additional earnest money of $_____________________ must be deposited by Buyer with escrow agent on or before ____________________,_________. If Buyer fails to deposit the earnest money as required by this contract, Buyer will be in default.

6. **TITLE POLICY:** Seller shall furnish to Buyer at ❑ Seller's ❑ Buyer's expense an owner policy of title insurance (the Title Policy) issued by ____(the Title Company) in the amount of the Sales Price, dated at or after closing, insuring Buyer against loss under the provisions of the Title Policy, subject to the promulgated exclusions (including existing building and zoning ordinances) and the following exceptions:
A. Restrictive covenants common to the platted subdivision in which the Property is located.
B. The standard printed exception for standby fees, taxes and assessments.
C. Liens created as part of the financing described in Paragraph 4.
D. Terms and provisions of the Documents including the assessments and platted easements.
E. Reservations or exceptions otherwise permitted by this contract or as may be approved by Buyer in writing.
F. The standard printed exception as to discrepancies, conflicts, shortages in area or boundary lines, encroachments or protrusions, or overlapping improvements.
G. The standard printed exception as to marital rights.
H. The standard printed exception as to waters, tidelands, beaches, streams, and related matters.
Within 20 days after the Title Company receives a copy of this contract, Seller shall furnish to Buyer a commitment for title insurance (the Commitment) and, at Buyer's expense, legible copies of restrictive covenants and documents evidencing exceptions in the Commitment other than the standard printed exceptions. Seller authorizes the Title Company to mail or hand deliver the Commitment and related documents to Buyer at Buyer's address shown below. If the Commitment is not delivered to Buyer within the specified time, the time for delivery will be automatically extended up to 15 days. Buyer will have 5 days after the receipt of the Commitment to object in writing to matters disclosed in the Commitment.
Buyer may object to existing building and zoning ordinances and items 6A through 6H above if Buyer determines that any such ordinance or item prohibits the following use or activity:_______________
____
____.
Buyer's failure to object within the time allowed will constitute a waiver of Buyer's right to object; except that

the requirements in Schedule C of the Commitment will not be deemed to have been waived. Seller shall cure the timely objections of Buyer or any third party lender within 15 days after Seller receives the objections and the Closing Date will be extended as necessary. If objections are not cured by the extended Closing Date, this contract will terminate and the earnest money will be refunded to Buyer unless Buyer elects to waive the objections.

NOTICE TO SELLER AND BUYER:

(1) Broker advises Buyer to have an abstract of title covering the Property examined by an attorney of Buyer's selection, or Buyer should be furnished with or obtain a Title Policy. If a Title Policy is furnished, the Commitment should be promptly reviewed by an attorney of Buyer's choice due to the time limitations on Buyer's right to object.

(2) If the Property is situated in a utility or other statutorily created district providing water, sewer, drainage, or flood control facilities and services, Chapter 49 of the Texas Water Code requires Seller to deliver and Buyer to sign the statutory notice relating to the tax rate, bonded indebtedness, or standby fee of the district prior to final execution of this contract.

(3) If the Property abuts the tidally influenced waters of the state, Section 33.135, Texas Natural Resources Code, requires a notice regarding coastal area property to be included in the contract. An addendum either promulgated by TREC or required by the parties should be used.

(4) Buyer is advised that the presence of wetlands, toxic substances, including asbestos and wastes or other environmental hazards or the presence of a threatened or endangered species or its habitat may affect Buyer's intended use of the Property. If Buyer is concerned about these matters, an addendum either promulgated by TREC or required by the parties should be used.

(5) If the Property is located outside the limits of a municipality, Seller notifies Buyer under §5.011, Texas Property Code, that the Property may now or later be included in the extraterritorial jurisdiction of a municipality and may now or later be subject to annexation by the municipality. Each municipality maintains a map that depicts its boundaries and extraterritorial jurisdiction. To determine if the Property is located within a municipality's extraterritorial jurisdiction or is likely to be located within a municipality's extraterritorial jurisdiction, contact all municipalities located in the general proximity of the Property for further information.

(6) Unless expressly prohibited in writing by the parties, Seller may continue to show the Property for sale and to receive, negotiate and accept back-up offers.

(7) Any residential service contract that is purchased in connection with this transaction should be reviewed for the scope of coverage, exclusions and limitations. **The purchase of a residential service contract is optional. Similar coverage may be purchased from various companies authorized to do business in Texas.**

7. **PROPERTY CONDITION:**

A. INSPECTIONS, ACCESS AND UTILITIES: Buyer may have the Property inspected by an inspector selected by Buyer, licensed by TREC or otherwise permitted by law to make such inspections. Seller shall permit access to the Property at reasonable times for inspection, repairs and treatment and for reinspection after repairs and treatment have been completed. Seller shall pay for turning on utilities for inspection and reinspection.

B. SELLER'S DISCLOSURE NOTICE PURSUANT TO SECTION 5.008, TEXAS PROPERTY CODE (Notice)(check one box only):

❑ (1) Buyer has received the Notice.

❑ (2) Buyer has not received the Notice. Within _____ days after the effective date of this contract, Seller shall deliver the Notice to Buyer. If Buyer does not receive the Notice, Buyer may terminate this contract at any time prior to the closing. If Seller delivers the Notice, Buyer may terminate this contract for any reason within seven days after Buyer receives the Notice or prior to the closing, whichever first occurs.

❑ (3) The Texas Property Code does not require this Seller to furnish the Notice.

C. SELLER'S DISCLOSURE OF LEAD-BASED PAINT AND LEAD-BASED PAINT HAZARDS is required by Federal law for a residential dwelling constructed prior to 1978. An addendum providing such disclosure ❑ is ❑ is not attached.

D. ACCEPTANCE OF PROPERTY CONDITION: (check one box only):

❑ (1) In addition to any earnest money deposited with escrow agent, Buyer has paid Seller $_______________ (the "Option Fee") for the unrestricted right to terminate this contract by giving notice of termination to Seller within ______ days after the effective date of this contract. If Buyer gives notice of termination within the time specified, the Option Fee will not be refunded, however, any earnest money will be refunded to Buyer. If Buyer does not give notice of termination within the time specified, Buyer will be deemed to have accepted the Property in its current condition and the Option Fee ❑ will ❑ will not be credited to the Sales Price at closing.

❑ (2) Buyer accepts the Property in its present condition; provided Seller, at Seller's expense, shall complete the following repairs and treatment: ____
____
____.

E. LENDER REQUIRED REPAIRS AND TREATMENTS (REPAIRS).Unless otherwise agreed in writing, neither party is obligated to pay for lender required repairs or treatments for wood destroying insects. If the cost of lender required repairs exceeds 5% of the Sales Price, Buyer may terminate this contract.

F. COMPLETION OF REPAIRS AND TREATMENT. Unless otherwise agreed by the parties in writing, Seller shall complete all agreed repairs and treatment prior to the Closing Date. Repairs and treatments must be performed by persons who regularly provide such repairs or treatments. At Buyer's election, any transferable warranties received by Seller with respect to the repairs will be transferred to Buyer at Buyer's expense. If Seller fails to complete any agreed repairs and treatment prior to the Closing Date, Buyer may do so and the Closing Date will be extended up to 15 days, if necessary, to complete repairs and treatment.

G. REPAIRS TO COMMON ELEMENTS. After Buyer receives all reports of needed repairs to Common Elements and Limited Common Elements that are not the responsibility of Seller, Buyer will have 7 days to deliver notice to Seller that Buyer will terminate the contract unless Buyer receives written confirmation from the Association that such repairs will be made in a reasonable time at no cost to Buyer. If Buyer delivers such notice, Seller will have _____ days after receipt of such notice to cause to be delivered to Buyer written confirmation of the Association's commitment to repair. If Buyer does not deliver such notice to Seller, Buyer will be deemed to have accepted the Property without such repairs. If required by Buyer and written confirmation of repairs is not delivered to Buyer as required above, Buyer may terminate this contract and the earnest money will be refunded to Buyer.

8. **BROKERS' FEES:** All obligations of the parties for payment of brokers' fees are contained in separate written agreements.

9. **CLOSING:** The closing of the sale will be on or before ______________________________, __________, or within 7 days after objections to matters disclosed in the Commitment or by the survey have been cured, whichever date is later (the Closing Date). *If financing or assumption approval has been obtained pursuant to Paragraph 4,* the Closing Date will be extended up to 15 days if necessary to comply with lender's closing requirements, for example: appraisal, survey, insurance policies, lender-required repairs, closing documents. If either party fails to close this sale by the Closing Date, the non-defaulting party will be entitled to exercise the remedies contained in Paragraph 15. At closing Seller shall furnish tax statements or certificates showing no delinquent taxes and a general warranty deed conveying good and indefeasible title showing no additional exceptions to those permitted in Paragraph 6.

10. **POSSESSION:** Seller shall deliver possession of the Property to Buyer on ________________________ in its present or required repaired condition, ordinary wear and tear excepted. Any possession by Buyer prior to closing or by Seller after closing which is not authorized by a temporary lease form promulgated by TREC or required by the parties will establish a tenancy at sufferance relationship between the parties. *Consult your insurance agent prior to change of ownership or possession as insurance coverage may be limited or terminated. The absence of a written lease or appropriate insurance coverage may expose the parties to economic loss.*

11. **SPECIAL PROVISIONS:** (Insert only factual statements and business details applicable to this sale. TREC rules prohibit licensees from adding factual statements or business details for which a contract

addendum, lease or other form has been promulgated by TREC for mandatory use.)

12. SETTLEMENT AND OTHER EXPENSES:

A. The following expenses must be paid at or prior to closing:

(1) Appraisal fees will be paid by ______________________________.

(2) The total of loan discount fees (including any Texas Veterans' Housing Assistance Program Participation Fee) may not exceed ______% of the loan of which Seller shall pay ____________ and Buyer shall pay the remainder. The total of any buydown fees may not exceed ____________ which will be paid by ______________________________.

(3) Seller's Expenses: Releases of existing liens, including prepayment penalties and recording fees; release of Seller's loan liability; tax statements or certificates; preparation of deed; one-half of escrow fee; and other expenses stipulated to be paid by Seller under other provisions of this contract.

(4) Buyer's Expenses: Loan application, origination and commitment fees; loan assumption costs; preparation and recording of deed of trust to secure assumption; lender required expenses incident to new loans, including PMI premium, preparation of loan documents, loan related inspection fee, recording fees, tax service and research fees, warehouse or underwriting fees, copies of restrictions and easements, amortization schedule, premiums for mortgagee title policies and endorsements required by lender, credit reports, photos; required premiums for flood and hazard insurance; required reserve deposit for insurance premiums and ad valorem taxes; interest on all monthly installment notes from date of disbursements to one month prior to dates of first monthly payments; customary Program Loan costs for Buyer; one-half of escrow fee; and other expenses stipulated to be paid by Buyer under other provisions of this contract.

B. Any Association transfer or processing fee will be paid by ______________________________.

C. If any expense exceeds an amount expressly stated in this contract for such expense to be paid by a party, that party may terminate this contract unless the other party agrees to pay such excess. In no event will Buyer pay charges and fees expressly prohibited by the Texas Veteran's Housing Assistance Program or other governmental loan program regulations.

13. PRORATIONS: Taxes for the current year, interest, maintenance fees, regular condominium assessments, dues and rents will be prorated through the Closing Date. If taxes for the current year vary from the amount prorated at closing, the parties shall adjust the prorations when tax statements for the current year are available. *If a loan is assumed* and the lender maintains an escrow account, the escrow account must be transferred to Buyer without any deficiency. Buyer shall reimburse Seller for the amount in the transferred account. Cash reserves from regular condominium assessments for deferred maintenance or capital improvements established by the Association will not be credited to Seller. Any special condominium assessment due and unpaid at closing will be the obligation of Seller. Buyer shall pay the premium for a new insurance policy. If taxes are not paid at or prior to closing, Buyer will be obligated to pay taxes for the current year.

14. CASUALTY LOSS: If any part of the Unit which Seller is solely obligated to maintain and repair under the terms of the Declaration is damaged or destroyed by fire or other casualty, Seller shall restore the same to its previous condition as soon as reasonably possible, but in any event by the Closing Date. If Seller is unable to do so without fault, Buyer may terminate this contract and the earnest money will be refunded to Buyer. If any part of the Common Elements or Limited Common Elements adjoining the Unit described in Paragraph 2A is damaged or destroyed by fire or other casualty loss, Buyer will have 7 days from receipt of notice of such casualty loss within which to notify Seller in writing that the contract will be terminated unless Buyer receives written confirmation from the Association that the damaged condition will be restored to its previous condition within a reasonable time at no cost to Buyer. Unless Buyer gives such notice within such time, Buyer will be deemed to have accepted the Property without confirmation of such restoration. Seller will have 7 days from the date of receipt of Buyer's notice within which to cause to be delivered to Buyer such confirmation. If required by Buyer and written confirmation is not delivered to Buyer as required above, Buyer may terminate this contract and the earnest money will be refunded to Buyer. Seller's obligations under this paragraph are independent of any obligations of Seller under Paragraph 7.

Residential Condominium Contract Concerning____Page Seven 11-8-99
(Address of Property)

15. **DEFAULT:** If Buyer fails to comply with this contract, Buyer will be in default, and Seller may either (a) enforce specific performance, seek such other relief as may be provided by law, or both, or (b) terminate this contract and receive the earnest money as liquidated damages, thereby releasing both parties from this contract. If, due to factors beyond Seller's control, Seller fails within the time allowed to make any non-casualty repairs or deliver the Commitment, Buyer may either (a) extend the time for performance up to 15 days and the Closing Date will be extended as necessary or (b) terminate this contract as the sole remedy and receive the earnest money. If Seller fails to comply with this contract for any other reason, Seller will be in default and Buyer may either (a) enforce specific performance, seek such other relief as may be provided by law, or both, or (b) terminate this contract and receive the earnest money, thereby releasing both parties from this contract.

16. **DISPUTE RESOLUTION:** It is the policy of the State of Texas to encourage the peaceable resolution of disputes through alternative dispute resolution procedures. The parties are encouraged to use an addendum approved by TREC to submit to mediation disputes which cannot be resolved in good faith through informal discussion.

17. **ATTORNEY'S FEES:** The prevailing party in any legal proceeding brought under or with respect to the transaction described in this contract is entitled to recover from the non-prevailing party all costs of such proceeding and reasonable attorney's fees.

18. **ESCROW:** The earnest money is deposited with escrow agent with the understanding that escrow agent is not (a) a party to this contract and does not have any liability for the performance or nonperformance of any party to this contract, (b) liable for interest on the earnest money and (c) liable for any loss of earnest money caused by the failure of any financial institution in which the earnest money has been deposited unless the financial institution is acting as escrow agent. At closing, the earnest money must be applied first to any cash down payment, then to Buyer's closing costs and any excess refunded to Buyer. If both parties make written demand for the earnest money, escrow agent may require payment of unpaid expenses incurred on behalf of the parties and a written release of liability of escrow agent from all parties. If one party makes written demand for the earnest money, escrow agent shall give notice of the demand by providing to the other party a copy of the demand. If escrow agent does not receive written objection to the demand from the other party within 30 days after notice to the other party, escrow agent may disburse the earnest money to the party making demand reduced by the amount of unpaid expenses incurred on behalf of the party receiving the earnest money and escrow agent may pay the same to the creditors. If escrow agent complies with the provisions of this paragraph, each party hereby releases escrow agent from all adverse claims related to the disbursal of the earnest money. Escrow agent's notice to the other party will be effective when deposited in the U. S. Mail, postage prepaid, certified mail, return receipt requested, addressed to the other party at such party's address shown below. Notice of objection to the demand will be deemed effective upon receipt by escrow agent.

19. **REPRESENTATIONS:** Seller represents that as of the Closing Date (a) there will be no liens, assessments or security interests against the Property which will not be satisfied out of the sales proceeds, unless securing payment of any loan assumed by Buyer; (b) assumed loan(s) will not be in default; (c) the present amount of the regular condominium assessment is $ ____________________ which will be current; and (d) Seller has no knowledge of any misrepresentation or errors in the Certificate or any material changes in the information contained therein. If any representation in this contract or the Certificate is untrue on the Closing Date, this contract may be terminated by Buyer and the earnest money will be refunded to Buyer. All representations contained in this contract will survive closing.

20. **FEDERAL TAX REQUIREMENT:** If Seller is a "foreign person", as defined by applicable law, or if Seller fails to deliver an affidavit that Seller is not a "foreign person", then Buyer shall withhold from the sales proceeds an amount sufficient to comply with applicable tax law and deliver the same to the Internal Revenue Service together with appropriate tax forms. IRS regulations require filing written reports if cash in excess of specified amounts is received in the transaction.

21. **AGREEMENT OF PARTIES:** This contract contains the entire agreement of the parties and cannot be changed except by their written agreement. Addenda which are a part of this contract are (list): ________
____.

Residential Condominium Contract Concerning____ Page Eight 11-8-99
(Address of Property)

22. CONSULT YOUR ATTORNEY: Real estate licensees cannot give legal advice. This contract is intended to be legally binding. READ IT CAREFULLY. If you do not understand the effect of this contract, consult your attorney BEFORE signing.

Buyer's Attorney is:______________________________ Seller's Attorney is:______________________________

23. NOTICES: All notices from one party to the other must be in writing and are effective when mailed to, hand-delivered at, or transmitted by facsimile machine as follows:

To Buyer at:

____

____

____

Telephone: (___)____________________

Facsimile: (___)____________________

To Seller at:

____

____

____

Telephone: (___)____________________

Facsimile:(___)____________________

EXECUTED the ______day of _______________________,_________ (THE EFFECTIVE DATE). (BROKER: FILL IN THE DATE OF FINAL ACCEPTANCE.)

____
Buyer

____
Buyer

____
Seller

____
Seller

BROKER INFORMATION AND RATIFICATION OF FEE

Listing Broker has agreed to pay Other Broker ________________________ of the total sales price when Listing Broker's fee is received. Escrow Agent is authorized and directed to pay Other Broker from Listing Broker's fee at closing.

____
Other Broker License No.

represents ❑ Seller as Listing Broker's subagent
❑ Buyer only as Buyer's agent

____
Associate Telephone

____
Broker Address

____
Telephone Facsimile

____
Listing Broker License No.

represents ❑ Seller and Buyer as an intermediary
❑ Seller only as Seller's agent

____
Listing Associate Telephone

____
Selling Associate Telephone

____
Broker Address

____
Telephone Facsimile

RECEIPT

Receipt of ❑ Contract and ❑ $ __________Earnest Money in the form of ________________is acknowledged.

Escrow Agent: ______________________________ Date: ____________________________,______

By:______________________________

____
Address

____
City State Zip Code

Telephone: (_____)____________________

Facsimile: (_____)____________________

PROMULGATED BY THE TEXAS REAL ESTATE COMMISSION (TREC) 06-15-98

ADDENDUM FOR "BACK-UP" CONTRACT

ADDENDUM TO CONTRACT BETWEEN THE UNDERSIGNED PARTIES CONCERNING PROPERTY AT

____

(Street Address and City)

A. The Contract to which this Addendum is attached (the "Back-Up Contract") is binding upon execution by the parties, and the earnest money and any Option Fee must be paid as provided in the Back-Up Contract. The Back-Up Contract is contingent upon the termination of a previous contract (the "First Contract") between Seller and ____________________________________, dated ________________________, _______, for the sale of Property. Except as provided by this Addendum, neither party is required to perform under the Back-Up Contract while it is contingent upon the First Contract.

B. If the First Contract terminates on or before 5:00 p.m. on ____________________________, ______ (the "Contingency Date"), the Back-Up Contract will no longer be contingent upon the termination of the First Contract. Seller must notify Buyer immediately of the termination of the First Contract. For purposes of performance, the effective date of the Back-Up Contract will be deemed to be the date Buyer receives notice of termination of the First Contract or the Contingency Date, whichever is earlier.

C. If the First Contract does not terminate by the Contingency Date, the Back-Up Contract terminates and the earnest money will be refunded to Buyer.

D. An amendment or modification of the First Contract will not terminate the First Contract.

E. If Buyer has the unrestricted right to terminate under Paragraph 7D(1), the time for giving notice of termination begins on the effective date of the Back-Up Contract, continues through the deemed effective date of the Back-Up Contract and ends upon the expiration of the number of days specified in Paragraph 7D(1).

F. For purposes of this Addendum, time is of the essence. Strict compliance with the times for performance stated herein is required.

____________________	____________________
Buyer	Seller
____________________	____________________
Buyer	Seller

The form of this addendum has been approved by the Texas Real Estate Commission. Such approval relates to this form only. No representation is made as to the legal validity or adequacy of any provision in any specific transaction. It is not suitable for complex transactions. Extensive riders or additions are not to be used. (06-98)Texas Real Estate Commission, P.O. Box 12188, Austin, TX 78711-2188, 1-800-250-8732 or (512)459-6544 (http:\\www.trec.state.tx.us) TREC No. 11-3. This form replaces TREC No. 11-2.

03-17-92

ADDENDUM FOR

RELEASE OF LIABILITY ON ASSUMPTION OF FHA, VA OR CONVENTIONAL LOAN

RESTORATION OF SELLER'S ENTITLEMENT FOR VA GUARANTEED LOAN

PROMULGATED BY THE TEXAS REAL ESTATE COMMISSION (TREC)

ADDENDUM TO EARNEST MONEY CONTRACT BETWEEN THE UNDERSIGNED PARTIES CONCERNING THE PROPERTY AT____
(Street Address and City)

☐ **A. RELEASE OF SELLER'S LIABILITY ON LOAN TO BE ASSUMED:**

Within __________ days from the effective date of this contract Seller and Buyer shall apply for release of Seller's liability from (a) any conventional lender, (b) VA and any lender whose loan has been guaranteed by VA, or (c) FHA and any lender whose loan has been insured by FHA. Seller and Buyer shall furnish all required information and documents. If any release of liability has not been approved by the Closing Date: (check 1 or 2 below)

☐ 1. This contract shall terminate and the Earnest Money shall be refunded to Buyer.

☐ 2. Failure to obtain release approval shall not delay closing and Seller and Buyer shall continue to seek release of Seller's liability.

☐ **B. RESTORATION OF SELLERS ENTITLEMENT FOR VA LOAN:**

Within _________ days from the effective date of this contract Seller and Buyer shall apply for restoration of Seller's VA entitlement and shall furnish all information and documents required by VA. If restoration has not been approved by the Closing Date: (check 1 or 2 below)

☐ 1. This contract shall terminate and the Earnest Money shall be refunded to Buyer.

☐ 2. Failure to obtain restoration approval shall not delay closing and Seller and Buyer shall continue to seek restoration of Seller's VA entitlement.

NOTICE: VA will not restore Seller's VA entitlement unless Buyer: (a) is a veteran, (b) has sufficient unused VA entitlement and (c) is otherwise qualified. If Seller desires release of liability from VA and the lender together with restoration of VA entitlement, paragraphs A and B should be used.

Seller shall pay the cost of securing the release and restoration. If Seller's cost will exceed $ ____________________, and Buyer declines to pay the excess, Seller may (a) waive release or restoration, (b) pay the excess, or (c) terminate this contract and the Earnest Money shall be refunded to Buyer.

Seller's deed shall contain any loan assumption clause required by FHA, VA or any lender. The provisions of this addendum are enforceable after closing.

____________________	____________________
Buyer	Seller
____________________	____________________
Buyer	Seller

The form of this Addendum has been approved by the Texas Real Estate Commission for use with similarly approved or promulgated contract forms. Such approval relates to this form only. No representation is made as to the legal validity or adequacy of any provision in any specific transactions. It is not suitable for complex transactions. (03-92) TREC No. 12-1. This form replaces TREC No. 12-0.

12-05-94

PROMULGATED BY THE TEXAS REAL ESTATE COMMISSION (TREC)
P.O. BOX 12188, AUSTIN, TX 78711-2188

ADDENDUM FOR COASTAL AREA PROPERTY

ADDENDUM TO EARNEST MONEY CONTRACT BETWEEN THE UNDERSIGNED PARTIES CONCERNING THE PROPERTY AT

____

____

(Location of Property)

IN ACCORDANCE WITH SECTION 33.1 35, TEXAS NATURAL RESOURCES CODE, THE FOLLOWING NOTICE IS INCLUDED AS PART OF THE CONTRACT:

NOTICE REGARDING COASTAL AREA PROPERTY

1. The real property described in and subject to this contract adjoins and shares a common boundary with the tidally influenced submerged lands of the state. The boundary is subject to change and can be determined accurately only by a survey on the ground made by a licensed state land surveyor in accordance with the original grant from the sovereign. The owner of the property described in this contract may gain or lose portions of the tract because of changes in the boundary.

2. The seller, transferor, or grantor has no knowledge of any prior fill as it relates to the property described in and subject to this contract except: ______________________________
____
____.

3. State law prohibits the use, encumbrance, construction, or placing of any structure in, on, or over state-owned submerged lands below the applicable tide line, without proper permission.

4. The purchaser or grantee is hereby advised to seek the advice of an attorney or other qualified person as to the legal nature and effect of the facts set forth in this notice on the property described in and subject to this contract. Information regarding the location of the applicable tide line as to the property described in and subject to this contract may be obtained from the surveying division of the General Land Office in Austin.

______________________ Buyer	______________________ Seller
______________________ Buyer	______________________ Seller

This form has been approved by the Texas Real Estate Commission for use with similarly approved or promulgated contract forms. Such approval relates to this form only. No representation is made as to the legal validity or adequacy of any provision in any specific transactions. It is not suitable for complex transactions. (12-94) TREC No. 33-0.

12-05-94

PROMULGATED BY THE TEXAS REAL ESTATE COMMISSION (TREC)
P.O. BOX 12188, AUSTIN, TX 78711-2188

ADDENDUM FOR
PROPERTY LOCATED SEAWARD OF THE GULF INTRACOASTAL WATERWAY

ADDENDUM TO EARNEST MONEY CONTRACT BETWEEN THE UNDERSIGNED PARTIES CONCERNING THE PROPERTY AT

____

____

(Location of Property)

IN ACCORDANCE WITH SECTION 61.0 25, TEXAS NATURAL RESOURCES CODE, THE FOLLOWING STATEMENT IS INCLUDED AS PART OF THE CONTRACT:

The real property described in this contract is located seaward of the Gulf Intracoastal Waterway to its southernmost point and then seaward of the longitudinal line also known as 97 degrees, 12', 19" which runs southerly to the international boundary from the intersection of the centerline of the Gulf Intracoastal Waterway and the Brownsville Ship Channel. If the property is in close proximity to a beach fronting the Gulf of Mexico, the purchaser is hereby advised that the public has acquired a right of use or easement to or over the area of any public beach by prescription, dedication, or presumption, or has retained a right by virtue of continuous right in the public since time immemorial, as recognized in law and custom.

The extreme seaward boundary of natural vegetation that spreads continuously inland customarily marks the landward boundary of the public easement. If there is no clearly marked natural vegetation line, the landward boundary of the easement is as provided by Sections 61.016 and 61.017, Natural Resources Code.

State law prohibits any obstruction, barrier, restraint, or interference with the use of the public easement, including the placement of structures seaward of the landward boundary of the easement. STRUCTURES ERECTED SEAWARD OF THE VEGETATION LINE (OR OTHER APPLICABLE EASEMENT BOUNDARY) OR THAT BECOME SEAWARD OF THE VEGETATION LINE AS A RESULT OF NATURAL PROCESSES ARE SUBJECT TO A LAWSUIT BY THE STATE OF TEXAS TO REMOVE THE STRUCTURES.

The purchaser is hereby notified that the purchaser should seek the advice of an attorney or other qualified person before executing this contract or instrument of conveyance as to the relevance of these statutes and facts to the value of the property the purchaser is hereby purchasing or contracting to purchase.

______________________	______________________
Buyer	Seller
______________________	______________________
Buyer	Seller

This form has been approved by the Texas Real Estate Commission for use with similarly approved or promulgated contract forms. Such approval relates to this form only. No representation is made as to the legal validity or adequacy of any provision in any specific transactions. It is not suitable for complex transactions. (12-94) TREC No. 34-0.

Transaction 9: 80% Conventional Without PMI

Utilizing: TREC 24-4, 16-3

Karl Leroy Leonard and his wife, Martha Ann Davidson, want to purchase the new home just built by Newtown Builders, Inc. The home has never been occupied. The transaction will be structured using the New Home Contract (Completed Construction) form.

The new home, located at 12863 Westover Drive in El Paso, 79901, is subject to mandatory membership in an owners' association. The property is identified as Lot 53, Block 18 in Section 8 of Pecos-Sun Addition in El Paso county. The buyers already live in the neighborhood and know everything that they need to know about the association and waive their right of termination.

The buyers will obtain an 80 percent LTV conventional loan with a 15-year amortization and an interest rate of 7.5 percent. They are willing to pay the builder's asking price of $284,500. They will apply for the loan within three days after the effective date of the contract and expect that they can receive approval within 20 days after the effective date of the contract. Closing can take place on or before April 15. Possession will take place on April 1. The buyer will pay $50 rent per day payable in advance. They will pay $100 per day for any holding over. A security deposit of $2,000 will be deposited prior to the move-in. The buyers own no pets and will not acquire any until after they close and take ownership of the property.

The buyers will deposit $14,225 with Buyer's Choice Title Company, who will issue an owner's title policy at closing. The title policy and survey will be obtained at the expense of the seller. The buyers want two days to examine the survey. They want to make certain they can park their class A motorhome in the driveway.

The buyers accept the property in its present condition, provided that the seller furnish certification that the property is free of wood destroying insects.

The seller warrants the property to be free of structural and mechanical defects for five full years after the date of closing. During that period the seller, at the seller's sole expense, will correct any malfunction or failure of any component of the house.

The seller has furnished the information to complete the required insulation addendum. You will not actually complete the addendum for the transaction, but it has been included and will be listed in paragraph 21.

The buyers want to review copies of all documents that they will be asked to sign at closing. They want these no less than 48 hours prior to closing.

The seller will pay for the appraisal. The buyers anticipate that a loan will be available with no discount points. Because the buyers are making a down payment equal to 20 percent of the purchase price, no PMI is required.

The buyers will have the contract reviewed by their attorney, Harry Hawkeye, prior to signing the agreement.

The buyers are represented by their buyer's broker, Barry Betterbuy. The builder is not represented by a licensee. The buyer's broker will be paid according to the provisions of the buyer's representation agreement signed by the buyers and Barry.

The buyers will receive notices at their current home address, and the seller will receive notices at the on-site sales office in the subdivision.

Although Barry encouraged them to incorporate the mediation addendum, the parties decline. They feel that everything will go smoothly and know that if it doesn't, they can always agree to mediation if the need arises.

PROMULGATED BY THE TEXAS REAL ESTATE COMMISSION (TREC) 06-22-00

NEW HOME CONTRACT

(Completed Construction)

NOTICE: Not For Use For Condominium Transactions

1. **PARTIES:** ______________________________ (Seller) agrees to sell and convey to ______________________________(Buyer) and Buyer agrees to buy from Seller the property described below.

2. **PROPERTY:** Lot _____, Block ____, ______________________________Addition, City of ______________________________, ______________________ County, Texas, known as ______________________________ (Address/Zip Code), or as described on attached exhibit, together with the improvements, fixtures and all other property located thereon. All property sold by this contract is called the "Property."
   Mandatory Membership in an Owners' Association: (Check one box only):
   ❑ The Property is not subject to mandatory membership in an owners' association.
   ❑ The TREC Addendum For Property Subject To Mandatory Membership In An Owners' Association is attached.
   NOTICE TO BUYER: If the Property is subject to mandatory membership in an owners' association, Seller notifies Buyer under §5.012, Texas Property Code, that, as a purchaser of property in the residential community in which the Property is located, you are obligated to be a member of an owners' association. Restrictive covenants governing the use and occupancy of the Property and a dedicatory instrument governing the establishment, maintenance, and operation of this residential community have been or will be recorded in the Real Property Records of the county in which the Property is located. Copies of the restrictive covenants and dedicatory instrument may be obtained from the county clerk. You are obligated to pay assessments to the owners' association. The amount of the assessments is subject to change. Your failure to pay the assessments could result in a lien on and the foreclosure of the Property.

3. **SALES PRICE:**
   A. Cash portion of Sales Price payable by Buyer at closing . . . . $____________
   B. Sum of all financing described below (excluding any FHA Mortgage Insurance Premium [MIP], VA funding fee, or Private Mortgage Insurance Premium [PMI]) . . . $____________
   C. Sales Price (Sum of A and B) . . . . $____________

4. **FINANCING:** Within _____ days after the effective date of this contract Buyer shall apply for all third party financing and make every reasonable effort to obtain financing. Financing will be deemed to have been obtained when the lender determines that Buyer has satisfied all of lender's financial requirements (those items relating to Buyer's net worth, income and creditworthiness). If financing (including any financed PMI premium) is not obtained within _____ days after the effective date hereof, this contract will terminate and the earnest money will be refunded to Buyer. Each note to be executed hereunder must be secured by vendor's and deed of trust liens.
   The portion of Sales Price not payable in cash will be paid as follows: (Check applicable boxes below)
   ❑ A. THIRD PARTY FINANCING:
   ❑ (1) This contract is subject to approval for Buyer of a third party first mortgage loan having a loan-to-value ratio not to exceed ______ % as established by such third party (excluding any financed PMI premium), due in full in _____ year(s), with interest not to exceed ____% per annum for the first _____year(s) of the loan. The loan will be ❑ with ❑ without PMI.
   ❑ (2) This contract is subject to approval for Buyer of a third party second mortgage loan having a loan-to-value ratio not to exceed_____ % as established by such third party (excluding any financed PMI premium), due in full in _____ year(s), with interest not to exceed _____ % per annum for the first _____ year(s) of the loan. The loan will be ❑ with ❑ without PMI.
   ❑ B. FHA INSURED FINANCING: This contract is subject to approval for Buyer of a Section ______ FHA insured loan of not less than $_________________ (excluding any financed MIP), amortizable monthly for not less than _____ years, with interest not to exceed _______% per annum for the first ______ year(s) of the Loan.
   As required by HUD-FHA, if FHA valuation is unknown, *"It is expressly agreed that, notwithstanding any other provisions of this contract, the purchaser* (Buyer) *shall not be obligated to complete the purchase of the property described herein or to incur any penalty by forfeiture of earnest money deposits or otherwise unless the purchaser* (Buyer) *has been given in accordance with HUD/FHA*

New Home (Completed Construction) Contract Concerning____Page Two 06-22-00
(Address of Property)

or VA requirements a written statement issued by the Federal Housing Commissioner, Department of Veterans Affairs, or a Direct Endorsement Lender setting forth the appraised value of the Property of not less than $________________. The purchaser (Buyer) *shall have the privilege and option of proceeding with consummation of the contract without regard to the amount of the appraised valuation. The appraised valuation is arrived at to determine the maximum mortgage the Department of Housing and Urban Development will insure. HUD does not warrant the value or the condition of the Property. The purchaser* (Buyer) *should satisfy himself/herself that the price and the condition of the Property are acceptable."* If the FHA appraised value of the Property (excluding closing costs and MIP) is less than the Sales Price (3C above), Seller may reduce the Sales Price to an amount equal to the FHA appraised value (excluding closing costs and MIP) and the parties to the sale shall close the sale at such lower Sales Price with appropriate adjustments to 3A and 3B above.

❑ C. VA GUARANTEED FINANCING: This contract is subject to approval for Buyer of a VA guaranteed loan of not less than $____________(excluding any financed Funding Fee), amortizable monthly for not less than _____ years, with interest not to exceed _____ % per annum for the first _____ year(s) of the Loan.

VA NOTICE TO BUYER: *"It is expressly agreed that, notwithstanding any other provisions of this contract, the Buyer shall not incur any penalty by forfeiture of earnest money or otherwise or be obligated to complete the purchase of the Property described herein, if the contract purchase price or cost exceeds the reasonable value of the Property established by the Department of Veterans Affairs. The Buyer shall, however, have the privilege and option of proceeding with the consummation of this contract without regard to the amount of the reasonable value established by the Department of Veterans Affairs."*

If Buyer elects to complete the purchase at an amount in excess of the reasonable value established by VA, Buyer shall pay such excess amount in cash from a source which Buyer agrees to disclose to the VA and which Buyer represents will not be from borrowed funds except as approved by VA. If VA reasonable value of the Property is less than the Sales Price (3C above), Seller may reduce the Sales Price to an amount equal to the VA reasonable value and the parties to the sale shall close at such lower Sales Price with appropriate adjustments to 3A and 3B above.

❑ D. TEXAS VETERANS' HOUSING ASSISTANCE PROGRAM LOAN: This contract is subject to approval for Buyer of a Texas Veterans' Housing Assistance Program Loan (the Program Loan) of $______________ for a period of at least ______________ years at the interest rate established by the Texas Veterans' Land Board at the time of closing.

❑ E. SELLER FINANCING: A promissory note from Buyer to Seller of $__________________, bearing ________% interest per annum, secured by vendor's and deed of trust liens, in accordance with the terms and conditions set forth in the attached TREC Seller Financing Addendum. If an owner policy of title insurance is furnished, Buyer shall furnish Seller with a mortgagee policy of title insurance.

❑ F. CREDIT APPROVAL ON SELLER FINANCING: Within ______ days after the effective date of this contract, Buyer shall deliver to Seller ❑ credit report ❑ verification of employment, including salary ❑ verification of funds on deposit in financial institutions ❑ current financial statement to establish Buyer's creditworthiness for seller financing and ❑ ______________________________
____.

If Buyer's documentation is not delivered within the specified time, Seller may terminate this contract by notice to Buyer within 7 days after expiration of the time for delivery, and the earnest money will be paid to Seller. If this contract is not so terminated, Seller will be deemed to have accepted Buyer's credit. If the documentation is timely delivered, and Seller determines in Seller's sole discretion that Buyer's credit is unacceptable, Seller may terminate this contract by notice to Buyer within 7 days after expiration of the time for delivery and the earnest money will be refunded to Buyer. If Seller does not so terminate this contract, Seller will be deemed to have accepted Buyer's credit. Buyer hereby authorizes any credit reporting agency to furnish to Seller at Buyer's sole expense copies of Buyer's credit reports.

5. **EARNEST MONEY:** Buyer shall deposit $_______________ as earnest money with _______________ ________________________________ at ____(Address), as escrow agent, upon execution of this contract by both parties. Additional earnest money of $____________ must be deposited by Buyer with escrow agent on or before______________________, _____. If Buyer fails to deposit the earnest money as required by this contract, Buyer will be in default.

6. TITLE POLICY AND SURVEY:

❑ A. TITLE POLICY: Seller shall furnish to Buyer at ❑ Seller's ❑ Buyer's expense an owner policy of title insurance (the Title Policy) issued by _______________________________________ (the Title Company) in the amount of the Sales Price, dated at or after closing, insuring Buyer against loss under the provisions of the Title Policy, subject to the promulgated exclusions (including existing building and zoning ordinances) and the following exceptions:

(1) Restrictive covenants common to the platted subdivision in which the Property is located.
(2) The standard printed exception for standby fees, taxes and assessments.
(3) Liens created as part of the financing described in Paragraph 4.
(4) Utility easements created by the dedication deed or plat of the subdivision in which the Property is located.
(5) Reservations or exceptions otherwise permitted by this contract or as may be approved by Buyer in writing.
(6) The standard printed exception as to discrepancies, conflicts, shortages in area or boundary lines, encroachments or protrusions, or overlapping improvements.
(7) The standard printed exception as to marital rights.
(8) The standard printed exception as to waters, tidelands, beaches, streams, and related matters.

Within 20 days after the Title Company receives a copy of this contract, Seller shall furnish to Buyer a commitment for title insurance (the Commitment) and, at Buyer's expense, legible copies of restrictive covenants and documents evidencing exceptions in the Commitment other than the standard printed exceptions. Seller authorizes the Title Company to mail or hand deliver the Commitment and related documents to Buyer at Buyer's address shown below. If the Commitment is not delivered to Buyer within the specified time, the time for delivery will be automatically extended up to 15 days. Buyer will have 7 days after the receipt of the Commitment to object in writing to matters disclosed in the Commitment.

❑ B. SURVEY: (Check one box only)

❑ (1) Within ______ days after Buyer's receipt of a survey furnished to a third-party lender at ❑ Seller's ❑ Buyer's expense, Buyer may object in writing to any matter shown on the survey which constitutes a defect or encumbrance to title.

❑ (2) Within ____ days after the effective date of this contract, Buyer may object in writing to any matter which constitutes a defect or encumbrance to title shown on a survey obtained by Buyer at Buyer's expense.

The survey must be made by a Registered Professional Land Surveyor acceptable to the Title Company and any lender. Utility easements created by the dedication deed and plat of the subdivision in which the Property is located will not be a basis for objection.

Buyer may object to existing building and zoning ordinances, items 6A(1) through (8) above and matters shown on the survey if Buyer determines that any such ordinance, items or matter prohibits the following use or activity:____
____
____.

Buyer's failure to object under Paragraph 6A or 6B within the time allowed will constitute a waiver of Buyer's right to object; except that the requirements in Schedule C of the Commitment will not be deemed to have been waived. Seller shall cure the timely objections of Buyer or any third party lender within 15 days from the date Seller receives the objections and the Closing Date will be extended as necessary. If objections are not cured by the extended Closing Date, this contract will terminate and the earnest money will be refunded to Buyer unless Buyer elects to waive the objections.

NOTICE TO SELLER AND BUYER:

(1) Broker advises Buyer to have an abstract of title covering the Property examined by an attorney of Buyer's selection, or Buyer should be furnished with or obtain a Title Policy. If a Title Policy is furnished, the Commitment should be promptly reviewed by an attorney of Buyer's choice due to the time limitations on Buyer's right to object.

(2) If the Property is situated in a utility or other statutorily created district providing water, sewer, drainage, or flood control facilities and services, Chapter 49 of the Texas Water Code requires Seller to deliver and Buyer to sign the statutory notice relating to the tax rate, bonded indebtedness, or standby fee of the district prior to final execution of this contract.

New Home (Completed Construction) Contract Concerning_______________________________________ Page Four 06-22-00
(Address of Property)

(3) If the Property abuts the tidally influenced waters of the state, Section 33.135, Texas Natural Resources Code, requires a notice regarding coastal area property to be included in the contract. An addendum either promulgated by TREC or required by the parties should be used.

(4) Buyer is advised that the presence of wetlands, toxic substances including asbestos and wastes or other environmental hazards or the presence of a threatened or endangered species or its habitat may affect Buyer's intended use of the Property. If Buyer is concerned about these matters, an addendum either promulgated by TREC or required by the parties should be used.

(5) If the Property is located outside the limits of a municipality, Seller notifies Buyer under §5.011, Texas Property Code, that the Property may now or later be included in the extraterritorial jurisdiction of a municipality and may now or later be subject to annexation by the municipality. Each municipality maintains a map that depicts its boundaries and extraterritorial jurisdiction. To determine if the Property is located within a municipality's extraterritorial jurisdiction or is likely to be located within a municipality's extraterritorial jurisdiction, contact all municipalities located in the general proximity of the Property for further information.

(6) Unless expressly prohibited in writing by the parties, Seller may continue to show the Property for sale and to receive, negotiate and accept back-up offers.

(7) Any residential service contract that is purchased in connection with this transaction should be reviewed for the scope of coverage, exclusions and limitations. **The purchase of a residential service contract is optional. Similar coverage may be purchased from various companies authorized to do business in Texas**.

7. PROPERTY CONDITION:

A. INSPECTIONS, ACCESS AND UTILITIES: Buyer, at Buyer's expense, may have the Property inspected by inspectors selected by Buyer, licensed by TREC or otherwise permitted by law to make such inspections. Seller shall permit access to the Property at reasonable times for inspections, repairs and treatment and for reinspections after repairs and treatment have been completed. Seller shall pay for turning on utilities for inspections and reinspections.

B. ACCEPTANCE OF PROPERTY CONDITION: (check one box only):

❑ (1) In addition to any earnest money deposited with escrow agent, Buyer has paid Seller $____________ (the "Option Fee") for the unrestricted right to terminate this contract by giving notice of termination to Seller within _______ days after the effective date of this contract. If Buyer gives notice of termination within the time specified, the Option Fee will not be refunded, however, any earnest money will be refunded to Buyer. If Buyer does not give notice of termination within the time specified, Buyer will be deemed to have accepted the Property in its current condition and the Option Fee ❑ will ❑ will not be credited to the Sales Price at closing.

❑ (2) Buyer accepts the Property in its present condition; provided Seller, at Seller's expense, shall complete the following repairs and treatment: ____
____.

C. LENDER REQUIRED REPAIRS AND TREATMENTS (REPAIRS): Unless otherwise agreed in writing, neither party is obligated to pay for lender required repairs or treatments for wood destroying insects. If the cost of lender required repairs exceeds 5% of the Sales Price, Buyer may terminate this contract.

D. COMPLETION OF REPAIRS AND TREATMENT. Unless otherwise agreed in writing, Seller shall complete all agreed repairs and treatment prior to the Closing Date. Repairs and treatments must be performed by persons who regularly provide such repairs or treatments. At Buyer's election, any transferable warranties received by Seller with respect to the repairs will be transferred to Buyer at Buyer's expense. If Seller fails to complete any agreed repairs and treatment prior to the Closing Date, Buyer may do so and the Closing Date will be extended up to 15 days, if necessary, to complete repairs and treatment.

E. WARRANTIES: Except as expressly set forth in Paragraph 11, or as attached to this contract, Seller makes no other express warranties. Seller agrees to assign to Buyer at closing all assignable manufacturer warranties.

F. INSULATION: As required by Federal Trade Commission Regulations, the information relating to the insulation installed or to be installed in the home being purchased under this contract is as follows:

(1) Exterior walls of improved living areas: insulated with ________________________ insulation to a thickness of _______ inches which yields an R-Value of _______.

(2) Walls in other areas of the home: insulated with ____________________________ insulation to a thickness of ______ inches which yields an R-Value of ______.

(3) Ceilings in improved living areas: insulated with ______________________________ insulation to a thickness of ________ inches which yields an R-Value of _______.
(4) Floors of improved living areas not applied to a slab foundation: insulated with ____________ _____________ insulation to a thickness of _______ inches which yields an R-Value of _______.
(5) Other insulated areas: insulated with ____________________________ insulation to a thickness of _______ inches which yields an R-Value of _______.

All stated R-Values are based on information provided by the manufacturer of the insulation.

8. **BROKERS' FEES:** All obligations of the parties for payment of brokers' fees are contained in separate written agreements.

9. **CLOSING:** The closing of the sale will be on or before ___________________________,_____, or within 7 days after objections to matters disclosed in the Commitment or by the survey have been cured, whichever date is later (the Closing Date). *If financing has been obtained pursuant to Paragraph 4,* the Closing Date will be extended up to 15 days if necessary to comply with lender's closing requirements (for example, appraisal, survey, insurance policies, lender-required repairs, closing documents).If either party fails to close this sale by the Closing Date, the non-defaulting party will be entitled to exercise the remedies contained in Paragraph 15. At closing Seller shall furnish tax statements or certificates showing no delinquent taxes and a general warranty deed conveying good and indefeasible title showing no additional exceptions to those permitted in Paragraph 6.

10. **POSSESSION:** Seller shall deliver possession of the Property to Buyer on ____________________ in its present or required repaired condition, ordinary wear and tear excepted. Any possession by Buyer prior to closing or by Seller after closing which is not authorized by a temporary lease form promulgated by TREC or required by the parties will establish a tenancy at sufferance relationship between the parties. *Consult your insurance agent prior to change of ownership or possession as insurance coverage may be limited or terminated. The absence of a written lease or appropriate insurance coverage may expose the parties to economic loss.*

11. **SPECIAL PROVISIONS:** (Insert only factual statements and business details applicable to this sale. TREC rules prohibit licensees from adding factual statements or business details for which a contract addendum, lease or other form has been promulgated by TREC for mandatory use.)

12. **SETTLEMENT AND OTHER EXPENSES:**

A. The following expenses must be paid at or prior to closing:

(1) Loan appraisal fees will be paid by ____.

(2) The total of the loan discount and buydown fees (including any Texas Veterans' Housing Assistance Program Participation Fee) may not exceed ______% of the loan of which Seller shall pay _________________ and Buyer shall pay the remainder. The total of any buydown fees may not exceed ________________ which will be paid by ______________________________.

(3) Seller's Expenses:

(a) All Sales: Lender, FHA or VA completion requirements, releases of existing liens, including prepayment penalties and recording fees; tax statements or certificates; preparation of deed; one-half of escrow fee; those expenses Buyer is prohibited by FHA or VA from paying; and other expenses stipulated to be paid by Seller under other provisions of this contract.

(b) VA Loan Sales: Those expenses stated in 3(a) above and other expenses VA regulation prohibits Buyer from paying.

(4) Buyer's Expenses:

(a) All Sales: Expenses incident to any loan, including application, origination, and commitment fees; interest on the notes from date of disbursement to one month prior to date of first monthly payments; recording fees; endorsements required by lender; copies of easements and restrictions; mortgagee title policy; loan-related inspection fees; credit reports; all prepaid items, including required premiums for flood and hazard insurance, reserve deposits for insurance,

New Home (Completed Construction) Contract Concerning______________________________ Page Six 06-22-00
(Address of Property)

ad valorem taxes and special governmental assessments; tax deletion; EPA endorsement; final compliance inspection; other expenses stipulated to be paid by Buyer under other provisions of this contract.

(b) Conventional Loan Sales: Expenses noted above and other loan-related expenses, including PMI premiums, photos, amortization schedules, one-half of escrow fee, preparation of loan documents, courier fee, repair inspections, underwriting fee and wire transfer.

(c) FHA Loan Sales: Expenses noted above and other loan-related expenses, including photos, amortization schedules, one-half of escrow fee, preparation of loan documents, courier fee and repair inspections.

B. The VA Loan Funding Fee or FHA Mortgage Insurance Premium (MIP) not to exceed __________will be paid by Buyer, and ❑ paid in cash at closing ❑ added to the amount of the loan or ❑ paid as follows: ____
____.

C. If any expense exceeds an amount stated in this contract for such expense to be paid by a party, that party may terminate this contract unless the other party agrees to pay such excess. In no event will Buyer pay charges and fees expressly prohibited by FHA, VA or other governmental loan program regulations.

13. **PRORATIONS AND ROLLBACK TAXES**:

A. PRORATIONS: Taxes for the current year, maintenance fees, assessments, dues and rents will be prorated through the Closing Date. If taxes for the current year vary from the amount prorated at closing, the parties shall adjust the prorations when tax statements for the current year are available. If taxes are not paid at or prior to closing, Buyer will be obligated to pay taxes for the current year.

B. ROLLBACK TAXES: If Seller's change in use of the Property prior to closing or denial of a special use valuation on the Property results in additional taxes, penalties or interest (Assessments) for periods prior to closing, the Assessments will be the obligation of Seller. Obligations imposed by this paragraph will survive closing.

14. **CASUALTY LOSS:** If any part of the Property is damaged or destroyed by fire or other casualty after the effective date of this contract, Seller shall restore the Property to its previous condition as soon as reasonably possible, but in any event by the Closing Date. If Seller fails to do so due to factors beyond Seller's control, Buyer may either (a) terminate this contract and the earnest money will be refunded to Buyer (b) extend the time for performance up to 15 days and the Closing Date will be extended as necessary or (c) accept the Property in its damaged condition and accept an assignment of insurance proceeds. Seller's obligations under this paragraph are independent of any obligations of Seller under Paragraph 7.

15. **DEFAULT:** If Buyer fails to comply with this contract, Buyer will be in default, and Seller may either (a) enforce specific performance, seek such other relief as may be provided by law, or both, or (b) terminate this contract and receive the earnest money as liquidated damages, thereby releasing both parties from this contract. If, due to factors beyond Seller's control, Seller fails within the time allowed to make any non-casualty repairs or deliver the Commitment, Buyer may either (a) extend the time for performance up to 15 days and the Closing Date will be extended as necessary or (b) terminate this contract as the sole remedy and receive the earnest money. If Seller fails to comply with this contract for any other reason, Seller will be in default and Buyer may either (a) enforce specific performance, seek such other relief as may be provided by law, or both, or (b) terminate this contract and receive the earnest money, thereby releasing both parties from this contract.

16. **DISPUTE RESOLUTION:** It is the policy of the State of Texas to encourage the peaceable resolution of disputes through alternative dispute resolution procedures. The parties are encouraged to use an addendum approved by TREC to submit to mediation disputes which cannot be resolved in good faith through informal discussion.

17. **ATTORNEY'S FEES:** The prevailing party in any legal proceeding brought under or with respect to the transaction described in this contract is entitled to recover from the non-prevailing party all costs of such proceeding and reasonable attorney's fees.

New Home (Completed Construction) Contract Concerning____Page Seven 06-22-00
(Address of Property)

18. **ESCROW:** The earnest money is deposited with escrow agent with the understanding that escrow agent is not (a) a party to this contract and does not have any liability for the performance or nonperformance of any party to this contract, (b) liable for interest on the earnest money and (c) liable for any loss of earnest money caused by the failure of any financial institution in which the earnest money has been deposited unless the financial institution is acting as escrow agent. At closing, the earnest money must be applied first to any cash down payment, then to Buyer's closing costs and any excess refunded to Buyer. If both parties make written demand for the earnest money, escrow agent may require payment of unpaid expenses incurred on behalf of the parties and a written release of liability of escrow agent from all parties. If one party makes written demand for the earnest money, escrow agent shall give notice of the demand by providing to the other party a copy of the demand. If escrow agent does not receive written objection to the demand from the other party within 30 days after notice to the other party, escrow agent may disburse the earnest money to the party making demand reduced by the amount of unpaid expenses incurred on behalf of the party receiving the earnest money and escrow agent may pay the same to the creditors. If escrow agent complies with the provisions of this paragraph, each party hereby releases escrow agent from all adverse claims related to the disbursal of the earnest money. Escrow agent's notice to the other party will be effective when deposited in the U. S. Mail, postage prepaid, certified mail, return receipt requested, addressed to the other party at such party's address shown below. Notice of objection to the demand will be deemed effective upon receipt by escrow agent.

19. **REPRESENTATIONS:** Seller represents that as of the Closing Date there will be no liens, assessments, or security interests against the Property which will not be satisfied out of the sales proceeds. If any representation in this contract is untrue on the Closing Date, this contract may be terminated by Buyer and the earnest money will be refunded to Buyer. All representations contained in this contract will survive closing.

20. **FEDERAL TAX REQUIREMENT:** If Seller is a "foreign person", as defined by applicable law, or if Seller fails to deliver an affidavit that Seller is not a "foreign person", then Buyer shall withhold from the sales proceeds an amount sufficient to comply with applicable tax law and deliver the same to the Internal Revenue Service together with appropriate tax forms. IRS regulations require filing written reports if cash in excess of specified amounts is received in the transaction.

21. **AGREEMENT OF PARTIES:** This contract contains the entire agreement of the parties and cannot be changed except by their written agreement. Addenda which are a part of this contract are (list): ________
____
____.

22. **CONSULT YOUR ATTORNEY:** Real estate licensees cannot give legal advice. This contract is intended to be legally binding. READ IT CAREFULLY. If you do not understand the effect of this contract, consult your attorney BEFORE signing.

Buyer's Attorney is:______________________________ Seller's Attorney is:______________________________

23. **NOTICES:** All notices from one party to the other must be in writing and are effective when mailed to, hand-delivered at, or transmitted by facsimile machine as follows:

To Buyer at:

____
____
____

Telephone:(___) ______________________

Facsimile: (___)______________________

To Seller at:

____
____
____

Telephone: (___) ______________________

Facsimile: (___)______________________

New Home (Complete Construction) Contract Concerning____Page Eight 06-22-00
(Address of Property)

EXECUTED the _____day of ____________________,_______ (THE EFFECTIVE DATE). (BROKER: FILL IN THE DATE OF FINAL ACCEPTANCE.)

This contract is subject to Chapter 27, Texas Property Code. The provisions of that chapter may affect your right to recover damages arising from the performance of this contract. If you have a complaint concerning a construction defect arising from the performance of this contract and that defect has not been corrected through normal warranty service, you must provide notice regarding the defect to the contractor by certified mail, return receipt requested, not later than the 60th day before the date you file suit to recover damages in a court of law. The notice must refer to Chapter 27, Texas Property Code, and must describe the construction defect. If requested by the contractor, you must provide the contractor an opportunity to inspect and cure the defect as provided by Section 27.004, Texas Property Code.

____
Buyer

____
Buyer

____
Seller

____
Seller

The form of this contract has been approved by the Texas Real Estate Commission. Such approval relates to this contract form only. TREC forms are intended for use only by trained real estate licensees. No representation is made as to the legal validity or adequacy of any provision in any specific transaction. It is not suitable for complex transactions. Extensive riders or additions are not to be used. Texas Real Estate Commission, P.O. Box 12188, Austin, TX 78711-2188, 1-800-250-8732 or (512) 459-6544 (http://www.trec.state.tx.us) TREC NO. 24-4. This form replaces TREC NO. 24-3.

BROKER INFORMATION AND RATIFICATION OF FEE

Listing Broker has agreed to pay Other Broker ______________________ of the total sales price when Listing Broker's fee is received. Escrow Agent is authorized and directed to pay Other Broker from Listing Broker's fee at closing.

____
Other Broker License No.
represents ❑ Seller as Listing Broker's subagent
❑ Buyer only as Buyer's agent

____
Associate Telephone

____
Broker Address

____
Telephone Facsimile

____
Listing Broker License No.
represents ❑ Seller and Buyer as an intermediary
❑ Seller only as Seller's agent

____
Listing Associate Telephone

____
Selling Associate Telephone

____
Broker Address

____
Telephone Facsimile

RECEIPT

Receipt of ❑ Contract and ❑ $__________ Earnest Money in the form of____________ is acknowledged.

Escrow Agent: ________________________________ Date: ______________________,_____

By:________________________________

________________________________ Telephone: (_____) ______________________
Address

________________________________ Facsimile: (_____)______________________
City State Zip Code

12-07-98

(NOTICE: For use only when BUYER occupies the property for no more than 90 days PRIOR to closing)

BUYER'S TEMPORARY RESIDENTIAL LEASE

PROMULGATED BY THE TEXAS REAL ESTATE COMMISSION (TREC)

1. **PARTIES:** The parties to this Lease are ______________________________ (Landlord) and ______________________________(Tenant).
2. **LEASE:** Landlord leases to Tenant the Property described in the Contract between Landlord as Seller and Tenant as Buyer dated ______________, ______,and known as ______________________________(address).
3. **TERM:** The term of this Lease commences on ______________________ and terminates as specified in Paragraph 18.
4. **RENTAL:** Rental will be $ ______________ per day. Upon commencement of this Lease, Tenant shall pay to Landlord the full amount of rental of $ ______________ for the anticipated term of the Lease (commencement date to the closing date specified in Paragraph 9 of the Contract). If the actual term of this Lease differs from the anticipated term, rent will be prorated and paid at closing through the actual closing date. No portion of the rental will be applied to payment of any items covered by the Contract.
5. **SECURITY DEPOSIT:** Tenant has paid to Landlord $ ______________ as a deposit to secure performance of this Lease by Tenant. If this Lease is terminated before the closing, Landlord may use the deposit to satisfy Tenant's obligations under this Lease. Landlord shall refund to Tenant any unused portion of the deposit together with an itemized list of all deductions from the deposit within 30 days after Tenant (a) surrenders possession of the Property and (b) provides Landlord written notice of Tenant's forwarding address. If this Lease is terminated by the closing of the sale of the Property, the unused portion of the deposit will be refunded to Tenant at closing, together with an itemized list of all deductions from the deposit. <u>NOTICE</u>: The security deposit must be in addition to the earnest money under the Contract.
6. **UTILITIES:** Tenant shall pay all utility connections, deposits and charges except ______________________________, which Landlord shall pay.
7. **USE OF PROPERTY:** Tenant may use the Property only for single family dwelling purposes. Tenant may not assign this Lease or sublet any part of the Property.
8. **PETS:** Tenant may not keep pets on the Property except ______________________
9. **CONDITION OF PROPERTY**: Tenant accepts the Property in its present condition and state of repair, but Landlord shall make all repairs and improvements required by the Contract. If this Lease is terminated prior to closing, Tenant shall surrender possession of the Property to Landlord in its present condition, as improved by Landlord, except normal wear and tear and any casualty loss.
10. **ALTERATIONS:** Tenant may not: (a) make any holes or drive nails into the woodwork, floors, walls or ceilings (b) alter, paint or decorate the Property or (c) install improvements or fixtures without the prior written consent of Landlord. Any improvements or fixtures placed on the Property during the Lease become a part of the Property.
11. **SPECIAL PROVISIONS:**

12. **INSPECTIONS:** Landlord may enter at reasonable times to inspect, replace, repair or complete the improvements.
13. **LAWS:** Tenant shall comply with all applicable laws, restrictions, ordinances, rules and regulations with respect to the Property.
14. **REPAIRS AND MAINTENANCE:** <u>Tenant shall bear all expense of repairing and maintaining the Property, including but not limited to yard, trees and shrubs, unless otherwise required by the Texas Property Code. Tenant shall promptly repair at Tenant's expense any damage to the Property caused directly or indirectly by any act or omission of the Tenant or any person other than Landlord, Landlord's agents or invitees.</u>

Buyer's Temporary Residential Lease____Page Two 12-07-98
(Address of Property)

15. **INDEMNITY:** Tenant indemnifies Landlord from the claims of all third parties for injury or damage to the person or property of such third party arising from the use or occupancy of the Property by Tenant. This indemnification includes attorney's fees, costs and expenses incurred by Landlord.
16. **INSURANCE:** Landlord and Tenant shall each maintain such insurance on the contents and Property as each party may deem appropriate during the term of this Lease. NOTE: CONSULT YOUR INSURANCE AGENT PRIOR TO CLOSING. Possession of the Property by Buyer as Tenant may change insurance policy coverage.
17. **DEFAULT:** If Tenant fails to perform or observe any provision of this Lease and fails, within 24 hours after notice by Landlord, to commence and diligently pursue to remedy such failure, Tenant will be in default.
18. **TERMINATION:** This Lease terminates upon (a) closing of the sale under the Contract, (b) termination of the Contract prior to closing, (c) Tenant's default under this Lease, or (d) Tenant's default under the Contract, whichever occurs first. Upon termination other than by closing of the sale, Tenant shall surrender possession of the Property.
19. **HOLDING OVER:** Any possession by Tenant after termination creates a tenancy at sufferance and will not operate to renew or extend this Lease. Tenant shall pay $ ____________________ per day during the period of any possession after termination as damages, in addition to any other remedies to which Landlord is entitled.
20. **ATTORNEY'S FEES:** The prevailing party in any legal proceeding brought under or with respect to the transaction described in this Lease is entitled to recover from the non-prevailing party all costs of such proceeding and reasonable attorney's fees.
21. **SMOKE DETECTORS:** The Texas Property Code requires Landlord to install smoke detectors in certain locations within the Property at Landlord's expense. Tenant expressly waives Landlord's duty to inspect and repair smoke detectors.
22. **SECURITY DEVICES:** The requirements of the Texas Property Code relating to security devices do not apply to a residential lease for a term of 90 days or less.
23. **CONSULT YOUR ATTORNEY:** Real estate licensees cannot give legal advice. This Lease is intended to be legally binding. READ IT CAREFULLY. If you do not understand the effect of this Lease, consult your attorney BEFORE signing.
24. **NOTICES:** All notices under this Lease from one party to the other must be in writing and are effective when delivered or transmitted by facsimile machine as follows:

To Landlord:	**To Tenant:**
______________________________	______________________________
______________________________	______________________________
______________________________	______________________________
Facsimile:(_____)__________________	Facsimile:(_____)__________________

EXECUTED the ______ day of ________________________________ .

______________________________	______________________________
Landlord	Tenant
______________________________	______________________________
Landlord	Tenant

The form of this contract has been approved by the Texas Real Estate Commission. TREC forms are intended for use only by trained real estate licensees. Such approval relates to this contract form only. No representation is made as to the legal validity or adequacy of any provision in any specific transaction. It is not suitable for complex transactions. Extensive riders or additions are not to be used. (12-98) Texas Real Estate Commission, P.O. Box 12188, Austin, TX 78711-2188, 1-800-250-8732 or (512)459-6544 (http://www.trec.state.tx.us) TREC NO. 16-3 This form replaces TREC NO. 16-2.

01A TREC NO. 16-3

Transaction 10: 90% Conventional Fixed Rate Loan with PMI

Utilizing: TREC 20-4, 28-0, 33-0, 34-0, 35-1, 36-1

Russell Alan Janes and his spouse, Anna Marie Janes, have agreed to sell their gulf-front home to Peter Paul Prospect and his spouse, Priscilla Bea Prospect, for $387,800. The Prospects will obtain a 90 percent conventional loan. It will require one discount point, which will be paid by the buyers. The buyers will also pay for the appraisal. The loan will be a 30-year fixed rate at 7 percent.

The property is located at 12656 Rolling Waves Lane in Galveston County, Texas. It is more fully described as Lot 6, Block 6, Sandy Dunes Addition, Section 2 of Galveston County, Texas. Although it is located outside the city limits, it has a Galveston, Texas, mailing address. The zip code is 77573. The house was built in 1981.

Because the property is subject to membership in and the assessments of a very active homeowners' association, the Prospects want the sellers to furnish the resale certificate from the association with a copy of the bylaws, annual budget, rules and regulations, restrictive covenants and the certificate of insurance for the association's liability policy. This will be obtained within 15 days after the effective date of the contract. The seller will pay the HOA transfer fee of $100. The annual maintenance fee of $600 is payable to ABC Management Company by January 31 each year.

The sellers will remove the leased security system from the property prior to closing and have agreed to leave the bedspread that matches the draperies in the master bedroom.

The buyers have selected Buyer's Choice Title Company to hold their $25,000 earnest money deposit and want them to issue the owner's title policy at closing. They request two days to examine the survey required by the lender. They anticipate they can get loan approval in 30 days and close in 35 days if they make a loan application within four days after the effective date of the contract. The buyers will pay for the survey. The sellers will pay for the owners' title policy. Possession will be granted at funding.

The Prospects do not like the looks of some of the plants on the property and want to have the soil tested for toxic materials. They can have the tests performed and get the results within 20 days after the effective date of the contract.

In exchange for the payment of $500 to the seller, the buyers want an unrestricted five-day right to inspect the property. If they find anything that they consider unusual, they want to be able to terminate the purchase agreement without forfeiture of their earnest money. If they proceed to closing, the $500 will be credited to the purchase price.

The property has been listed by Smooth Sales Realty, Inc., who also has a buyer representation agreement with the Prospects. Both parties have signed a written authorization to permit the broker to function as an intermediary and to allow the broker to appoint Susan Smart, salesperson, to work with the sellers and Sammy Sharp, broker associate, to work with and advise the buyers. The broker has given the parties the proper written notification of who has been appointed to whom to give advice.

The seller furnished the seller's disclosure form prior to the offer being made. The parties are all very reasonable people and will probably get to the closing table without a hitch; however, to be on the safe side, they ask the brokers to make the agreement for mediation a part of their contract and have agreed to select a mutually acceptable mediator when and if the need arises.

The buyers will take the prepared offer to their attorney, Rachel Review, prior to signing.

At the advice of the attorney, the buyers require that all documents be prepared and made available to them 48 hours prior to closing for review. They also want to have the opportunity to do a walk-through inspection during the four hours immediately preceding closing. They will close on or before April 4.

PROMULGATED BY THE TEXAS REAL ESTATE COMMISSION (TREC) 11-8-99

ONE TO FOUR FAMILY RESIDENTIAL CONTRACT (RESALE)
ALL CASH, ASSUMPTION, THIRD PARTY CONVENTIONAL OR SELLER FINANCING

NOTICE: Not For Use For Condominium Transactions

1. **PARTIES:** ______________________________ (Seller) agrees to sell and convey to ______________________________(Buyer) and Buyer agrees to buy from Seller the property described below.

2. **PROPERTY:** Lot ____________, Block _____, ______________________________ Addition, City of ______________________________, ____________________ County, Texas, known as ______________________________ (Address/Zip Code), or as described on attached exhibit, together with the following items, if any: curtains and rods, draperies and rods, valances, blinds, window shades, screens, shutters, awnings, wall-to-wall carpeting, mirrors fixed in place, ceiling fans, attic fans, mail boxes, television antennas and satellite dish system with controls and equipment, permanently installed heating and air-conditioning units, window air-conditioning units, built-in security and fire detection equipment, plumbing and lighting fixtures including chandeliers, water softener, stove, built-in kitchen equipment, garage door openers with controls, built-in cleaning equipment, all swimming pool equipment and maintenance accessories, shrubbery, landscaping, permanently installed outdoor cooking equipment, built-in fireplace screens, artificial fireplace logs and all other property owned by Seller and attached to the above described real property except the following property which is not included: ______________________________
____
____
______________________________.

All property sold by this contract is called the "Property." The Property ❑ is ❑ is not subject to mandatory membership in an owners' association. The TREC Addendum For Property Subject To Mandatory Membership In An Owners' Association ❑ is ❑ is not attached.
NOTICE TO BUYER: If the Property is subject to mandatory membership in an owners' association, Seller notifies Buyer under §5.012, Texas Property Code, that, as a purchaser of property in the residential community in which the Property is located, you are obligated to be a member of an owners' association. Restrictive covenants governing the use and occupancy of the Property and a dedicatory instrument governing the establishment, maintenance, and operation of this residential community have been or will be recorded in the Real Property Records of the county in which the Property is located. Copies of the restrictive covenants and dedicatory instrument may be obtained from the county clerk. You are obligated to pay assessments to the owners' association. The amount of the assessments is subject to change. Your failure to pay the assessments could result in a lien on and the foreclosure of the Property.

3. **SALES PRICE:**
   A. Cash portion of Sales Price payable by Buyer at closing . . . . $____________
   B. Sum of all financing described below
      (excluding any private mortgage insurance [PMI] premium) . . . . $____________
   C. Sales Price (Sum of A and B) . . . . $____________

4. **FINANCING:** Within _____ days after the effective date of this contract Buyer shall apply for all third party financing or noteholder's approval of any assumption and make every reasonable effort to obtain financing or assumption approval. Financing or assumption approval will be deemed to have been obtained when the lender determines that Buyer has satisfied all of lender's financial requirements (those items relating to Buyer's net worth, income and creditworthiness). If financing (including any financed PMI premium) or assumption approval is not obtained within ______ days after the effective

date hereof, this contract will terminate and the earnest money will be refunded to Buyer. Each note to be executed hereunder must be secured by vendor's and deed of trust liens.

The portion of Sales Price not payable in cash will be paid as follows: (Check applicable boxes below)

❑ A. THIRD PARTY FINANCING:

❑ (1) This contract is subject to approval for Buyer of a third party first mortgage loan having a loan-to-value ratio not to exceed ____ % as established by such third party (excluding any financed PMI premium), due in full in _____ year(s), with interest not to exceed _____ % per annum for the first _____ year(s) of the loan. The loan will be ❑ with ❑ without PMI.

❑ (2) This contract is subject to approval for Buyer of a third party second mortgage loan having a loan-to-value ratio not to exceed ______ % as established by such third party (excluding any financed PMI premium), due in full in ______ year(s), with interest not to exceed ______ % per annum for the first _____ year(s) of the loan. The loan will be ❑ with ❑ without PMI.

❑ B. TEXAS VETERANS' HOUSING ASSISTANCE PROGRAM LOAN: This contract is subject to approval for Buyer of a Texas Veterans' Housing Assistance Program Loan (the Program Loan) of $_______________ for a period of at least ____________ years at the interest rate established by the Texas Veterans' Land Board at the time of closing.

❑ C. SELLER FINANCING: A promissory note from Buyer to Seller of $____________, bearing ____ % interest per annum, secured by vendor's and deed of trust liens, in accordance with the terms and conditions set forth in the attached TREC Seller Financing Addendum. If an owner policy of title insurance is furnished, Buyer shall furnish Seller with a mortgagee policy of title insurance.

❑ D. ASSUMPTION:

❑ (1) Buyer shall assume the unpaid principal balance of a first lien promissory note payable to ____
which unpaid balance at closing will be $ _____________ . The total current monthly payment including principal, interest and any reserve deposits is $ _______________ .
Buyer's initial payment will be the first payment due after closing.

❑ (2) Buyer shall assume the unpaid principal balance of a second lien promissory note payable to ____
which unpaid balance at closing will be $ _______________ . The total current monthly payment including principal, interest and any reserve deposits is $ _______________ .
Buyer's initial payment will be the first payment due after closing.

Buyer's assumption of an existing note includes all obligations imposed by the deed of trust securing the note.

If the unpaid principal balance(s) of any assumed loan(s) as of the Closing Date varies from the loan balance(s) stated above, the ❑ cash payable at closing ❑ Sales Price will be adjusted by the amount of any variance; provided, if the total principal balance of all assumed loans varies in an amount greater than $350.00 at closing, either party may terminate this contract and the earnest money will be refunded to Buyer unless the other party elects to eliminate the excess in the variance by an appropriate adjustment at closing. If the noteholder requires (a) payment of an assumption fee in excess of $ ____________in D(1) above or $ _______________ in D(2) above and Seller declines to pay such excess, or (b) an increase in the interest rate to more than _____ % in D(1) above, or _____ % in D(2) above, or (c) any other modification of the loan documents, Buyer may terminate this contract and the earnest money will be refunded to Buyer. A vendor's lien and deed of trust to secure assumption will be required which shall automatically be released on execution and delivery of a release by noteholder. If Seller is released from liability on any assumed note, the vendor's lien and deed of trust to secure assumption will not be required.

One to Four Family Residential Contract Concerning____ Page Three 11-8-99
(Address of Property)

NOTICE TO BUYER: The monthly payments, interest rates or other terms of some loans may be adjusted by the lender at or after closing. If you are concerned about the possibility of future adjustments, do not sign the contract without examining the notes and deeds of trust.
NOTICE TO SELLER: Your liability to pay the note assumed by Buyer will continue unless you obtain a release of liability from the lender. If you are concerned about future liability, you should use the TREC Release of Liability Addendum.

❑ E. CREDIT APPROVAL ON ASSUMPTION OR SELLER FINANCING: Within _____ days after the effective date of this contract, Buyer shall deliver to Seller ❑ credit report ❑ verification of employment, including salary ❑ verification of funds on deposit in financial institutions ❑ current financial statement to establish Buyer's creditworthiness for assumption approval or seller financing and ❑ ____
____
____.

If Buyer's documentation is not delivered within the specified time, Seller may terminate this contract by notice to Buyer within 7 days after expiration of the time for delivery, and the earnest money will be paid to Seller. If this contract is not so terminated, Seller will be deemed to have accepted Buyer's credit. If the documentation is timely delivered, and Seller determines in Seller's sole discretion that Buyer's credit is unacceptable, Seller may terminate this contract by notice to Buyer within 7 days after expiration of the time for delivery and the earnest money will be refunded to Buyer. If Seller does not so terminate this contract, Seller will be deemed to have accepted Buyer's credit. Buyer hereby authorizes any credit reporting agency to furnish to Seller at Buyer's sole expense copies of Buyer's credit reports.

5. **EARNEST MONEY:** Buyer shall deposit $________________ as earnest money with _____________ ____________________________________ at ____ (Address), as escrow agent, upon execution of this contract by both parties. Additional earnest money of $______________ must be deposited by Buyer with escrow agent on or before _____________________, ________. If Buyer fails to deposit the earnest money as required by this contract, Buyer will be in default.

6. **TITLE POLICY AND SURVEY:**

❑ A. TITLE POLICY: Seller shall furnish to Buyer at ❑ Seller's ❑ Buyer's expense an owner policy of title insurance (the Title Policy) issued by ____ (the Title Company) in the amount of the Sales Price, dated at or after closing, insuring Buyer against loss under the provisions of the Title Policy, subject to the promulgated exclusions (including existing building and zoning ordinances) and the following exceptions:

(1) Restrictive covenants common to the platted subdivision in which the Property is located.
(2) The standard printed exception for standby fees, taxes and assessments.
(3) Liens created as part of the financing described in Paragraph 4.
(4) Utility easements created by the dedication deed or plat of the subdivision in which the Property is located.
(5) Reservations or exceptions otherwise permitted by this contract or as may be approved by Buyer in writing.
(6) The standard printed exception as to discrepancies, conflicts, shortages in area or boundary lines, encroachments or protrusions, or overlapping improvements.
(7) The standard printed exception as to marital rights.
(8) The standard printed exception as to waters, tidelands, beaches, streams, and related matters.

Within 20 days after the Title Company receives a copy of this contract, Seller shall furnish to Buyer a commitment for title insurance (the Commitment) and, at Buyer's expense, legible copies of restrictive covenants and documents evidencing exceptions in the Commitment other than the

standard printed exceptions. Seller authorizes the Title Company to mail or hand deliver the Commitment and related documents to Buyer at Buyer's address shown below. If the Commitment is not delivered to Buyer within the specified time, the time for delivery will be automatically extended up to 15 days. Buyer will have 7 days after the receipt of the Commitment to object in writing to matters disclosed in the Commitment.

❑ B. SURVEY: (Check one box only)

❑ (1) Within _____ days after Buyer's receipt of a survey furnished to a third-party lender at ❑ Seller's ❑ Buyer's expense, Buyer may object in writing to any matter shown on the survey which constitutes a defect or encumbrance to title.

❑ (2) Within _____ days after the effective date of this contract, Buyer may object in writing to any matter which constitutes a defect or encumbrance to title shown on a survey obtained by Buyer at Buyer's expense.

The survey must be made by a Registered Professional Land Surveyor acceptable to the Title Company and any lender. Utility easements created by the dedication deed and plat of the subdivision in which the Property is located will not be a basis for objection.

Buyer may object to existing building and zoning ordinances, items 6A(1) through (8) above and matters shown on the survey if Buyer determines that any such ordinance, items or matters prohibits the following use or activity: ____
____
____.

Buyer's failure to object under Paragraph 6A or 6B within the time allowed will constitute a waiver of Buyer's right to object; except that the requirements in Schedule C of the Commitment will not be deemed to have been waived. Seller shall cure the timely objections of Buyer or any third party lender within 15 days from the date Seller receives the objections and the Closing Date will be extended as necessary. If objections are not cured by the extended Closing Date, this contract will terminate and the earnest money will be refunded to Buyer unless Buyer elects to waive the objections.

NOTICE TO SELLER AND BUYER:

(1) Broker advises Buyer to have an abstract of title covering the Property examined by an attorney of Buyer's selection, or Buyer should be furnished with or obtain a Title Policy. If a Title Policy is furnished, the Commitment should be promptly reviewed by an attorney of Buyer's choice due to the time limitations on Buyer's right to object.

(2) If the Property is situated in a utility or other statutorily created district providing water, sewer, drainage, or flood control facilities and services, Chapter 49 of the Texas Water Code requires Seller to deliver and Buyer to sign the statutory notice relating to the tax rate, bonded indebtedness, or standby fee of the district prior to final execution of this contract.

(3) If the Property abuts the tidally influenced waters of the state, Section 33.135, Texas Natural Resources Code, requires a notice regarding coastal area property to be included in the contract. An addendum either promulgated by TREC or required by the parties should be used.

(4) Buyer is advised that the presence of wetlands, toxic substances, including asbestos and wastes or other environmental hazards or the presence of a threatened or endangered species or its habitat may affect Buyer's intended use of the Property. If Buyer is concerned about these matters, an addendum either promulgated by TREC or required by the parties should be used.

(5) If the Property is located outside the limits of a municipality, Seller notifies Buyer under §5.011, Texas Property Code, that the Property may now or later be included in the extraterritorial jurisdiction of a municipality and may now or later be subject to annexation by the municipality. Each municipality maintains a map that depicts its boundaries and extraterritorial jurisdiction. To determine if the Property is located within a municipality's extraterritorial jurisdiction or is likely to be located within a municipality's extraterritorial jurisdiction, contact all municipalities located in the general proximity of the Property for further information.

(6) Unless expressly prohibited in writing by the parties, Seller may continue to show the Property for sale and to receive, negotiate and accept back up offers.

One to Four Family Residential Contract Concerning____________________________________ Page Five 11-8-99
(Address of Property)

(7) Any residential service contract that is purchased in connection with this transaction should be reviewed for the scope of coverage, exclusions and limitations. **The purchase of a residential service contract is optional. Similar coverage may be purchased from various companies authorized to do business in Texas.**

7. **PROPERTY CONDITION:**

A. INSPECTIONS, ACCESS AND UTILITIES: Buyer may have the Property inspected by an inspector selected by Buyer, licensed by TREC or otherwise permitted by law to make such inspections. Seller shall permit access to the Property at reasonable times for inspection, repairs and treatment and for reinspection after repairs and treatment have been completed. Seller shall pay for turning on utilities for inspection and reinspection.

B. SELLER'S DISCLOSURE NOTICE PURSUANT TO SECTION 5.008, TEXAS PROPERTY CODE (Notice) (check one box only):

❑ (1) Buyer has received the Notice.

❑ (2) Buyer has not received the Notice. Within _______ days after the effective date of this contract, Seller shall deliver the Notice to Buyer. If Buyer does not receive the Notice, Buyer may terminate this contract at any time prior to the closing. If Seller delivers the Notice, Buyer may terminate this contract for any reason within 7 days after Buyer receives the Notice or prior to the closing, whichever first occurs.

❑ (3) The Texas Property Code does not require this Seller to furnish the Notice.

C. SELLER'S DISCLOSURE OF LEAD-BASED PAINT AND LEAD-BASED PAINT HAZARDS is required by Federal law for a residential dwelling constructed prior to 1978. An addendum providing such disclosure ❑ is ❑ is not attached.

D. ACCEPTANCE OF PROPERTY CONDITION: (check one box only):

❑ (1) In addition to any earnest money deposited with escrow agent, Buyer has paid Seller $____________ (the "Option Fee") for the unrestricted right to terminate this contract by giving notice of termination to Seller within _______ days after the effective date of this contract. If Buyer gives notice of termination within the time specified, the Option Fee will not be refunded, however, any earnest money will be refunded to Buyer. If Buyer does not give notice of termination within the time specified, Buyer will be deemed to have accepted the Property in its current condition and the Option Fee ❑ will ❑ will not be credited to the Sales Price at closing.

❑ (2) Buyer accepts the Property in its present condition; provided Seller, at Seller's expense, shall complete the following repairs and treatment: ______________________________
____
____
____.

E. LENDER REQUIRED REPAIRS AND TREATMENTS (REPAIRS): Unless otherwise agreed in writing, neither party is obligated to pay for lender required repairs or treatments for wood destroying insects. If the cost of lender required repairs exceeds 5% of the Sales Price, Buyer may terminate this contract.

F. COMPLETION OF REPAIRS AND TREATMENT. Unless otherwise agreed by the parties in writing, Seller shall complete all agreed repairs and treatment prior to the Closing Date. Repairs and treatments must be performed by persons who regularly provide such repairs or treatments. At Buyer's election, any transferable warranties received by Seller with respect to the repairs will be transferred to Buyer at Buyer's expense. If Seller fails to complete any agreed repairs and treatment prior to the Closing Date, Buyer may do so and the Closing Date will be extended up to 15 days, if necessary, to complete repairs and treatment or treatments for wood destroying insects.

8. **BROKERS' FEES:** All obligations of the parties for payment of brokers' fees are contained in separate written agreements.

9. **CLOSING:** The closing of the sale will be on or before ______________________, ______, or within 7 days after objections to matters disclosed in the Commitment or by the survey have been cured, whichever date is later (the Closing Date). *If financing or assumption approval has been obtained pursuant to Paragraph 4,* the Closing Date will be extended up to 15 days if necessary to comply with lender's closing requirements (for example, appraisal, survey, insurance policies, lender-required repairs, closing documents). If either party fails to close this sale by the Closing Date, the non-defaulting party will be entitled to exercise the remedies contained in Paragraph 15. At closing Seller shall furnish tax statements or certificates showing no delinquent taxes and a general warranty deed conveying good and indefeasible title showing no additional exceptions to those permitted in Paragraph 6.

10. **POSSESSION:** Seller shall deliver possession of the Property to Buyer on ________________ in its present or required repaired condition, ordinary wear and tear excepted. Any possession by Buyer prior to closing or by Seller after closing which is not authorized by a temporary lease form promulgated by TREC or required by the parties will establish a tenancy at sufferance relationship between the parties. *Consult your insurance agent prior to change of ownership or possession as insurance coverage may be limited or terminated. The absence of a written lease or appropriate insurance coverage may expose the parties to economic loss.*

11. **SPECIAL PROVISIONS:** (Insert only factual statements and business details applicable to this sale. TREC rules prohibit licensees from adding factual statements or business details for which a contract addendum, lease or other form has been promulgated by TREC for mandatory use.)

12. **SETTLEMENT AND OTHER EXPENSES:**
   A. The following expenses must be paid at or prior to closing:
      (1) Appraisal fees will be paid by ______________________________________.
      (2) The total of loan discount fees (including any Texas Veterans' Housing Assistance Program Participation Fee) may not exceed ________% of the loan of which Seller shall pay _____________ and Buyer shall pay the remainder. The total of any buydown fees may not exceed _____________which will be paid by ____________________________.
      (3) Seller's Expenses: Releases of existing liens, including prepayment penalties and recording fees; release of Seller's loan liability; tax statements or certificates; preparation of deed; one-half of escrow fee; and other expenses stipulated to be paid by Seller under other provisions of this contract.
      (4) Buyer's Expenses: Loan application, origination and commitment fees; loan assumption costs; preparation and recording of deed of trust to secure assumption; lender required expenses

One to Four Family Residential Contract Concerning_______________________________Page Seven 11-8-99
(Address of Property)

incident to new loans, including PMI premium, preparation of loan documents, loan related inspection fee, recording fees, tax service and research fees, warehouse or underwriting fees, copies of restrictions and easements, amortization schedule, premiums for mortgagee title policies and endorsements required by lender, credit reports, photos; required premiums for flood and hazard insurance; required reserve deposit for insurance premiums and ad valorem taxes; interest on all monthly installment notes from date of disbursements to one month prior to dates of first monthly payments; customary Program Loan costs for Buyer; one-half of escrow fee; and other expenses stipulated to be paid by Buyer under other provisions of this contract.

B. If any expense exceeds an amount expressly stated in this contract for such expense to be paid by a party, that party may terminate this contract unless the other party agrees to pay such excess. In no event will Buyer pay charges and fees expressly prohibited by the Texas Veterans' Housing Assistance Program or other governmental loan program regulations.

13. **PRORATIONS**: Taxes for the current year, interest, maintenance fees, assessments, dues and rents will be prorated through the Closing Date. If taxes for the current year vary from the amount prorated at closing, the parties shall adjust the prorations when tax statements for the current year are available. *If a loan is assumed* and the lender maintains an escrow account, the escrow account must be transferred to Buyer without any deficiency. Buyer shall reimburse Seller for the amount in the transferred account. Buyer shall pay the premium for a new insurance policy. If taxes are not paid at or prior to closing, Buyer will be obligated to pay taxes for the current year.

14. **CASUALTY LOSS:** If any part of the Property is damaged or destroyed by fire or other casualty loss after the effective date of the contract, Seller shall restore the Property to its previous condition as soon as reasonably possible, but in any event by the Closing Date. If Seller fails to do so due to factors beyond Seller's control, Buyer may either (a) terminate this contract and the earnest money will be refunded to Buyer (b) extend the time for performance up to 15 days and the Closing Date will be extended as necessary or (c) accept the Property in its damaged condition and accept an assignment of insurance proceeds. Seller's obligations under this paragraph are independent of any obligations of Seller under Paragraph 7.

15. **DEFAULT:** If Buyer fails to comply with this contract, Buyer will be in default, and Seller may either (a) enforce specific performance, seek such other relief as may be provided by law, or both, or (b) terminate this contract and receive the earnest money as liquidated damages, thereby releasing both parties from this contract. If, due to factors beyond Seller's control, Seller fails within the time allowed to make any non-casualty repairs or deliver the Commitment, Buyer may either (a) extend the time for performance up to 15 days and the Closing Date will be extended as necessary or (b) terminate this contract as the sole remedy and receive the earnest money. If Seller fails to comply with this contract for any other reason, Seller will be in default and Buyer may either (a) enforce specific performance, seek such other relief as may be provided by law, or both, or (b) terminate this contract and receive the earnest money, thereby releasing both parties from this contract.

16. **DISPUTE RESOLUTION:** It is the policy of the State of Texas to encourage the peaceable resolution of disputes through alternative dispute resolution procedures. The parties are encouraged to use an addendum approved by TREC to submit to mediation disputes which cannot be resolved in good faith through informal discussion.

17. **ATTORNEY'S FEES:** The prevailing party in any legal proceeding brought under or with respect to the transaction described in this contract is entitled to recover from the non-prevailing party all costs of such proceeding and reasonable attorney's fees.

Initialed for identification by Buyer__________ and Seller__________ 01A TREC NO. 20-4

18. **ESCROW:** The earnest money is deposited with escrow agent with the understanding that escrow agent is not (a) a party to this contract and does not have any liability for the performance or nonperformance of any party to this contract, (b) liable for interest on the earnest money and (c) liable for any loss of earnest money caused by the failure of any financial institution in which the earnest money has been deposited unless the financial institution is acting as escrow agent. At closing, the earnest money must be applied first to any cash down payment, then to Buyer's closing costs and any excess refunded to Buyer. If both parties make written demand for the earnest money, escrow agent may require payment of unpaid expenses incurred on behalf of the parties and a written release of liability of escrow agent from all parties. If one party makes written demand for the earnest money, escrow agent shall give notice of the demand by providing to the other party a copy of the demand. If escrow agent does not receive written objection to the demand from the other party within 30 days after notice to the other party, escrow agent may disburse the earnest money to the party making demand reduced by the amount of unpaid expenses incurred on behalf of the party receiving the earnest money and escrow agent may pay the same to the creditors. If escrow agent complies with the provisions of this paragraph, each party hereby releases escrow agent from all adverse claims related to the disbursal of the earnest money. Escrow agent's notice to the other party will be effective when deposited in the U. S. Mail, postage prepaid, certified mail, return receipt requested, addressed to the other party at such party's address shown below. Notice of objection to the demand will be deemed effective upon receipt by escrow agent.

19. **REPRESENTATIONS:** Seller represents that as of the Closing Date (a) there will be no liens, assessments, or security interests against the Property which will not be satisfied out of the sales proceeds unless securing payment of any loans assumed by Buyer and (b) assumed loans will not be in default. If any representation in this contract is untrue on the Closing Date, this contract may be terminated by Buyer and the earnest money will be refunded to Buyer. All representations contained in this contract will survive closing.

20. **FEDERAL TAX REQUIREMENT:** If Seller is a "foreign person," as defined by applicable law, or if Seller fails to deliver an affidavit that Seller is not a "foreign person," then Buyer shall withhold from the sales proceeds an amount sufficient to comply with applicable tax law and deliver the same to the Internal Revenue Service together with appropriate tax forms. IRS regulations require filing written reports if cash in excess of specified amounts is received in the transaction.

21. **AGREEMENT OF PARTIES:** This contract contains the entire agreement of the parties and cannot be changed except by their written agreement. Addenda which are a part of this contract are (list):

____

____

____

____

____

____.

22. **CONSULT YOUR ATTORNEY:** Real estate licensees cannot give legal advice. This contract is intended to be legally binding. READ IT CAREFULLY. If you do not understand the effect of this contract, consult your attorney BEFORE signing.

Buyer's
Attorney is:_______________________

Seller's
Attorney is:_______________________

One to Four Family Residential Contract Concerning______________________________________ Page Nine 11-8-99
(Address of Property)

23. **NOTICES:** All notices from one party to the other must be in writing and are effective when mailed to, hand-delivered at, or transmitted by facsimile machine as follows:

To Buyer at:	**To Seller at:**
______________________	______________________
______________________	______________________
______________________	______________________
Telephone:(___)______________	Telephone:(___)______________
Facsimile:(___) ______________	Facsimile:(___) ______________

EXECUTED the _____day of __________________, ______ (THE EFFECTIVE DATE). (BROKER: FILL IN THE DATE OF FINAL ACCEPTANCE.)

______________________ Buyer	______________________ Seller
______________________ Buyer	______________________ Seller

The form of this contract has been approved by the Texas Real Estate Commission. TREC forms are intended for use only by trained real estate licensees. No representation is made as to the legal validity or adequacy of any provision in any specific transactions. It is not suitable for complex transactions. Texas Real Estate Commission, P.O. Box 12188, Austin, TX 78711-2188, 1-800-250-8732 or (512) 459-6544 (http://www.trec.state.tx.us)TREC NO. 20-4. This form replaces TREC NO. 20-3.

BROKER INFORMATION AND RATIFICATION OF FEE

Listing Broker has agreed to pay Other Broker ______________________ of the total sales price when Listing Broker's fee is received. Escrow Agent is authorized and directed to pay Other Broker from Listing Broker's fee at closing.

______________________ Other Broker License No.	______________________ Listing Broker License No.
represents ❑ Seller as Listing Broker's subagent ❑ Buyer only as Buyer's agent	represents ❑ Seller and Buyer as an intermediary ❑ Seller only as Seller's agent
	______________________ Listing Associate Telephone
______________________ Associate Telephone	______________________ Selling Associate Telephone
______________________ Broker Address	______________________ Broker Address
______________________ Telephone Facsimile	______________________ Telephone Facsimile

RECEIPT

Receipt of ❑ Contract and ❑ $__________ Earnest Money in the form of ______________________ is acknowledged.

Escrow Agent: ______________________ Date: ______________________, ______

By: ______________________

______________________ Telephone: (____) ______________________
Address

______________________ Facsimile: (____) ______________________
City State Zip

10-25-93

ENVIRONMENTAL ASSESSMENT, THREATENED OR ENDANGERED SPECIES, AND WETLANDS ADDENDUM

PROMULGATED BY THE TEXAS REAL ESTATE COMMISSION (TREC)

ADDENDUM TO EARNEST MONEY CONTRACT BETWEEN THE UNDERSIGNED PARTIES CONCERNING THE PROPERTY AT ______________________________

(Address)

☐ A. ENVIRONMENTAL ASSESSMENT: Buyer, at Buyer's expense, may obtain an Environmental Assessment Report prepared by an environmental specialist.

☐ B. THREATENED OR ENDANGERED SPECIES: Buyer, at Buyer's expense, may obtain a report from a natural resources professional to determine if there are any threatened o r endangered species or their habitats as defined by the Texas Parks and wildlife Department or the U.S. Fish and Wildlife Service.

☐ C. WETLANDS: Buyer, at Buyer's expense, may obtain a report from an environmental specialist to determine if there are wetlands, as defined by federal or state law or regulation.

Within ________ days after the Effective Date of the contract, Buyer may terminate the contract by furnishing Seller a copy of any report noted above that adversely affects the use of the Property and the Earnest Money shall be refunded to Buyer. If Buyer does not furnish Seller a copy of the unacceptable report within the prescribed time and give Seller notice that Buyer has terminated the contract, Buyer shall be deemed to have accepted the Property.

______________________	______________________
Buyer	Seller
______________________	______________________
Buyer	Seller

The form of this addendum has been approved by the Texas Real Estate Commission for use only with similarly approved o r promulgated forms of contracts. No representation is made as to the legal validity or adequacy of any provision in any specific transactions. It is not suitable for complex transactions. (10-93) TREC No. 28-0.

01A TREC No. 28-0

PROMULGATED BY THE TEXAS REAL ESTATE COMMISSION (TREC)
P.O. BOX 12188, AUSTIN, TX 78711-2188

12-05-94

ADDENDUM FOR
COASTAL AREA PROPERTY

ADDENDUM TO EARNEST MONEY CONTRACT BETWEEN THE UNDERSIGNED PARTIES CONCERNING THE PROPERTY AT

____

____

(Location of Property)

IN ACCORDANCE WITH SECTION 33.1 35, TEXAS NATURAL RESOURCES CODE, THE FOLLOWING NOTICE IS INCLUDED AS PART OF THE CONTRACT:

NOTICE REGARDING COASTAL AREA PROPERTY

1. The real property described in and subject to this contract adjoins and shares a common boundary with the tidally influenced submerged lands of the state. The boundary is subject to change and can be determined accurately only by a survey on the ground made by a licensed state land surveyor in accordance with the original grant from the sovereign. The owner of the property described in this contract may gain or lose portions of the tract because of changes in the boundary.

2. The seller, transferor, or grantor has no knowledge of any prior fill as it relates to the property described in and subject to this contract except: ____.

3. State law prohibits the use, encumbrance, construction, or placing of any structure in, on, or over state-owned submerged lands below the applicable tide line, without proper permission.

4. The purchaser or grantee is hereby advised to seek the advice of an attorney or other qualified person as to the legal nature and effect of the facts set forth in this notice on the property described in and subject to this contract. Information regarding the location of the applicable tide line as to the property described in and subject to this contract may be obtained from the surveying division of the General Land Office in Austin.

________________ Buyer	________________ Seller
________________ Buyer	________________ Seller

This form has been approved by the Texas Real Estate Commission for use with similarly approved or promulgated contract forms. Such approval relates to this form only. No representation is made as to the legal validity or adequacy of any provision in any specific transactions. It is not suitable for complex transactions. (12-94) TREC No. 33-0.

12-05-94

PROMULGATED BY THE TEXAS REAL ESTATE COMMISSION (TREC)
P.O. BOX 12188, AUSTIN, TX 78711-2188

ADDENDUM FOR PROPERTY LOCATED SEAWARD OF THE GULF INTRACOASTAL WATERWAY

ADDENDUM TO EARNEST MONEY CONTRACT BETWEEN THE UNDERSIGNED PARTIES CONCERNING THE PROPERTY AT

____

____

(Location of Property)

IN ACCORDANCE WITH SECTION 61.0 25, TEXAS NATURAL RESOURCES CODE, THE FOLLOWING STATEMENT IS INCLUDED AS PART OF THE CONTRACT:

The real property described in this contract is located seaward of the Gulf Intracoastal Waterway to its southernmost point and then seaward of the longitudinal line also known as 97 degrees, 12', 19" which runs southerly to the international boundary from the intersection of the centerline of the Gulf Intracoastal Waterway and the Brownsville Ship Channel. If the property is in close proximity to a beach fronting the Gulf of Mexico, the purchaser is hereby advised that the public has acquired a right of use or easement to or over the area of any public beach by prescription, dedication, or presumption, or has retained a right by virtue of continuous right in the public since time immemorial, as recognized in law and custom.

The extreme seaward boundary of natural vegetation that spreads continuously inland customarily marks the landward boundary of the public easement. If there is no clearly marked natural vegetation line, the landward boundary of the easement is as provided by Sections 61.016 and 61.017, Natural Resources Code.

State law prohibits any obstruction, barrier, restraint, or interference with the use of the public easement, including the placement of structures seaward of the landward boundary of the easement. STRUCTURES ERECTED SEAWARD OF THE VEGETATION LINE (OR OTHER APPLICABLE EASEMENT BOUNDARY) OR THAT BECOME SEAWARD OF THE VEGETATION LINE AS A RESULT OF NATURAL PROCESSES ARE SUBJECT TO A LAWSUIT BY THE STATE OF TEXAS TO REMOVE THE STRUCTURES.

The purchaser is hereby notified that the purchaser should seek the advice of an attorney or other qualified person before executing this contract or instrument of conveyance as to the relevance of these statutes and facts to the value of the property the purchaser is hereby purchasing or contracting to purchase.

_______________	_______________
Buyer	Seller
_______________	_______________
Buyer	Seller

This form has been approved by the Texas Real Estate Commission for use with similarly approved or promulgated contract forms. Such approval relates to this form only. No representation is made as to the legal validity or adequacy of any provision in any specific transactions. It is not suitable for complex transactions. (12-94) TREC No. 34-0.

06-15-98

PROMULGATED BY THE TEXAS REAL ESTATE COMMISSION (TREC)

AGREEMENT FOR MEDIATION

ADDENDUM TO CONTRACT CONCERNING THE PROPERTY AT

____

(Street Address and City)

The parties to the Contract and any broker who signs this addendum agree to negotiate in good faith in an effort to resolve any dispute related to the Contract that may arise between the parties or between a party and a broker.

If the dispute cannot be resolved by negotiation, the parties to the dispute shall submit the dispute to mediation before resorting to litigation.

This Agreement for Mediation will survive closing.

❑ If the need for mediation arises, the parties to the dispute shall choose a mutually acceptable mediator and shall share the cost of mediation services equally.

❑ If the need for mediation arises, mediation services will be provided by ______________________ ____________________and the parties to the dispute shall share the cost of mediation services equally.

NOTE: Mediation is a voluntary dispute resolution process in which the parties to the dispute meet with an impartial person, called a mediator, who would help to resolve the dispute informally and confidentially. Mediators facilitate the resolution of disputes but cannot impose binding decisions. The parties to the dispute must agree before any settlement is binding.

Date: ______________________________

______________________ Buyer	______________________ Seller
______________________ Buyer	______________________ Seller
______________________ Other Broker	______________________ Listing Broker
By: ______________________	By: ______________________

The form of this addendum has been approved for voluntary use by the Texas Real Estate Commission for use only with similarly approved or promulgated forms of contracts. No representation is made as to the legal validity or adequacy of any provision in any specific transactions. (06-98) Texas Real Estate Commission, P.O. Box 12188, Austin, TX 78711-2188, 1-800-250-8732 or (512)459-6544. (http://www.trec.state.tx.us) TREC No. 35-1. This form replaces TREC No. 35-0.

PROMULGATED BY THE TEXAS REAL ESTATE COMMISSION (TREC) 09-01-99

ADDENDUM FOR PROPERTY SUBJECT TO MANDATORY MEMBERSHIP IN AN OWNERS' ASSOCIATION

(NOT FOR USE WITH CONDOMINIUMS)

ADDENDUM TO CONTRACT CONCERNING THE PROPERTY AT

____
(Street Address and City)

____
(Name of Owners' Association)

A. **SUBDIVISION INFORMATION:** "Subdivision Information" means: (i) the restrictions applying to the subdivision, (ii) the bylaws and rules of the Owners' Association, and (iii) a resale certificate, all of which were provided by the Owners' Association in compliance with Section 207.003 of the Texas Property Code no more than three months before the date of their delivery to Buyer.

(Check only one box):

❑ 1. Within ________ days after the effective date of the contract, Seller shall at Seller's expense deliver the Subdivision Information to Buyer. If Buyer does not receive the Subdivision Information, Buyer may terminate the contract at any time prior to closing. If Seller delivers the Subdivision Information, Buyer may terminate the contract for any reason within 7 days after Buyer receives the Subdivision Information or prior to closing, whichever first occurs.

❑ 2. Buyer has received and approved the Subdivision Information before signing the contract.

❑ 3. Buyer does not require delivery of the Subdivision Information **and waives the right of termination under this Addendum**.

If Seller becomes aware of any material changes in the Subdivision Information, Seller shall immediately give notice to Buyer. Buyer may terminate the contract prior to closing by giving written notice to Seller if: (i) any of the Subdivision Information provided was not true; or (ii) any material adverse change in the Subdivision Information occurs prior to closing.

B. **TRANSFER FEES:** Buyer shall pay any Owners' Association transfer fee not to exceed $ ____________, and Seller agrees to pay any excess.

NOTICE TO BUYER REGARDING REPAIRS BY THE OWNERS' ASSOCIATION: The Owners' Association may have the sole responsibility to make certain repairs to the Property. If you are concerned about the condition of any part of the Property which the Owners' Association is required to repair, you should not sign the contract unless you are satisfied that the Owners' Association will make the desired repairs.

______________________	______________________
Buyer	Seller
______________________	______________________
Buyer	Seller

The form of this addendum has been approved by the Texas Real Estate Commission for use only with similarly approved or promulgated forms of contracts. Such approval relates to this contract form only. TREC forms are intended for use only by trained real estate licensees. No representation is made as to the legal validity or adequacy of any provision in any specific transactions. It is not suitable for complex transactions.(09-99)Texas Real Estate Commission, P.O. Box 12188, Austin, TX 78711-2188, 1-800-250-8732 or (512) 459-6544 (http://www.trec.state.tx.us) TREC No. 36-1.This form replaces TREC No. 36-0.

01A TREC No. 36-1

PART 6

Estimating Seller Net and Buyer Move-In

Buyers and sellers are interested in the bottom line and expect the real estate licensee to give a reasonably accurate estimate of those numbers. To be able to provide this information to the client or customer, the licensee needs to become comfortable with calculating closing costs, prepaids, and lender-required reserve deposits. One must be familiar with HUD's Uniform Settlement Statement, which must be used in all transactions covered by the RESPA rules. These rules cover the vast majority of transactions structured with the promulgated forms we have been studying.

To estimate the costs accurately, carefully examine the purchase agreement, know the typical charges incurred with the particular type of financing involved in the transaction, obtain a title insurance rate card and obtain accurate numbers for the ad valorem taxes, homeowners' association maintenance fee and homeowner's insurance policy premium.

Most title insurance companies provide real estate licensees with charts to use in estimating closing costs. For our example we will use the HUD form. By using this form for estimating purposes, your client or customer will be familiar with it when it is presented in its final form at closing. Familiarity with the form contributes to a smoother closing experience.

One of the most commonly encountered transactions involves a buyer's purchasing a single-family, previously occupied home with funds obtained from a 90 percent conventional loan. Transaction 10 in Part Five of this book fits the description *typical* and is used for this example. In our example we round all line items to the nearest dollar. Rounding is acceptable for giving estimates. Exact numbers must be used at closing.

THE SELLER'S SIDE

The listing agent will be concerned with accurately estimating the bottom line for the seller. To do this, begin by itemizing the applicable costs on the back of the statement. In Transaction 10, the seller has charges at the following lines:

703	**Commission** (using a commission rate of 7%) Sales price of \$387,800 × .07 = \$27,146	\$ 27,146
1107	**Attorney's Fee** Preparation of General Warranty Deed and Release	\$ 130
1110	**Owner's Title Insurance Policy Premium** Calculated on sale price using title insurance rate card; using current rate card	\$ 2,885
1111	**Escrow Fee** Determined by title company	\$ 75
1113	**Messenger** Determined by title company	\$ 45
1201	**Recording Fees** Release of lien	\$ 20

Enter these numbers in the column labeled "Paid from Seller's Funds at Settlement" on the back of the Uniform Settlement Statement. Total the column and enter your total on the front of the Uniform Settlement Statement at line 502.

On the front of the Uniform Settlement Statement, enter the contract sale price at line 401. The seller paid the homeowners' association maintenance fee of \$660 on January 1. We use a closing date of April 4 and need to prorate the homeowners' association maintenance fee with the seller paying through the day of closing as stipulated in paragraph 13 of the contract. The seller has had the benefit of January 1 through April 4. The buyer will reimburse the seller for the remaining portion of the year.

To calculate the amount involved, we shall use a "banker's year" of 360 days. For the remaining days in April, we subtract the closing date from 30.

April		May-December		Days Due
30 days − 4 = 26	+	240 (30 × 8)	=	266

The annual fee of \$660 is divided by 360 days and multiplied by the days due to calculate the amount the buyer will be charged and the seller will be credited at lines 409 and 109.

$$\$660 \div 360 \text{ days} \times 266 \text{ days due} = \$488 \text{ (rounded)}$$

The seller has an outstanding loan balance of \$86,000 after the April 1 payment has been made. The loan is at 8 percent interest and has no prepayment penalty. To calculate the payoff to enter at line 504, we must calculate four days of interest and add it to the principal balance outstanding.

$$\text{Loan amount } \$86{,}000 \times .08 = \$6{,}880 \text{ annual interest}$$

$$\$6{,}880 \div 360 \text{ days} \times 4 \text{ days due} = \$76 \text{ (rounded)}$$

$$\$86{,}000 + \$76 = \$86{,}076 \text{ total payoff}$$

Paragraph 13 also calls for the ad valorem taxes to be prorated through the day of closing, April 4. The annual tax bill for this property is \$5,648. To prorate the tax bill, count the days from January 1 through April 4, calculate the dollar amount of tax per day and calculate the total amount of tax that will be charged to the seller at line 510 and credited to the buyer at line 210.

Jan		Feb		Mar		Apr	
30	+	30	+	30	+	4	= 94 days due

Annual tax	÷ 360	= \$ per day	× days due	= lines 510 and 210
\$5,648	÷ 360	= \$15.69	× 94	= \$1,475 (rounded)

Now you may total all lines in the 400 series and enter your total at lines 420 and 601. Total all lines in the 500 series and enter your total at lines 520 and 602. Subtract line 602 from line 601 and enter your answer at line 603. Check the box that indicates cash "To" the seller at line 603 and you are ready to give a solid, accurate estimate to your seller client.

THE BUYER'S SIDE

Again, begin on the back of the statement. The purchase agreement and a title company closing cost estimating sheet with typical numbers are invaluable tools.

The 800 series of line items relate to costs associated with the buyer's new loan.

801	**Loan Origination Fee** \$349,000 × .01 = \$3,490	\$ 3,490
802	**Loan Discount** Paragraph 12B calls for the buyer to pay 1 discount point. \$349,000 × .01 = \$3,490	\$ 3,490
803	**Appraisal Fee**	\$ 300
804	**Credit Report**	\$ 75
806	**Mortgage Insurance Premium** You are told by the loan officer that the PMI premium will be .5 points if paid by the buyer in cash at closing. \$349,000 × .005 = \$1,745	\$ 1,745
808	**Amortization Schedule**	\$ 20

The 900 and 1000 series cover the prepaids and the reserve items to be deposited with the lender.

901	**Prepaid Interest From** April 4 to May 1 = 26 days due New loan of \$349,000 × .07 ÷ 360 × 26 days due = \$1,764 (rounded)	\$ 1,764
903	**Hazard Insurance Premium** This amount represents the first year's annual premium. Check with an insurance agent for the appropriate premium in your area.	\$ 1,725
1001	**Hazard Insurance Deposit** Two months is typical. \$1,725 ÷ 12 = \$144 per month (rounded) × 2 = \$288	\$ 288
1003	**City Property Taxes** Lenders typically require the prorated amount on line 210 plus the balance of the month of closing plus the month until the first payment comes due plus two months in advance. January through April + May + 2 months = 7 months	\$ 3,297
1105	**Document Preparation** Legal fees for the preparation of the note and deed of trust.	\$ 200
1109	**Lender's Coverage** The lender requires a mortgagee's title policy to give the lender assurance that it is in first lien position.	\$ 175
1111	**Escrow Fee**	\$ 75
1113	**Messenger**	\$ 45

1201	**Recording Fees** Paid to the county clerk's office to record the Deed of Trust ($35) and the General Warranty Deed ($23).	$ 58
1204	**Tax Service Fee**	$ 115
1301	**Survey** Every buyer should require a survey prior to closing. Lenders require a survey as a part of the loan package.	$ 325

Enter these numbers in the column labeled "Paid from the Borrower's Funds at Settlement" on the back of the Uniform Settlement Statement. Total the column and enter your total on the front of the Uniform Settlement Statement at line 103.

On the front of the Uniform Settlement Statement, enter the contract sale price at line 101. At line 201 enter the earnest money recited in paragraph 5 of the purchase agreement, and enter the amount from paragraph 3B on line 202. The prorated items should be entered on lines 109 (maintenance fee) and 210 (property tax). You are now ready to total the borrower's side.

Total all lines in the 100 series and enter the number at line 120 and at line 301. Total all lines in the 200 series and enter the number at line 220 and at line 302. To accurately estimate the amount the buyer will need to bring to the closing in the form of a cashier's check, subtract line 302 from line 301 and enter the difference at line 303. Check the box that indicates cash "From" the borrower. Check your completed statement with the answer key in Appendix C.

For a further discussion of finding your way through and completing a closing statement, we recommend Chapter 14 in *Mastering Real Estate Mathematics,* sixth edition, by Ventolo, Tamper and Alloway, published by the Real Estate Education Company® of Chicago. Chapter 13 of the same book will help you prorate taxes, interest, insurance, homeowners' association maintenance fees and rents.

Good luck and happy selling!

A. Settlement Statement

U.S. Department of Housing and Urban Development

OMB No. 2502-0265

B. Type of Loan	6. File Number	7. Loan Number	8. Mortgage Insurance Case Number
1. ☐ FHA 2. ☐ FmHA 3. ☐ Conv. Unins. 4. ☐ VA 5. ☒ Conv. Ins.			

C. **Note:** This form is furnished to give you a statement of actual settlement costs. Amounts paid to and by the settlement agent are shown. Items marked "(p.o.c.)" were paid outside the closing; they are shown here for informational purposes and are not included in the totals.

D. Name and Address of Borrower	E. Name and Address of Seller Tax I.D. No.	F. Name and Address of Lender
232-36-3775 Peter Paul Prospect, et ux Priscilla Bea Prospect 654 Broadway Galveston	492-56-6667 Russell Alan James, et ux Anna Marie James 12656 Rolling Waves Lane Galveston	Deep Pocket Mortgage Company 6000 Money Lane Galveston, Texas

G. Property Location	H. Settlement Agent and Agent Identification Number	
12656 Rolling Waves Lane Galveston, Texas 77573	Buyer's Choice Title Company	
	Place of Settlement: Galveston, Texas	I. Settlement Date: April 4

J. Summary of Borrower's Transaction		K. Summary of Seller's Transaction	
100. Gross Amount Due From Borrower		**400. Gross Amount Due To Seller**	
101. Contract sales price	*	401. Contract sales price	*
102. Personal property		402. Personal property	
103. Settlement charges to borrower (line 1400)	*	403.	
104. Option fee paid	*<500>	404. Option fee received	*<500>
105.		405.	
Adjustments for items paid by seller in advance		**Adjustments for items paid by seller in advance**	
106. City/town taxes to		406. City/town taxes to	
107. County taxes to		407. County taxes to	
108. Assessments to		408. Assessments to	
109. Maintenance fee 4/4-12/31	*	409. Maintenance fee 4/4-12/31	*
110.		410.	
111.		411.	
112.		412.	
120. Gross Amount Due From Borrower	*	**420. Gross Amount Due To Seller**	*
200. Amounts Paid By Or In Behalf Of Borrower		**500. Reductions In Amount Due To Seller**	
201. Deposit or earnest money	*	501. Excess deposit (see instructions)	
202. Principal amount of new loan(s)	*	502. Settlement charges to seller (line 1400)	*
203. Existing loan(s) taken subject to		503. Existing loan(s) taken subject to	
204.		504. Payoff of first mortgage loan	*
205.		505. Payoff of second mortgage loan	
206.		506.	
207.		507.	
208.		508.	
209.		509.	
Adjustments for items unpaid by seller		**Adjustments for items unpaid by seller**	
210. City/town taxes 1/1 through 4/4	*	510. City/town taxes 1/1 through 4/4	*
211. County taxes to		511. County taxes to	
212. Assessments to		512. Assessments to	
213.		513.	
214.		514.	
215.		515.	
216.		516.	
217.		517.	
218.		518.	
219.		519.	
220. Total Paid By/For Borrower	*	**520. Total Reduction Amount Due Seller**	*
300. Cash At Settlement From/To Borrower		**600. Cash At Settlement To/From Seller**	
301. Gross Amount due from borrower (line 120)	*	601. Gross amount due to seller (line 420)	*
302. Less amounts paid by/for borrower (line 220)	(*)	602. Less reductions in amt. due seller (line 520)	*)
303. Cash ☒ From ☐ To Borrower	*	**603. Cash** ☒ To ☐ From Seller	*

L. Settlement Charges	Paid From Borrower's Funds at Settlement	Paid From Seller's Funds at Settlement
700. Total Sales/Broker's Commission based on price $ @ % =		
Division of Commission (line 700) as follows:		
701. $ to		
702. $ to		
703. Commission paid at Settlement		*
704.		
800. Items Payable In Connection With Loan		
801. Loan Origination Fee 1 % of new loan (rounded)	*	
802. Loan Discount 1 % of new loan (rounded)	*	
803. Appraisal Fee to	*	
804. Credit Report to	*	
805. Lender's Inspection Fee		
806. Mortgage Insurance Application Fee to 1/2% of new loan	*	
807. Assumption Fee		
808. Amortization schedule	*	
809.		
810.		
811.		
900. Items Required By Lender To Be Paid In Advance		
901. Interest from 4/4 to 5/1 @$ /day	*	
902. Mortgage Insurance Premium for months to		
903. Hazard Insurance Premium for 1 year years to	*	
904. years to		
905.		
1000. Reserves Deposited With Lender		
1001. Hazard Insurance 2 months @ $ per month	*	
1002. Mortgage Insurance months @ $ per month		
1003. City property taxes 7 months @ $ per month (rounded)	*	
1004. County property taxes months @ $ per month		
1005. Annual assessments months @ $ per month		
1006. months @ $ per month		
1007. months @ $ per month		
1008. months @ $ per month		
1100. Title Charges		
1101. Settlement or closing fee to		
1102. Abstract or title search to		
1103. Title examination to		
1104. Title insurance binder to		
1105. Document preparation to For note and deed of trust	*	
1106. Notary fees to		
1107. Attorney's fees to For deed and release		*
(includes above items numbers:		
1108. Title insurance to		
(includes above items numbers:		
1109. Lender's coverage $	*	
1110. Owner's coverage $		*
1111. Escrow Fee to	*	*
1112. Restrictions to		
1113. Messenger to	*	*
1200. Government Recording and Transfer Charges		
1201. Recording fees: Deed $ Borrower ; Mortgage $ Borrower ; Releases $ Seller	*	*
1202. City/county tax/stamps: Deed $; Mortgage $		
1203. State tax/stamps: Deed $; Mortgage $		
1204. Tax service fee	*	
1205.		
1300. Additional Settlement Charges		
1301. Survey to ABC Survey Company	*	
1302. Pest inspection to		
1303.		
1304.		
1305.		
1400. Total Settlement Charges (enter on lines 103, Section J and 502, Section K)	*	*

Appendix A

Additional Texas Real Estate Commission Promulgated Forms

21-4	One to Four Family Residential Contract (Resale) FHA Insured or VA Guaranteed Financing	12/99
23-4	New Home Contract (Incomplete Construction)	06/00
24-4	New Home Contract (Completed Construction)	06/00
25-3	Farm and Ranch Contract	12/99
30-2	Residential Condominium Contract (Resale) All Cash, Assumption, Third Party Conventional or Seller Financing	12/99
31-2	Residential Condominium Contract (Resale) FHA Insured or VA Guaranteed Financing	12/99
32-0	Condominium Resale Certificate	8/94
9-4	Unimproved Property Contract	12/99

11-08-99

PROMULGATED BY THE TEXAS REAL ESTATE COMMISSION (TREC)

ONE TO FOUR FAMILY RESIDENTIAL CONTRACT (RESALE)
FHA INSURED OR VA GUARANTEED FINANCING

Notice: Not For Use For Condominium Transactions

1. **PARTIES:** ______________________________ (Seller) agrees to sell and convey to ______________________________ (Buyer) and Buyer agrees to buy from Seller the Property described below.

2. **PROPERTY:** Lot ________, Block ________, ______________________________Addition, City of ______________________________, ______________________ County, Texas, known as ______________________________ (Address/Zip Code), or as described on attached exhibit, together with the following items, if any: curtains and rods, draperies and rods, valances, blinds, window shades, screens, shutters, awnings, wall-to-wall carpeting, mirrors fixed in place, ceiling fans, attic fans, mail boxes, television antennas and satellite dish system with controls and equipment, permanently installed heating and air conditioning units, window air conditioning units, built-in security and fire detection equipment, plumbing and lighting fixtures, including chandeliers, water softener, stove, built-in kitchen equipment, garage door openers with controls, built-in cleaning equipment, all swimming pool equipment and maintenance accessories, shrubbery, landscaping, permanently installed outdoor cooking equipment, built-in fireplace screens, artificial fireplace logs and all other property owned by Seller and attached to the above described real property except the following property which is not included:______________________________
______________________________.

All property sold by this contract is called the "Property." The Property ❑ is ❑ is not subject to mandatory membership in an owners' association. The TREC Addendum For Property Subject To Mandatory Membership In An Owners' Association ❑ is ❑ is not attached.

NOTICE TO BUYER: If the Property is subject to mandatory membership in an owners' association, Seller notifies Buyer under §5.012, Texas Property Code, that, as a purchaser of property in the residential community in which the Property is located, you are obligated to be a member of an owners' association. Restrictive covenants governing the use and occupancy of the Property and a dedicatory instrument governing the establishment, maintenance, and operation of this residential community have been or will be recorded in the Real Property Records of the county in which the Property is located. Copies of the restrictive covenants and dedicatory instrument may be obtained from the county clerk. You are obligated to pay assessments to the owners' association. The amount of the assessments is subject to change. Your failure to pay the assessments could result in a lien on and the foreclosure of the Property.

3. **SALES PRICE:**
   A. Cash portion of the Sales Price payable by Buyer at closing . . . . $______________
   B. Sum of all financing described below (excluding VA Funding Fee or FHA Mortgage Insurance Premium [MIP]) . . . . $______________
   C. Sales Price (Sum of A and B) . . . . $______________

4. **FINANCING:** Within ________ days after the effective date of this contract Buyer shall apply for and make every reasonable effort to obtain financing. Financing will be deemed to have been obtained when the lender has determined that Buyer has satisfied all of lender's financial requirements (those items relating to Buyer's net worth, income and creditworthiness). If financing (including any financed MIP or Funding Fee) is not obtained within ________ days after the effective date hereof, this contract will terminate and the earnest money will refunded to Buyer. The portion of the Sales Price not payable in cash will be paid as follows: (Check applicable boxes below)

   ❑ A. FHA INSURED FINANCING: This contract is subject to approval for Buyer of a Section ________ FHA insured loan of not less than $______________ (excluding any financed MIP), amortizable monthly for not less than ______ years, with interest not to exceed ________% per annum for the first ________year(s) of the loan.

   As required by HUD-FHA, if FHA valuation is unknown, *"It is expressly agreed that, notwithstanding any other provisions of this contract, the purchaser* (Buyer) *shall not be obligated to complete the purchase of the Property described herein or to incur any penalty by forfeiture of earnest money*

FHA or VA Residential Contract Concerning____Page Two 11-08-99
(Address of Property)

deposits or otherwise unless the purchaser (Buyer) *has been given in accordance with HUD/FHA or VA requirements a written statement issued by the Federal Housing Commissioner, Department of Veterans Affairs, or a Direct Endorsement Lender setting forth the appraised value of the Property of not less than $_______________. The purchaser* (Buyer) *shall have the privilege and option of proceeding with consummation of the contract without regard to the amount of the appraised valuation. The appraised valuation is arrived at to determine the maximum mortgage the Department of Housing and Urban Development will insure. HUD does not warrant the value or the condition of the Property. The purchaser* (Buyer) *should satisfy himself/herself that the price and the condition of the Property are acceptable."* If the FHA appraised value of the Property (excluding closing costs and MIP) is less than the Sales Price (3C above), Seller may reduce the Sales Price to an amount equal to the FHA appraised value (excluding closing costs and MIP) and the parties to the sale shall close the sale at such lower Sales Price with appropriate adjustments to 3A and 3B above.

❑ B. VA GUARANTEED FINANCING: This contract is subject to approval for Buyer of a VA guaranteed loan of not less than $___________(excluding any financed Funding Fee), amortizable monthly for not less than_____ years, with interest not to exceed _____ % per annum for the first _____ year(s) of the loan.

VA NOTICE TO BUYER: *"It is expressly agreed that, notwithstanding any other provisions of this contract, the Buyer shall not incur any penalty by forfeiture of earnest money or otherwise or be obligated to complete the purchase of the Property described herein, if the contract purchase price or cost exceeds the reasonable value of the Property established by the Department of Veterans Affairs. The Buyer shall, however, have the privilege and option of proceeding with the consummation of this contract without regard to the amount of the reasonable value established by the Department of Veterans Affairs."*

If Buyer elects to complete the purchase at an amount in excess of the reasonable value established by VA, Buyer shall pay such excess amount in cash from a source which Buyer agrees to disclose to the VA and which Buyer represents will not be from borrowed funds except as approved by VA. If VA reasonable value of the Property is less than the Sales Price (3C above), Seller may reduce the Sales Price to an amount equal to the VA reasonable value and the parties to the sale shall close at such lower Sales Price with appropriate adjustments to 3A and 3B above.

❑ C. TEXAS VETERANS' HOUSING ASSISTANCE PROGRAM LOAN: This contract is subject to approval for Buyer of a Texas Veterans' Housing Assistance Program Loan of $_____________ for a period of at least ______ years at the interest rate established by the Texas Veterans' Land Board at the time of closing.

5. **EARNEST MONEY:** Buyer shall deposit $______________ as earnest money with _______________ ______________________________ at ______________________________ (Address), as escrow agent, upon execution of this contract by both parties. Additional earnest money of $ __________________ must be deposited by Buyer with escrow agent on or before __________________ , _____. If Buyer fails to deposit the earnest money as required by this contract, Buyer will be in default.

6. **TITLE POLICY AND SURVEY:**

❑ A. TITLE POLICY: Seller shall furnish to Buyer at ❑ Seller's ❑ Buyer's expense an owner policy of title insurance (the Title Policy) issued by ______________________________ (the Title Company) in the amount of the Sales Price, dated at or after closing, insuring Buyer against loss under the provisions of the Title Policy, subject to the promulgated exclusions (including existing building and zoning ordinances) and the following exceptions:

(1) Restrictive covenants common to the platted subdivision in which the Property is located.
(2) The standard printed exception for standby fees, taxes and assessments.
(3) Liens created as part of the financing described in Paragraph 4.
(4 Utility easements created by the dedication deed or plat of the subdivision in which the Property is located.
(5) Reservations or exceptions otherwise permitted by this contract or as may be approved by Buyer in writing.
(6) The standard printed exception as to discrepancies, conflicts, shortages in area or boundary lines, encroachments or protrusions, or overlapping improvements.
(7) The standard printed exception as to marital rights.
(8) The standard printed exception as to waters, tidelands, beaches, streams, and related matters.

FHA or VA Residential Contract Concerning____ Page Three 11-08-99
(Address of Property)

Within 20 days after the Title Company receives a copy of this contract, Seller shall furnish to Buyer a commitment for title insurance (the Commitment) and, at Buyer's expense, legible copies of restrictive covenants and documents evidencing exceptions in the Commitment other than the standard printed exceptions. Seller authorizes the Title Company to mail or hand deliver the Commitment and related documents to Buyer at Buyer's address shown below. If the Commitment is not delivered to Buyer within the specified time, the time for delivery will be automatically extended up to 15 days. Buyer will have 7 days after the receipt of the Commitment to object in writing to matters disclosed in the Commitment.

❑ B. SURVEY: Within ________ days after Buyer's receipt of a survey furnished to a third-party lender at ❑ Seller's ❑ Buyer's expense, Buyer may object in writing to any matter shown on the survey which constitutes a defect or encumbrance to title.
The survey must be made by a Registered Professional Land Surveyor acceptable to the Title Company and any lender. Utility easements created by the dedication deed and plat of the subdivision in which the Property is located will not be a basis for objection.

Buyer may object to existing building and zoning ordinances, items 6A(1) through (8) above and matters shown on the survey if Buyer determines that any such ordinance, items or matters prohibits the following use or activity:____
____.

Buyer's failure to object under Paragraph 6A or 6B within the time allowed will constitute a waiver of Buyer's right to object; except that the requirements in Schedule C of the Commitment will not be deemed to have been waived. Seller shall cure the timely objections of Buyer or any third party lender within 15 days from the date Seller receives the objections and the Closing Date will be extended as necessary. If objections are not cured by the extended Closing Date, this contract will terminate and the earnest money will be refunded to Buyer unless Buyer elects to waive the objections.

NOTICE TO SELLER AND BUYER:

(1) Broker advises Buyer to have an abstract of title covering the Property examined by an attorney of Buyer's selection, or Buyer should be furnished with or obtain a Title Policy. If a Title Policy is furnished, the Commitment should be promptly reviewed by an attorney of Buyer's choice due to the time limitations on Buyer's right to object.

(2) If the Property is situated in a utility or other statutorily created district providing water, sewer, drainage, or flood control facilities and services, Chapter 49 of the Texas Water Code requires Seller to deliver and Buyer to sign the statutory notice relating to the tax rate, bonded indebtedness, or standby fee of the district prior to final execution of this contract.

(3) If the Property abuts the tidally influenced waters of the state, Section 33.135, Texas Natural Resources Code, requires a notice regarding coastal area property to be included in the contract. An addendum either promulgated by TREC or required by the parties should be used.

(4) Buyer is advised that the presence of wetlands, toxic substances including asbestos and wastes or other environmental hazards or the presence of a threatened or endangered species or its habitat may affect Buyer's intended use of the Property. If Buyer is concerned about these matters, an addendum either promulgated by TREC or required by the parties should be used.

(5) If the Property is located outside the limits of a municipality, Seller notifies Buyer under §5.011, Texas Property Code, that the Property may now or later be included in the extraterritorial jurisdiction of a municipality and may now or later be subject to annexation by the municipality. Each municipality maintains a map that depicts its boundaries and extraterritorial jurisdiction. To determine if the Property is located within a municipality's extraterritorial jurisdiction or is likely to be located within a municipality's extraterritorial jurisdiction, contact all municipalities located in the general proximity of the Property for further information.

(6) Unless expressly prohibited in writing by the parties, Seller may continue to show the Property for sale and to receive, negotiate and accept back-up offers.

(7) Any residential service contract that is purchased in connection with this transaction should be reviewed for the scope of coverage, exclusions and limitations. **The purchase of a residential service contract is optional. Similar coverage may be purchased from various companies authorized to do business in Texas.**

7. **PROPERTY CONDITION:**
A. INSPECTIONS, ACCESS AND UTILITIES: Buyer may have the Property inspected by an inspector

Initialed for identification by Buyer________ and Seller________ 01A TREC NO. 21-4

selected by Buyer, licensed by TREC or otherwise permitted by law to make such inspections. Seller shall permit access to the Property at reasonable times for inspection, repairs and treatment and for reinspection after repairs and treatment have been completed. Seller shall pay for turning on utilities for inspection and reinspection.

B. SELLER'S DISCLOSURE NOTICE PURSUANT TO SECTION 5.008, TEXAS PROPERTY CODE (Notice) (check one box only):

❑ (1) Buyer has received the Notice.

❑ (2) Buyer has not received the Notice. Within _______ days after the effective date of this contract, Seller shall deliver the Notice to Buyer. If Buyer does not receive the Notice, Buyer may terminate this contract at any time prior to the closing. If Seller delivers the Notice, Buyer may terminate this contract for any reason within 7 days after Buyer receives the Notice or prior to the closing, whichever first occurs.

❑ (3) The Texas Property Code does not require this Seller to furnish the Notice.

C. SELLER'S DISCLOSURE OF LEAD-BASED PAINT AND LEAD-BASED PAINT HAZARDS is required by Federal law for a residential dwelling constructed prior to 1978. An addendum providing such disclosure ❑ is ❑ is not attached.

D. ACCEPTANCE OF PROPERTY CONDITION: (check one box only):

❑ (1) In addition to any earnest money deposited with escrow agent, Buyer has paid Seller $_____________ (the "Option Fee") for the unrestricted right to terminate this contract by giving notice of termination to Seller within _______ days after the effective date of this contract. If Buyer gives notice of termination within the time specified, the Option Fee will not be refunded, however, any earnest money will be refunded to Buyer. If Buyer does not give notice of termination within the time specified, Buyer will be deemed to have accepted the Property in its current condition and the Option Fee ❑ will ❑ will not be credited to the Sales Price at closing.

❑ (2) Buyer accepts the Property in its present condition; provided Seller, at Seller's expense, shall complete the following repairs and treatment: ____
____
____.

E. LENDER REQUIRED REPAIRS AND TREATMENTS (REPAIRS): Unless otherwise agreed in writing, neither party is obligated to pay for lender required repairs or treatments for wood destroying insects. If the cost of lender required repairs exceeds 5% of the Sales Price, Buyer may terminate this contract.

F. COMPLETION OF REPAIRS AND TREATMENT. Unless otherwise agreed by the parties in writing, Seller shall complete all agreed repairs and treatment prior to the Closing Date. Repairs and treatments must be performed by persons who regularly provide such repairs or treatments. At Buyer's election, any transferable warranties received by Seller with respect to the repairs will be transferred to Buyer at Buyer's expense. If Seller fails to complete any agreed repairs and treatment prior to the Closing Date, Buyer may do so and the Closing Date will be extended up to 15 days, if necessary, to complete repairs and treatment.

8. **BROKERS' FEES:** All obligations of the parties for payment of brokers' fees are contained in separate written agreements.

9. **CLOSING:** The closing of the sale will be on or before ____________________________, ______, or within 7 days after objections to matters disclosed in the Commitment or by the survey have been cured, whichever date is later (the Closing Date). *If financing has been obtained pursuant to Paragraph 4,* the Closing Date will be extended up to 15 days if necessary to comply with lender's closing requirements, for example: appraisal, survey, insurance policies, lender-required repairs, closing documents). If either party fails to close this sale by the Closing Date, the non-defaulting party will be entitled to exercise the remedies contained in Paragraph 15. At closing Seller shall furnish tax statements or certificates showing no delinquent taxes and a general warranty deed conveying good and indefeasible title showing no additional exceptions to those permitted in Paragraph 6.

10. **POSSESSION:** Seller shall deliver possession of the Property to Buyer on __________________ in its present or required repaired condition, ordinary wear and tear excepted. Any possession by Buyer prior to closing or by Seller after closing which is not authorized by a temporary lease form promulgated by TREC or required by the parties will establish a tenancy at sufferance relationship between the parties. *Consult your insurance agent prior to change of ownership or possession as insurance*

coverage may be limited or terminated. The absence of a written lease or appropriate insurance coverage may expose the parties to economic loss.

11. **SPECIAL PROVISIONS:** (Insert only factual statements and business details applicable to this sale. TREC rules prohibit licensees from adding factual statements or business details for which a contract addendum, lease or other form has been promulgated by TREC for mandatory use.)

12. **SETTLEMENT AND OTHER EXPENSES:**
   A. The following expenses must be paid at or prior to closing:
      (1) Appraisal fees will be paid by ______________________________.
      (2) The total of the loan discount fees (including any Texas Veterans' Housing Assistance Program Participation Fee) may not exceed _________% of the loan of which Seller shall pay ___________and Buyer shall pay the remainder. The total of any buydown fees may not exceed ______________ which will be paid by ______________________________.
      (3) Seller's Expenses: Releases of existing liens, including prepayment penalties and recording fees; tax statements or certificates; preparation of deed; one-half of escrow fee; expenses FHA or VA prohibits Buyer to pay; and other expenses stipulated to be paid by Seller under other provisions of this contract.
      (4) Buyer's Expenses: Interest on the note(s) from date of disbursement to one month prior to dates of first monthly payments, expenses stipulated to be paid by Buyer under other provisions of this contract; any customary Texas Veterans' Housing Assistance Program Loan costs for Buyer; and premiums for mortgagee title policy and endorsements required by lender.
         (a) FHA Buyer: All prepaid items required by applicable HUD-FHA or other regulations, including required premiums for flood and hazard insurance, reserve deposits for other insurance, ad valorem taxes and special governmental assessments; expenses incident to any loan, including preparation of loan documents, recording fees, copies of restrictions and easements, amortization schedule, loan origination fee, loan commitment fee, credit reports, photos, loan related inspection fee; and one-half of escrow fee.
         (b) VA Buyer: All prepaid items,including required premiums for flood and hazard insurance, reserve deposits for other insurance, ad valorem taxes and special governmental assessments; expenses incident to any loan, including credit reports, recording fees, loan origination fee, loan related inspection fees.
   B. The VA Loan Funding Fee or FHA Mortgage Insurance Premium (MIP) not to exceed ___________ will be paid by Buyer, and ❑ paid in cash at closing ❑ added to the amount of the loan or ❑ paid as follows: ____
   ____.
   C. If any expense exceeds an amount expressly stated in this contract for such expense to be paid by a party, that party may terminate this contract unless the other party agrees to pay such excess. In no event will Buyer pay charges and fees expressly prohibited by FHA, VA or other governmental loan program regulations.

13. **PRORATIONS**: Taxes for the current year, maintenance fees, assessments, dues and rents will be prorated through the Closing Date. If taxes for the current year vary from the amount prorated at closing, the parties will adjust the prorations when tax statements for the current year are available. If taxes are not paid at or prior to closing, Buyer will be obligated to pay taxes for the current year.

14. **CASUALTY LOSS:** If any part of the Property is damaged or destroyed by fire or other casualty loss after the effective date of the contract, Seller shall restore the Property to its previous condition as soon as

reasonably possible, but in any event by the Closing Date. If Seller fails to do so due to factors beyond Seller's control, Buyer may either (a) terminate this contract and the earnest money will be refunded to Buyer (b) extend the time for performance up to 15 days and the Closing Date will be extended as necessary or (c) accept the Property in its damaged condition and accept an assignment of insurance proceeds. Seller's obligations under this paragraph are independent of any obligations of Seller under Paragraph 7.

15. **DEFAULT:** If Buyer fails to comply with this contract, Buyer will be in default, and Seller may either (a) enforce specific performance, seek such other relief as may be provided by law, or both, or (b) terminate this contract and receive the earnest money as liquidated damages, thereby releasing both parties from this contract. If, due to factors beyond Seller's control, Seller fails within the time allowed to make any non-casualty repairs or deliver the Commitment, Buyer may either (a) extend the time for performance up to 15 days and the Closing Date will be extended as necessary or (b) terminate this contract as the sole remedy and receive the earnest money. If Seller fails to comply with this contract for any other reason, Seller will be in default and Buyer may either (a) enforce specific performance, seek such other relief as may be provided by law, or both, or (b) terminate this contract and receive the earnest money, thereby releasing both parties from this contract.

16. **DISPUTE RESOLUTION:** It is the policy of the State of Texas to encourage the peaceable resolution of disputes through alternative dispute resolution procedures. The parties are encouraged to use an addendum approved by TREC to submit to mediation disputes which cannot be resolved in good faith through informal discussion.

17. **ATTORNEY'S FEES:** The prevailing party in any legal proceeding brought under or with respect to the transaction described in this contract is entitled to recover from the non-prevailing party all costs of such proceeding and reasonable attorney's fees.

18. **ESCROW:** The earnest money is deposited with escrow agent with the understanding that escrow agent is not (a) a party to this contract and does not have any liability for the performance or nonperformance of any party to this contract, (b) liable for interest on the earnest money and (c) liable for any loss of earnest money caused by the failure of any financial institution in which the earnest money has been deposited unless the financial institution is acting as escrow agent. At closing, the earnest money must be applied first to any cash down payment, then to Buyer's closing costs and any excess refunded to Buyer. If both parties make written demand for the earnest money, escrow agent may require payment of unpaid expenses incurred on behalf of the parties and a written release of liability of escrow agent from all parties. If one party makes written demand for the earnest money, escrow agent shall give notice of the demand by providing to the other party a copy of the demand. If escrow agent does not receive written objection to the demand from the other party within 30 days after notice to the other party, escrow agent may disburse the earnest money to the party making demand reduced by the amount of unpaid expenses incurred on behalf of the party receiving the earnest money and escrow agent may pay the same to the creditors. If escrow agent complies with the provisions of this paragraph, each party hereby releases escrow agent from all adverse claims related to the disbursal of the earnest money. Escrow agent's notice to the other party will be effective when deposited in the U. S. Mail, postage prepaid, certified mail, return receipt requested, addressed to the other party at such party's address shown below. Notice of objection to the demand will be deemed effective upon receipt by escrow agent.

19. **REPRESENTATIONS:** Seller represents that as of the Closing Date there will be no liens, assessments, or security interests against the Property which will not be satisfied out of the sales proceeds. If any representation in this contract is untrue on the Closing Date, this contract may be terminated by Buyer and the earnest money will be refunded to Buyer. All representations contained in this contract will survive closing.

20. **FEDERAL TAX REQUIREMENT:** If Seller is a "foreign person", as defined by applicable law, or if Seller fails to deliver an affidavit that Seller is not a "foreign person", then Buyer shall withhold from the sales proceeds an amount sufficient to comply with applicable tax law and deliver the same to the Internal Revenue Service together with appropriate tax forms. IRS regulations require filing written reports if cash in excess of specified amounts is received in the transaction.

21. **AGREEMENT OF PARTIES:** This contract contains the entire agreement of the parties and cannot be changed except by their written agreement. Addenda which are a part of this contract are (list): ______
____.

FHA or VA Residential Contract Concerning________________________________Page Seven 11-08-99
(Address of Property)

22. **CONSULT YOUR ATTORNEY:** Real estate licensees cannot give legal advice. This contract is intended to be legally binding. READ IT CAREFULLY. If you do not understand the effect of this contract, consult your attorney BEFORE signing.

Buyer's Attorney is: ______________________ Seller's Attorney is: ______________________

23. **NOTICES:** All notices from one party to the other must be in writing and are effective when mailed to, hand-delivered at, or transmitted by facsimile machine as follows:

To Buyer at:

____

____

____

Telephone:(___)______________________

Facsimile:(___)______________________

To Seller at:

____

____

____

Telephone:(___)______________________

Facsimile: (___)______________________

EXECUTED the __________day of ______________________, ______ (THE EFFECTIVE DATE). (BROKER: FILL IN THE DATE OF FINAL ACCEPTANCE.)

______________________ Buyer

______________________ Buyer

______________________ Seller

______________________ Seller

The form of this contract has been approved by the Texas Real Estate Commission. Such approval relates to this contract form only. TREC forms are intended for use only by trained real estate licensees. No representation is made as to the legal validity or adequacy of any provision in any specific transaction. It is not suitable for complex transactions. Extensive riders or additions are not to be used. Texas Real Estate Commission, P.O. Box 12188, Austin, TX 78711-2188, 1-800-250-8732 or (512) 459-6544 (http://www.trec.state.tx.us) TREC NO. 21-4. This form replaces TREC NO. 21-3.

BROKER INFORMATION AND RATIFICATION OF FEE

Listing Broker has agreed to pay Other Broker ______________________ of the total sales price when Listing Broker's fee is received. Escrow Agent is authorized and directed to pay Other Broker from Listing Broker's fee at closing.

____
Other Broker License No.

represents
- ☐ Seller as Listing Broker's subagent
- ☐ Buyer only as Buyer's agent

____
Associate Telephone

____
Broker Address

____
Telephone Facsimile

____
Listing Broker License No.

represents
- ☐ Seller and Buyer as an intermediary
- ☐ Seller only as Seller's agent

____
Listing Associate Telephone

____
Selling Associate Telephone

____
Broker Address

____
Telephone Facsimile

RECEIPT

Receipt of ☐ Contract and ☐ $_________ Earnest Money in the form of______________________is acknowledged.

Escrow Agent: ______________________ Date: ______________________, ______

By:______________________

____
Address

Telephone: (___)______________________

____
City State Zip Code

Facsimile: (___)______________________

06-22-00

PROMULGATED BY THE TEXAS REAL ESTATE COMMISSION (TREC)

NEW HOME CONTRACT

(Incomplete Construction)

NOTICE: Not For Use For Condominium Transactions or Closings Prior to Completion of Construction

1. **PARTIES:** ______________________________ (Seller) agrees to sell and convey to ______________________________(Buyer) and Buyer agrees to buy from Seller the property described below.

2. **PROPERTY:** Lot ____________, Block _____, ______________________________ Addition, City of ______________________________, ______________________________ County, Texas, known as ______________________________ (Address/Zip Code), or as described on attached exhibit, together with the improvements, fixtures and all other property located thereon. All property sold by this contract is called the "Property."
Mandatory Membership in an Owners' Association: (Check one box only):
❑ The Property is not subject to mandatory membership in an owners' association.
❑ The TREC Addendum For Property Subject To Mandatory Membership In An Owners' Association is attached.
NOTICE TO BUYER: If the Property is subject to mandatory membership in an owners' association, Seller notifies Buyer under §5.012, Texas Property Code, that, as a purchaser of property in the residential community in which the Property is located, you are obligated to be a member of an owners' association. Restrictive covenants governing the use and occupancy of the Property and a dedicatory instrument governing the establishment, maintenance, and operation of this residential community have been or will be recorded in the Real Property Records of the county in which the Property is located. Copies of the restrictive covenants and dedicatory instrument may be obtained from the county clerk. You are obligated to pay assessments to the owners' association. The amount of the assessments is subject to change. Your failure to pay the assessments could result in a lien on and the foreclosure of the Property.

3. **SALES PRICE:**
   A. Cash portion of Sales Price payable by Buyer at closing . . . . $____________
   B. Sum of all financing described below (excluding any FHA Mortgage Insurance Premium [MIP], VA funding fee, or Private Mortgage Insurance Premium [PMI]) . . . $____________
   C. Sales Price (Sum of A and B) . . . . $____________

4. **FINANCING:** Within _____ days after the effective date of this contract Buyer shall apply for all third party financing and make every reasonable effort to obtain financing. Financing will be deemed to have been obtained when the lender determines that Buyer has satisfied all of lender's financial requirements (those items relating to Buyer's net worth, income and creditworthiness). If financing (including any financed PMI premium) is not obtained within____ days after the effective date hereof, this contract will terminate and the earnest money will be refunded to Buyer. Each note to be executed hereunder must be secured by vendor's and deed of trust liens.
The portion of Sales Price not payable in cash will be paid as follows: (Check applicable boxes below)
❑ A. THIRD PARTY FINANCING:
   ❑ (1) This contract is subject to approval for Buyer of a third party first mortgage loan having a loan-to-value ratio not to exceed ________ % as established by such third party (excluding any financed PMI premium), due in full in _____ year(s), with interest not to exceed _____ % per annum for the first _____ year(s) of the loan. The loan will be ❑ with ❑ without PMI.
   ❑ (2) This contract is subject to approval for Buyer of a third party second mortgage loan having a loan-to-value ratio not to exceed _____ % as established by such third party (excluding any financed PMI premium), due in full in ______ year(s), with interest not to exceed ______ % per annum for the first _____ year(s) of the loan. The loan will be ❑ with ❑ without PMI.
❑ B. FHA INSURED FINANCING: This contract is subject to approval for Buyer of a Section ______ FHA insured loan of not less than $_______________ (excluding any financed MIP), amortizable monthly for not less than _____ years, with interest not to exceed ______ % per annum for the first _______ year(s) of the Loan.
As required by HUD-FHA, if FHA valuation is unknown, "It is expressly agreed that, notwithstanding any other provisions of this contract, the purchaser (Buyer) *shall not be obligated to complete the purchase of the property described herein or to incur any penalty by forfeiture of earnest money*

deposits or otherwise unless the purchaser (Buyer) *has been given in accordance with HUD/FHA or VA requirements a written statement issued by the Federal Housing Commissioner, Department of Veterans Affairs, or a Direct Endorsement Lender setting forth the appraised value of the Property of not less than $ ____________. The purchaser (Buyer) shall have the privilege and option of proceeding with consummation of the contract without regard to the amount of the appraised valuation. The appraised valuation is arrived at to determine the maximum mortgage the Department of Housing and Urban Development will insure. HUD does not warrant the value or the condition of the property. The purchaser* (Buyer) *should satisfy himself/herself that the price and the condition of the Property are acceptable."* If the FHA appraised value of the Property (excluding closing costs and MIP) is less than the Sales Price (3C above), Seller may reduce the Sales Price to an amount equal to the FHA appraised value (excluding closing costs and MIP) and the parties to the sale shall close the sale at such lower Sales Price with appropriate adjustments to 3A and 3B above.

❑ C. VA GUARANTEED FINANCING: This contract is subject to approval for Buyer of a VA guaranteed loan of not less than $___________ (excluding any financed Funding Fee), amortizable monthly for not less than _____ years, with interest not to exceed _____ % per annum for the first ______ year(s) of the Loan.

VA NOTICE TO BUYER: *"It is expressly agreed that, notwithstanding any other provisions of this contract, the Buyer shall not incur any penalty by forfeiture of earnest money or otherwise or be obligated to complete the purchase of the Property described herein, if the contract purchase price or cost exceeds the reasonable value of the Property established by the Department of Veterans Affairs. The Buyer shall, however, have the privilege and option of proceeding with the consummation of this contract without regard to the amount of the reasonable value established by the Department of Veterans Affairs."*

If Buyer elects to complete the purchase at an amount in excess of the reasonable value established by VA, Buyer shall pay such excess amount in cash from a source which Buyer agrees to disclose to the VA and which Buyer represents will not be from borrowed funds except as approved by VA. If VA reasonable value of the Property is less than the Sales Price (3C above), Seller may reduce the Sales Price to an amount equal to the VA reasonable value and the parties to the sale shall close at such lower Sales Price with appropriate adjustments to 3A and 3B above.

❑ D. TEXAS VETERANS' HOUSING ASSISTANCE PROGRAM LOAN: This contract is subject to approval for Buyer of a Texas Veterans' Housing Assistance Program Loan (the Program Loan) of $____________ for a period of at least ______ years at the interest rate established by the Texas Veterans' Land Board at the time of closing.

❑ E. SELLER FINANCING: A promissory note from Buyer to Seller of $______________, bearing ______% interest per annum, secured by vendor's and deed of trust liens, in accordance with the terms and conditions set forth in the attached TREC Seller Financing Addendum. If an owner policy of title insurance is furnished, Buyer shall furnish Seller with a mortgagee policy of title insurance.

❑ F. CREDIT APPROVAL ON SELLER FINANCING: Within _______ days after the effective date of this contract, Buyer shall deliver to Seller ❑ credit report ❑ verification of employment, including salary ❑ verification of funds on deposit in financial institutions ❑ current financial statement to establish Buyer's creditworthiness for seller financing and ❑ ______________________________
____.
If Buyer's documentation is not delivered within the specified time, Seller may terminate this contract by notice to Buyer within 7 days after expiration of the time for delivery, and the earnest money will be paid to Seller. If this contract is not so terminated, Seller will be deemed to have accepted Buyer's credit. If the documentation is timely delivered, and Seller determines in Seller's sole discretion that Buyer's credit is unacceptable, Seller may terminate this contract by notice to Buyer within 7 days after expiration of the time for delivery and the earnest money will be refunded to Buyer. If Seller does not so terminate this contract, Seller will be deemed to have accepted Buyer's credit. Buyer hereby authorizes any credit reporting agency to furnish to Seller at Buyer's sole expense copies of Buyer's credit reports.

5. **EARNEST MONEY:** Buyer shall deposit $_____________ as earnest money with ________________ __________________ at ____ (Address), as escrow agent, upon execution of this contract by both parties. Additional earnest money of $______________must be

New Home (Incomplete Construction) Contract Concerning______________________________ Page Three 06-22-00
(Address of Property)

deposited by Buyer with escrow agent on or before ____________________, _______. If Buyer fails to deposit the earnest money as required by this contract, Buyer will be in default.

6. TITLE POLICY AND SURVEY:

❑ A. TITLE POLICY: Seller shall furnish to Buyer at ❑ Seller's ❑ Buyer's expense an owner policy of title insurance (the Title Policy) issued by ____________________________________(the Title Company) in the amount of the Sales Price, dated at or after closing, insuring Buyer against loss under the provisions of the Title Policy, subject to the promulgated exclusions (including existing building and zoning ordinances) and the following exceptions:

(1) Restrictive covenants common to the platted subdivision in which the Property is located.
(2) The standard printed exception for standby fees, taxes and assessments.
(3) Liens created as part of the financing described in Paragraph 4.
(4) Utility easements created by the dedication deed or plat of the subdivision in which the Property is located.
(5) Reservations or exceptions otherwise permitted by this contract or as may be approved by Buyer in writing.
(6) The standard printed exception as to discrepancies, conflicts, shortages in area or boundary lines, encroachments or protrusions, or overlapping improvements.
(7) The standard printed exception as to marital rights.
(8) The standard printed exception as to waters, tidelands, beaches, streams, and related matters.

Within 20 days after the Title Company receives a copy of this contract, Seller shall furnish to Buyer a commitment for title insurance (the Commitment) and, at Buyer's expense, legible copies of restrictive covenants and documents evidencing exceptions in the Commitment other than the standard printed exceptions. Seller authorizes the Title Company to mail or hand deliver the Commitment and related documents to Buyer at Buyer's address shown below. If the Commitment is not delivered to Buyer within the specified time, the time for delivery will be automatically extended up to 15 days. Buyer will have 7 days after the receipt of the Commitment to object in writing to matters disclosed in the Commitment.

❑ B. SURVEY: (Check one box only)

❑ (1) Within ______ days after Buyer's receipt of a survey furnished to a third-party lender at ❑ Seller's ❑ Buyer's expense, Buyer may object in writing to any matter shown on the survey which constitutes a defect or encumbrance to title.

❑ (2) Within _____ days after the effective date of this contract, Buyer may object in writing to any matter which constitutes a defect or encumbrance to title shown on a survey obtained by Buyer at Buyer's expense.

The survey must be made by a Registered Professional Land Surveyor acceptable to the Title Company and any lender. Utility easements created by the dedication deed and plat of the subdivision in which the Property is located will not be a basis for objection.

Buyer may object to existing building and zoning ordinances, items 6A(1) through (8) above and matters shown on the survey if Buyer determines that any such ordinance, items or matter prohibits the following use or activity: ____
____.

Buyer's failure to object under Paragraph 6A or 6B within the time allowed will constitute a waiver of Buyer's right to object; except that the requirements in Schedule C of the Commitment will not be deemed to have been waived. Seller will cure the timely objections of Buyer or any third party lender within 15 days after Seller receives the objections and the Closing Date will be extended as necessary. If objections are not cured by the extended Closing Date, this contract will terminate and the earnest money will be refunded to Buyer unless Buyer elects to waive the objections.

NOTICE TO SELLER AND BUYER:

(1) Broker advises Buyer to have an abstract of title covering the Property examined by an attorney of Buyer's selection, or Buyer should be furnished with or obtain a Title Policy. If a Title Policy is furnished, the Commitment should be promptly reviewed by an attorney of Buyer's choice due to the time limitations on Buyer's right to object.

(2) If the Property is situated in a utility or other statutorily created district providing water, sewer, drainage, or flood control facilities and services, Chapter 49 of the Texas Water Code requires Seller to deliver and Buyer to sign the statutory notice relating to the tax rate, bonded indebtedness, or standby fee of the district prior to final execution of this contract.

(3) If the Property abuts the tidally influenced waters of the state, Section 33.135, Texas Natural Resources Code, requires a notice regarding coastal area property to be included in the contract. An addendum either promulgated by TREC or required by the parties should be used.

(4) Buyer is advised that the presence of wetlands, toxic substances, including asbestos and wastes or other environmental hazards or the presence of a threatened or endangered species or its habitat may affect Buyer's intended use of the Property. If Buyer is concerned about these matters, an addendum either promulgated by TREC or required by the parties should be used.

(5) If the Property is located outside the limits of a municipality, Seller notifies Buyer under §5.011, Texas Property Code, that the Property may now or later be included in the extraterritorial jurisdiction of a municipality and may now or later be subject to annexation by the municipality. Each municipality maintains a map that depicts its boundaries and extraterritorial jurisdiction. To determine if the Property is located within a municipality's extraterritorial jurisdiction or is likely to be located within a municipality's extraterritorial jurisdiction, contact all municipalities located in the general proximity of the Property for further information.

(6) Unless expressly prohibited in writing by the parties, Seller may continue to show the Property for sale and to receive, negotiate and accept back-up offers.

(7) Any residential service contract that is purchased in connection with this transaction should be reviewed for the scope of coverage, exclusions and limitations. **The purchase of a residential service contract is optional. Similar coverage may be purchased from various companies authorized to do business in Texas.**

7. PROPERTY CONDITION:

A. INSPECTIONS AND ACCESS: Buyer, at Buyer's expense, may have the Property inspected by inspectors selected by Buyer, licensed by TREC or otherwise permitted by law to make such inspections. Seller shall permit access to the Property at reasonable times for inspections and for reinspections.

B. CONSTRUCTION DOCUMENTS: Seller shall complete all improvements with due diligence in accordance with the plans and specifications, finish-out schedules or allowances initialed by the parties, incorporated by reference and identified as ____, together with the following changes or alternates:____ and any other change orders agreed to in writing (called the Construction Documents).

C. COST ADJUSTMENTS: Increase in costs resulting from change orders or items selected by Buyer which exceed the allowances specified in the Construction Documents will be paid by Buyer as follows:
____
____
____.
A decrease in costs resulting from change orders and unused allowances will reduce Sales Price and loan amount accordingly.

D. BUYER'S SELECTIONS: If the Construction Documents permit selections by Buyer, Buyer's selections will conform to Seller's normal standards as set out in the Construction Documents or will not, in Seller's judgment, adversely affect the marketability of the Property. Buyer will make required selections within ______ days after receipt of written notice from Seller.

E. COMPLETION: Seller must commence construction no later than ____ days after loan approval. The improvements will be substantially completed in accordance with the Construction Documents and ready for occupancy not later than ___________________,______. The improvements will be deemed to be substantially completed in accordance with the Construction Documents upon the final inspection and approval by all applicable governmental authorities and any lender. Construction delays caused by Buyer's acts or omissions, acts of God, fire or other casualty, strikes, boycotts or nonavailability of materials for which no substitute of comparable quality and price is available will be added to the time allowed for substantial completion of the construction. However, in no event may the time for substantial completion extend beyond the Closing Date. Seller may substitute materials, equipment and appliances of comparable quality for those specified in the Construction Documents.

F. WARRANTIES: Except as expressly set forth in Paragraph 11, or as attached to this contract, Seller makes no other express warranties. Seller agrees to assign to Buyer at closing all assignable manufacturer warranties.

G. INSULATION: As required by Federal Trade Commission Regulations, the information relating to the

insulation installed or to be installed in the home being purchased under this contract is as follows:
(1) Exterior walls of improved living areas: insulated with __________________________ insulation to a thickness of ________ inches which yields an R-Value of ________.
(2) Walls in other areas of the home: insulated with _______________________________ insulation to a thickness of _______ inches which yields an R-Value of _______.
(3) Ceilings in improved living areas: insulated with _______________________________ insulation to a thickness of ________ inches which yields an R-Value of ________.
(4) Floors of improved living areas not applied to a slab foundation: insulated with ____________ ______________ insulation to a thickness of ________ inches which yields an R-Value of ________.
(5) Other insulated areas: insulated with ___________________________ insulation to a thickness of _______ inches which yields an R-Value of ________.
All stated R-Values are based on information provided by the manufacturer of the insulation.

8. **BROKERS' FEES:** All obligations of the parties for payment of brokers' fees are contained in separate written agreements.

9. **CLOSING:** The closing of the sale will be on or before ____________________________,______, or within 7 days after objections to matters disclosed in the Commitment or by the survey have been cured, whichever date is later (the Closing Date). *If financing has been obtained pursuant to Paragraph 4,* the Closing Date will be extended up to 15 days if necessary to comply with lender's closing requirements (for example, appraisal, survey, insurance policies, lender-required repairs, closing documents). If either party fails to close this sale by the Closing Date, the non-defaulting party will be entitled to exercise the remedies contained in Paragraph 15. At closing Seller shall furnish tax statements or certificates showing no delinquent taxes, and a general warranty deed conveying good and indefeasible title showing no additional exceptions to those permitted in Paragraph 6.

10. **POSSESSION:** Seller shall deliver possession of the Property to Buyer on ________________________. Any possession by Buyer prior to closing or by Seller after closing which is not authorized by a temporary lease form promulgated by TREC or required by the parties will establish a tenancy at sufferance relationship between the parties. *Consult your insurance agent prior to change of ownership or possession as insurance coverage may be limited or terminated. The absence of a written lease or appropriate insurance coverage may expose the parties to economic loss.*

11. **SPECIAL PROVISIONS:** (Insert only factual statements and business details applicable to this sale. TREC rules prohibit licensees from adding factual statements or business details for which a contract addendum, lease or other form has been promulgated by TREC for mandatory use.)

12. **SETTLEMENT AND OTHER EXPENSES:**
A. The following expenses must be paid at or prior to closing:
(1) Loan appraisal fees will be paid by ____.
(2) The total of the loan discount and buydown fees (including any Texas Veterans' Housing Assistance Program Participation Fee) may not exceed _______% of the loan of which Seller shall pay ____________________ and Buyer shall pay the remainder. The total of any buydown fees may not exceed __________________ which will be paid by _________________.
(3) Seller's Expenses:
(a) All Sales: Lender, FHA or VA completion requirements, releases of existing liens, including prepayment penalties and recording fees; tax statements or certificates; preparation of deed; one-half of escrow fee; those expenses Buyer is prohibited by FHA or VA from paying; and other expenses stipulated to be paid by Seller under other provisions of this contract.
(b) VA Loan Sales: Those expenses stated in 3(a) above and other expenses VA regulation prohibits Buyer from paying.

(4) Buyer's Expenses:

(a) All Sales: Expenses incident to any loan, including application, origination, and commitment fees; interest on the notes from date of disbursement to one month prior to date of first monthly payments; recording fees; endorsements required by lender; copies of easements and restrictions; mortgagee title policy; loan-related inspection fees; credit reports; all prepaid items, including required premiums for flood and hazard insurance, reserve deposits for insurance, ad valorem taxes and special governmental assessments; tax deletion; EPA endorsement; final compliance inspection; other expenses stipulated to be paid by Buyer under other provisions of this contract.

(b) Conventional Loan Sales: Expenses noted above and other loan-related expenses, including PMI premiums, photos, amortization schedules, one-half of escrow fee, preparation of loan documents, courier fee, repair inspections, underwriting fee and wire transfer.

(c) FHA Loan Sales: Expenses noted above and other loan-related expenses, including photos, amortization schedules, one-half of escrow fee, preparation of loan documents, courier fee and repair inspections.

B. The VA Loan Funding Fee or FHA Mortgage Insurance Premium (MIP) not to exceed ___________will be paid by Buyer, and ❑ paid in cash at closing ❑ added to the amount of the loan or ❑ paid as follows: ____

____.

C. If any expense exceeds an amount stated in this contract for such expense to be paid by a party, that party may terminate this contract unless the other party agrees to pay such excess. In no event will Buyer pay charges and fees expressly prohibited by FHA, VA or other governmental loan program regulations.

13. PRORATIONS AND ROLLBACK TAXES:

A. PRORATIONS: Taxes for the current year, maintenance fees, assessments, dues and rents will be prorated through the Closing Date. If taxes for the current year vary from the amount prorated at closing, the parties shall adjust the prorations when tax statements for the current year are available. If taxes are not paid at or prior to closing, Buyer will be obligated to pay taxes for the current year.

B. ROLLBACK TAXES: If Seller's change in use of the Property prior to closing or denial of a special use valuation on the Property results in additional taxes, penalties or interest (Assessments) for periods prior to closing, the Assessments will be the obligation of Seller. Obligations imposed by this paragraph will survive closing.

14. CASUALTY LOSS: If any part of the Property is damaged or destroyed by fire or other casualty after the effective date of this contract, Seller shall restore the Property to its previous condition as soon as reasonably possible, but in any event by the Closing Date. If Seller fails to do so due to factors beyond Seller's control, Buyer may either (a) terminate this contract and the earnest money will be refunded to Buyer (b) extend the time for performance up to 15 days and the Closing Date will be extended as necessary or (c) accept the Property in its damaged condition and accept an assignment of insurance proceeds. Seller's obligations under this paragraph are independent of any obligations of Seller under Paragraph 7.

15. DEFAULT: If Buyer fails to comply with this contract, Buyer will be in default, and Seller may either (a) enforce specific performance, seek such other relief as may be provided by law, or both, or (b) terminate this contract and receive the earnest money as liquidated damages, thereby releasing both parties from this contract. If, due to factors beyond Seller's control, Seller fails within the time allowed to make any non-casualty repairs or deliver the Commitment, Buyer may either (a) extend the time for performance up to 15 days and the Closing Date will be extended as necessary or (b) terminate this contract as the sole remedy and receive the earnest money. If Seller fails to comply with this contract for any other reason, Seller will be in default and Buyer may either (a) enforce specific performance, seek such other relief as may be provided by law, or both, or (b) terminate this contract and receive the earnest money, thereby releasing both parties from this contract.

16. DISPUTE RESOLUTION: It is the policy of the State of Texas to encourage the peaceable resolution of disputes through alternative dispute resolution procedures. The parties are encouraged to use an addendum approved by TREC to submit to mediation disputes which cannot be resolved in good faith through informal discussion.

New Home (Incomplete Construction) Contract Concerning______________________________ Page Seven 06-22-00
(Address of Property)

17. **ATTORNEY'S FEES:** The prevailing party in any legal proceeding brought under or with respect to the transaction described in this contract is entitled to recover from the non-prevailing party all costs of such proceeding and reasonable attorney's fees.

18. **ESCROW:** The earnest money is deposited with escrow agent with the understanding that escrow agent is not (a) a party to this contract and does not have any liability for the performance or nonperformance of any party to this contract, (b) liable for interest on the earnest money and (c) liable for any loss of earnest money caused by the failure of any financial institution in which the earnest money has been deposited unless the financial institution is acting as escrow agent. At closing, the earnest money must be applied first to any cash down payment, then to Buyer's closing costs and any excess refunded to Buyer. If both parties make written demand for the earnest money, escrow agent may require payment of unpaid expenses incurred on behalf of the parties and a written release of liability of escrow agent from all parties. If one party makes written demand for the earnest money, escrow agent shall give notice of the demand by providing to the other party a copy of the demand. If escrow agent does not receive written objection to the demand from the other party within 30 days after notice to the other party, escrow agent may disburse the earnest money to the party making demand reduced by the amount of unpaid expenses incurred on behalf of the party receiving the earnest money and escrow agent may pay the same to the creditors. If escrow agent complies with the provisions of this paragraph, each party hereby releases escrow agent from all adverse claims related to the disbursal of the earnest money. Escrow agent's notice to the other party will be effective when deposited in the U. S. Mail, postage prepaid, certified mail, return receipt requested, addressed to the other party at such party's address shown below. Notice of objection to the demand will be deemed effective upon receipt by escrow agent.

19. **REPRESENTATIONS:** Seller represents that as of the Closing Date there will be no liens, assessments, or security interests against the Property which will not be satisfied out of the sales proceeds. If any representation in this contract is untrue on the Closing Date, this contract may be terminated by Buyer and the earnest money will be refunded to Buyer. All representations contained in this contract will survive closing.

20. **FEDERAL TAX REQUIREMENT:** If Seller is a "foreign person", as defined by applicable law, or if Seller fails to deliver an affidavit that Seller is not a "foreign person", then Buyer shall withhold from the sales proceeds an amount sufficient to comply with applicable tax law and deliver the same to the Internal Revenue Service together with appropriate tax forms. IRS regulations require filing written reports if cash in excess of specified amounts is received in the transaction.

21. **AGREEMENT OF PARTIES:** This contract contains the entire agreement of the parties and cannot be changed except by their written agreement. Addenda which are a part of this contract are (list):
____
____.

22. **CONSULT YOUR ATTORNEY:** Real estate licensees cannot give legal advice. This contract is intended to be legally binding. READ IT CAREFULLY. If you do not understand the effect of this contract, consult your attorney BEFORE signing.

Buyer's Attorney is:______________________________ Seller's Attorney is:______________________________

23. **NOTICES:** All notices from one party to the other must be in writing and are effective when mailed to, hand-delivered at, or transmitted by facsimile machine as follows:

To Buyer at:

____
____
____

Telephone: (___) ______________________

Facsimile: (___)______________________

To Seller at:

____
____
____

Telephone: (___) ______________________

Facsimile:(___) ______________________

New Home (Incomplete Construction) Contract Concerning________________________________ Page Eight 06-22-00
(Address of Property)

EXECUTED the _____ day of ____________________, ______ (THE EFFECTIVE DATE). (BROKER: FILL IN THE DATE OF FINAL ACCEPTANCE.)

This contract is subject to Chapter 27, Texas Property Code. The provisions of that chapter may affect your right to recover damages arising from the performance of this contract. If you have a complaint concerning a construction defect arising from the performance of this contract and that defect has not been corrected through normal warranty service, you must provide notice regarding the defect to the contractor by certified mail, return receipt requested, not later than the 60th day before the date you file suit to recover damages in a court of law. The notice must refer to Chapter 27, Texas Property Code, and must describe the construction defect. If requested by the contractor, you must provide the contractor an opportunity to inspect and cure the defect as provided by Section 27.004, Texas Property Code.

____
Buyer

____
Buyer

____
Seller

____
Seller

The form of this contract has been approved by the Texas Real Estate Commission. Such approval relates to this contract form only. TREC forms are intended for use only by trained real estate licensees. No representation is made as to the legal validity or adequacy of any provision in any specific transaction. It is not suitable for complex transactions. Extensive riders or additions are not to be used. Texas Real Estate Commission, P.O. Box 12188, Austin, TX 78711-2188, 1-800-250-8732 or (512) 459-6544 (http://www.trec.state.tx.us) TREC NO. 23-4. This form replaces TREC NO. 23-3.

BROKER INFORMATION AND RATIFICATION OF FEE

Listing Broker has agreed to pay Other Broker ____________________ of the total sales price when Listing Broker's fee is received. Escrow Agent is authorized and directed to pay Other Broker from Listing Broker's fee at closing.

____
Other Broker License No.
represents ❑ Seller as Listing Broker's subagent
❑ Buyer only as Buyer's agent

____
Associate Telephone

____
Broker Address

____
Telephone Facsimile

____
Listing Broker License No.
represents ❑ Seller and Buyer as an intermediary
❑ Seller only as Seller's agent

____
Listing Associate Telephone

____
Selling Associate Telephone

____
Broker Address

____
Telephone Facsimile

RECEIPT

Receipt of ❑ Contract and ❑ $__________ Earnest Money in the form of______________is acknowledged.

Escrow Agent: ______________________ Date: ______________, ______

By:______________________

______________________ Telephone: (___)______________
Address

______________________ Facsimile: (___)______________
City State Zip Code

PROMULGATED BY THE TEXAS REAL ESTATE COMMISSION (TREC) 06-22-00

EQUAL HOUSING OPPORTUNITY

NEW HOME CONTRACT

(Completed Construction)

NOTICE: Not For Use For Condominium Transactions

1. **PARTIES:** ______________________________ (Seller) agrees to sell and convey to ______________________________(Buyer) and Buyer agrees to buy from Seller the property described below.

2. **PROPERTY:** Lot _____, Block ____, ______________________________Addition, City of ____________________, ____________________ County, Texas, known as ______________________________ (Address/Zip Code), or as described on attached exhibit, together with the improvements, fixtures and all other property located thereon. All property sold by this contract is called the "Property."
Mandatory Membership in an Owners' Association: (Check one box only):
❑ The Property is not subject to mandatory membership in an owners' association.
❑ The TREC Addendum For Property Subject To Mandatory Membership In An Owners' Association is attached.
NOTICE TO BUYER: If the Property is subject to mandatory membership in an owners' association, Seller notifies Buyer under §5.012, Texas Property Code, that, as a purchaser of property in the residential community in which the Property is located, you are obligated to be a member of an owners' association. Restrictive covenants governing the use and occupancy of the Property and a dedicatory instrument governing the establishment, maintenance, and operation of this residential community have been or will be recorded in the Real Property Records of the county in which the Property is located. Copies of the restrictive covenants and dedicatory instrument may be obtained from the county clerk. You are obligated to pay assessments to the owners' association. The amount of the assessments is subject to change. Your failure to pay the assessments could result in a lien on and the foreclosure of the Property.

3. **SALES PRICE:**
A. Cash portion of Sales Price payable by Buyer at closing . . . . $__________
B. Sum of all financing described below (excluding any FHA Mortgage Insurance Premium [MIP], VA funding fee, or Private Mortgage Insurance Premium [PMI]) . . . $__________
C. Sales Price (Sum of A and B) . . . . $__________

4. **FINANCING:** Within _____ days after the effective date of this contract Buyer shall apply for all third party financing and make every reasonable effort to obtain financing. Financing will be deemed to have been obtained when the lender determines that Buyer has satisfied all of lender's financial requirements (those items relating to Buyer's net worth, income and creditworthiness). If financing (including any financed PMI premium) is not obtained within _____ days after the effective date hereof, this contract will terminate and the earnest money will be refunded to Buyer. Each note to be executed hereunder must be secured by vendor's and deed of trust liens.
The portion of Sales Price not payable in cash will be paid as follows: (Check applicable boxes below)
❑ A. THIRD PARTY FINANCING:
❑ (1) This contract is subject to approval for Buyer of a third party first mortgage loan having a loan-to-value ratio not to exceed ______ % as established by such third party (excluding any financed PMI premium), due in full in _____ year(s), with interest not to exceed ____% per annum for the first _____year(s) of the loan. The loan will be ❑ with ❑ without PMI.
❑ (2) This contract is subject to approval for Buyer of a third party second mortgage loan having a loan-to-value ratio not to exceed_____ % as established by such third party (excluding any financed PMI premium), due in full in ____ year(s), with interest not to exceed _____ % per annum for the first _____ year(s) of the loan. The loan will be ❑ with ❑ without PMI.
❑ B. FHA INSURED FINANCING: This contract is subject to approval for Buyer of a Section ______ FHA insured loan of not less than $__________________ (excluding any financed MIP), amortizable monthly for not less than _____ years, with interest not to exceed _______% per annum for the first _______ year(s) of the Loan.
As required by HUD-FHA, if FHA valuation is unknown, *"It is expressly agreed that, notwithstanding any other provisions of this contract, the purchaser* (Buyer) *shall not be obligated to complete the purchase of the property described herein or to incur any penalty by forfeiture of earnest money deposits or otherwise unless the purchaser* (Buyer) *has been given in accordance with HUD/FHA*

or VA requirements a written statement issued by the Federal Housing Commissioner, Department of Veterans Affairs, or a Direct Endorsement Lender setting forth the appraised value of the Property of not less than $_______________. The purchaser (Buyer) *shall have the privilege and option of proceeding with consummation of the contract without regard to the amount of the appraised valuation. The appraised valuation is arrived at to determine the maximum mortgage the Department of Housing and Urban Development will insure. HUD does not warrant the value or the condition of the Property. The purchaser* (Buyer) *should satisfy himself/herself that the price and the condition of the Property are acceptable."* If the FHA appraised value of the Property (excluding closing costs and MIP) is less than the Sales Price (3C above), Seller may reduce the Sales Price to an amount equal to the FHA appraised value (excluding closing costs and MIP) and the parties to the sale shall close the sale at such lower Sales Price with appropriate adjustments to 3A and 3B above.

❑ C. VA GUARANTEED FINANCING: This contract is subject to approval for Buyer of a VA guaranteed loan of not less than $____________(excluding any financed Funding Fee), amortizable monthly for not less than _____ years, with interest not to exceed ______ % per annum for the first _____ year(s) of the Loan.

VA NOTICE TO BUYER: *"It is expressly agreed that, notwithstanding any other provisions of this contract, the Buyer shall not incur any penalty by forfeiture of earnest money or otherwise or be obligated to complete the purchase of the Property described herein, if the contract purchase price or cost exceeds the reasonable value of the Property established by the Department of Veterans Affairs. The Buyer shall, however, have the privilege and option of proceeding with the consummation of this contract without regard to the amount of the reasonable value established by the Department of Veterans Affairs."*

If Buyer elects to complete the purchase at an amount in excess of the reasonable value established by VA, Buyer shall pay such excess amount in cash from a source which Buyer agrees to disclose to the VA and which Buyer represents will not be from borrowed funds except as approved by VA. If VA reasonable value of the Property is less than the Sales Price (3C above), Seller may reduce the Sales Price to an amount equal to the VA reasonable value and the parties to the sale shall close at such lower Sales Price with appropriate adjustments to 3A and 3B above.

❑ D. TEXAS VETERANS' HOUSING ASSISTANCE PROGRAM LOAN: This contract is subject to approval for Buyer of a Texas Veterans' Housing Assistance Program Loan (the Program Loan) of $______________ for a period of at least ______________ years at the interest rate established by the Texas Veterans' Land Board at the time of closing.

❑ E. SELLER FINANCING: A promissory note from Buyer to Seller of $_________________, bearing ________% interest per annum, secured by vendor's and deed of trust liens, in accordance with the terms and conditions set forth in the attached TREC Seller Financing Addendum. If an owner policy of title insurance is furnished, Buyer shall furnish Seller with a mortgagee policy of title insurance.

❑ F. CREDIT APPROVAL ON SELLER FINANCING: Within ______ days after the effective date of this contract, Buyer shall deliver to Seller ❑ credit report ❑ verification of employment, including salary ❑ verification of funds on deposit in financial institutions ❑ current financial statement to establish Buyer's creditworthiness for seller financing and ❑ __________________________
____.

If Buyer's documentation is not delivered within the specified time, Seller may terminate this contract by notice to Buyer within 7 days after expiration of the time for delivery, and the earnest money will be paid to Seller. If this contract is not so terminated, Seller will be deemed to have accepted Buyer's credit. If the documentation is timely delivered, and Seller determines in Seller's sole discretion that Buyer's credit is unacceptable, Seller may terminate this contract by notice to Buyer within 7 days after expiration of the time for delivery and the earnest money will be refunded to Buyer. If Seller does not so terminate this contract, Seller will be deemed to have accepted Buyer's credit. Buyer hereby authorizes any credit reporting agency to furnish to Seller at Buyer's sole expense copies of Buyer's credit reports.

5. **EARNEST MONEY:** Buyer shall deposit $_______________ as earnest money with _______________ _______________________________ at _______________________________(Address), as escrow agent, upon execution of this contract by both parties. Additional earnest money of $____________ must be deposited by Buyer with escrow agent on or before_____________________, _____. If Buyer fails to deposit the earnest money as required by this contract, Buyer will be in default.

6. TITLE POLICY AND SURVEY:

❑ A. TITLE POLICY: Seller shall furnish to Buyer at ❑ Seller's ❑ Buyer's expense an owner policy of title insurance (the Title Policy) issued by ______________________________ (the Title Company) in the amount of the Sales Price, dated at or after closing, insuring Buyer against loss under the provisions of the Title Policy, subject to the promulgated exclusions (including existing building and zoning ordinances) and the following exceptions:

(1) Restrictive covenants common to the platted subdivision in which the Property is located.
(2) The standard printed exception for standby fees, taxes and assessments.
(3) Liens created as part of the financing described in Paragraph 4.
(4) Utility easements created by the dedication deed or plat of the subdivision in which the Property is located.
(5) Reservations or exceptions otherwise permitted by this contract or as may be approved by Buyer in writing.
(6) The standard printed exception as to discrepancies, conflicts, shortages in area or boundary lines, encroachments or protrusions, or overlapping improvements.
(7) The standard printed exception as to marital rights.
(8) The standard printed exception as to waters, tidelands, beaches, streams, and related matters.

Within 20 days after the Title Company receives a copy of this contract, Seller shall furnish to Buyer a commitment for title insurance (the Commitment) and, at Buyer's expense, legible copies of restrictive covenants and documents evidencing exceptions in the Commitment other than the standard printed exceptions. Seller authorizes the Title Company to mail or hand deliver the Commitment and related documents to Buyer at Buyer's address shown below. If the Commitment is not delivered to Buyer within the specified time, the time for delivery will be automatically extended up to 15 days. Buyer will have 7 days after the receipt of the Commitment to object in writing to matters disclosed in the Commitment.

❑ B. SURVEY: (Check one box only)

❑ (1) Within ______ days after Buyer's receipt of a survey furnished to a third-party lender at ❑ Seller's ❑ Buyer's expense, Buyer may object in writing to any matter shown on the survey which constitutes a defect or encumbrance to title.

❑ (2) Within ____ days after the effective date of this contract, Buyer may object in writing to any matter which constitutes a defect or encumbrance to title shown on a survey obtained by Buyer at Buyer's expense.

The survey must be made by a Registered Professional Land Surveyor acceptable to the Title Company and any lender. Utility easements created by the dedication deed and plat of the subdivision in which the Property is located will not be a basis for objection.

Buyer may object to existing building and zoning ordinances, items 6A(1) through (8) above and matters shown on the survey if Buyer determines that any such ordinance, items or matter prohibits the following use or activity:______________________________
____
______________________________.

Buyer's failure to object under Paragraph 6A or 6B within the time allowed will constitute a waiver of Buyer's right to object; except that the requirements in Schedule C of the Commitment will not be deemed to have been waived. Seller shall cure the timely objections of Buyer or any third party lender within 15 days from the date Seller receives the objections and the Closing Date will be extended as necessary. If objections are not cured by the extended Closing Date, this contract will terminate and the earnest money will be refunded to Buyer unless Buyer elects to waive the objections.

NOTICE TO SELLER AND BUYER:

(1) Broker advises Buyer to have an abstract of title covering the Property examined by an attorney of Buyer's selection, or Buyer should be furnished with or obtain a Title Policy. If a Title Policy is furnished, the Commitment should be promptly reviewed by an attorney of Buyer's choice due to the time limitations on Buyer's right to object.

(2) If the Property is situated in a utility or other statutorily created district providing water, sewer, drainage, or flood control facilities and services, Chapter 49 of the Texas Water Code requires Seller to deliver and Buyer to sign the statutory notice relating to the tax rate, bonded indebtedness, or standby fee of the district prior to final execution of this contract.

(3) If the Property abuts the tidally influenced waters of the state, Section 33.135, Texas Natural Resources Code, requires a notice regarding coastal area property to be included in the contract. An addendum either promulgated by TREC or required by the parties should be used.

(4) Buyer is advised that the presence of wetlands, toxic substances including asbestos and wastes or other environmental hazards or the presence of a threatened or endangered species or its habitat may affect Buyer's intended use of the Property. If Buyer is concerned about these matters, an addendum either promulgated by TREC or required by the parties should be used.

(5) If the Property is located outside the limits of a municipality, Seller notifies Buyer under §5.011, Texas Property Code, that the Property may now or later be included in the extraterritorial jurisdiction of a municipality and may now or later be subject to annexation by the municipality. Each municipality maintains a map that depicts its boundaries and extraterritorial jurisdiction. To determine if the Property is located within a municipality's extraterritorial jurisdiction or is likely to be located within a municipality's extraterritorial jurisdiction, contact all municipalities located in the general proximity of the Property for further information.

(6) Unless expressly prohibited in writing by the parties, Seller may continue to show the Property for sale and to receive, negotiate and accept back-up offers.

(7) Any residential service contract that is purchased in connection with this transaction should be reviewed for the scope of coverage, exclusions and limitations. **The purchase of a residential service contract is optional. Similar coverage may be purchased from various companies authorized to do business in Texas.**

7. PROPERTY CONDITION:

A. INSPECTIONS, ACCESS AND UTILITIES: Buyer, at Buyer's expense, may have the Property inspected by inspectors selected by Buyer, licensed by TREC or otherwise permitted by law to make such inspections. Seller shall permit access to the Property at reasonable times for inspections, repairs and treatment and for reinspections after repairs and treatment have been completed. Seller shall pay for turning on utilities for inspections and reinspections.

B. ACCEPTANCE OF PROPERTY CONDITION: (check one box only):

❑ (1) In addition to any earnest money deposited with escrow agent, Buyer has paid Seller $____________ (the "Option Fee") for the unrestricted right to terminate this contract by giving notice of termination to Seller within _______ days after the effective date of this contract. If Buyer gives notice of termination within the time specified, the Option Fee will not be refunded, however, any earnest money will be refunded to Buyer. If Buyer does not give notice of termination within the time specified, Buyer will be deemed to have accepted the Property in its current condition and the Option Fee ❑ will ❑ will not be credited to the Sales Price at closing.

❑ (2) Buyer accepts the Property in its present condition; provided Seller, at Seller's expense, shall complete the following repairs and treatment: ______________________________________
____.

C. LENDER REQUIRED REPAIRS AND TREATMENTS (REPAIRS): Unless otherwise agreed in writing, neither party is obligated to pay for lender required repairs or treatments for wood destroying insects. If the cost of lender required repairs exceeds 5% of the Sales Price, Buyer may terminate this contract.

D. COMPLETION OF REPAIRS AND TREATMENT. Unless otherwise agreed in writing, Seller shall complete all agreed repairs and treatment prior to the Closing Date. Repairs and treatments must be performed by persons who regularly provide such repairs or treatments. At Buyer's election, any transferable warranties received by Seller with respect to the repairs will be transferred to Buyer at Buyer's expense. If Seller fails to complete any agreed repairs and treatment prior to the Closing Date, Buyer may do so and the Closing Date will be extended up to 15 days, if necessary, to complete repairs and treatment.

E. WARRANTIES: Except as expressly set forth in Paragraph 11, or as attached to this contract, Seller makes no other express warranties. Seller agrees to assign to Buyer at closing all assignable manufacturer warranties.

F. INSULATION: As required by Federal Trade Commission Regulations, the information relating to the insulation installed or to be installed in the home being purchased under this contract is as follows:

(1) Exterior walls of improved living areas: insulated with ________________________insulation to a thickness of _______ inches which yields an R-Value of _______.

(2) Walls in other areas of the home: insulated with ____________________________insulation to a thickness of ______ inches which yields an R-Value of ______.

New Home (Completed Construction) Contract Concerning____ Page Five 06-22-00
(Address of Property)

(3) Ceilings in improved living areas: insulated with ________________________ insulation to a thickness of ________ inches which yields an R-Value of ________.

(4) Floors of improved living areas not applied to a slab foundation: insulated with ________________________ insulation to a thickness of ________ inches which yields an R-Value of ________.

(5) Other insulated areas: insulated with ________________________ insulation to a thickness of ________ inches which yields an R-Value of ________.

All stated R-Values are based on information provided by the manufacturer of the insulation.

8. **BROKERS' FEES:** All obligations of the parties for payment of brokers' fees are contained in separate written agreements.

9. **CLOSING:** The closing of the sale will be on or before ________________________, ______, or within 7 days after objections to matters disclosed in the Commitment or by the survey have been cured, whichever date is later (the Closing Date). *If financing has been obtained pursuant to Paragraph 4,* the Closing Date will be extended up to 15 days if necessary to comply with lender's closing requirements (for example, appraisal, survey, insurance policies, lender-required repairs, closing documents).If either party fails to close this sale by the Closing Date, the non-defaulting party will be entitled to exercise the remedies contained in Paragraph 15. At closing Seller shall furnish tax statements or certificates showing no delinquent taxes and a general warranty deed conveying good and indefeasible title showing no additional exceptions to those permitted in Paragraph 6.

10. **POSSESSION:** Seller shall deliver possession of the Property to Buyer on ________________________ in its present or required repaired condition, ordinary wear and tear excepted. Any possession by Buyer prior to closing or by Seller after closing which is not authorized by a temporary lease form promulgated by TREC or required by the parties will establish a tenancy at sufferance relationship between the parties. *Consult your insurance agent prior to change of ownership or possession as insurance coverage may be limited or terminated. The absence of a written lease or appropriate insurance coverage may expose the parties to economic loss.*

11. **SPECIAL PROVISIONS:** (Insert only factual statements and business details applicable to this sale. TREC rules prohibit licensees from adding factual statements or business details for which a contract addendum, lease or other form has been promulgated by TREC for mandatory use.)

12. **SETTLEMENT AND OTHER EXPENSES:**

A. The following expenses must be paid at or prior to closing:

(1) Loan appraisal fees will be paid by ____.

(2) The total of the loan discount and buydown fees (including any Texas Veterans' Housing Assistance Program Participation Fee) may not exceed ______% of the loan of which Seller shall pay ____________________ and Buyer shall pay the remainder. The total of any buydown fees may not exceed ____________________ which will be paid by ______________________________.

(3) Seller's Expenses:

(a) All Sales: Lender, FHA or VA completion requirements, releases of existing liens, including prepayment penalties and recording fees; tax statements or certificates; preparation of deed; one-half of escrow fee; those expenses Buyer is prohibited by FHA or VA from paying; and other expenses stipulated to be paid by Seller under other provisions of this contract.

(b) VA Loan Sales: Those expenses stated in 3(a) above and other expenses VA regulation prohibits Buyer from paying.

(4) Buyer's Expenses:

(a) All Sales: Expenses incident to any loan, including application, origination, and commitment fees; interest on the notes from date of disbursement to one month prior to date of first monthly payments; recording fees; endorsements required by lender; copies of easements and restrictions; mortgagee title policy; loan-related inspection fees; credit reports; all prepaid items, including required premiums for flood and hazard insurance, reserve deposits for insurance, ad valorem taxes and special governmental assessments; tax deletion; EPA endorsement; final compliance inspection; other expenses stipulated to be paid by Buyer under other provisions of this contract.

(b) Conventional Loan Sales: Expenses noted above and other loan-related expenses, including PMI premiums, photos, amortization schedules, one-half of escrow fee, preparation of loan documents, courier fee, repair inspections, underwriting fee and wire transfer.

(c) FHA Loan Sales: Expenses noted above and other loan-related expenses, including photos, amortization schedules, one-half of escrow fee, preparation of loan documents, courier fee and repair inspections.

B. The VA Loan Funding Fee or FHA Mortgage Insurance Premium (MIP) not to exceed ___________ will be paid by Buyer, and ❑ paid in cash at closing ❑ added to the amount of the loan or ❑ paid as follows:
____
____.

C. If any expense exceeds an amount stated in this contract for such expense to be paid by a party, that party may terminate this contract unless the other party agrees to pay such excess. In no event will Buyer pay charges and fees expressly prohibited by FHA, VA or other governmental loan program regulations.

13. **PRORATIONS AND ROLLBACK TAXES**:

A. PRORATIONS: Taxes for the current year, maintenance fees, assessments, dues and rents will be prorated through the Closing Date. If taxes for the current year vary from the amount prorated at closing, the parties shall adjust the prorations when tax statements for the current year are available. If taxes are not paid at or prior to closing, Buyer will be obligated to pay taxes for the current year.

B. ROLLBACK TAXES: If Seller's change in use of the Property prior to closing or denial of a special use valuation on the Property results in additional taxes, penalties or interest (Assessments) for periods prior to closing, the Assessments will be the obligation of Seller. Obligations imposed by this paragraph will survive closing.

14. **CASUALTY LOSS:** If any part of the Property is damaged or destroyed by fire or other casualty after the effective date of this contract, Seller shall restore the Property to its previous condition as soon as reasonably possible, but in any event by the Closing Date. If Seller fails to do so due to factors beyond Seller's control, Buyer may either (a) terminate this contract and the earnest money will be refunded to Buyer (b) extend the time for performance up to 15 days and the Closing Date will be extended as necessary or (c) accept the Property in its damaged condition and accept an assignment of insurance proceeds. Seller's obligations under this paragraph are independent of any obligations of Seller under Paragraph 7.

15. **DEFAULT:** If Buyer fails to comply with this contract, Buyer will be in default, and Seller may either (a) enforce specific performance, seek such other relief as may be provided by law, or both, or (b) terminate this contract and receive the earnest money as liquidated damages, thereby releasing both parties from this contract. If, due to factors beyond Seller's control, Seller fails within the time allowed to make any non-casualty repairs or deliver the Commitment, Buyer may either (a) extend the time for performance up to 15 days and the Closing Date will be extended as necessary or (b) terminate this contract as the sole remedy and receive the earnest money. If Seller fails to comply with this contract for any other reason, Seller will be in default and Buyer may either (a) enforce specific performance, seek such other relief as may be provided by law, or both, or (b) terminate this contract and receive the earnest money, thereby releasing both parties from this contract.

16. **DISPUTE RESOLUTION:** It is the policy of the State of Texas to encourage the peaceable resolution of disputes through alternative dispute resolution procedures. The parties are encouraged to use an addendum approved by TREC to submit to mediation disputes which cannot be resolved in good faith through informal discussion.

17. **ATTORNEY'S FEES:** The prevailing party in any legal proceeding brought under or with respect to the transaction described in this contract is entitled to recover from the non-prevailing party all costs of such proceeding and reasonable attorney's fees.

New Home (Completed Construction) Contract Concerning______________________________ Page Seven 06-22-00
(Address of Property)

18. **ESCROW:** The earnest money is deposited with escrow agent with the understanding that escrow agent is not (a) a party to this contract and does not have any liability for the performance or nonperformance of any party to this contract, (b) liable for interest on the earnest money and (c) liable for any loss of earnest money caused by the failure of any financial institution in which the earnest money has been deposited unless the financial institution is acting as escrow agent. At closing, the earnest money must be applied first to any cash down payment, then to Buyer's closing costs and any excess refunded to Buyer. If both parties make written demand for the earnest money, escrow agent may require payment of unpaid expenses incurred on behalf of the parties and a written release of liability of escrow agent from all parties. If one party makes written demand for the earnest money, escrow agent shall give notice of the demand by providing to the other party a copy of the demand. If escrow agent does not receive written objection to the demand from the other party within 30 days after notice to the other party, escrow agent may disburse the earnest money to the party making demand reduced by the amount of unpaid expenses incurred on behalf of the party receiving the earnest money and escrow agent may pay the same to the creditors. If escrow agent complies with the provisions of this paragraph, each party hereby releases escrow agent from all adverse claims related to the disbursal of the earnest money. Escrow agent's notice to the other party will be effective when deposited in the U. S. Mail, postage prepaid, certified mail, return receipt requested, addressed to the other party at such party's address shown below. Notice of objection to the demand will be deemed effective upon receipt by escrow agent.

19. **REPRESENTATIONS:** Seller represents that as of the Closing Date there will be no liens, assessments, or security interests against the Property which will not be satisfied out of the sales proceeds. If any representation in this contract is untrue on the Closing Date, this contract may be terminated by Buyer and the earnest money will be refunded to Buyer. All representations contained in this contract will survive closing.

20. **FEDERAL TAX REQUIREMENT:** If Seller is a "foreign person", as defined by applicable law, or if Seller fails to deliver an affidavit that Seller is not a "foreign person", then Buyer shall withhold from the sales proceeds an amount sufficient to comply with applicable tax law and deliver the same to the Internal Revenue Service together with appropriate tax forms. IRS regulations require filing written reports if cash in excess of specified amounts is received in the transaction.

21. **AGREEMENT OF PARTIES:** This contract contains the entire agreement of the parties and cannot be changed except by their written agreement. Addenda which are a part of this contract are (list): ________

____

____.

22. **CONSULT YOUR ATTORNEY:** Real estate licensees cannot give legal advice. This contract is intended to be legally binding. READ IT CAREFULLY. If you do not understand the effect of this contract, consult your attorney BEFORE signing.

Buyer's Attorney is:______________________________

Seller's Attorney is:______________________________

23. **NOTICES:** All notices from one party to the other must be in writing and are effective when mailed to, hand-delivered at, or transmitted by facsimile machine as follows:

To Buyer at:

____

____

____

Telephone:(___) ______________________

Facsimile: (___)______________________

To Seller at:

____

____

____

Telephone: (___) ______________________

Facsimile: (___)______________________

New Home (Complete Construction) Contract Concerning______________________________ Page Eight 06-22-00
(Address of Property)

EXECUTED the _____day of ________________, _______ (THE EFFECTIVE DATE). (BROKER: FILL IN THE DATE OF FINAL ACCEPTANCE.)

This contract is subject to Chapter 27, Texas Property Code. The provisions of that chapter may affect your right to recover damages arising from the performance of this contract. If you have a complaint concerning a construction defect arising from the performance of this contract and that defect has not been corrected through normal warranty service, you must provide notice regarding the defect to the contractor by certified mail, return receipt requested, not later than the 60th day before the date you file suit to recover damages in a court of law. The notice must refer to Chapter 27, Texas Property Code, and must describe the construction defect. If requested by the contractor, you must provide the contractor an opportunity to inspect and cure the defect as provided by Section 27.004, Texas Property Code.

____
Buyer

____
Buyer

____
Seller

____
Seller

The form of this contract has been approved by the Texas Real Estate Commission. Such approval relates to this contract form only. TREC forms are intended for use only by trained real estate licensees. No representation is made as to the legal validity or adequacy of any provision in any specific transaction. It is not suitable for complex transactions. Extensive riders or additions are not to be used. Texas Real Estate Commission, P.O. Box 12188, Austin, TX 78711-2188, 1-800-250-8732 or (512) 459-6544 (http://www.trec.state.tx.us) TREC NO. 24-4. This form replaces TREC NO. 24-3.

BROKER INFORMATION AND RATIFICATION OF FEE

Listing Broker has agreed to pay Other Broker ________________ of the total sales price when Listing Broker's fee is received. Escrow Agent is authorized and directed to pay Other Broker from Listing Broker's fee at closing.

____
Other Broker License No.
represents ❑ Seller as Listing Broker's subagent
❑ Buyer only as Buyer's agent

____
Associate Telephone

____
Broker Address

____
Telephone Facsimile

____
Listing Broker License No.
represents ❑ Seller and Buyer as an intermediary
❑ Seller only as Seller's agent

____
Listing Associate Telephone

____
Selling Associate Telephone

____
Broker Address

____
Telephone Facsimile

RECEIPT

Receipt of ❑ Contract and ❑ $_________ Earnest Money in the form of____________ is acknowledged.

Escrow Agent: ______________________ Date: ________________, _____

By:______________________

______________________ Telephone: (____) ______________
Address

______________________ Facsimile: (____)______________
City State Zip Code

01A TREC NO. 24-4

11-08-99

PROMULGATED BY THE TEXAS REAL ESTATE COMMISSION (TREC)

EQUAL HOUSING OPPORTUNITY

FARM AND RANCH CONTRACT

1. **PARTIES:** ____________________ (Seller) agrees to sell and convey to ____________________(Buyer) and Buyer agrees to buy from Seller the property described below.

2. **PROPERTY:** The land situated in ____________________County, Texas, described as follows:

or as described on attached exhibit, together with all improvements thereon and all rights, privileges and appurtenances pertaining thereto, including but not limited to: water rights, claims and permits, easements, all rights and obligations of applicable government programs and cooperative or association memberships. Included with the sale are the following items, if any: windmills and tanks, domestic water systems, curtains and rods, draperies and rods, valances, blinds, window shades, screens, shutters, awnings, wall-to-wall carpeting, mirrors fixed in place, ceiling fans, attic fans, mail boxes, television antennas and satellite dish with controls and equipment, permanently installed heating and air conditioning units, window air conditioning units, built-in security and fire detection equipment, plumbing and lighting fixtures, including chandeliers, water softener, stove, built-in kitchen equipment, garage door openers with controls, built-in cleaning equipment, all swimming pool equipment and maintenance accessories, shrubbery, landscaping, permanently installed outdoor cooking equipment, built-in fireplace screens, artificial fireplace logs and all other property owned by Seller and attached to the above described real property.

The following crops and equipment are included:____________________
____________________.

The following property is not included:____________________
____________________.

All property sold by this contract is called the "Property." The Property will be conveyed subject to the following exceptions, reservations, conditions and restrictions (if none, insert "none"):

A. Minerals, Royalties, and Timber Interests:

(1) Presently outstanding in third parties:

(2) To be additionally retained by Seller:

B. Mineral Leases:

C. Surface Leases:

D. Easements:

E. Restrictions, Zoning Ordinances or other Exceptions:

3. SALES PRICE:

A. Cash portion of Sales Price payable by Buyer at closing .... $____________

B. (1) Sum of all financing described in Paragraph 4 .... $_________

(2) Less: face amount of any lender required stock .... <_________>

(3) Difference between B(1) and B(2) .... $____________

C. Sales Price [sum of A and B(3)] .... $____________

D. The Sales Price ☐ will ☐ will not be adjusted based on the survey required by Paragraph 6B, and the number of acres over or under ______ acres will be multiplied by $__________ per acre. The result thereof will be added to or subtracted from the Sales Price, and the cash amount set out in 3A will be adjusted accordingly; however, if the amount set out in 3A is to be adjusted by more than 10%, either party may terminate this contract and the earnest money will be refunded to Buyer.

4. FINANCING: Within _____ days after the effective date of this contract Buyer shall apply for all third party financing or noteholder's approval of any assumption and make every reasonable effort to obtain financing or assumption approval. Financing or assumption approval will be deemed to have been obtained when the lender determines that Buyer has satisfied all of lender's financial requirements (those items relating to Buyer's net worth, income and creditworthiness). If financing (including the face amount of any lender required stock) or assumption approval is not obtained within_____ days after the effective date hereof, this contract will terminate and the earnest money will be refunded to Buyer. Each note to be executed hereunder must be secured by vendor's and deed of trust liens.

The portion of Sales Price not payable in cash will be paid as follows: (Check applicable boxes below)

☐ A. THIRD PARTY FINANCING:

☐ (1) This contract is subject to approval for Buyer of a third party first lien note of $__________ (including the face amount of any lender required stock) payable at _______ intervals for not less than _____ years with the initial interest rate not to exceed _____ % per annum.

☐ (2) This contract is subject to approval for Buyer of a third party second lien note of $________________ (including the face amount of any lender required stock) payable at _________ intervals for not less than _____ years with the initial interest rate not to exceed _____ % per annum.

☐ B. SELLER FINANCING: A promissory note from Buyer to Seller of $__________________, bearing _____% interest per annum, secured by vendor's and deed of trust liens, in accordance with the terms and conditions set forth in the attached TREC Seller Financing Addendum. If an owner policy of title insurance is furnished, Buyer shall furnish Seller with a mortgagee policy of title insurance.

☐ C. ASSUMPTION:

☐ (1) Buyer shall assume the unpaid principal balance of a first lien promissory note payable to ______________________________ dated __________________, which unpaid balance at closing will be $____________ (including the face amount of any lender required stock). The total current monthly payment including principal, interest and any reserve deposits is $ __________. Buyer's initial payment will be the first payment due after closing.

☐ (2) Buyer shall assume the unpaid principal balance of a second lien promissory note payable to ______________________________dated __________________, which unpaid balance at closing will be $__________ (including the face amount of any lender required stock). The total current monthly payment including principal, interest and any reserve deposits is $ _____________. Buyer's initial payment will be the first payment due after closing.

If any assumed loan initially required the purchase of lender's stock, the sale of the Property will include such stock.

Buyer's assumption of an existing note includes all obligations imposed by the deed of trust securing the note. If the unpaid principal balance(s) of any assumed loan(s) as of the Closing Date varies from the loan balance(s) stated above, the ☐ cash payable at closing ☐ Sales Price will be adjusted by the amount of any variance; provided, if the total principal balance of all assumed loans varies in an amount greater than $500.00 at closing, either party may terminate this contract and the earnest money will be refunded to Buyer unless the other party elects to eliminate the excess in the variance by an appropriate adjustment at closing. If the noteholder on assumption requires (a) Buyer to pay an assumption fee in excess of $__________ in C(l) above or $__________ in C(2) above, and Seller declines to pay such excess or (b) an increase in the interest rate to more than _____% in C(l) above or ______% in C(2) above, or (c) any other modification of the loan documents, Buyer may terminate this contract and the earnest money will be refunded to Buyer. A vendor's lien and deed of trust to secure assumption will be required, which will automatically be released on execution and delivery of a release by noteholder. If Seller is released from liability on any assumed note, the vendor's lien and deed of trust to secure assumption will not be required.

NOTICE TO BUYER: The payments, interest rates or other terms of some loans may be adjusted by the lender at or after closing. If you are concerned about the possibility of future adjustments, do not sign the contract without examining the notes and deeds of trust.

NOTICE TO SELLER: Your liability to pay the note assumed by Buyer will continue unless you obtain a release of liability from the lender. If you are concerned about future liability, you should use the TREC Release of Liability Addendum.

❑ D. CREDIT APPROVAL ON ASSUMPTION OR SELLER FINANCING: Within _______ days after the effective date of this contract, Buyer shall deliver to Seller ❑ credit report ❑ verification of employment, including salary ❑ verification of funds on deposit in financial institutions ❑ current financial statement to establish Buyer's creditworthiness for assumption approval or seller financing and ❑ __________

____

____.

If Buyer's documentation is not delivered within the specified time, Seller may terminate this contract by notice to Buyer within 7 days after expiration of the time for delivery, and the earnest money will be paid to Seller. If this contract is not so terminated, Seller will be deemed to have accepted Buyer's credit. If the documentation is timely delivered, and Seller determines in Seller's sole discretion that Buyer's credit is unacceptable, Seller may terminate this contract by notice to Buyer within 7 days after expiration of the time for delivery and the earnest money will be refunded to Buyer. If Seller does not so terminate this contract, Seller will be deemed to have accepted Buyer's credit. Buyer hereby authorizes any credit reporting agency to furnish to Seller at Buyer's sole expense copies of Buyer's credit reports.

5. **EARNEST MONEY:** Buyer shall deposit $______________ as earnest money with ______________ ________________________________ at ________________________________ (Address), as escrow agent, upon execution of this contract by both parties. Additional earnest money of $___________ must be deposited by Buyer with escrow agent on or before ___________________, ______. If Buyer fails to deposit the earnest money as required by this contract, Buyer will be in default.

6. **TITLE POLICY AND SURVEY:**

❑ A. TITLE POLICY: Seller shall furnish to Buyer at ❑ Seller's ❑ Buyer's expense an owner policy of title insurance (the Title Policy) issued by ________________________________(the Title Company) in the amount of the Sales Price, dated at or after closing, insuring Buyer against loss under the provisions of the Title Policy, subject to the promulgated exclusions (including existing building and zoning ordinances) and the following exceptions:

(1) The standard printed exception for standby fees, taxes and assessments.
(2) Liens created as part of the financing described in Paragraph 4.
(3) Those matters specifically described in Paragraph 2.
(4) The standard printed exception as to discrepancies, conflicts, shortages in area or boundary lines, encroachments or protrusions, or overlapping improvements.
(5) The standard printed exception as to marital rights.
(6) The standard printed exception as to waters, tidelands, beaches, streams, and related matters.

Within 20 days after the Title Company receives a copy of this contract, Seller shall furnish to Buyer a commitment for title insurance (the Commitment) and, at Buyer's expense, legible copies of restrictive covenants and documents evidencing exceptions in the Commitment other than the standard printed exceptions. Seller authorizes the Title Company to mail or hand deliver the Commitment and related documents to Buyer at Buyer's address shown below. If the Commitment is not delivered to Buyer within the specified time, the time for delivery will be automatically extended up to 15 days.

❑ B. SURVEY: (Check one box only)

❑ (1) Within _____ days after the effective date of this contract, Buyer shall obtain a survey at Buyer's expense.

❑ (2) Within _____ days after the effective date of this contract, Seller shall cause a survey to be delivered to Buyer at Seller's expense.

❑ (3) Within _____ days after the effective date of this contract, Seller will deliver to Buyer the existing survey plat of the Property dated ___________________________, _____, which ❑ will ❑ will not be recertified to a date subsequent to the effective date of this contract at the expense of ❑ Buyer ❑ Seller.

The survey must be made by a Registered Professional Land Surveyor acceptable to the Title Company and any lender.

Buyer will have 7 days after the receipt of the latter of the Commitment or survey to object in writing to matters disclosed in the Commitment or survey except for those matters specifically described in Paragraph 2. Buyer's failure to object under Paragraph 6 within the time allowed will constitute a waiver of Buyer's right to object; except that the requirements in Schedule C of the Commitment will not be deemed to have been waived. Seller shall cure the timely objections of Buyer or any third party lender within 20 days after Seller receives the objections and the Closing Date will be extended as necessary. If objections are not cured by the extended Closing Date, this contract will terminate and the earnest money will be refunded to Buyer unless Buyer elects to waive the objections.

❑ C. ABSTRACT OF TITLE: TREC Addendum for Abstract of Title, or an addendum required by the parties, is attached.

NOTICE TO SELLER AND BUYER:

(1) Broker advises Buyer to have an abstract of title covering the Property examined by an attorney of Buyer's selection, or Buyer should be furnished with or obtain a Title Policy. If a Title Policy is furnished, the Commitment should be promptly reviewed by an attorney of Buyer's choice due to the time limitations on Buyer's right to object.

(2) If the Property is situated in a utility or other statutorily created district providing water, sewer, drainage, or flood control facilities and services, Chapter 49 of the Texas Water Code requires Seller to deliver and the Buyer to sign the statutory notice relating to the tax rate, bonded indebtedness, or standby fee of the district prior to final execution of this contract.

(3) Eligibility for government farm program benefits may depend upon compliance with a soil conservation plan for the Property. Buyer is advised to determine whether the property is subject to and in compliance with a plan before signing this contract.

(4) Buyer is advised that the presence of wetlands, toxic substances, including asbestos and wastes or other environmental hazards or the presence of a threatened or endangered species or its habitat may affect Buyer's intended use of the Property. If Buyer is concerned about these matters, an addendum either promulgated by TREC or required by the parties should be used.

(5) If the Property is located outside the limits of a municipality, Seller notifies Buyer under §5.011, Texas Property Code, that the Property may now or later be included in the extraterritorial jurisdiction of a municipality and may now or later be subject to annexation by the municipality. Each municipality maintains a map that depicts its boundaries and extraterritorial jurisdiction. To determine if the Property is located within a municipality's extraterritorial jurisdiction or is likely to be located within a municipality's extraterritorial jurisdiction, contact all municipalities located in the general proximity of the Property for further information.

(6) If the Property abuts the tidally influenced submerged lands of the state, Section 33.135, Texas Natural Resources Code, requires a notice regarding coastal area property to be included in the contract. An addendum either promulgated by TREC or required by the parties should be used.

(7) Unless expressly prohibited in writing by the parties, Seller may continue to show the Property for sale and to receive, negotiate and accept back-up offers.

(8) Any residential service contract that is purchased in connection with this transaction should be reviewed for the scope of coverage, exclusions and limitations. **The purchase of a residential service contract is optional. Similar coverage may be purchased from various companies authorized to do business in Texas**.

7. **PROPERTY CONDITION:**

A. INSPECTIONS, ACCESS AND UTILITIES: Buyer may have the Property inspected by an inspector selected by Buyer, licenced by TREC or otherwise permitted by law to make such inspections. Seller shall permit access to the Property at reasonable times for inspection, repairs and treatment and for reinspection after repairs and treatment have been completed. Seller shall pay for turning on utilities for inspection and reinspection.

B. SELLER'S DISCLOSURE NOTICE PURSUANT TO SECTION 5.008, TEXAS PROPERTY CODE (Notice) (check one box only):

❑ (1) Buyer has received the Notice.

❑ (2) Buyer has not received the Notice. Within _____ days after the effective date of this contract, Seller shall deliver the Notice to Buyer. If Buyer does not receive the Notice, Buyer may terminate this contract at any time prior to the closing. If Seller delivers the Notice, Buyer may terminate this contract for any reason within 7 days after Buyer receives the Notice or prior to the closing, whichever first occurs.

❑ (3) The Texas Property Code does not require this Seller to furnish the Notice.

C. SELLER'S DISCLOSURE OF LEAD-BASED PAINT AND LEAD-BASED PAINT HAZARDS is required by Federal law for a residential dwelling constructed prior to 1978. An addendum providing such disclosure ❑ is ❑ is not attached.

D. ACCEPTANCE OF PROPERTY CONDITION: (check one box only):

❑ (1) In addition to any earnest money deposited with escrow agent, Buyer has paid Seller $_____________ (the "Option Fee") for the (i) right to inspect the Property at Buyer's cost, (ii) right to conduct feasibility studies as Buyer deems necessary and (iii) unrestricted right to terminate this contract by giving notice of termination to Seller within ________ days after the effective date of this contract. If Buyer gives notice of termination within the time specified, the Option Fee will not be refunded, however, any earnest money will be refunded to Buyer. If Buyer does not give notice of termination within the time specified, Buyer will be deemed to have accepted the Property in its current condition and the Option Fee ❑ will ❑ will not be credited to the Sales Price at closing.

❑ (2) Buyer accepts the Property in its present condition; provided Seller, at Seller's expense, shall complete the following repairs and treatment: ____________________________________

____

____.

E. LENDER REQUIRED REPAIRS AND TREATMENTS (REPAIRS): Unless otherwise agreed in writing, neither party is obligated to pay for lender required repairs or treatments for wood destroying insects. If the cost of lender required repairs exceeds 5% of the Sales Price, Buyer may terminate this contract.

F. COMPLETION OF REPAIRS AND TREATMENT. Unless otherwise agreed by the parties in writing, Seller shall complete all agreed repairs and treatment prior to the Closing Date. Repairs and treatments must be performed by persons who regularly provide such repairs or treatments. At Buyer's election, any transferable warranties received by Seller with respect to the repairs will be transferred to Buyer at Buyer's expense. If Seller fails to complete any agreed repairs and treatment prior to the Closing Date, Buyer may do so and the Closing Date will be extended up to 15 days, if necessary, to complete repairs and treatment.

8. **BROKERS' FEES:** All obligations of the parties for payment of brokers' fees are contained in separate written agreements.

9. **CLOSING:** The closing of the sale will be on or before ____________________________, ________, or within 7 days after objections to matters disclosed in the Commitment or by the survey have been cured, whichever date is later (the Closing Date). *If financing or assumption approval has been obtained pursuant to Paragraph 4,* the Closing Date will be extended up to 15 days if necessary to comply with lender's closing requirements (for example, appraisal, survey, insurance policies, lender-required repairs, closing documents). If either party fails to close this sale by the Closing Date, the non-defaulting party will be entitled to exercise the remedies contained in Paragraph 15. At closing Seller shall furnish tax statements or certificates showing no delinquent taxes, and a general warranty deed conveying good and indefeasible title showing no additional exceptions to those permitted in Paragraph 6.

10. **POSSESSION:** Seller shall deliver possession of the Property to Buyer on ______________________ in its present or required repaired condition, ordinary wear and tear excepted. Any possession by Buyer prior to closing or by Seller after closing which is not authorized by a temporary lease form promulgated by TREC or required by the parties will establish a tenancy at sufferance relationship between the parties. *Consult your insurance agent prior to change of ownership or possession as insurance coverage may be limited or terminated. The absence of a written lease or appropriate insurance coverage may expose the parties to economic loss.*

11. SPECIAL PROVISIONS: (Insert only factual statements and business details applicable to this sale. TREC rules prohibit licensees from adding factual statements or business details for which a contract addendum, lease or other form has been promulgated by TREC for mandatory use.)

12. SETTLEMENT AND OTHER EXPENSES:

A. The following expenses must be paid at or prior to closing:

(1) Appraisal fees will be paid by ______________________________.

(2) The total of loan discount fees (including any Texas Veterans' Housing Assistance Program Participation Fee) may not exceed _____% of the loan of which Seller shall pay ___________ and Buyer shall pay the remainder. The total of any buydown fees may not exceed ___________which will be paid by ______________________________.

(3) Seller's Expenses: Releases of existing liens, including prepayment penalties and recording fees; release of Seller's loan liability; tax statements or certificates; preparation of deed; one-half of escrow fee; and other expenses stipulated to be paid by Seller under other provisions of this contract.

(4) Buyer's Expenses: Loan application, origination and commitment fees; loan assumption costs; preparation and recording of deed of trust to secure assumption; lender required expenses incident to new loans, including PMI premium, preparation of loan documents, recording fees, tax service and research fees, warehouse or underwriting fees, copies of restrictions and easements, amortization schedule, premiums for mortgagee title policies and endorsements required by lender, credit reports, photos; required premiums for flood and hazard insurance; required reserve deposit for insurance premiums and ad valorem taxes; interest on all monthly installment notes from date of disbursements to one month prior to dates of first monthly payments; customary Program Loan costs for Buyer; one-half of escrow fee; and other expenses stipulated to be paid by Buyer under other provisions of this contract.

B. If any expense exceeds an amount expressly stated in this contract for such expense to be paid by a party, that party may terminate this contract unless the other party agrees to pay such excess. In no event will Buyer pay charges and fees expressly prohibited by the Texas Veterans' Housing Assistance Program or other governmental loan program regulations.

13. PRORATIONS AND ROLLBACK TAXES:

A. PRORATIONS: Taxes for the current year, interest, maintenance fees, assessments, dues and rents will be prorated through the Closing Date. If taxes for the current year vary from the amount prorated at closing, the parties shall adjust the prorations when tax statements for the current year are available. *If a loan is assumed* and the lender maintains an escrow account, the escrow account must be transferred to Buyer without any deficiency. Buyer shall reimburse Seller for the amount in the transferred account. Buyer shall pay the premium for a new insurance policy. If taxes are not paid at or prior to closing, Buyer will be obligated to pay taxes for the current year.

B. ROLLBACK TAXES: If this sale or Buyer's use of the Property after closing results in the assessment of additional taxes, penalties or interest (Assessments) for periods prior to closing, the Assessments will be the obligation of Buyer. If Seller's change in use of the Property prior to closing or denial of a special use valuation on the Property claimed by Seller results in Assessments for periods prior to closing, the Assessments will be the obligation of Seller. Obligations imposed by this paragraph will survive closing.

14. CASUALTY LOSS: If any part of the Property is damaged or destroyed by fire or other casualty loss after the effective date of the contract, Seller shall restore the Property to its previous condition as soon as reasonably possible, but in any event by the Closing Date. If Seller fails to do so due to factors beyond Seller's control, Buyer may either (a) terminate this contract and the earnest money will be refunded to Buyer (b) extend the time for performance up to 15 days and the Closing Date will be extended as necessary or (c) accept the Property in its damaged condition and accept an assignment of insurance proceeds. Seller's obligations under this paragraph are independent of any obligations of Seller under Paragraph 7.

15. **DEFAULT:** If Buyer fails to comply with this contract, Buyer will be in default, and Seller may either (a) enforce specific performance, seek such other relief as may be provided by law, or both, or (b) terminate this contract and receive the earnest money as liquidated damages, thereby releasing both parties from this contract. If, due to factors beyond Seller's control, Seller fails within the time allowed to make any non-casualty repairs or deliver the Commitment, Buyer may either (a) extend the time for performance up to 15 days and the Closing Date will be extended as necessary or (b) terminate this contract as the sole remedy and receive the earnest money. If Seller fails to comply with this contract for any other reason, Seller will be in default and Buyer may either (a) enforce specific performance, seek such other relief as may be provided by law, or both, or (b) terminate this contract and receive the earnest money, thereby releasing both parties from this contract.

16. **DISPUTE RESOLUTION:** It is the policy of the State of Texas to encourage the peaceable resolution of disputes through alternative dispute resolution procedures. The parties are encouraged to use an addendum approved by TREC to submit to mediation disputes which cannot be resolved in good faith through informal discussion.

17. **ATTORNEY'S FEES:** The prevailing party in any legal proceeding brought under or with respect to the transaction described in this contract is entitled to recover from the non-prevailing party all costs of such proceeding and reasonable attorney's fees.

18. **ESCROW:** The earnest money is deposited with escrow agent with the understanding that escrow agent is not (a) a party to this contract and does not have any liability for the performance or nonperformance of any party to this contract, (b) liable for interest on the earnest money and (c) liable for any loss of earnest money caused by the failure of any financial institution in which the earnest money has been deposited unless the financial institution is acting as escrow agent. At closing, the earnest money must be applied first to any cash down payment, then to Buyer's closing costs and any excess refunded to Buyer. If both parties make written demand for the earnest money, escrow agent may require payment of unpaid expenses incurred on behalf of the parties and a written release of liability of escrow agent from all parties. If one party makes written demand for the earnest money, escrow agent shall give notice of the demand by providing to the other party a copy of the demand. If escrow agent does not receive written objection to the demand from the other party within 30 days after notice to the other party, escrow agent may disburse the earnest money to the party making demand reduced by the amount of unpaid expenses incurred on behalf of the party receiving the earnest money and escrow agent may pay the same to the creditors. If escrow agent complies with the provisions of this paragraph, each party hereby releases escrow agent from all adverse claims related to the disbursal of the earnest money. Escrow agent's notice to the other party will be effective when deposited in the U. S. Mail, postage prepaid, certified mail, return receipt requested, addressed to the other party at such party's address shown below. Notice of objection to the demand will be deemed effective upon receipt by escrow agent.

19. **REPRESENTATIONS:** Seller represents that as of the Closing Date (a) there will be no liens, assessments, or security interests against the Property which will not be satisfied out of the Sales Price unless securing payment of any loans assumed by Buyer and (b) assumed loans will be without default. If any representation in this contract is untrue on the Closing Date, this contract may be terminated by Buyer and the Earnest Money will be refunded to Buyer. All representations contained in this contract will survive closing.

20. **FEDERAL TAX REQUIREMENT:** If Seller is a "foreign person", as defined by applicable law, or if Seller fails to deliver an affidavit that Seller is not a "foreign person", then Buyer shall withhold from the sales proceeds an amount sufficient to comply with applicable tax law and deliver the same to the Internal Revenue Service together with appropriate tax forms. IRS regulations require filing written reports if cash in excess of specified amounts is received in the transaction.

21. **AGREEMENT OF PARTIES:** This contract contains the entire agreement of the parties and cannot be changed except by their written agreement. Addenda which are a part of this contract are (list):________

____

____

____.

22. **CONSULT YOUR ATTORNEY:** Real estate licensees cannot give legal advice. This is intended to be a legally binding contract. READ IT CAREFULLY. If you do not understand the effect of this contract, consult

your attorney BEFORE signing.

Buyer's Attorney is:______________________ Seller's Attorney is:______________________

23. NOTICES: All notices from the parties to each other must be in writing and are effective when mailed to, hand-delivered at, or transmitted by facsimile machine as follows:

To Buyer at:

____

____

____

Telephone: (___)______________________

Facsimile: (___)______________________

To Seller at:

____

____

____

Telephone: (___) ______________________

Facsimile:(___) ______________________

EXECUTED the _____day of _________________, _____ (THE EFFECTIVE DATE). (BROKER: FILL IN THE DATE OF FINAL ACCEPTANCE.)

______________________ Buyer

______________________ Seller

______________________ Buyer

______________________ Seller

BROKER INFORMATION AND RATIFICATION OF FEE

Listing Broker has agreed to pay Other Broker ______________________ of the total sales price when Listing Broker's fee is received. Escrow Agent is authorized and directed to pay Other Broker from Listing Broker's fee at closing.

____
Other Broker License No.

represents ☐ Seller as Listing Broker's subagent
☐ Buyer only as Buyer's agent

____
Associate Telephone

____
Broker Address

____
Telephone Facsimile

____
Listing Broker License No.

represents ☐ Seller and Buyer as an intermediary
☐ Seller only as Seller's agent

____
Listing Associate Telephone

____
Selling Associate Telephone

____
Broker Address

____
Telephone Facsimile

RECEIPT

Receipt of ☐ Contract and ☐ $__________ Earnest Money in the form of__________________is acknowledged.

Escrow Agent: ______________________ Date: __________________,______

By:______________________

____
Address

Telephone: (_____)______________________

____
City State Zip Code

Facsimile: (_____) ______________________

NOTICE: Not For Use Where Seller Owns Fee Simple Title To Land Beneath Unit 11-8-99
PROMULGATED BY THE TEXAS REAL ESTATE COMMISSION (TREC)

RESIDENTIAL CONDOMINIUM CONTRACT (RESALE)
ALL CASH, ASSUMPTION, THIRD PARTY CONVENTIONAL OR SELLER FINANCING

1. **PARTIES:** ______________________________ (Seller) agrees to sell and convey to ______________________________ (Buyer) and Buyer agrees to buy from Seller the property described below.

2. **PROPERTY AND CONDOMINIUM DOCUMENTS:**
   A. Condominium Unit ________, in Building ________, of ______________________________, a condominium project, located at ______________________________ (Address/Zip Code), City of ______________________________, ______________________________ County, Texas, described in the Condominium Declaration and Plat and any amendments thereto of record in said County; together with such Unit's undivided interest in the Common Elements designated by the Declaration, including those areas reserved as Limited Common Elements appurtenant to the Unit and such other rights to use the Common Elements which have been specifically assigned to the Unit in any other manner. Parking areas assigned to the Unit are: ______________________________.
   The property includes the following items owned by Seller, if any: curtains and rods, draperies and rods, valances, blinds, window shades, screens, shutters, awnings, wall-to-wall carpeting, mirrors fixed in place, ceiling fans, attic fans, mail boxes, television antennas and satellite dish system with controls and equipment, permanently installed heating and air conditioning units, window air conditioning units, built-in security and fire detection equipment, plumbing and lighting fixtures including chandeliers, water softener, stove, built-in kitchen equipment, garage door openers with controls, built-in cleaning equipment, all swimming pool equipment and maintenance accessories, shrubbery, landscaping, permanently installed outdoor cooking equipment, built-in fireplace screens, artificial fireplace logs and all other personal property owned by Seller and attached to the Unit or located in the Unit and given as collateral for any indebtedness which will remain in effect after closing except the following property which is not included:
   ____
   ______________________________.
   All property sold by this contract is called the "Property".
   B. The Declaration, Bylaws and any Rules of the Association are called "Documents". (Check one box only):
   ❑ (1) Buyer has received a copy of the Documents. Buyer is advised to read the Documents before signing the contract.
   ❑ (2) Buyer has not received a copy of the Documents. Seller shall deliver the Documents to Buyer within ______ days after the effective date of the contract. Buyer may cancel the contract before the sixth day after Buyer receives the Documents by hand-delivering or mailing written notice of cancellation to Seller by certified United States mail, return receipt requested.
   C. The Resale Certificate from the condominium owners association (the Association) is called the "Certificate". The Certificate must be in a form promulgated by TREC or required by the parties. The Certificate must have been prepared no more than three months before the date it is delivered to Buyer and must contain at a minimum the information required by Section 82.157 of the Texas Property Code. (Check one box only):
   ❑ (1) Buyer has received the Certificate.
   ❑ (2) Buyer has not received the Certificate. Seller shall deliver the Certificate to Buyer within _____ days after the effective date of the contract. Buyer may cancel the contract before the sixth day after the date Buyer receives the Certificate by hand-delivering or mailing written notice of cancellation to Seller by certified United States mail, return receipt requested.
   ❑ (3) Buyer has received Seller's affidavit that Seller requested information from the Association concerning its financial condition as required by the Texas Property Code, and that the Association did not provide a Certificate or information required in the Certificate. Buyer and Seller agree to waive the requirement to furnish the Certificate.

3. **SALES PRICE:**
   A. Cash portion of Sales Price payable by Buyer at closing . . . . $______________
   B. Sum of all financing described below
   (excluding any private mortgage insurance [PMI] premium) . . . . $______________
   C. Sales Price (Sum of A and B) . . . . $______________

Residential Condominium Contract Concerning____Page Two 11-8-99
(Address of Property)

4. **FINANCING:** Within _____ days after the effective date of this contract Buyer shall apply for all third party financing or noteholder's approval of any assumption and make every reasonable effort to obtain financing or assumption approval. Financing or assumption approval will be deemed to have been obtained when the lender determines that Buyer has satisfied all of lender's financial requirements (those items relating to Buyer's net worth, income and creditworthiness). If financing (including any financed PMI premium) or assumption approval is not obtained within _____ days after the effective date hereof, this contract will terminate and the earnest money will be refunded to Buyer. Each note to be executed hereunder must be secured by vendor's and deed of trust liens.
The portion of Sales Price not payable in cash will be paid as follows: (Check applicable boxes below)
❑ A. THIRD PARTY FINANCING:
❑ (1) This contract is subject to approval for Buyer of a third party first mortgage loan having a loan-to-value ratio not to exceed _______ % as established by such third party (excluding any financed PMI premium), due in full in _____ year(s), with interest not to exceed _____ % per annum for the first _____ year(s) of the loan. The loan will be ❑ with ❑ without PMI.
❑ (2) This contract is subject to approval for Buyer of a third party second mortgage loan having a loan-to-value ratio not to exceed _____ % as established by such third party (excluding any financed PMI premium), due in full in ______ year(s), with interest not to exceed _______ % per annum for the first _____ year(s) of the loan. The loan will be ❑ with ❑ without PMI.
❑ B. TEXAS VETERANS' HOUSING ASSISTANCE PROGRAM LOAN: This contract is subject to approval for Buyer of a Texas Veterans' Housing Assistance Program Loan (the Program Loan) of $________________for a period of at least ________ years at the interest rate established by the Texas Veterans' Land Board at the time of closing.
❑ C. SELLER FINANCING: A promissory note from Buyer to Seller of $__________________, bearing _______ % interest per annum, secured by vendor's and deed of trust liens, in accordance with the terms and conditions set forth in the attached TREC Seller Financing Addendum. If an owner policy of title insurance is furnished, Buyer shall furnish Seller with a mortgagee policy of title insurance.
❑ D. ASSUMPTION:
❑ (1) Buyer shall assume the unpaid principal balance of a first lien promissory note payable to ____ which unpaid balance at closing will be $ ______________ . The total current monthly payment including principal, interest and any reserve deposits is $ _______________ . Buyer's initial payment will be the first payment due after closing.
❑ (2) Buyer shall assume the unpaid principal balance of a second lien promissory note payable to ____ which unpaid balance at closing will be $ _______________ . The total current monthly payment including principal, interest and any reserve deposits is $ _______________ . Buyer's initial payment will be the first payment due after closing.
Buyer's assumption of an existing note includes all obligations imposed by the deed of trust securing the note.
If the unpaid principal balance(s) of any assumed loan(s) as of the Closing Date varies from the loan balance(s) stated above, the ❑ cash payable at closing ❑ Sales Price will be adjusted by the amount of any variance; provided, if the total principal balance of all assumed loans varies in an amount greater than $350.00 at closing, either party may terminate this contract and the earnest money will be refunded to Buyer unless the other party elects to eliminate the excess in the variance by an appropriate adjustment at closing. If the noteholder requires (a) payment of an assumption fee in excess of $ _______________in D(1) above or $ _______________ in D(2) above and Seller declines to pay such excess, or (b) an increase in the interest rate to more than _____ % in D(1) above, or _____ % in D(2) above, or (c) any other modification of the loan documents, Buyer may terminate this contract and the earnest money will be refunded to Buyer. A vendor's lien and deed of trust to secure assumption will be required which shall automatically be released on execution and delivery of a release by noteholder. If Seller is released from liability on any assumed note, the vendor's lien and deed of trust to secure assumption will not be required.
NOTICE TO BUYER: The monthly payments, interest rates or other terms of some loans may be adjusted by the lender at or after closing. If you are concerned about the possibility of

Initialed for identification by Buyer__________ and Seller__________ 01A TREC NO. 30-2

future adjustments, do not sign the contract without examining the notes and deeds of trust.
NOTICE TO SELLER: Your liability to pay the note assumed by Buyer will continue unless you obtain a release of liability from the lender. If you are concerned about future liability, you should use the TREC Release of Liability Addendum.

❑ E. CREDIT APPROVAL ON ASSUMPTION OR SELLER FINANCING: Within ______ days after the effective date of this contract, Buyer shall deliver to Seller ❑ credit report ❑ verification of employment, including salary ❑ verification of funds on deposit in financial institutions ❑ current financial statement to establish Buyer's creditworthiness for assumption approval or seller financing and ❑ ____

____

____.

If Buyer's documentation is not delivered within the specified time, Seller may terminate this contract by notice to Buyer within 7 days after expiration of the time for delivery, and the earnest money will be paid to Seller. If this contract is not so terminated, Seller will be deemed to have accepted Buyer's credit. If the documentation is timely delivered, and Seller determines in Seller's sole discretion that Buyer's credit is unacceptable, Seller may terminate this contract by notice to Buyer within 7 days after expiration of the time for delivery and the earnest money will be refunded to Buyer. If Seller does not so terminate this contract, Seller will be deemed to have accepted Buyer's credit. Buyer hereby authorizes any credit reporting agency to furnish to Seller at Buyer's sole expense copies of Buyer's credit reports.

5. **EARNEST MONEY:** Buyer shall deposit $___________ as earnest money with ____________________ ____________________ at ____________________ (Address), as escrow agent, upon execution of this contract by both parties. Additional earnest money of $____________________ must be deposited by Buyer with escrow agent on or before ____________________, ________. If Buyer fails to deposit the earnest money as required by this contract, Buyer will be in default.

6. **TITLE POLICY:** Seller shall furnish to Buyer at ❑ Seller's ❑ Buyer's expense an owner policy of title insurance (the Title Policy) issued by ____________________(the Title Company) in the amount of the Sales Price, dated at or after closing, insuring Buyer against loss under the provisions of the Title Policy, subject to the promulgated exclusions (including existing building and zoning ordinances) and the following exceptions:
A. Restrictive covenants common to the platted subdivision in which the Property is located.
B. The standard printed exception for standby fees, taxes and assessments.
C. Liens created as part of the financing described in Paragraph 4.
D. Terms and provisions of the Documents including the assessments and platted easements.
E. Reservations or exceptions otherwise permitted by this contract or as may be approved by Buyer in writing.
F. The standard printed exception as to discrepancies, conflicts, shortages in area or boundary lines, encroachments or protrusions, or overlapping improvements.
G. The standard printed exception as to marital rights.
H. The standard printed exception as to waters, tidelands, beaches, streams, and related matters.

Within 20 days after the Title Company receives a copy of this contract, Seller shall furnish to Buyer a commitment for title insurance (the Commitment) and, at Buyer's expense, legible copies of restrictive covenants and documents evidencing exceptions in the Commitment other than the standard printed exceptions. Seller authorizes the Title Company to mail or hand deliver the Commitment and related documents to Buyer at Buyer's address shown below. If the Commitment is not delivered to Buyer within the specified time, the time for delivery will be automatically extended up to 15 days. Buyer will have 5 days after the receipt of the Commitment to object in writing to matters disclosed in the Commitment.
Buyer may object to existing building and zoning ordinances and items 6A through 6H above if Buyer determines that any such ordinance or item prohibits the following use or activity:____________________

____

____.

Buyer's failure to object within the time allowed will constitute a waiver of Buyer's right to object; except that the requirements in Schedule C of the Commitment will not be deemed to have been waived. Seller shall cure the timely objections of Buyer or any third party lender within 15 days after Seller receives the objections and the Closing Date will be extended as necessary. If objections are not cured by the extended Closing Date, this contract will terminate and the earnest money will be refunded to Buyer unless Buyer elects to waive the objections.

NOTICE TO SELLER AND BUYER:

(1) Broker advises Buyer to have an abstract of title covering the Property examined by an attorney of Buyer's selection, or Buyer should be furnished with or obtain a Title Policy. If a Title Policy is furnished, the Commitment should be promptly reviewed by an attorney of Buyer's choice due to the time limitations on Buyer's right to object.

(2) If the Property is situated in a utility or other statutorily created district providing water, sewer, drainage, or flood control facilities and services, Chapter 49 of the Texas Water Code requires Seller to deliver and Buyer to sign the statutory notice relating to the tax rate, bonded indebtedness, or standby fee of the district prior to final execution of this contract.

(3) If the Property abuts the tidally influenced waters of the state, Section 33.135, Texas Natural Resources Code, requires a notice regarding coastal area property to be included in the contract. An addendum either promulgated by TREC or required by the parties should be used.

(4) Buyer is advised that the presence of wetlands, toxic substances, including asbestos and wastes or other environmental hazards or the presence of a threatened or endangered species or its habitat may affect Buyer's intended use of the Property. If Buyer is concerned about these matters, an addendum either promulgated by TREC or required by the parties should be used.

(5) If the Property is located outside the limits of a municipality, Seller notifies Buyer under §5.011, Texas Property Code, that the Property may now or later be included in the extraterritorial jurisdiction of a municipality and may now or later be subject to annexation by the municipality. Each municipality maintains a map that depicts its boundaries and extraterritorial jurisdiction. To determine if the Property is located within a municipality's extraterritorial jurisdiction or is likely to be located within a municipality's extraterritorial jurisdiction, contact all municipalities located in the general proximity of the Property for further information.

(6) Unless expressly prohibited in writing by the parties, Seller may continue to show the Property for sale and to receive, negotiate and accept back-up offers.

(7) Any residential service contract that is purchased in connection with this transaction should be reviewed for the scope of coverage, exclusions and limitations. **The purchase of a residential service contract is optional. Similar coverage may be purchased from various companies authorized to do business in Texas.**

7. **PROPERTY CONDITION:**

A. INSPECTIONS, ACCESS AND UTILITIES: Buyer may have the Property inspected by an inspector selected by Buyer, licensed by TREC or otherwise permitted by law to make such inspections. Seller shall permit access to the Property at reasonable times for inspection, repairs and treatment and for reinspection after repairs and treatment have been completed. Seller shall pay for turning on utilities for inspection and reinspection.

B. SELLER'S DISCLOSURE NOTICE PURSUANT TO SECTION 5.008, TEXAS PROPERTY CODE (Notice)(check one box only):

❑ (1) Buyer has received the Notice.

❑ (2) Buyer has not received the Notice. Within _____ days after the effective date of this contract, Seller shall deliver the Notice to Buyer. If Buyer does not receive the Notice, Buyer may terminate this contract at any time prior to the closing. If Seller delivers the Notice, Buyer may terminate this contract for any reason within seven days after Buyer receives the Notice or prior to the closing, whichever first occurs.

❑ (3) The Texas Property Code does not require this Seller to furnish the Notice.

C. SELLER'S DISCLOSURE OF LEAD-BASED PAINT AND LEAD-BASED PAINT HAZARDS is required by Federal law for a residential dwelling constructed prior to 1978. An addendum providing such disclosure ❑ is ❑ is not attached.

D. ACCEPTANCE OF PROPERTY CONDITION: (check one box only):

☐ (1) In addition to any earnest money deposited with escrow agent, Buyer has paid Seller $______________ (the "Option Fee") for the unrestricted right to terminate this contract by giving notice of termination to Seller within _____ days after the effective date of this contract. If Buyer gives notice of termination within the time specified, the Option Fee will not be refunded, however, any earnest money will be refunded to Buyer. If Buyer does not give notice of termination within the time specified, Buyer will be deemed to have accepted the Property in its current condition and the Option Fee ☐ will ☐ will not be credited to the Sales Price at closing.

☐ (2) Buyer accepts the Property in its present condition; provided Seller, at Seller's expense, shall complete the following repairs and treatment: ________________________________
____
____.

E. LENDER REQUIRED REPAIRS AND TREATMENTS (REPAIRS).Unless otherwise agreed in writing, neither party is obligated to pay for lender required repairs or treatments for wood destroying insects. If the cost of lender required repairs exceeds 5% of the Sales Price, Buyer may terminate this contract.

F. COMPLETION OF REPAIRS AND TREATMENT. Unless otherwise agreed by the parties in writing, Seller shall complete all agreed repairs and treatment prior to the Closing Date. Repairs and treatments must be performed by persons who regularly provide such repairs or treatments. At Buyer's election, any transferable warranties received by Seller with respect to the repairs will be transferred to Buyer at Buyer's expense. If Seller fails to complete any agreed repairs and treatment prior to the Closing Date, Buyer may do so and the Closing Date will be extended up to 15 days, if necessary, to complete repairs and treatment.

G. REPAIRS TO COMMON ELEMENTS. After Buyer receives all reports of needed repairs to Common Elements and Limited Common Elements that are not the responsibility of Seller, Buyer will have 7 days to deliver notice to Seller that Buyer will terminate the contract unless Buyer receives written confirmation from the Association that such repairs will be made in a reasonable time at no cost to Buyer. If Buyer delivers such notice, Seller will have _____ days after receipt of such notice to cause to be delivered to Buyer written confirmation of the Association's commitment to repair. If Buyer does not deliver such notice to Seller, Buyer will be deemed to have accepted the Property without such repairs. If required by Buyer and written confirmation of repairs is not delivered to Buyer as required above, Buyer may terminate this contract and the earnest money will be refunded to Buyer.

8. **BROKERS' FEES:** All obligations of the parties for payment of brokers' fees are contained in separate written agreements.

9. **CLOSING:** The closing of the sale will be on or before ____________________________, __________, or within 7 days after objections to matters disclosed in the Commitment or by the survey have been cured, whichever date is later (the Closing Date). *If financing or assumption approval has been obtained pursuant to Paragraph 4,* the Closing Date will be extended up to 15 days if necessary to comply with lender's closing requirements, for example: appraisal, survey, insurance policies, lender-required repairs, closing documents. If either party fails to close this sale by the Closing Date, the non-defaulting party will be entitled to exercise the remedies contained in Paragraph 15. At closing Seller shall furnish tax statements or certificates showing no delinquent taxes and a general warranty deed conveying good and indefeasible title showing no additional exceptions to those permitted in Paragraph 6.

10. **POSSESSION:** Seller shall deliver possession of the Property to Buyer on ______________________ in its present or required repaired condition, ordinary wear and tear excepted. Any possession by Buyer prior to closing or by Seller after closing which is not authorized by a temporary lease form promulgated by TREC or required by the parties will establish a tenancy at sufferance relationship between the parties. *Consult your insurance agent prior to change of ownership or possession as insurance coverage may be limited or terminated. The absence of a written lease or appropriate insurance coverage may expose the parties to economic loss.*

11. **SPECIAL PROVISIONS:** (Insert only factual statements and business details applicable to this sale. TREC rules prohibit licensees from adding factual statements or business details for which a contract

addendum, lease or other form has been promulgated by TREC for mandatory use.)

12. **SETTLEMENT AND OTHER EXPENSES:**
A. The following expenses must be paid at or prior to closing:
(1) Appraisal fees will be paid by ______________________________.
(2) The total of loan discount fees (including any Texas Veterans' Housing Assistance Program Participation Fee) may not exceed ______% of the loan of which Seller shall pay ____________ and Buyer shall pay the remainder. The total of any buydown fees may not exceed ___________ which will be paid by ______________________________.
(3) Seller's Expenses: Releases of existing liens, including prepayment penalties and recording fees; release of Seller's loan liability; tax statements or certificates; preparation of deed; one-half of escrow fee; and other expenses stipulated to be paid by Seller under other provisions of this contract.
(4) Buyer's Expenses: Loan application, origination and commitment fees; loan assumption costs; preparation and recording of deed of trust to secure assumption; lender required expenses incident to new loans, including PMI premium, preparation of loan documents, loan related inspection fee, recording fees, tax service and research fees, warehouse or underwriting fees, copies of restrictions and easements, amortization schedule, premiums for mortgagee title policies and endorsements required by lender, credit reports, photos; required premiums for flood and hazard insurance; required reserve deposit for insurance premiums and ad valorem taxes; interest on all monthly installment notes from date of disbursements to one month prior to dates of first monthly payments; customary Program Loan costs for Buyer; one-half of escrow fee; and other expenses stipulated to be paid by Buyer under other provisions of this contract.
B. Any Association transfer or processing fee will be paid by ______________________________.
C. If any expense exceeds an amount expressly stated in this contract for such expense to be paid by a party, that party may terminate this contract unless the other party agrees to pay such excess. In no event will Buyer pay charges and fees expressly prohibited by the Texas Veteran's Housing Assistance Program or other governmental loan program regulations.

13. **PRORATIONS**: Taxes for the current year, interest, maintenance fees, regular condominium assessments, dues and rents will be prorated through the Closing Date. If taxes for the current year vary from the amount prorated at closing, the parties shall adjust the prorations when tax statements for the current year are available. *If a loan is assumed* and the lender maintains an escrow account, the escrow account must be transferred to Buyer without any deficiency. Buyer shall reimburse Seller for the amount in the transferred account. Cash reserves from regular condominium assessments for deferred maintenance or capital improvements established by the Association will not be credited to Seller. Any special condominium assessment due and unpaid at closing will be the obligation of Seller. Buyer shall pay the premium for a new insurance policy. If taxes are not paid at or prior to closing, Buyer will be obligated to pay taxes for the current year.

14. **CASUALTY LOSS:** If any part of the Unit which Seller is solely obligated to maintain and repair under the terms of the Declaration is damaged or destroyed by fire or other casualty, Seller shall restore the same to its previous condition as soon as reasonably possible, but in any event by the Closing Date. If Seller is unable to do so without fault, Buyer may terminate this contract and the earnest money will be refunded to Buyer. If any part of the Common Elements or Limited Common Elements adjoining the Unit described in Paragraph 2A is damaged or destroyed by fire or other casualty loss, Buyer will have 7 days from receipt of notice of such casualty loss within which to notify Seller in writing that the contract will be terminated unless Buyer receives written confirmation from the Association that the damaged condition will be restored to its previous condition within a reasonable time at no cost to Buyer. Unless Buyer gives such notice within such time, Buyer will be deemed to have accepted the Property without confirmation of such restoration. Seller will have 7 days from the date of receipt of Buyer's notice within which to cause to be delivered to Buyer such confirmation. If required by Buyer and written confirmation is not delivered to Buyer as required above, Buyer may terminate this contract and the earnest money will be refunded to Buyer. Seller's obligations under this paragraph are independent of any obligations of Seller under Paragraph 7.

15. **DEFAULT:** If Buyer fails to comply with this contract, Buyer will be in default, and Seller may either (a) enforce specific performance, seek such other relief as may be provided by law, or both, or (b) terminate this contract and receive the earnest money as liquidated damages, thereby releasing both parties from this contract. If, due to factors beyond Seller's control, Seller fails within the time allowed to make any non-casualty repairs or deliver the Commitment, Buyer may either (a) extend the time for performance up to 15 days and the Closing Date will be extended as necessary or (b) terminate this contract as the sole remedy and receive the earnest money. If Seller fails to comply with this contract for any other reason, Seller will be in default and Buyer may either (a) enforce specific performance, seek such other relief as may be provided by law, or both, or (b) terminate this contract and receive the earnest money, thereby releasing both parties from this contract.

16. **DISPUTE RESOLUTION:** It is the policy of the State of Texas to encourage the peaceable resolution of disputes through alternative dispute resolution procedures. The parties are encouraged to use an addendum approved by TREC to submit to mediation disputes which cannot be resolved in good faith through informal discussion.

17. **ATTORNEY'S FEES:** The prevailing party in any legal proceeding brought under or with respect to the transaction described in this contract is entitled to recover from the non-prevailing party all costs of such proceeding and reasonable attorney's fees.

18. **ESCROW:** The earnest money is deposited with escrow agent with the understanding that escrow agent is not (a) a party to this contract and does not have any liability for the performance or nonperformance of any party to this contract, (b) liable for interest on the earnest money and (c) liable for any loss of earnest money caused by the failure of any financial institution in which the earnest money has been deposited unless the financial institution is acting as escrow agent. At closing, the earnest money must be applied first to any cash down payment, then to Buyer's closing costs and any excess refunded to Buyer. If both parties make written demand for the earnest money, escrow agent may require payment of unpaid expenses incurred on behalf of the parties and a written release of liability of escrow agent from all parties. If one party makes written demand for the earnest money, escrow agent shall give notice of the demand by providing to the other party a copy of the demand. If escrow agent does not receive written objection to the demand from the other party within 30 days after notice to the other party, escrow agent may disburse the earnest money to the party making demand reduced by the amount of unpaid expenses incurred on behalf of the party receiving the earnest money and escrow agent may pay the same to the creditors. If escrow agent complies with the provisions of this paragraph, each party hereby releases escrow agent from all adverse claims related to the disbursal of the earnest money. Escrow agent's notice to the other party will be effective when deposited in the U. S. Mail, postage prepaid, certified mail, return receipt requested, addressed to the other party at such party's address shown below. Notice of objection to the demand will be deemed effective upon receipt by escrow agent.

19. **REPRESENTATIONS:** Seller represents that as of the Closing Date (a) there will be no liens, assessments or security interests against the Property which will not be satisfied out of the sales proceeds, unless securing payment of any loan assumed by Buyer; (b) assumed loan(s) will not be in default; (c) the present amount of the regular condominium assessment is $ __________________ which will be current; and (d) Seller has no knowledge of any misrepresentation or errors in the Certificate or any material changes in the information contained therein. If any representation in this contract or the Certificate is untrue on the Closing Date, this contract may be terminated by Buyer and the earnest money will be refunded to Buyer. All representations contained in this contract will survive closing.

20. **FEDERAL TAX REQUIREMENT:** If Seller is a "foreign person", as defined by applicable law, or if Seller fails to deliver an affidavit that Seller is not a "foreign person", then Buyer shall withhold from the sales proceeds an amount sufficient to comply with applicable tax law and deliver the same to the Internal Revenue Service together with appropriate tax forms. IRS regulations require filing written reports if cash in excess of specified amounts is received in the transaction.

21. **AGREEMENT OF PARTIES:** This contract contains the entire agreement of the parties and cannot be changed except by their written agreement. Addenda which are a part of this contract are (list): ________
____.

Residential Condominium Contract Concerning____Page Eight 11-8-99
(Address of Property)

22. **CONSULT YOUR ATTORNEY:** Real estate licensees cannot give legal advice. This contract is intended to be legally binding. READ IT CAREFULLY. If you do not understand the effect of this contract, consult your attorney BEFORE signing.

Buyer's Attorney is:______________________________

Seller's Attorney is:______________________________

23. **NOTICES:** All notices from one party to the other must be in writing and are effective when mailed to, hand-delivered at, or transmitted by facsimile machine as follows:

To Buyer at:

____

____

____

Telephone: (___)______________________

Facsimile: (___)______________________

To Seller at:

____

____

____

Telephone: (___)______________________

Facsimile:(___)______________________

EXECUTED the _____day of ____________________,________ (THE EFFECTIVE DATE). (BROKER: FILL IN THE DATE OF FINAL ACCEPTANCE.)

____
Buyer

____
Buyer

____
Seller

____
Seller

BROKER INFORMATION AND RATIFICATION OF FEE

Listing Broker has agreed to pay Other Broker ______________________ of the total sales price when Listing Broker's fee is received. Escrow Agent is authorized and directed to pay Other Broker from Listing Broker's fee at closing.

____
Other Broker License No.

represents
- ❑ Seller as Listing Broker's subagent
- ❑ Buyer only as Buyer's agent

____
Associate Telephone

____
Broker Address

____
Telephone Facsimile

____
Listing Broker License No.

represents
- ❑ Seller and Buyer as an intermediary
- ❑ Seller only as Seller's agent

____
Listing Associate Telephone

____
Selling Associate Telephone

____
Broker Address

____
Telephone Facsimile

RECEIPT

Receipt of ❑ Contract and ❑ $ _________Earnest Money in the form of ________________is acknowledged.

Escrow Agent: ______________________________ Date: ______________________________,______

By:______________________________

____
Address

____
City State Zip Code

Telephone: (_____)______________________

Facsimile: (_____)______________________

NOTICE: Not For Use Where Seller Owns Fee Simple Title To Land Beneath Unit 11-8-99
PROMULGATED BY THE TEXAS REAL ESTATE COMMISSION (TREC)

RESIDENTIAL CONDOMINIUM CONTRACT (RESALE)
FHA INSURED OR VA GUARANTEED FINANCING

1. PARTIES: ________________________________ (Seller) agrees to sell and convey to ________________________________ (Buyer) and Buyer agrees to buy from Seller the property described below.

2. PROPERTY AND CONDOMINIUM DOCUMENTS:

A. Condominium Unit ______, in Building ______, of ______________________________, a condominium project, located at ______________________________ (Address/Zip Code), City of ______________________, ____________________ County, Texas, described in the Condominium Declaration and Plat and any amendments thereto of record in said County; together with such Unit's undivided interest in the Common Elements designated by the Declaration, including those areas reserved as Limited Common Elements appurtenant to the Unit and such other rights to use the Common Elements which have been specifically assigned to the Unit in any other manner. Parking areas assigned to the Unit are: ____________________. The property includes the following items owned by Seller, if any: curtains and rods, draperies and rods, valances, blinds, window shades, screens, shutters, awnings, wall-to-wall carpeting, mirrors fixed in place, ceiling fans, attic fans, mail boxes, television antennas and satellite dish system with controls and equipment, permanently installed heating and air conditioning units, window air conditioning units, built-in security and fire detection equipment, plumbing and lighting fixtures including chandeliers, water softener, stove, built-in kitchen equipment, garage door openers with controls, built-in cleaning equipment, all swimming pool equipment and maintenance accessories, shrubbery, landscaping, permanently installed outdoor cooking equipment, built-in fireplace screens, artificial fireplace logs and all other property owned by Seller and attached to the Unit or located in the Unit and given as collateral for any indebtedness which will remain in effect after closing except the following property which is not included: ____________________
____.
All property sold by this contract is called the "Property".

B. The Declaration, Bylaws and any Rules of the Association are called "Documents". (Check one box only):

❑ (1) Buyer has received a copy of the Documents. Buyer is advised to read the Documents before signing the contract.

❑ (2) Buyer has not received a copy of the Documents. Seller shall deliver the Documents to Buyer within _____ days after the effective date of the contract. Buyer may cancel the contract before the sixth day after Buyer receives the Documents by hand-delivering or mailing written notice of cancellation to Seller by certified United States mail, return receipt requested.

C. The Resale Certificate from the condominium owners association (the Association) is called the "Certificate". The Certificate must be in a form promulgated by TREC or required by the parties. The Certificate must have been prepared no more than three months before the date it is delivered to Buyer and must contain at a minimum the information required by Section 82.157 of the Texas Property Code. (Check one box only):

❑ (1) Buyer has received the Certificate.

❑ (2) Buyer has not received the Certificate. Seller shall deliver the Certificate to Buyer within ____days after the effective date of the contract. Buyer may cancel the contract before the sixth day after the date Buyer receives the Certificate by hand-delivering or mailing written notice of cancellation to Seller by certified United States mail, return receipt requested.

❑ (3) Buyer has received Seller's affidavit that Seller requested information from the Association concerning its financial condition as required by the Texas Property Code, and that the Association did not provide a Certificate or information required in the Certificate. Buyer and Seller agree to waive the requirement to furnish the Certificate.

3. SALES PRICE:

A. Cash portion of the Sales Price payable by Buyer at closing . . . . $____________

B. Sum of all financing described below
(excluding VA Funding Fee or FHA Mortgage Insurance Premium [MIP]) . . . . $____________

C. Sales Price (Sum of A and B) . . . . $____________

4. **FINANCING:** Within ______ days after the effective date of this contract Buyer shall apply for and make every reasonable effort to obtain financing. Financing will be deemed to have been obtained when the lender has determined that Buyer has satisfied all of lender's financial conditions (those items relating to Buyer's net worth, income and creditworthiness). If financing (including any financed MIP or Funding Fee) is not obtained within ______ days after the effective date hereof, this contract will terminate and the earnest money will be refunded to Buyer. The portion of the Sales Price not payable in cash shall be paid as follows: (Check applicable boxes below)

❑ A. FHA INSURED FINANCING: This contract is subject to approval for Buyer of a Section__________ FHA insured loan of not less than $______________ (excluding any financed MIP), amortizable monthly for not less than ______ years, with interest not to exceed _____ % per annum for the first _____ year(s) of the loan.

As required by HUD-FHA, if FHA valuation is unknown, *"It is expressly agreed that, notwithstanding any other provisions of this contract, the purchaser* (Buyer) *shall not be obligated to complete the purchase of the Property described herein or to incur any penalty by forfeiture of earnest money deposits or otherwise unless the purchaser* (Buyer) *has been given in accordance with HUD/FHA or VA requirements a written statement issued by the Federal Housing Commissioner, Department of Veterans Affairs, or a Direct Endorsement Lender setting forth the appraised value of the Property of not less than $________________. The purchaser* (Buyer) *shall have the privilege and option of proceeding with consummation of the contract without regard to the amount of the appraised valuation. The appraised valuation is arrived at to determine the maximum mortgage the Department of Housing and Urban Development will insure. HUD does not warrant the value or the condition of the Property. The purchaser* (Buyer) *should satisfy himself/herself that the price and the condition of the Property are acceptable."*

If the FHA appraised value of the Property (excluding closing costs and MIP) is less than the Sales Price (3C above), Seller may reduce the Sales Price to an amount equal to the FHA appraised value (excluding closing costs and MIP) and the parties to the sale shall close the sale at such lower Sales Price with appropriate adjustments to 3A and 3B above.

❑ B. VA GUARANTEED FINANCING: This contract is subject to approval for Buyer of a VA guaranteed loan of not less than $____________(excluding any financed Funding Fee), amortizable monthly for not less than _____ years, with interest not to exceed ____ % per annum for the first _____ year(s) of the loan.

VA NOTICE TO BUYER: *"It is expressly agreed that, notwithstanding any other provisions of this contract, the Buyer shall not incur any penalty by forfeiture of earnest money or otherwise or be obligated to complete the purchase of the Property described herein, if the contract purchase price or cost exceeds the reasonable value of the Property established by the Department of Veterans Affairs. The Buyer shall, however, have the privilege and option of proceeding with the consummation of this contract without regard to the amount of the reasonable value established by the Department of Veterans Affairs."*

If Buyer elects to complete the purchase at an amount in excess of the reasonable value established by VA, Buyer shall pay such excess amount in cash from a source which Buyer agrees to disclose to the VA and which Buyer represents will not be from borrowed funds except as approved by VA. If VA reasonable value of the Property is less than the Sales Price (3C above), Seller may reduce the Sales Price to an amount equal to the VA reasonable value and the parties to the sale shall close at such lower Sales Price with appropriate adjustments to 3A and 3B above.

❑ C. TEXAS VETERANS' HOUSING ASSISTANCE PROGRAM LOAN: This contract is subject to approval for Buyer of a Texas Veterans' Housing Assistance Program Loan of $______________for a period of at least ___________ years at the interest rate established by the Texas Veterans' Land Board at the time of closing.

5. **EARNEST MONEY:** Buyer shall deposit $___________as Earnest Money with___________________ ____________________________ at ____ (Address), as Escrow Agent, upon execution of this contract by both parties. Additional Earnest Money of $_____________ must be deposited by Buyer with Escrow Agent on or before _________________, _______. If Buyer fails to deposit the Earnest Money as required by this contract, Buyer will be in default.

6. **TITLE POLICY:** Seller shall furnish to Buyer at ❑ Seller's ❑ Buyer's expense an owner policy of title insurance (the Title Policy) issued by ____(the

Title Company) in the amount of the Sales Price, dated at or after closing, insuring Buyer against loss under the provisions of the Title Policy, subject to the promulgated exclusions (including existing building and zoning ordinances) and the following exceptions:

A. Restrictive covenants common to the platted subdivision in which the Property is located.
B. The standard printed exception for standby fees, taxes and assessments.
C. Liens created as part of the financing described in Paragraph 4.
D. Terms and provisions of the Documents including the assessments and platted easements.
E. Reservations or exceptions otherwise permitted by this contract or as may be approved by Buyer in writing.
F. The standard printed exception as to discrepancies, conflicts, shortages in area or boundary lines, encroachments or protrusions, or overlapping improvements.
G. The standard printed exception as to marital rights.
H. The standard printed exception as to waters, tidelands, beaches, streams, and related matters.

Within 20 days after the Title Company receives a copy of this contract, Seller shall furnish to Buyer a commitment for title insurance (the Commitment) and, at Buyer's expense, legible copies of restrictive covenants and documents evidencing exceptions in the Commitment other than the standard printed exceptions. Seller authorizes the Title Company to mail or hand deliver the Commitment and related documents to Buyer at Buyer's address shown below. If the Commitment is not delivered to Buyer within the specified time, the time for delivery will be automatically extended up to 15 days. Buyer will have 5 days after the receipt of the Commitment to object in writing to matters disclosed in the Commitment.
Buyer may object to existing building and zoning ordinances and items 6A through 6H above if Buyer determines that any such ordinance or item prohibits the following use or activity:____________________
____.
Buyer's failure to object within the time allowed will constitute a waiver of Buyer's right to object; except that the requirements in Schedule C of the Commitment will not be deemed to have been waived. Seller shall cure the timely objections of Buyer or any third party lender within 15 days after Seller receives the objections and the Closing Date will be extended as necessary. If objections are not cured by the extended Closing Date, this contract will terminate and the earnest money will be refunded to Buyer unless Buyer elects to waive the objections.

NOTICE TO SELLER AND BUYER:

(1) Broker advises Buyer to have an abstract covering the Property examined by an attorney of Buyer's selection, or Buyer should be furnished with or obtain a Title Policy. If a Title Policy is furnished, the Commitment should be promptly reviewed by an attorney of Buyer's choice due to the time limitations on Buyer's right to object.

(2) If the Property is situated in a utility or other statutorily created district providing water, sewer, drainage, or flood control facilities and services, Chapter 49 of the Texas Water Code requires Seller to deliver and Buyer to sign the statutory notice relating to the tax rate, bonded indebtedness, or standby fee of the district prior to final execution of this contract.

(3) If the Property abuts the tidally influenced waters of the state, Section 33.135, Texas Natural Resources Code, requires a notice regarding coastal area property to be included in the contract. An addendum either promulgated by TREC or required by the parties should be used.

(4) Buyer is advised that the presence of wetlands, toxic substances, including asbestos and wastes or other environmental hazards or the presence of a threatened or endangered species or its habitat may affect Buyer's intended use of the Property. If Buyer is concerned about these matters, an addendum either promulgated by TREC or required by the parties should be used.

(5) If the Property is located outside the limits of a municipality, Seller notifies Buyer under §5.011, Texas Property Code, that the Property may now or later be included in the extraterritorial jurisdiction of a municipality and may now or later be subject to annexation by the municipality. Each municipality maintains a map that depicts its boundaries and extraterritorial jurisdiction. To determine if the Property is located within a municipality's extraterritorial jurisdiction or is likely to be located within a municipality's extraterritorial jurisdiction, contact all municipalities located in the general proximity of the Property for further information.

(6) Unless expressly prohibited in writing by the parties, Seller may continue to show the Property for sale and to receive, negotiate and accept back-up offers.

(7) Any residential service contract that is purchased in connection with this transaction should be reviewed for the scope of coverage, exclusions and limitations. **The purchase of a residential service contract is optional. Similar coverage may be purchased from various companies authorized to do business in Texas.**

FHA or VA Financed Residential Condominium Contract Concerning________________________________ Page Four 11-8-99
(Address of Property)

7. PROPERTY CONDITION:

A. INSPECTIONS, ACCESS AND UTILITIES: Buyer may have the Property inspected by an inspector selected by Buyer, licensed by TREC or otherwise permitted by law to make such inspections. Seller shall permit access to the Property at reasonable times for inspection, repairs and treatment and for reinspection after repairs and treatment have been completed. Seller shall pay for turning on utilities for inspection and reinspection.

B. SELLER'S DISCLOSURE NOTICE PURSUANT TO SECTION 5.008, TEXAS PROPERTY CODE (Notice)(check one box only):

❑ (1) Buyer has received the Notice.

❑ (2) Buyer has not received the Notice. Within ______ days after the effective date of this contract, Seller shall deliver the Notice to Buyer. If Buyer does not receive the Notice, Buyer may terminate this contract at any time prior to the closing. If Seller delivers the Notice, Buyer may terminate this contract for any reason within seven days after Buyer receives the Notice or prior to the closing, whichever first occurs.

❑ (3) The Texas Property Code does not require this Seller to furnish the Notice.

C. SELLER'S DISCLOSURE OF LEAD-BASED PAINT AND LEAD-BASED PAINT HAZARDS is required by Federal law for a residential dwelling constructed prior to 1978. An addendum providing such disclosure ❑ is ❑ is not attached.

D. ACCEPTANCE OF PROPERTY CONDITION: (check one box only):

❑ (1) In addition to any earnest money deposited with escrow agent, Buyer has paid Seller $ ______________ (the "Option Fee") for the unrestricted right to terminate this contract by giving notice of termination to Seller within _____ days after the effective date of this contract. If Buyer gives notice of termination within the time specified, the Option Fee will not be refunded, however, any earnest money will be refunded to Buyer. If Buyer does not give notice of termination within the time specified, Buyer will be deemed to have accepted the Property in its current condition and the Option Fee ❑ will ❑ will not be credited to the Sales Price at closing.

❑ (2) Buyer accepts the Property in its present condition; provided Seller, at Seller's expense, shall complete the following repairs and treatment:________________________________
____
____.

E. LENDER REQUIRED REPAIRS AND TREATMENTS (REPAIRS). Unless otherwise agreed in writing, neither party is obligated to pay for lender required repairs or treatments for wood destroying insects. If the cost of lender required repairs exceeds 5% of the Sales Price, Buyer may terminate this contract.

F. COMPLETION OF REPAIRS AND TREATMENT. Unless otherwise agreed by the parties in writing, Seller shall complete all agreed repairs and treatment prior to the Closing Date. Repairs and treatments must be performed by persons who regularly provide such repairs or treatments. At Buyer's election, any transferable warranties received by Seller with respect to the repairs will be transferred to Buyer at Buyer's expense. If Seller fails to complete any agreed repairs and treatment prior to the Closing Date, Buyer may do so and the Closing Date will be extended up to 15 days, if necessary, to complete repairs and treatment.

G. REPAIRS TO COMMON ELEMENTS. After Buyer receives all reports of needed repairs to Common Elements and Limited Common Elements that are not the responsibility of Seller, Buyer will have 7 days to deliver notice to Seller that Buyer will terminate the contract unless Buyer receives written confirmation from the Association that such repairs will be made in a reasonable time at no cost to Buyer. If Buyer delivers such notice, Seller will have _____ days after receipt of such notice to cause to be delivered to Buyer written confirmation of the Association's commitment to repair. If Buyer does not deliver such notice to Seller, Buyer will be deemed to have accepted the Property without such repairs. If required by Buyer and written confirmation of repairs is not delivered to Buyer as required above, Buyer may terminate this contract and the earnest money will be refunded to Buyer.

8. BROKERS' FEES: All obligations of the parties for payment of brokers' fees are contained in separate written agreements.

Initialed for identification by Buyer__________ and Seller__________ **01A** TREC NO. 31-2

FHA or VA Financed Residential Condominium Contract Concerning____Page Five 11-8-99
(Address of Property)

9. **CLOSING:** The closing of the sale will be on or before ______________________, ________, or within 7 days after objections to matters disclosed in the Commitment or by the survey have been cured, whichever date is later (the Closing Date). *If financing or assumption approval has been obtained pursuant to Paragraph 4,* the Closing Date will be extended up to 15 days if necessary to comply with lender's closing requirements (for example, appraisal, survey, insurance policies, lender-required repairs, closing documents). If either party fails to close this sale by the Closing Date, the non-defaulting party will be entitled to exercise the remedies contained in Paragraph 15. At closing Seller shall furnish tax statements or certificates showing no delinquent taxes and a general warranty deed conveying good and indefeasible title showing no additional exceptions to those permitted in Paragraph 6.

10. **POSSESSION:** Seller shall deliver possession of the Property to Buyer on ____________________ in its present or required repaired condition, ordinary wear and tear excepted. Any possession by Buyer prior to closing or by Seller after closing which is not authorized by a temporary lease form promulgated by TREC or required by the parties will establish a tenancy at sufferance relationship between the parties. *Consult your insurance agent prior to change of ownership or possession as insurance coverage may be limited or terminated. The absence of a written lease or appropriate insurance coverage may expose the parties to economic loss.*

11. **SPECIAL PROVISIONS:** (Insert only factual statements and business details applicable to this sale. TREC rules prohibit licensees from adding factual statements or business details for which a contract addendum, lease or other form has been promulgated by TREC for mandatory use.)

12. **SETTLEMENT AND OTHER EXPENSES:**

A. The following expenses must be paid at or prior to closing:

(1) Appraisal fees will be paid by ____.

(2) The total of the loan discount fees (including any Texas Veterans' Housing Assistance Program Participation Fee) may not exceed ____% of the loan of which Seller shall pay ____________and Buyer shall pay the remainder. The total of any buydown fees may not exceed___________which will be paid by _________________________.

(3) Seller's Expenses: FHA or VA required repairs and any other inspections, reports or repairs required of Seller by this contract; releases of existing liens, including prepayment penalties and recording fees; tax statements or certificates; preparation of deed; one-half of escrow fee; expenses FHA or VA prohibits Buyer to pay; tax statements or certificates; and other expenses stipulated to be paid by Seller under other provisions of this contract.

(4) Buyer's Expenses: Interest on the note(s) from date of disbursement to one month prior to dates of first monthly payments, expenses stipulated to be paid by Buyer under other provisions of this contract; any customary Texas Veterans' Housing Assistance Program Loan costs for Buyer; and premiums for mortgagee title policy and endorsements required by lender.

(a) FHA Buyer: All prepaid items required by applicable HUD-FHA or other regulations, including required premiums for flood and hazard insurance, reserve deposits for other insurance, ad valorem taxes and special governmental assessments; expenses incident to any loan, including preparation of loan documents, recording fees, copies of restrictions and easements, amortization schedule, loan origination fee, loan commitment fee, credit reports, photos, loan related inspection fee; and one-half of escrow fee.

(b) VA Buyer: All prepaid items, including required premiums for flood and hazard insurance, reserve deposits for other insurance, ad valorem taxes and special governmental assessments; expenses incident to any loan: for example, credit reports, recording fees, loan origination fee, loan related inspection fees.

B. Any Association transfer or processing fee will be paid by ______________________________.

C. The VA Loan Funding Fee or FHA Mortgage Insurance Premium (MIP) not to exceed $____________ will be paid by Buyer, and ❑ paid in cash at closing ❑ added to the amount of the loan or ❑ paid as follows: ____.

D. If any expense exceeds an amount expressly stated in this contract for such expense to be paid by a party, that party may terminate this contract unless the other party agrees to pay such excess. In no event will Buyer pay charges and fees expressly prohibited by the Texas Veteran's Housing Assistance Program or other governmental loan program regulations.

13. **PRORATIONS**: Taxes for the current year, interest, maintenance fees, regular condominium assessments, dues and rents will be prorated through the Closing Date. If taxes for the current year vary from the amount prorated at closing, the parties shall adjust the prorations when tax statements for the current year are available. Cash reserves from regular condominium assessments for deferred maintenance or capital improvements established by the Association will not be credited to Seller. Any special condominium assessment due and unpaid at closing will be the obligation of Seller. Buyer shall pay the premium for a new insurance policy. If taxes are not paid at or prior to closing, Buyer will be obligated to pay taxes for the current year.

14. **CASUALTY LOSS:** If any part of the Unit which Seller is solely obligated to maintain and repair under the terms of the Declaration is damaged or destroyed by fire or other casualty, Seller shall restore the same to its previous condition as soon as reasonably possible, but in any event by the Closing Date. If Seller is unable to do so without fault, Buyer may terminate this contract and the earnest money will be refunded to Buyer. If any part of the Common Elements or Limited Common Elements adjoining the Unit described in Paragraph 2A is damaged or destroyed by fire or other casualty loss, Buyer will have 7 days from receipt of notice of such casualty loss within which to notify Seller in writing that the contract will be terminated unless Buyer receives written confirmation from the Association that the damaged condition will be restored to its previous condition within a reasonable time at no cost to Buyer. Unless Buyer gives such notice within such time, Buyer will be deemed to have accepted the Property without confirmation of such restoration. Seller will have 7 days from the date of receipt of Buyer's notice within which to cause to be delivered to Buyer such confirmation. If required by Buyer and written confirmation is not delivered to Buyer as required above, Buyer may terminate this contract and the earnest money will be refunded to Buyer. Seller's obligations under this paragraph are independent of any obligations of Seller under Paragraph 7.

15. **DEFAULT:** If Buyer fails to comply with this contract, Buyer will be in default, and Seller may either (a) enforce specific performance, seek such other relief as may be provided by law, or both, or (b) terminate this contract and receive the earnest money as liquidated damages, thereby releasing both parties from this contract. If, due to factors beyond Seller's control, Seller fails within the time allowed to make any non-casualty repairs or deliver the Commitment, Buyer may either (a) extend the time for performance up to 15 days and the Closing Date will be extended as necessary or (b) terminate this contract as the sole remedy and receive the earnest money. If Seller fails to comply with this contract for any other reason, Seller will be in default and Buyer may either (a) enforce specific performance, seek such other relief as may be provided by law, or both, or (b) terminate this contract and receive the earnest money, thereby releasing both parties from this contract.

FHA or VA Financed Residential Condominium Contract Concerning______________________________ Page Seven 11-8-99
(Address of Property)

16. **DISPUTE RESOLUTION:** It is the policy of the State of Texas to encourage the peaceable resolution of disputes through alternative dispute resolution procedures. The parties are encouraged to use an addendum approved by TREC to submit to mediation disputes which cannot be resolved in good faith through informal discussion.

17. **ATTORNEY'S FEES:** The prevailing party in any legal proceeding brought under or with respect to the transaction described in this contract is entitled to recover from the non-prevailing party all costs of such proceeding and reasonable attorney's fees.

18. **ESCROW:** The earnest money is deposited with escrow agent with the understanding that escrow agent is not (a) a party to this contract and does not have any liability for the performance or nonperformance of any party to this contract, (b) liable for interest on the earnest money and (c) liable for any loss of earnest money caused by the failure of any financial institution in which the earnest money has been deposited unless the financial institution is acting as escrow agent. At closing, the earnest money must be applied first to any cash down payment, then to Buyer's closing costs and any excess refunded to Buyer. If both parties make written demand for the earnest money, escrow agent may require payment of unpaid expenses incurred on behalf of the parties and a written release of liability of escrow agent from all parties. If one party makes written demand for the earnest money, escrow agent shall give notice of the demand by providing to the other party a copy of the demand. If escrow agent does not receive written objection to the demand from the other party within 30 days after notice to the other party, escrow agent may disburse the earnest money to the party making demand reduced by the amount of unpaid expenses incurred on behalf of the party receiving the earnest money and escrow agent may pay the same to the creditors. If escrow agent complies with the provisions of this paragraph, each party hereby releases escrow agent from all adverse claims related to the disbursal of the earnest money. Escrow agent's notice to the other party will be effective when deposited in the U. S. Mail, postage prepaid, certified mail, return receipt requested, addressed to the other party at such party's address shown below. Notice of objection to the demand will be deemed effective upon receipt by escrow agent.

19. **REPRESENTATIONS:** Seller represents that as of the Closing Date (a) there will be no liens, assessments or security interests against the Property which will not be satisfied out of the sales proceeds; (b) the present amount of the regular condominium assessment is $ ____________________ which will be current; (c) Seller has no knowledge of any misrepresentation or errors in the Certificate or any material changes in the information contained therein. If any representation in this contract or the Certificate is untrue on the Closing Date, this contract may be terminated by Buyer and the earnest money will be refunded to Buyer. All representations contained in this contract will survive closing.

20. **FEDERAL TAX REQUIREMENT:** If Seller is a "foreign person", as defined by applicable law, or if Seller fails to deliver an affidavit that Seller is not a "foreign person", then Buyer shall withhold from the sales proceeds an amount sufficient to comply with applicable tax law and deliver the same to the Internal Revenue Service together with appropriate tax forms. IRS regulations require filing written reports if cash in excess of specified amounts is received in the transaction.

21. **AGREEMENT OF PARTIES:** This contract contains the entire agreement of the parties and cannot be changed except by their written agreement. Addenda which are a part of this contract are (list): ________
____
____.

22. **CONSULT YOUR ATTORNEY:** Real estate licensees cannot give legal advice. This contract is intended to be legally binding. READ IT CAREFULLY. If you do not understand the effect of this contract, consult your attorney BEFORE signing.

Buyer's Attorney is:______________________________ Seller's Attorney is:______________________________

FHA or VA Financed Residential Condominium Contract Concerning______________________________Page Eight 11-8-99
(Address of Property)

23. **NOTICES:** All notices from one party to the other must be in writing and are effective when mailed to, hand-delivered at, or transmitted by facsimile machine as follows:

To Buyer at: **To Seller at:**

______________________ ______________________

______________________ ______________________

______________________ ______________________

Telephone: (___) ______________ Telephone: (___)______________

Facsimile: (___)______________ Facsimile:(___) ______________

EXECUTED the ______day of ____________________,________ (THE EFFECTIVE DATE). (BROKER: FILL IN THE DATE OF FINAL ACCEPTANCE.)

______________________ ______________________
Buyer Seller

______________________ ______________________
Buyer Seller

The form of this contract has been approved by the Texas Real Estate Commission. Such approval relates to this contract form only. TREC forms are intended for use only by trained real estate licensees. No representation is made as to the legal validity or adequacy of any provision in any specific transaction. It is not suitable for complex transactions. Extensive riders or additions are not to be used. Texas Real Estate Commission, P.O. Box 12188, Austin, TX 78711-2188, 1-800-250-8732 or (512) 459-6544 (http://www.trec.state.tx.us) TREC NO. 31-2. This form replaces TREC NO. 31-1.

BROKER INFORMATION AND RATIFICATION OF FEE

Listing Broker has agreed to pay Other Broker ____________________ of the total sales price when Listing Broker's fee is received. Escrow Agent is authorized and directed to pay Other Broker from Listing Broker's fee at closing.

______________________ ______________________
Other Broker License No. Listing Broker License No.
represents ❑ Seller as Listing Broker's subagent represents ❑ Seller and Buyer as an intermediary
❑ Buyer only as Buyer's agent ❑ Seller only as Seller's agent

____
Listing Associate Telephone

______________________ ______________________
Associate Telephone Selling Associate Telephone

______________________ ______________________
Broker Address Broker Address

______________________ ______________________
Telephone Facsimile Telephone Facsimile

RECEIPT

Receipt of ❑ Contract and ❑ $__________ Earnest Money in the form of____________________ is acknowledged.

Escrow Agent: ______________________ Date: ____________________,________

By:______________________

______________________ Telephone: (___)______________
Address

______________________ Facsimile: (___)______________
City State Zip Code

EQUAL HOUSING OPPORTUNITY

CONDOMINIUM RESALE CERTIFICATE

04-18-94

PROMULGATED BY THE TEXAS REAL ESTATE COMMISSION (TREC)

Condominium Certificate concerning Condominium Unit __________, in Building ____________, of ____________ ____, a condominium project, located at ______________________ ______________________________ (Address), City of ______________________________, ____________________, County, Texas, on behalf of the condominium owners association (the Association) by the Association's governing body (the Board).

A. The Declaration ☐ does ☐ does not contain a right of first refusal or other restraint that restricts the right to transfer the Unit. If a right of first refusal or other restraint exists, see Section _____ of the Declaration.

B. The periodic common expense assessment for the Unit is $______________ per ____________.

C. There ☐ is ☐ is not a common expense or special assessment due and unpaid by the Seller to the Association. The total unpaid amount is $_______________ and is for ____.

D. Other amounts ☐ are ☐ are not payable by Seller to the Association. The total unpaid amount is $______________ and is for ____.

E. Capital expenditures approved by the Association for the next 12 months are $_______________.

F. Reserves for capital expenditures are $___________________; of this amount $_____________________ has been designated for ____.

G. The current operating budget of the Association is attached.

H. The amount of unsatisfied judgments against the Association is $_______________________.

I. There ☐ are ☐ are not any suits pending against the Association. The nature of the suits is ____________________ ____.

J. The Association ☐ does ☐ does not provide insurance coverage for the benefit of unit owners as per the attached summary from the Association's insurance agent.

K. The Board ☐ has ☐ has no knowledge of alterations or improvements to the Unit or to the limited common elements assigned to the Unit or any portion of the project that violate any provision of the Declaration, by-laws or rules of the Association. Known violations are: ____ ____.

L. The Board ☐ has ☐ has not received notice from a governmental authority concerning violations of health or building codes with respect to the Unit, the limited common elements assigned to the Unit, or any other portion of the condominium project. Notices received are: ____ ____.

M. The remaining term of any leasehold estate that affects the condominium is _______________________ and the provisions governing an extension or renewal of the lease are:____ ____ ____.

N. The name, mailing address and telephone number of the Association's managing agent are:

____

(Name) (Telephone Number)

____

(Mailing Address)

REQUIRED ATTACHMENTS:

1. Operating Budget
2. Insurance Summary

(Name of Condominium Owners Association)

NOTICE: The Certificate must be prepared no more than three months before the date it is delivered to Buyer.

By: ________________________________

____

Title

Received:________________________________19___

____

Buyer

____

Mailing Address

____

Buyer

____

Date Phone No.

The form of this certificate has been approved by the Texas Real Estate Commission for use only with similarly approved or promulgated forms of contracts. No representation is made as to the legal validity or adequacy of any provision in any specific transactions. (04-94) TREC No. 32-0.

11-8-99

EQUAL HOUSING OPPORTUNITY

PROMULGATED BY THE TEXAS REAL ESTATE COMMISSION (TREC)

UNIMPROVED PROPERTY CONTRACT

NOTICE: Not For Use For Condominium Transactions

1. **PARTIES:** ______________________________ (Seller) agrees to sell and convey to ______________________________(Buyer) and Buyer agrees to buy from Seller the property described below.

2. **PROPERTY:** Lot ____________, Block _____, ______________________Addition, City of ______________________, ______________________ County, Texas, known as ______________________(Address/Zip Code), or as described on attached exhibit, (the Property). The Property ❑ is ❑ is not subject to mandatory membership in an owners' association. The TREC Addendum For Property Subject To Mandatory Membership In An Owners' Association ❑ is ❑ is not attached.
NOTICE TO BUYER: If the Property is subject to mandatory membership in an owners' association, Seller notifies Buyer under §5.012, Texas Property Code, that, as a purchaser of property in the residential community in which the Property is located, you are obligated to be a member of an owners' association. Restrictive covenants governing the use and occupancy of the Property and a dedicatory instrument governing the establishment, maintenance, and operation of this residential community have been or will be recorded in the Real Property Records of the county in which the Property is located. Copies of the restrictive covenants and dedicatory instrument may be obtained from the county clerk. You are obligated to pay assessments to the owners' association. The amount of the assessments is subject to change. Your failure to pay the assessments could result in a lien on and the foreclosure of the Property.

3. **SALES PRICE:**
A. Cash portion of Sales Price payable by Buyer at closing . . . . $____________
B. Sum of all financing described below . . . . $____________
C. Sales Price (Sum of A and B) . . . . $____________

4. **FINANCING:** Within _____ days after the effective date of this contract Buyer shall apply for all third party financing or noteholder's approval of any assumption and make every reasonable effort to obtain financing or assumption approval. Financing or assumption approval will be deemed to have been obtained when the lender determines that Buyer has satisfied all of lender's financial requirements (those items relating to Buyer's net worth, income and creditworthiness) If financing or assumption approval is not obtained within _______ days after the effective date hereof, this contract will terminate and the earnest money will be refunded to Buyer. Each note to be executed hereunder must be secured by vendor's and deed of trust liens. The portion of Sales Price not payable in cash will be paid as follows: (Check applicable boxes below)
❑ A. THIRD PARTY FINANCING:
❑ (1) This contract is subject to approval for Buyer of a third party loan in an amount not to exceed _____ % of the Sales Price, evidenced by a third party first lien promissory note of not less than $ ______________, due in full in _____ year(s), with interest not to exceed _____ % per annum for the first _____ year(s) of the loan.
❑ (2) This contract is subject to approval for Buyer of a third party loan in an amount not to exceed _____ % of the Sales Price, evidenced by a third party second lien promissory note of not less than $ ____________ , due in full in _____year(s), with interest not to exceed _____ % per annum for the first _____ year(s) of the loan.
❑ B. SELLER FINANCING: A promissory note from Buyer to Seller of $___________, bearing _____% interest per annum, secured by vendor's and deed of trust liens, in accordance with the terms and conditions set forth in the attached TREC Seller Financing Addendum. If an owner policy of title insurance is furnished, Buyer shall furnish Seller with a mortgagee policy of title insurance.
❑ C. ASSUMPTION:
❑ (1) Buyer shall assume the unpaid principal balance of a first lien promissory note payable to ______________________________ which unpaid balance at closing will be $ _____________. The total current monthly payment including principal, interest and any reserve deposits is $ ______________ . Buyer's initial payment will be the first payment due after closing.

☐ (2) Buyer shall assume the unpaid principal balance of a second lien promissory note payable to ____________________________________ which unpaid balance at closing will be $ ______________. The total current monthly payment including principal, interest and any reserve deposits is $______________. Buyer's initial payment will be the first payment due after closing.

Buyer's assumption of an existing note includes all obligations imposed by the deed of trust securing the note.

If the unpaid principal balance(s) of any assumed loan(s) as of the Closing Date varies from the loan balance(s) stated above, the ☐ cash payable at closing ☐ Sales Price will be adjusted by the amount of any variance; provided, if the total principal balance of all assumed loans varies in an amount greater than $350.00 at closing, either party may terminate this contract and the earnest money will be refunded to Buyer unless the other party elects to eliminate the excess in the variance by an appropriate adjustment at closing. If the noteholder requires (a) payment of an assumption fee in excess of $ ______________ in C(1) above or $ ______________ in C(2) above and Seller declines to pay such excess, or (b) an increase in the interest rate to more than ______ % in C(1) above, or ______ % in C(2) above, or (c) any other modification of the loan documents, Buyer may terminate this contract and the earnest money will be refunded to Buyer. A vendor's lien and deed of trust to secure assumption will be required which shall automatically be released on execution and delivery of a release by noteholder. If Seller is released from liability on any assumed note, the vendor's lien and deed of trust to secure assumption will not be required.

NOTICE TO BUYER: The monthly payments, interest rates or other terms of some loans may be adjusted by the lender at or after closing. If you are concerned about the possibility of future adjustments, do not sign the contract without examining the notes and deeds of trust.

NOTICE TO SELLER: Your liability to pay the note assumed by Buyer will continue unless you obtain a release of liability from the lender. If you are concerned about future liability, you should use the TREC Release of Liability Addendum.

☐ D. CREDIT APPROVAL ON ASSUMPTION OR SELLER FINANCING: Within ______ days after the effective date of this contract, Buyer shall deliver to Seller ☐ credit report ☐ verification of employment, including salary ☐ verification of funds on deposit in financial institutions ☐ current financial statement to establish Buyer's creditworthiness or assumption approval or seller financing and ☐ ____.

If Buyer's documentation is not delivered within the specified time, Seller may terminate this contract by notice to Buyer within 7 days after expiration of the time for delivery, and the earnest money will be paid to Seller. If this contract is not so terminated, Seller will be deemed to have accepted Buyer's credit. If the documentation is timely delivered, and Seller determines in Seller's sole discretion that Buyer's credit is unacceptable, Seller may terminate this contract by notice to Buyer within 7 days after expiration of the time for delivery and the earnest money will be refunded to Buyer. If Seller does not so terminate this contract, Seller will be deemed to have accepted Buyer's credit. Buyer hereby authorizes any credit reporting agency to furnish to Seller at Buyer's sole expense copies of Buyer's credit reports.

5. **EARNEST MONEY:** Buyer shall deposit $__________ as earnest money with ____________________ ____________________________ at ____________________________________ (Address), as escrow agent, upon execution of this contract by both parties. Additional earnest money of $______________ must be deposited by Buyer with escrow agent on or before ________________, _____. If Buyer fails to deposit the earnest money as required by this contract, Buyer will be in default.

6. **TITLE POLICY AND SURVEY:**

☐ A. TITLE POLICY: Seller shall furnish to Buyer at ☐ Seller's ☐ Buyer's expense an owner policy of title insurance (the Title Policy) issued by______________________________________ (the Title Company) in the amount of the Sales Price, dated at or after closing, insuring Buyer against loss under the provisions of the Title Policy, subject to the promulgated exclusions (including existing building and zoning ordinances) and the following exceptions:

(1) Restrictive covenants common to the platted subdivision in which the Property is located.

(2) The standard printed exception for standby fees, taxes and assessments.

(3) Liens created as part of the financing described in Paragraph 4.
(4) Utility easements created by the dedication deed or plat of the subdivision in which the Property is located.
(5) Reservations or exceptions otherwise permitted by this contract or as may be approved by Buyer in writing.
(6) The standard printed exception as to discrepancies, conflicts, shortages in area or boundary lines, encroachments or protrusions, or overlapping improvements.
(7) The standard printed exception as to marital rights.
(8) The standard printed exception as to waters, tidelands, beaches, streams, and related matters.

Within 20 days after the Title Company receives a copy of this contract, Seller shall furnish to Buyer a commitment for title insurance (the Commitment) and, at Buyer's expense, legible copies of restrictive covenants and documents evidencing exceptions in the Commitment other than the standard printed exceptions. Seller authorizes the Title Company to mail or hand deliver the Commitment and related documents to Buyer at Buyer's address shown below. If the Commitment is not delivered to Buyer within the specified time, the time for delivery will be automatically extended up to 15 days.

❑ B. SURVEY: (Check one box only)

❑ (1) Within ______ days after the effective date of this contract, Buyer shall obtain a survey at Buyer's expense.

❑ (2) Within _____ days after the effective date of this contract, Seller shall cause a survey to be delivered to Buyer at Seller's expense.

❑ (3) Within _____ days after the effective date of this contract, Seller will deliver to Buyer the existing survey plat of the Property dated ________________________, ________, which ❑ will ❑ will not be recertified to a date subsequent to the effective date of this contract at the expense of ❑ Buyer ❑ Seller.

The survey must be made by a Registered Professional Land Surveyor acceptable to the Title Company and any lender.

Buyer may object to existing building and zoning ordinances, items 6A(1) through (8) above and matters shown on the survey if Buyer determines that any such ordinance, items or matters prohibits the following use or activity: ____
____.

Buyer will have 7 days after the receipt of the latter of the Commitment or survey to object in writing to matters disclosed in the Commitment or survey. Buyer's failure to object under Paragraph 6 within the time allowed will constitute a waiver of Buyer's right to object; except that the requirements in Schedule C of the Commitment will not be deemed to have been waived. Seller shall cure the timely objections of Buyer or any third party lender within 20 days after Seller receives the objections and the Closing Date will be extended as necessary. If objections are not cured by the extended Closing Date, this contract will terminate and the earnest money will be refunded to Buyer unless Buyer elects to waive the objections.

NOTICE TO SELLER AND BUYER:

(1) Broker advises Buyer to have an abstract of title covering the Property examined by an attorney of Buyer's selection, or Buyer should be furnished with or obtain a Title Policy. If a Title Policy is furnished, the Commitment should be promptly reviewed by an attorney of Buyer's choice due to the time limitations on Buyer's right to object.
(2) If the Property is situated in a utility or other statutorily created district providing water, sewer, drainage, or flood control facilities and services, Chapter 49 of the Texas Water Code requires Seller to deliver and Buyer to sign the statutory notice relating to the tax rate, bonded indebtedness, or standby fee of the district prior to final execution of this contract.
(3) If the Property abuts the tidally influenced waters of the state, Section 33.135, Texas Natural Resources Code, requires a notice regarding coastal area property to be included in the contract. An addendum either promulgated by TREC or required by the parties should be used.
(4) Buyer is advised that the presence of wetlands, toxic substances, including asbestos and wastes or other environmental hazards or the presence of a threatened or endangered species or its habitat may affect Buyer's intended use of the Property. If Buyer is concerned about these matters, an addendum either promulgated by TREC or required by the parties should be used.

(5) If the Property is located outside the limits of a municipality, Seller notifies Buyer under §5.011, Texas Property Code, that the Property may now or later be included in the extraterritorial jurisdiction of a municipality and may now or later be subject to annexation by the municipality. Each municipality maintains a map that depicts its boundaries and extraterritorial jurisdiction. To determine if the Property is located within a municipality's extraterritorial jurisdiction or is likely to be located within a municipality's extraterritorial jurisdiction, contact all municipalities located in the general proximity of the Property for further information.

(6) Unless expressly prohibited in writing by the parties, Seller may continue to show the Property for sale and to receive, negotiate and accept back-up offers.

7. PROPERTY CONDITION:

A. INSPECTIONS, ACCESS AND UTILITIES: Buyer may have the Property inspected by an inspector selected by Buyer, licensed by TREC or otherwise permitted by law to make such inspections. Seller shall permit access to the Property at reasonable times for inspection, repairs and treatment and for reinspection after repairs and treatment have been completed. Seller shall pay for turning on utilities for inspection and reinspection.

B. ACCEPTANCE OF PROPERTY CONDITION: NOTICE: Buyer should determine the availability of utilities to the Property suitable to satisfy Buyer's needs. (check one box only):

❑ (1) In addition to any earnest money deposited with escrow agent, Buyer has paid Seller $____________ (the "Option Fee") for the unrestricted right to terminate this contract by giving notice of termination to Seller within _____ days after the effective date of this contract. If Buyer gives notice of termination within the time specified, the Option Fee will not be refunded, however, any earnest money will be refunded to Buyer. If Buyer does not give notice of termination within the time specified, Buyer will be deemed to have accepted the Property in its current condition and the Option Fee ❑ will ❑ will not be credited to the Sales Price at closing.

❑ (2) Buyer accepts the Property in its present condition.

8. BROKERS' FEES: All obligations of the parties for payment of brokers' fees are contained in separate written agreements.

9. CLOSING: The closing of the sale will be on or before ______________________________, ________, or within 7 days after objections to matters disclosed in the Commitment or by the survey have been cured, whichever date is later (the Closing Date). *If financing or assumption approval has been obtained pursuant to Paragraph 4,* the Closing Date will be extended up to 15 days if necessary to comply with lender's closing requirements. If either party fails to close this sale by the Closing Date, the non-defaulting party will be entitled to exercise the remedies contained in Paragraph 15. At closing Seller shall furnish tax statements or certificates showing no delinquent taxes and a general warranty deed conveying good and indefeasible title showing no additional exceptions to those permitted in Paragraph 6.

10. POSSESSION: Seller shall deliver possession of the Property to Buyer at closing and funding.

11. SPECIAL PROVISIONS: (Insert only factual statements and business details applicable to this sale. TREC rules prohibit licensees from adding factual statements or business details for which a contract addendum, lease or other form has been promulgated by TREC for mandatory use.)

12. SETTLEMENT AND OTHER EXPENSES:

A. The following expenses must be paid at or prior to closing:

(1) Appraisal fees will be paid by ______________________________.

(2) The total of loan discount fees may not exceed ______ % of the loan of which Seller shall pay ______________and Buyer shall pay the remainder. The total of any buydown fees may not exceed _____________which will be paid by ______________________________.

(3) Seller's Expenses: Releases of existing liens, including prepayment penalties and recording fees; release of Seller's loan liability; tax statements or certificates; preparation of deed; one-half of escrow fee; and other expenses stipulated to be paid by Seller under other provisions of this contract.

(4) Buyer's Expenses: Loan application, origination and commitment fees; loan assumption costs; preparation and recording of deed of trust to secure assumption; lender required expenses incident to new loans, including preparation of loan documents, recording fees, tax service and research fees, warehouse or underwriting fees, copies of restrictions and easements, amortization schedule, premiums for mortgagee title policies and endorsements required by lender, credit reports, photos; required premiums for flood and hazard insurance; required reserve deposit for insurance premiums and ad valorem taxes; interest on all monthly installment notes from date of disbursements to one month prior to dates of first monthly payments; one-half of escrow fee; and other expenses stipulated to be paid by Buyer under other provisions of this contract.

B. If any expense exceeds an amount expressly stated in this contract for such expense to be paid by a party, that party may terminate this contract unless the other party agrees to pay such excess. In no event will Buyer pay charges and fees expressly prohibited by governmental loan program regulations.

13. PRORATIONS AND ROLLBACK TAXES:

A. PRORATIONS: Taxes for the current year, interest, maintenance fees, assessments, dues and rents will be prorated through the Closing Date. If taxes for the current year vary from the amount prorated at closing, the parties shall adjust the prorations when tax statements for the current year are available. *If a loan is assumed* and the lender maintains an escrow account, the escrow account must be transferred to Buyer without any deficiency. Buyer shall reimburse Seller for the amount in the transferred account. Buyer shall pay the premium for a new insurance policy. If taxes are not paid at or prior to closing, Buyer will be obligated to pay taxes for the current year.

B. ROLLBACK TAXES: If this sale or Buyer's use of the Property after closing results in the assessment of additional taxes, penalties or interest (Assessments) for periods prior to closing, the Assessments will be the obligation of Buyer. If Seller's change in use of the Property prior to closing or denial of a special use valuation on the Property claimed by Seller results in Assessments for periods prior to closing, the Assessments will be the obligation of Seller. Obligations imposed by this paragraph will survive closing.

14. CASUALTY LOSS: If any part of the Property is damaged or destroyed by fire or other casualty loss after the effective date of the contract, Seller shall restore the Property to its previous condition as soon as reasonably possible, but in any event by the Closing Date. If Seller fails to do so due to factors beyond Seller's control, Buyer may either (a) terminate this contract and the earnest money will be refunded to Buyer (b) extend the time for performance up to 15 days and the Closing Date will be extended as necessary or (c) accept the Property in its damaged condition and accept an assignment of insurance proceeds. Seller's obligations under this paragraph are independent of any obligations of Seller under Paragraph 7.

15. DEFAULT: If Buyer fails to comply with this contract, Buyer will be in default, and Seller may either (a) enforce specific performance, seek such other relief as may be provided by law, or both, or (b) terminate this contract and receive the earnest money as liquidated damages, thereby releasing both parties from this contract. If, due to factors beyond Seller's control, Seller fails within the time allowed to make any non-casualty repairs or deliver the Commitment, Buyer may either (a) extend the time for performance up to 15 days and the Closing Date will be extended as necessary or (b) terminate this contract as the sole remedy and receive the earnest money. If Seller fails to comply with this contract for any other reason, Seller will be in default and Buyer may either (a) enforce specific performance, seek such other relief as may be provided by law, or both, or (b) terminate this contract and receive the earnest money, thereby releasing both parties from this contract.

Unimproved Property Contract Concerning____Page Six 11-8-99
(Address of Property)

16. **DISPUTE RESOLUTION:** It is the policy of the State of Texas to encourage the peaceable resolution of disputes through alternative dispute resolution procedures. The parties are encouraged to use an addendum approved by TREC to submit to mediation disputes which cannot be resolved in good faith through informal discussion.

17. **ATTORNEY'S FEES:** The prevailing party in any legal proceeding brought under or with respect to the transaction described in this contract is entitled to recover from the non-prevailing party all costs of such proceeding and reasonable attorney's fees.

18. **ESCROW:** The earnest money is deposited with escrow agent with the understanding that escrow agent is not (a) a party to this contract and does not have any liability for the performance or nonperformance of any party to this contract, (b) liable for interest on the earnest money and (c) liable for any loss of earnest money caused by the failure of any financial institution in which the earnest money has been deposited unless the financial institution is acting as escrow agent. At closing, the earnest money must be applied first to any cash down payment, then to Buyer's closing costs and any excess refunded to Buyer. If both parties make written demand for the earnest money, escrow agent may require payment of unpaid expenses incurred on behalf of the parties and a written release of liability of escrow agent from all parties. If one party makes written demand for the earnest money, escrow agent shall give notice of the demand by providing to the other party a copy of the demand. If escrow agent does not receive written objection to the demand from the other party within 30 days after notice to the other party, escrow agent may disburse the earnest money to the party making demand reduced by the amount of unpaid expenses incurred on behalf of the party receiving the earnest money and escrow agent may pay the same to the creditors. If escrow agent complies with the provisions of this paragraph, each party hereby releases escrow agent from all adverse claims related to the disbursal of the earnest money. Escrow agent's notice to the other party will be effective when deposited in the U. S. Mail, postage prepaid, certified mail, return receipt requested, addressed to the other party at such party's address shown below. Notice of objection to the demand will be deemed effective upon receipt by escrow agent.

19. **REPRESENTATIONS:** Seller represents that as of the Closing Date (a) there will be no liens, assessments, or security interests against the Property which will not be satisfied out of the sales proceeds unless securing payment of any loans assumed by Buyer and (b) assumed loans will not be in default. If any representation in this contract is untrue on the Closing Date, this contract may be terminated by Buyer and the earnest money will be refunded to Buyer. All representations contained in this contract will survive closing.

20. **FEDERAL TAX REQUIREMENT:** If Seller is a "foreign person", as defined by applicable law, or if Seller fails to deliver an affidavit that Seller is not a "foreign person", then Buyer shall withhold from the sales proceeds an amount sufficient to comply with applicable tax law and deliver the same to the Internal Revenue Service together with appropriate tax forms. IRS regulations require filing written reports if cash in excess of specified amounts is received in the transaction.

21. **AGREEMENT OF PARTIES:** This contract contains the entire agreement of the parties and cannot be changed except by their written agreement. Addenda which are a part of this contract are (list): ________
____
____
____.

22. **CONSULT YOUR ATTORNEY:** Real estate licensees cannot give legal advice. This contract is intended to be legally binding. READ IT CAREFULLY. If you do not understand the effect of this contract, consult your attorney BEFORE signing.

Buyer's Attorney is:______________________________ Seller's Attorney is:______________________________

Initialed for identification by Buyer__________ and Seller__________ **01A** TREC NO. 9-4

Unimproved Property Contract Concerning____Page Seven 11-8-99
(Address of Property)

23. **NOTICES:** All notices from one party to the other must be in writing and are effective when mailed to, hand-delivered at, or transmitted by facsimile machine as follows:

To Buyer at:

____

____

____

Telephone: (___)______________________

Facsimile: (___)______________________

To Seller at:

____

____

____

Telephone: (___)______________________

Facsimile: (___)______________________

EXECUTED the ______day of ___________________,______ (THE EFFECTIVE DATE). (BROKER: FILL IN THE DATE OF FINAL ACCEPTANCE.)

____
Buyer

____
Buyer

____
Seller

____
Seller

The form of this contract has been approved by the Texas Real Estate Commission. Such approval relates to this contract form only. TREC forms are intended for use only by trained real estate licensees. No representation is made as to the legal validity or adequacy of any provision in any specific transaction. It is not suitable for complex transactions. Extensive riders or additions are not to be used. Texas Real Estate Commission, P.O. Box 12188, Austin, TX 78711-2188, 1-800-250-8732 or (512) 459-6544 (http://www.trec.state.tx.us) TREC NO. 9-4. This form replaces TREC NO. 9-3.

BROKER INFORMATION AND RATIFICATION OF FEE

Listing Broker has agreed to pay Other Broker __________________________ of the total sales price when Listing Broker's fee is received. Escrow Agent is authorized and directed to pay Other Broker from Listing Broker's fee at closing.

____
Other Broker License No.

represents ☐ Seller as Listing Broker's subagent
☐ Buyer only as Buyer's agent

____
Associate Telephone

____
Broker Address

____
Telephone Facsimile

____
Listing Broker License No.

represents ☐ Seller and Buyer as an intermediary
☐ Seller only as Seller's agent

____
Listing Associate Telephone

____
Selling Associate Telephone

____
Broker Address

____
Telephone Facsimile

RECEIPT

Receipt of ☐ Contract and ☐ $_________ Earnest Money in the form of_________________________is acknowledged.

Escrow Agent: ______________________________________

By:____

____
Address

____
City State Zip Code

Date: __________________________,_________

Telephone: (___) _________________________

Facsimile: (___) _________________________

Appendix B

Answer Key

Answers to multiple choice questions at the end of Parts 1–4.

PART 1	PART 2	PART 3	PART 4
1. C	1. D	1. B	1. B
2. D	2. A	2. B	2. A
3. B	3. B	3. A	3. B
4. B	4. A	4. D	4. A
5. D	5. D	5. B	5. A
6. B	6. B	6. B	6. D
7. C	7. B	7. D	7. B
8. B	8. C	8. A	8. B
9. D	9. B	9. C	9. C
10. B	10. D	10. A	10. B

A. Settlement Statement

Part 6 Case Study

U.S. Department of Housing and Urban Development

Answer Key for Appendix C

OMB No. 2502-0265

B. Type of Loan	6. File Number	7. Loan Number	8. Mortgage Insurance Case Number
1. ☐ FHA 2. ☐ FmHA 3. ☐ Conv. Unins. 4. ☐ VA 5. ☒ Conv. Ins.			

C. Note: This form is furnished to give you a statement of actual settlement costs. Amounts paid to and by the settlement agent are shown. Items marked "(p.o.c.)" were paid outside the closing; they are shown here for informational purposes and are not included in the totals.

D. Name and Address of Borrower	E. Name and Address of Seller Tax I.D. No.	F. Name and Address of Lender
232-36-3775 Peter Paul Prospect, et ux Priscilla Bea Prospect 654 Broadway Galveston	492-56-6667 Russell Alan James, et ux Anna Marie James 12656 Rolling Waves Lane Galveston	Deep Pocket Mortgage Company 6000 Money Lane Galveston, Texas

G. Property Location	H. Settlement Agent and Agent Identification Number	
12656 Rolling Waves Lane Galveston, Texas 77573	Buyer's Choice Title Company	
	Place of Settlement: Galveston, Texas	I. Settlement Date: April 4

J. Summary of Borrower's Transaction		K. Summary of Seller's Transaction	
100. Gross Amount Due From Borrower		**400. Gross Amount Due To Seller**	
101. Contract sales price	* 387,800	401. Contract sales price	* 387,800
102. Personal property		402. Personal property	
103. Settlement charges to borrower (line 1400)	* 17,187	403.	
104 Option fee paid	* <500>	404 Option fee received	* <500>
105		405.	
Adjustments for items paid by seller in advance		**Adjustments for items paid by seller in advance**	
106. City/town taxes to		406. City/town taxes to	
107. County taxes to		407. County taxes to	
108. Assessments to		408. Assessments to	
109. Maintenance fee 4/4-12/31	* 488	409. Maintenance fee 4/4-12/31	* 488
110.		410.	
111.		411.	
112.		412.	
120. Gross Amount Due From Borrower	* 404,975	**420. Gross Amount Due To Seller**	* 387,788
200. Amounts Paid By Or In Behalf Of Borrower		**500. Reductions In Amount Due To Seller**	
201. Deposit or earnest money	* 25,000	501. Excess deposit (see instructions)	
202. Principal amount of new loan(s)	* 349,000	502. Settlement charges to seller (line 1400)	* 30,301
203. Existing loan(s) taken subject to		503. Existing loan(s) taken subject to	
204.		504. Payoff of first mortgage loan	* 86,076
205.		505. Payoff of second mortgage loan	
206.		506.	
207.		507.	
208.		508.	
209.		509.	
Adjustments for items unpaid by seller		**Adjustments for items unpaid by seller**	
210. City/town taxes 1/1 through 4/4	* 1,475	510. City/town taxes 1/1 through 4/4	* 1,475
211. County taxes to		511. County taxes to	
212. Assessments to		512. Assessments to	
213.		513.	
214.		514.	
215.		515.	
216.		516.	
217.		517.	
218.		518.	
219.		519.	
220. Total Paid By/For Borrower	* 375,475	**520. Total Reduction Amount Due Seller**	* 117,852
300. Cash At Settlement From/To Borrower		**600. Cash At Settlement To/From Seller**	
301. Gross Amount due from borrower (line 120)	* 404,975	601. Gross amount due to seller (line 420)	* 387,788
302. Less amounts paid by/for borrower (line 220)	* 375,475	602. Less reductions in amt. due seller (line 520)	* 117,852
303. Cash ☒ From ☐ To Borrower	* 29,500	**603. Cash** ☒ To ☐ From Seller	* 269,936

L. Settlement Charges	Paid From Borrower's Funds at Settlement	Paid From Seller's Funds at Settlement
700. Total Sales/Broker's Commission based on price $ @ % =		
Division of Commission (line 700) as follows:		
701. $ to		
702. $ to		
703. Commission paid at Settlement		* 27,146
704.		
800. Items Payable In Connection With Loan		
801. Loan Origination Fee 1 % of new loan (rounded)	* 3,490	
802. Loan Discount 1 % of new loan (rounded)	* 3,490	
803. Appraisal Fee to	* 300	
804. Credit Report to	* 75	
805. Lender's Inspection Fee		
806. Mortgage Insurance Application Fee to 1/2% of new loan	* 1,745	
807. Assumption Fee		
808. Amortization schedule	* 20	
809.		
810.		
811.		
900. Items Required By Lender To Be Paid In Advance		
901. Interest from 4/4 to 5/1 @$ /day	* 1,764	
902. Mortgage Insurance Premium for months to		
903. Hazard Insurance Premium for 1 year years to	* 1,725	
904. years to		
905.		
1000. Reserves Deposited With Lender		
1001. Hazard Insurance 2 months @ $ 144 per month	* 288	
1002. Mortgage Insurance months @ $ per month		
1003. City property taxes 7 months @ $ 471 per month (rounded)	* 3,297	
1004. County property taxes months @ $ per month		
1005. Annual assessments months @ $ per month		
1006. months @ $ per month		
1007. months @ $ per month		
1008. months @ $ per month		
1100. Title Charges		
1101. Settlement or closing fee to		
1102. Abstract or title search to		
1103. Title examination to		
1104. Title insurance binder to		
1105. Document preparation to For note and deed of trust	* 200	
1106. Notary fees to		
1107. Attorney's fees to For deed and release		* 130
(includes above items numbers:		
1108. Title insurance to		
(includes above items numbers:		
1109. Lender's coverage $ 349,000	* 175	
1110. Owner's coverage $ 387,800		* 2,885
1111. Escrow Fee to	* 75	* 75
1112. Restrictions to		
1113. Messenger to	* 45	* 45
1200. Government Recording and Transfer Charges		
1201. Recording fees: Deed $ Borrower ; Mortgage $ Borrower ; Releases $ Seller	* 58	* 20
1202. City/county tax stamps: Deed $; Mortgage $		
1203. State tax/stamps: Deed $; Mortgage $		
1204. Tax service fee	* 115	
1205.		
1300. Additional Settlement Charges		
1301. Survey to ABC Survey Company	* 325	
1302. Pest inspection to		
1303.		
1304.		
1305.		
1400. Total Settlement Charges (enter on lines 103, Section J and 502, Section K)	* 17,187	* 30,301